I0028087

Foucault Versus Freud

In *Foucault Versus Freud*, Jerome C. Wakefield offers a novel analysis of one of the great intellectual clashes of our times, the attack on Sigmund Freud's influential sexual theories by the eminent French philosopher and historian of ideas Michel Foucault.

Starting from Foucault's question, "What makes the psychoanalytic theory of incest acceptable to the bourgeois family?", and drawing on Foucault's relatively unexplored published lectures as well as his celebrated *History of Sexuality, Vol. 1*, Wakefield evaluates Foucault's argument that there is a continuity between the two-century medical anti-masturbation crusade and Freud's theory, providing the reader with an accessible introduction to Foucault's conceptual innovations including power/knowledge, the deployment of sexuality, and the use of surveillance and confession as tactics in medicalizing sexuality and reshaping family life.

Rather than allowing the argument to stay at the evidentially uncertain level one often finds in Foucault's writings, Wakefield undertakes close readings both of Freud's "seduction-theory" texts and later Oedipal-period texts to test whether Foucault's provocative arguments find support or disconfirmation. Despite identifying weaknesses in Foucault's position, Wakefield argues that a careful look at Freud's sexual theories through Foucault's theoretical lens changes forever the way one sees Freud's theory—and has the potential to help psychoanalysis move forward in a constructive way.

This book is written to be understandable for those who are not steeped in philosophy or familiar with Foucault's philosophy, offering a lucid introduction to Foucault's ideas and his clash with Freud that will be of interest to clinicians, students, and scholars alike.

Jerome C. Wakefield is university professor, professor of Social Work, affiliate professor of Philosophy, associate faculty in the Center for Bioethics in the School of Global Public Health, and honorary faculty in the Psychoanalytic Association of New York Affiliated with NYU Grossman School of Medicine, at New York University.

Psychological Issues
Series Editor: David L. Wolitsky

Members of the Editorial Board
Wilma Bucci Derner Institute, Adelphi University
Diana Diamond City University of New York
Morris Eagle Derner Institute, Adelphi University
Peter Fonagy University College London
Andrew Gerber Austen Riggs Center
Robert Holt New York University
Paolo Migone Editor, *Psicoterapia e Scienze Umane*
Fred Pine Albert Einstein College of Medicine

The basic mission of *Psychological Issues* is to contribute to the further development of psychoanalysis as a science, as a respected scholarly enterprise, as a theory of human behavior, and as a therapeutic method.

Over the past 50 years, the series has focused on fundamental aspects and foundations of psychoanalytic theory and clinical practice, as well as on work in related disciplines relevant to psychoanalysis. *Psychological Issues* does not aim to represent or promote a particular point of view. The contributions cover broad and integrative topics of vital interest to all psychoanalysts as well as to colleagues in related disciplines. They cut across particular schools of thought and tackle key issues, such as the philosophical underpinnings of psychoanalysis, psychoanalytic theories of motivation, conceptions of therapeutic action, the nature of unconscious mental functioning, psychoanalysis and social issues, and reports of original empirical research relevant to psychoanalysis. The authors often take a critical stance toward theories and offer a careful theoretical analysis and conceptual clarification of the complexities of theories and their clinical implications, drawing upon relevant empirical findings from psychoanalytic research as well as from research in related fields.

Series Editor David L. Wolitzky and the Editorial Board continues to invite contributions from social/behavioral sciences such as anthropology and sociology, from biological sciences such as physiology and the various brain sciences, and from scholarly humanistic disciplines such as philosophy, law, and ethics. Volumes 1–64 in this series were published by International Universities Press. Volumes 65–69 were published by Jason Aronson. For a full list of the titles published by Routledge in this series, please visit the Routledge website: https://www.routledge.com/Psychological-Issues/book-series/PSYCHISSUES

Foucault Versus Freud

Oedipal Theory and the Deployment
of Sexuality

Jerome C. Wakefield

Routledge
Taylor & Francis Group

LONDON AND NEW YORK

Designed cover image: Sigmund Freud © Freud Museum London; Michel Foucault © Christian Taillandier/L'Expres/Camera Press/Redux; a photo depicting Michel Foucault's seminar © David Horn.

First published 2025
by Routledge
4 Park Square, Milton Park, Abingdon, Oxon OX14 4RN

and by Routledge
605 Third Avenue, New York, NY 10158

Routledge is an imprint of the Taylor & Francis Group, an informa business

© 2025 Jerome Wakefield

The right of Jerome Wakefield to be identified as author of this work has been asserted in accordance with sections 77 and 78 of the Copyright, Designs and Patents Act 1988.

All rights reserved. No part of this book may be reprinted or reproduced or utilised in any form or by any electronic, mechanical, or other means, now known or hereafter invented, including photocopying and recording, or in any information storage or retrieval system, without permission in writing from the publishers.

Trademark notice: Product or corporate names may be trademarks or registered trademarks, and are used only for identification and explanation without intent to infringe.

British Library Cataloguing-in-Publication Data
A catalogue record for this book is available from the British Library

Library of Congress Cataloging-in-Publication Data
Names: Wakefield, Jerome C., author.
Title: Foucault versus Freud : Oedipal theory and the deployment of sexuality / Jerome C. Wakefield.
Description: Abingdon, Oxon ; New York, NY : Routledge, 2024. |
Series: Psychological issues | Includes bibliographical references and index. |
Identifiers: LCCN 2023059091 (print) | LCCN 2023059092 (ebook) |
ISBN 9781032769257 (hardback) | ISBN 9781032769233 (paperback) |
ISBN 9781003480396 (ebook)
Subjects: LCSH: Foucault, Michel, 1926-1984. | Freud, Sigmund, 1856-1939. |
Sex (Psychology) | Oedipus complex. | Psychoanalysis.
Classification: LCC BF175.5.S48 W35 2024 (print) | LCC BF175.5.S48 (ebook) |
DDC 155.3--dc23/eng/20240118
LC record available at https://lccn.loc.gov/2023059091
LC ebook record available at https://lccn.loc.gov/2023059092

ISBN: 978-1-032-76925-7 (hbk)
ISBN: 978-1-032-76923-3 (pbk)
ISBN: 978-1-003-48039-6 (ebk)

DOI: 10.4324/9781003480396

Typeset in Times New Roman
by MPS Limited, Dehradun

To the memory of Hubert Dreyfus and Michel Foucault, inspiring teachers who opened new vistas for philosophical exploration.

Contents

Acknowledgments

My interest in Continental philosophy—initially in the work of Maurice Merleau-Ponty but later focused on Michel Foucault—was encouraged by my amazingly dedicated, brilliant, and kind teacher, Hubert Dreyfus. Bert played a key historical role in engaging analytic philosophers with the problems posed by Continental philosophers. He certainly played this role in my life, to the point that, despite my thoroughly analytic philosophical training and inclination, I was teaching a Merleau-Ponty versus Freud course during summer session and was a Teaching Assistant in Bert's Foucault course at Berkeley. His prescient attacks on the limitations of early artificial intelligence efforts make me wish he was around now to weigh in on our newest AI revolution.

When he was visiting Berkeley in the years immediately before his death, Michel Foucault also showed me great kindness and encouragement. In our conversations he manifested a sensible and tempered approach that I find is often lost in his interpreters and followers. He was supportive to the extent, for example, of accompanying me to the library in the law school to help me translate medieval penitential texts from the Latin for my still-unpublished research on the history of thinking about ideal sexual performance (I only had two years of Latin in High School and almost failed!). His sense of contingency always amused me. The sentence I best recall from his seminar was not some profound insight into speaking truth to power but his throwaway comment that if the railroad had not been invented when it was, there would be no psychoanalysis (i.e., because that led to grappling with the nature of traumatic neuroses due to railroad accidents). We were discussing my coming to France to study when I received a letter from him in mid-1984 stating that he was ill but thankfully the doctors had told him it was not AIDS. They were wrong (or being kind?), and Foucault died shortly thereafter of an AIDS-related infection. This book is a belated continuation of my attempt to learn from our conversations.

I thank my wife Lisa Peters and sons Joshua and Zachary for being supportive and patient as I worked on this book.

My friend, frequent coauthor, and former student Jordan Conrad provided his usual astute and painstaking feedback on a draft of this book. His comments led to many improvements, for which I am grateful.

Finally, I thank Kate Hawes, senior publisher at Routledge, and her superbly effective and helpful editorial assistant, Georgina Clutterbuck, for their support in bringing this volume to fruition.

The author gratefully acknowledges permission to republish the following materials:

Excerpt(s) from *The History of Sexuality: Volume 1: An Introduction* by Michel Foucault, translated by Robert Hurley, translation copyright © 1978 by Penguin Random House LLC. Used by permission of Pantheon Books, an imprint of the Knopf Doubleday Publishing Group, a division of Penguin Random House LLC. All rights reserved.

Extracts from *La Volonté de savoir*, Michel Foucault © Editions Gallimard, Paris, 1976.

Excerpt(s) from *Power/Knowledge* by Michel Foucault, copyright © 1972, 1975, 1976, 1977 by Michel Foucault. This collection © 1980 by The Harvester Press. Used by permission of Pantheon Books, an imprint of the Knopf Doubleday Publishing Group, a division of Penguin Random House LLC. All rights reserved.

Excerpt(s) from *Abnormal: Lectures at the Collége de France, 1974–1975* by Michel Foucault, copyright © 2016 by Verso. Reproduced with permission of the Licensor through PLSclear.

Paris, le *15 . 1 . 84*

      M. Jerome Wakefield a participé au séminaire que
j'ai donné à l'Université de Californie (Berkeley) pendant
l'automne 1983. Il y a donné une présentation et j'ai eu l'occasion à plusieurs reprises de discuter de son travail avec lui.

      M. J. Wakefield m'a paru avoir une très solide
formation philosophique qui lui permet de réfléchir sur le
cadre méthodologique de ses recherches et d'en contrôler la
conceptualisation. Ses enquêtes empiriques ou historiques sont
pour lui l'occasion d'élaborations théoriques intéressantes.

      D'autre part, M.J. Wakefield a une connaissance à la
fois vaste et précise de la réflexion médicale et philosophique
sur la sexualité; il connaît bien la littérature classique
sur ce sujet et il est tout à fait familier avec les recherches
contemporaines. Ses capacités d'analyse et son aptitude à
exposer ses idées en font un chercheur de très grande
qualité.

Michel Foucault

Chapter 1

Introduction: Foucault Versus Freud

My primary goal in this book is to sympathetically reconstruct and critically evaluate Michel Foucault's attack on Sigmund Freud's influential theory of the Oedipus complex. In this introductory chapter, I pose Foucault's challenge to Freud in the form of Foucault's question as to why Oedipal theory was so widely accepted, and his novel approach to an answer in terms of the social power function served by the theory. I then offer a survey of background topics as preparation for the analyses to come. The survey includes a primer of Foucault's distinctive approach to the uses of scientific theory for social power ("power/knowledge"), his concept of the "deployment of sexuality" as a two-century phenomenon in which medico-scientific theories of sexuality were used for social control purposes (especially manifested in the medical crusade against masturbation), his rejection of the "repression hypothesis" concerning the Victorian reaction to sexuality, and his focus on the tactics of surveillance and confession as instruments of social control. I also survey Foucault's views of various components of Freud's theory, arguing that Foucault has a quite differentiated view of psychoanalysis's various doctrines, accepting some as constructive but taking Oedipal theory and the process of psychoanalytic confession as central targets of criticism.

Foucault's Question: Why was Freud's Oedipal Theory so Influential?

How should we understand the remarkable success of Freud's sexual theories? In his 1975 public lectures on nineteenth-century ideas of

DOI: 10.4324/9781003480396-1

sexual pathology published posthumously as *Abnormal* (2003), the French philosopher and historian of ideas Michel Foucault begins his tenth lecture (delivered 12 March 1975 at the College de France) by asking: *"What makes the psychoanalytic theory of incest acceptable to the bourgeois family?"* (2003, p. 263). By the "psychoanalytic theory of incest," Foucault refers, of course, to Sigmund Freud's extraordinarily influential theory of the Oedipus complex, in which, in the prototypical instance, Freud postulates that the boy in some inchoate sense desires to have sexual intercourse with his mother. Foucault offers a parenthetical spoiler, "danger comes from the child's desire," and then spends a large part of the lecture trying to explain this answer to his question. He returns to the question of the Oedipal theory's acceptance with additional thoughts in his most celebrated book, *History of Sexuality, Volume 1: An Introduction* (1978; hereafter *HS1*).

Foucault's account of Freud's Oedipal theory (or "incest theory") in his lecture is disorienting. He claims that Freud, who is widely acclaimed as the one who liberated us from the Victorian sexual prohibitions of the nineteenth century, in fact propounded theories that at a deeper level extended some features of the most outrageous part of the Victorian sexual nonsense, namely, the relentless medical campaign against child masturbation (or "masturbation crusade"): "I think, then, that the functioning of the theme of incest should be situated in the century-old practice of the crusade against masturbation. In the end, it is an episode, or in any case a turning point, in this crusade" (2003, p. 268). Thus, Foucault argues that the incest theory, although in some respects novel (a "turning point"), was fundamentally an extension (an "episode") of the doctrines and power tactics of the masturbation crusade, and was accepted for similar reasons. Foucault in turn explains the acceptance of the masturbation crusade as due to its functions of social regulation and the way that belief in its supposedly scientific doctrines about sex changed family power relationships to support emerging social values. Such alterations in power that result from changes in relationships due to accepting a scientific theory about human nature Foucault labels "power/knowledge." Foucault offers further explanations of the appeal of the Oedipal theory to the bourgeois family in *HS1*, but his explanations there (reviewed in Chapter 6) at best add detail to his earlier explanation in the lecture rather than renouncing or changing it.

In sum, Foucault argues, first, that the Oedipal theory extended the masturbation crusade in some important ways concerning its doctrinal substance and the tactics used in its application to the family. And second, he claims that, like the masturbation crusade and in fact parasitic on the masturbation crusade's wide acceptance, the incest theory's acceptance was due to the appeal of the power/knowledge that emerged from those crusade-like doctrines and tactics and how it continued to reshape family relationships in ways similar to the effects of the crusade.

If Foucault is correct, then a radical reconceptualization of the nature and historical-cultural role of Freud's theory would be warranted. Foucault's claim that Freud's sexual theories are continuous with the masturbation crusade challenges the notion of Freud as liberator from a period of sexual repression. Indeed, as we shall see, Foucault argues that no such period existed. He calls the claimed existence of such a period of repression of sex by society and the accompanying Freudian notion that individuals then repressed their sexual desires, yielding neurosis, the "repressive hypothesis." To dispel the idea that Freud liberated us from repression, Foucault attacks the repressive hypothesis. The first section of *HS1* is titled "We 'Other Victorians'," a play on the title of Steven Marcus's (1966) book, *The Other Victorians*, which portrays what is supposed to be the "underside" of Victorian culture comprised of those willing to write about sex, such as pornographers and diarists, who are taken to have violated the supposed sexual taboos of the repressive era. Foucault's point is that everyone was and is such an "other Victorian" because the repressive notion is a myth to begin with and sex was amply discussed—not just by pornographers—even if often it was discussed under the guise of thinking about how to repress it. The next section of *HS1* is titled "The Repressive Hypothesis," and here Foucault directly attacks the notion that such a repressive epoch actually existed, at least when looked at through the Foucauldian lens that focuses on discourse—or talking about sex. (Note that I use the French-inspired adjective "Foucauldian" rather than the English-expectable "Foucaultian" because the former has come to be the standard usage in the English-language scholarly literature.)

As Foucault's reference to the bourgeois family indicates, the Oedipal theory has been vastly influential over the last century well beyond its centrality to psychoanalysis and psychodynamic mental health treatment, with its influence extending across the humanities, literature, and the culture at large to the media and everyday life. This was already the case in the early twentieth century when D. H. Lawrence observed that "The Oedipus complex was a household word, the incest motive a commonplace of tea-table chat" and that it was "a common term, a topic of conversation ordinary in living rooms" (1921, pp. 3, 10). It remains so today, with frequent Oedipus-complex related references in popular television series ranging from "The Sopranos" (in which the mafia anti-hero has a dream that clearly points to Oedipal sexual desire) to "The Simpsons" (in one episode with an Oedipal theme, Lisa observes that Oedipus killed his father and married his mother, and Homer wonders who, in a case like that, pays for the wedding?). In the first episode of the popular 1987 British detective series, "Inspector Morse," the good Inspector, holding a copy of Sophocles's play *Oedipus the King*, explains the Oedipus complex to a colleague as part of his theory as to what might have motivated a suspect to commit a murder. Comments on psycho-analysis's extraordinary cultural influence by cultural icons, such as Andre Breton's quip in 1924 that "the fashion this winter is psycho-analysis" (1990, p. 94) and W. H. Auden's (1940) famous poetry line attributing to Freud the reshaping of our entire society's attitudes, reflect the success of the Oedipal theory.

This level of influence requires explanation. Generally, when one asks why a theory is accepted, one is asking for the evidence that supports the theory. Yet, many scholars, including me (Wakefield, 2023a), have argued—and Foucault seems to assume, even though he is somewhat evasive on this point because he does not see evidential evaluation as his concern—that there is not and never was enough remotely adequate scientific evidence to warrant belief in the Oedipal theory. Consequently, such scholars are confronted with the challenge of explaining why the theory had such an extraordinary influence on Western psychology and culture. Many have taken up this challenge, and some of the many answers proposed to Foucault's question by other distinguished critics of psychoanalysis are surveyed in Chapter 2.

In attempting in this book to reconstruct and rethink Foucault's power/knowledge answer to the question of why Freud's Oedipal theory was so appealing, my hope is to reach a deeper understanding of the nature and historical position of Freud's theory. Note that my aim is not primarily to do Foucault scholarship. Although acknowledging Foucault's views, I will not remain anchored to Foucault's elaborate network of background assumptions. Rather, I will use elements of Foucault's analysis as a starting point to reexamine Freud and to see whether Foucault directs us to an illuminating way of seeing Freud's Oedipal theory, irrespective of how doctrinally "Foucauldian" that way of seeing Freud may be.

To reconstruct Foucault's understanding of the Oedipal theory, I have to consider more than his view of the Oedipal theory itself. Foucault's tenth 1975 lecture builds closely on his analysis in the ninth lecture, delivered the week before, on the topic of the remarkable two-century medical anti-masturbation campaign, which Foucault labels the "masturbation crusade." In the lectures, Foucault argues that the incest theory is a functional extension of the masturbation crusade. He thus sees the appeal of the incest theory as consisting in large part of the appeal behind the masturbation crusade, simply shifted to the incest theory. Consequently, his explanation of the incest theory's acceptance in large part lies in his explanation of the crusade's acceptance plus an explanation of how the masturbation crusade could easily transform into the incest theory with its appeal communicated to its new form intact. The two lectures thus provide one integrated answer to Foucault's question and must both be considered. This in turn requires an in-depth appreciation of the nature and doctrines of the masturbation crusade itself, which I describe in Chapter 3. This is followed in Chapter 4 by an exposition and evaluation of Foucault's analysis of the crusade. I consider the arguments Foucault presents in both his tenth 1975 lecture and *HSI* specifically regarding the incest theory in Chapter 6.

One would assume that assessing the persuasiveness of Foucault's analysis of Freud surely requires identifying the evidence in Freud's theorizing on which Foucault's analysis is based. Yet, oddly enough, Foucault is quite reticent on this crucial point. Instead, he tends to state his hypotheses about Freud in an oracular fashion without specifying the evidence in Freud's work that supports his hypothesis, staying at a relatively superficial impressionistic level in characterizing Freud's theories. Several commentators have noted the fact that Foucault does not immerse himself in Freud's texts as he does in other texts he writes about, and conducts his analysis at a global level aloof from the details of Freud's work: "Foucault does not deal with the content of psychoanalysis" (Basaure, 2009, p. 357); "As for Foucault,...I don't see him being too concerned with Freud's position" (Jacques Lacan, as quoted in Grace, 2013, p. 226); Foucault did not analyze Freud's theories "as a body of ideas" but just as "a social institution" (Barrett, 1991, p. 115); "Psychoanalytic texts are rarely discussed and Freud is hardly mentioned" (Whitebook, 2003, p. 331); and even, "Foucault was never all that passionately interested in psychoanalysis" (Maurice Blanchot, as quoted in Miller, 1992, p. 58).

Yet, *HS1*'s analysis is clearly aimed at psychoanalysis and specifically is an attempt to demonstrate Foucault's construal of Freud's incest theory as the culmination of the two-century phenomenon that he calls "the deployment [*dispositif*] of sexuality" (alternatively translated as the "apparatus of sexuality"). During the deployment, medical and scientific theorizing about sexuality functioned as an instrument of social regulation and power ("power/knowledge"), giving rise to a network of practices of control such as surveillance, confession, and medicalization that intruded into family life. Although psychoanalysis is not often explicitly mentioned in *HS1*, Foucault indicates toward the end that *HS1*'s "history of the deployment of sexuality...can serve as an archaeology of psychoanalysis" (1978, p. 129). As Miller says, "psychoanalysis is at the heart of" Foucault's project on the history of sexuality and is indeed "the object of the enquiry" (1992, p. 58). Forrester observes that "we can immediately see that, behind every argument in this book, Foucault will be conducting an interrogation of psychoanalysis" (1980, p. 289). Asked whether in his view the history of sexuality culminates in psychoanalysis, Foucault answers,

"Certainly! A culminating point is arrived at here in the history of procedures that set sex and truth in relation. In our time there isn't a single one of the discourses on sexuality which isn't, in one way or another, oriented in relation to that of psychoanalysis."

(Foucault, 1980a, p. 219)

Foucault's lack of confrontation with Freud's text is thus not a matter of indifference or lack of importance, but a matter of style and lack of analytic rigor.

To evaluate Foucault's contentions about Freud, I attempt to bridge the crucial evidential gap in Foucault's argument between the magnitude of his claims and the lack of Freudian scholarship to support those claims. To address this gap, in Chapters 5 and 7, I offer detailed exegeses of relevant aspects of Freud's writings—specifically, his early theorizing about the actual neuroses in Chapter 5 and his later Oedipal analysis of the case of Little Hans in Chapter 7. I thus attempt to bring relevant Freudian textual sources to bear on the evaluation of Foucault's claim that Freudian theory is part of the deployment of sexuality and an extension of aspects of the masturbation crusade.

Beyond critically examining the nature and limits of Foucault's analysis of the Oedipal theory when tested against Freud's texts, I have several other goals in this book. The first is to fill a gap left in my previous scholarship on Freud's Oedipal theory. Although this book is an independent work that can be read without reference to my other books, *Foucault Versus Freud* completes a trilogy focused on Freud's defense of the Oedipal theory in his case history of Little Hans (Freud, 1909). Conceptualized within the trilogy, this book might fall in the middle. It can be considered a sequel to *Freud's Argument for the Oedipus Complex* (2023a), where I showed that Freud's arguments for the Oedipal theory lack scientific validity, thus raising the "appeal" puzzle that Foucault confronts. And, it can be considered a "prequel" to *Attachment, Sexuality, Power* (2023b), where I presented my own account of the workings of power/knowledge in the Hans case located within Foucault's framework but somewhat different from Foucault's analysis. In providing a neo-Foucauldian account of both the Hans case history and the subsequent cultural influence of the Oedipal theory, I failed to first acknowledge and address Foucault's own interpretation of the appeal of the Oedipal theory. This omission is remedied here.

The overarching goal of my Oedipal theory trilogy is to offer a systematic analysis that illuminates where Freud went wrong in his Oedipal theorizing and points to a constructive way forward for psychoanalysis as a clinical and scholarly field. In the end, I broadly agree with Foucault's judgment that Freud contributed to scientific advances in several areas including the excavation of unconscious meanings and a focus on childhood experiences rather than faulty genes as the source of adult emotional maladies, but that the Oedipal theory in the sexual form proposed by Freud—which Freud declared to be his greatest achievement—is not among those advances.

A further goal of this book is to give Foucault's 1975 lectures, which have been relatively ignored, the scholarly attention they deserve. To my knowledge, this book's analysis is the first extended discussion of the ninth and tenth 1975 lectures. The lectures were not available in print for many years, and they were immediately succeeded by *HS1* containing much new material, eclipsing the lectures. However, many insights and arguments in the lectures did not find their way into the book. Moreover, the masturbation crusade and Oedipus complex do not get the explicit focused attention in *HS1* that is lavished on them in the dedicated 1975 lectures.

Another goal is to introduce Foucault's provocative but often challenging writings about sexuality to an audience that includes psychologists and mental health clinicians, many of whom may not be familiar with his ideas. One obstacle to dissemination of Foucault's ideas in the psychological community is that Foucault's poetic and convoluted prose is often a challenge for English-speaking readers. Foucault does not lay out his arguments in the explicit way favored by Anglo-American philosophers and psychologists, which may be partly a matter of cultural styles. There is a story that once when Foucault was visiting Berkeley, he was asked by the American philosopher John Searle, who was known for the crystal clarity of his writing, "Michel, why don't you write more clearly?" Foucault answered, "John, if I wrote as clearly as you do, nobody would read me in France."

I have addressed this impediment in two ways. First, I quote extensively but selectively from Foucault's work, with clarity as a major criterion for choice of passages, and I simultaneously offer glosses to make the passages' meanings more transparent. Second, both Foucault himself in his interviews and some of his better expositors are admirably clear, and I quote heavily from such sources.

Another obstacle to mental health professionals accessing Foucault's ideas is the belief that Foucault's views are destructively antagonistic to the field's goals. Foucault is often classified as an anti-psychiatrist who does not believe in mental illness, or a relativist, post-modernist, or constructivist who denies that there is a truth for scientific psychology to reveal. Although Foucault sometimes overstates his claims and writes in a way that seems to confirm such popular views of his work, he denied that he was generally impugning psychiatry, that he was an anti-psychiatrist or anti-psychoanalyst, or that he was denying the validity of current theories or treatments. Rather, he was trying to understand how things came to be what they are, which might lead to critical insights but in itself is not necessarily a condemnation of current practices: "[T]he medicalization of madness…was connected with a whole series of social and economic processes…and practices of power. This fact in no way impugns the scientific validity or therapeutic effectiveness of psychiatry: it does not endorse psychiatry, but neither does it invalidate it" (1997, pp. 296–297).

In any event, thankfully these thorny methodological concerns need not enter essentially into the evaluation of the nature and quality of Foucault's substantive claims about Freud that I analyze here. I therefore set them aside to be taken up elsewhere. Foucault himself acknowledged that, when it comes to his rejection of the repressive hypothesis, it is a substantive claim the correctness of which must be determined by the evidence:

"All this is an illusion, it will be said, a hasty impression behind which a more discerning gaze will surely discover the same great machinery of repression….The answer will have to come out of a historical inquiry….Perhaps these historical analyses will end by dissipating what this cursory survey seems to suggest."

(1978, p. 72)

In making this book useful to Anglo-American readers and playing to my own strengths as primarily an analytic philosopher interested in the logic and validity of arguments, a caveat is that I drag Foucault's argument from its natural French setting into a more analytic-philosophy spirited framework to see what he has to offer from this perspective—this despite Foucault's disclaimer to an American audience that he never was an analytic philosopher. The result is that I will be ignoring most of the rich, complex, and often perplexing French philosophical scene of which Foucault was a part and which pushed his thinking in certain directions. In particular, I will not attempt to address Foucault's famous alliances and disputes regarding various psychoanalytic topics with such illustrious interlocutors as Sartre, Deleuze, Lacan, and Derrida, nor his complex relationships to structuralism, existential phenomenology (particularly Heidegger and Merleau-Ponty), and Marxism. Moreover, although Foucault often frames his discussion of psychoanalysis and the Oedipal theory in terms that reflect Lacan's version of psychoanalysis (despite having, like many of the rest of us, apparently been unsure whether he actually understood Lacan [Miller, 1992]), I will focus only on the implications for his clash with Freud. However, it appears that in the end Foucault saw Lacan's views, despite their many novelties, as suffering from similar problems to Freud's (e.g., some version of the repression hypothesis and an ahistorical universality). Moreover, I am concerned here with Foucault's ideas only during the phase of his writings in which "power/knowledge" was his central preoccupation, and not his earlier endeavors regarding, for example, epistemes and the rise of the sciences of man (see below). Happily, during this period his work is "much more concise and straightforward" (Forrester, 1980, p. 289) than the earlier work, thus more amenable to reconstruction and evaluation.

It should be noted that Foucault's account of the Oedipal theory does not fall into any neat intellectual category. He denied being Freudian, Marxist, or structuralist, thus placing himself outside the standard intellectual camps in France of his time. His arguments changed over time, consistent with his assertion that he is more an experimental thinker trying out ideas than he is a top-down systemic philosopher. Rather than systematization, he emphasizes the contingency and unpredictability of the tactics of social power embedded in the theories of the human sciences, as it responds to changing local conditions and merges into larger regulatory strategies: "There is nothing necessary in [the] order of ideas" (1998, p. 434).

In the remainder of this chapter, I offer background introductions to Freudian and Foucauldian topics as preparation for the analyses to come. These include a primer of relevant aspects of Foucault's distinctive approach to power, such as power/knowledge, the deployment of sexuality, and the explanation of theory acceptance in terms of consequent changes in social power arrangements.

Sigmund Freud's Theory of the Oedipus Complex

Sigmund Freud (1856–1939) was a brilliant nineteenth- and early-twentieth-century Viennese psychologist and philosopher who created a new framework for thinking about the mind that remains extraordinarily influential. He was a central figure in transforming psychology from a science of consciousness to a science acknowledging the existence of unconscious mental representations (Wakefield, 2018). His theory of the determination of behavior by possibly distorted unconscious mental representations of the self and others has become the basis for the field of cognitive social psychology and a forerunner of today's cognitive science (Wakefield, 1992). He developed illuminating theories of psychological conflict and defense, identifying the tactics people use to maintain the mind's equilibrium and self-image and manipulate the impressions of others. He also contributed a theory of unconscious affective and motivational processes that yield ambivalence, conflict, and compromises, and argued that these compromises sometimes generate symptoms. Freud explicitly and systematically challenged the dominant "constitutional degeneracy" approach to mental disorder of his time that explained psychopathology as a product of the individual's flawed biological inheritance from earlier generations, and he replaced it with "infantilism" that attributed etiology to occurrences in the early childhood years of an individual's psychological development. Whereas other leading thinkers of the time, such as Emil Kraepelin and Eugen Bleuler, focused primarily on the psychoses, Freud was the leading turn-of-the-century thinker regarding the psychoneuroses, thus paving the way for the movement of psychiatric practice into the community instead of being confined to the asylum.

Freud established the field of psychotherapy or "talk therapy," an approach to treatment that to this day can be as effective as psychiatric medication for many mental disorders, and elaborated ways of understanding obstacles to the therapeutic process, including important concepts such as "transference" and "resistance." Psychotherapy subsequently expanded well beyond the boundaries of psychoanalysis, but mostly within the same "talking therapy" framework. Virtually all of the thinkers who created the classic psychotherapies that diverged from psychoanalysis were themselves trained as analysts (e.g., Albert Ellis, Aaron Beck, Fritz Perls, Carl Rogers) but were forced to leave the fold when their novel ideas violated psychoanalysis's Freud-inspired intellectual rigidity. One might speculate that if it was not for Freud's obstinate insistence on the Oedipal theory, cognitive behavioral therapy, the currently dominant form of psychotherapy in the United

States and many other countries, which also explores unconscious "cognitive schemas" and "automatic thoughts," would be part of ego psychology and within the broader psychoanalytic tent today.

Freud postulated the Oedipus complex as a universal childhood psychosexual developmental stage applying to all children and all child–parent pairs. In this book, for simplicity of exposition and relevance to the evidence I closely examine, I limit my discussion to the mother-son dyad, thus to the "positive"—i.e, opposite-sex—Oedipus complex and to the sexual desire of a boy for his mother or female caregiver. This was the theory's original form and the only form that existed at the time of the Little Hans case history that is discussed at length later in this book. Freud's subsequent attempts to extend the theory to girls and to same-sex parental desire raise complex questions that will not be addressed here. These elaborations did not amend the heart of the theory as expressed in the original mother-son account considered here, but Freud himself expressed concerns that some of these extensions were not on as solid ground as the initial and prototypical case of a boy's desire for his mother.

The Oedipal theory is also the foundation of Freud's theory of the etiology of the psychoneuroses ("neurosogenesis"). Freud postulated that all later neurotic emotional suffering has its source in unresolved Oedipal feelings and conflicts. This view was the foundation of psychoanalysis's approach to treating neuroses for nearly a century, determining how patients' problems were interpreted in clinical interventions.

Freud believed that the discovery of the Oedipus complex was his central and most distinctive scientific contribution. Despite many changes to his theory over time, Freud never wavered as to the primacy of the Oedipus complex in his overall account of development and psychopathology. He affirmed the theory throughout his work, starting with an early statement in *The Interpretation of Dreams* ("Being in love with the one parent and hating the other are among the essential constituents ... determining the symptoms of the later neurosis" [Freud, 1900, p. 261]). In 1920, he added a note to his *Three Essays on the Theory of Sexuality* stating that "With the progress of psychoanalytic studies the importance of the Oedipus complex has become more and more clearly evident; its recognition has become the shibboleth that distinguishes the adherents of psychoanalysis from its opponents" (Freud, 1905, p. 226, n.1 [footnote added 1920]). He reaffirmed the theory's centrality to his legacy in his last work, published posthumously ("I venture to say that if psycho-analysis could boast of no other achievement than the discovery of the repressed Oedipus complex, that alone would give it a claim to be included among the precious new acquisitions of mankind" [Freud, 1940, pp. 192–193]).

Briefly, the theory's core is that boys normally experience a psychosexual developmental stage roughly between ages three and six in which the boy has intense incestuous sexual desire—not mere sensual pleasure in touch, but true erotic longing with some degree of inchoate physical premonition of intercourse despite lack of knowl-edge of the sex act—for his mother (equated here with the female caretaker of the child). From these incestuous sexual feelings, other components of the theory flow. The boy's desire triggers jealous rivalry and even murderous rage toward the father due to his possession of the mother. As a consequence of the boy's fantasies of getting rid of his father and replacing him in sexually possessing his mother, the son experiences intense anxiety due to fear of retribution and punishment by the father, which the child infers would take the form of castration, in which the boy's offending organ that is excited by the mother would be removed by the father. At the same time, the child experiences fear that his fantasies of getting rid of the father might somehow be realized, for the child also loves and needs his father.

The theory also holds that repression of the set of emotions, desires, and conflicts aroused during the Oedipal phase propels the boy's psychological development forward. For example, formation of a moral conscience occurs through unconscious identification with the father's values and prohibitions to avert his anger, and fear of the father leads to the boy's turning away from his mother as his sexual object choice and eventual shift of sexual interest to sexual objects outside the family of origin.

The Oedipal theory with its strict sexual formulation resonates with many partial and less-provocative truths with which it should not be confused. Many of the theoretical offshoots of psychoanalysis that broke with Freud rejected or reinterpreted the Oedipal theory, from object relations theory and self-psychology to feminist theory and attachment theory. It is clear that children do have sexual feelings in the form of pleasurable genital sensations, and that they sometimes experience feelings that resemble erotic interest in friends or a parent. Some rare pathologies of sexuality or aggression in childhood can look like Freud's description of the Oedipus complex gone astray. Occasionally there occurs overt incestuous sexualization of parent–child relationships. Other theoreticians, such as Heinz Kohut (1977), have suggested that the kinds of Oedipal feelings Freud described, although not a normal developmental stage as Freud claimed, do occur in certain children when there is an abnormal family environment that pathologically interferes with normal development of the self. Clinicians have undoubtedly occasionally seen such children who manifest Oedipal feelings and desires, although one must always be cautious about such interpretations given the tendency to see things from one's preset theoretical position and the power of suggestion. Other theoreticians, such as Karen Horney (1939), suggest that what may be misinterpreted as Oedipal psychosexual desires are in fact derived from social and emotional variables, such as envy of the privileges and dominance of adults. For example, children perceive adult gender roles and may express a desire to take over such roles, as in a boy saying that he wants to marry mommy. Most importantly, there are many routine developmental challenges that children must undergo that resemble aspects of Freud's described Oedipal stage, such as attachment to a parent as described by John Bowlby (1982). How a child negotiates the intense triadic relationship between the child and his parents can have momentous implications for the child's later emotional and relationship life. All these and many other Oedipal-like phenomena do occur.

Such alterations make the theory more commonsensical or make it more about pathology than a universal normal developmental stage. However, in abandoning what is uniquely provocative about the theory they undermine the ability of the Oedipus complex to play the essential role it does in Freud's broader developmental and neurosogenic theories. Rather than interpreting Freud's talk as elliptical for broader sensual feelings or feelings related to cultural gender norms, I take Freud's assertions as he clearly intended and insistently stated them, as literal statements about a child's sexual and aggressive feelings.

Does the Oedipus complex exist in anything like the form Freud proposed? In *Freud's Argument for the Oedipus Complex* (2023a), I closely examined the support presented by Freud for the existence of the Oedipus complex, reconstructing and evaluating each of the arguments in the case of Little Hans, in which Freud presented what he considered his best evidence for the Oedipus complex. I concluded that the arguments made sense in principle, but when compared to the actual case data they failed abysmally. There was not initially a good reason for believing the Oedipal theory, and subsequent evidence supports this negative conclusion (Eagle, 2018). So, I conclude that the Oedipus complex does not exist, at least in anything like the form Freud proposed and was never scientifically well supported. This yields the question of what explains the phenomenal success and influence of the theory—that is, why did a demonstrably false theory gain the degree of medical approval and cultural significance it did? This is where Foucault's theory of power/knowledge can usefully explain why a theory might be accepted due to its role in social power strategies rather than its evidential support.

In principle, one can analyze the power/knowledge in the deployment of a theory without denying the theory's truth. However, if Freud presented no credible evidence for the Oedipal theory, then this is all the more reason to suspect that there is an alternative explanation, such as one based on power/knowledge, for the theory's wide acceptance and influence.

Michel Foucault

The account I present here of Foucault's argument regarding the Oedipal theory can be read independently of any wider knowledge of Foucault's philosophical work or life. However, for those who are interested, I present some brief biographical notes.

Michel Foucault (1926–1984) was born in Poitiers, France, the son of a prominent surgeon—thus a family of the bourgeois social stratum. As a philosophy student in Paris at the prestigious École Normale Supérieure, Foucault attended the lectures of phenomenologist Maurice Merleau-Ponty and worked with philosophers Jean Hyppolite and Louis Althusser, studying Heidegger, Nietzsche, Marx, and Hegel. Despite bouts of depression and even a suicide attempt, perhaps linked to his struggle in coming to terms with his homosexuality, Foucault eventually earned degrees in both philosophy and psychology and went on for the doctorate in philosophy while teaching philosophy and working as a psychologist in Paris's Hôpital Sainte-Anne. While intermittently holding positions in French universities and teaching in several foreign countries, he completed his philosophy doctoral dissertation, which became his first major book, *History of Madness*, tracing how forms of unreason that posed a limit and challenge to rationality were medicalized and transformed into mental disorders. He was soon elected to a coveted academic position at the College de France where he was given a Chair with the self-designated title, "History and Systems of Thought." His duties consisted of about 12 public lectures each year on his research, and these lectures became well-attended public events. During much of his later life, Foucault was widely considered France's foremost—and most controversial—intellectual. He clashed with many of the leading French and European intellectuals of his time, including Jürgen Habermas, Jacques Derrida (with whom he did not speak for years, reputedly due to a dispute over an interpretation of Descartes's *cogito* argument), and Gilles Deleuze. Foucault was also an activist involved in many unpopular initiatives, such as working against the Algerian war and for homosexual rights and prison reform.

In the early 1980s, Foucault spent considerable time in the United States, particularly at the University of California, Berkeley, interacting with American philosophers such as Hubert Dreyfus and John Searle. (I was a graduate student at Berkeley at the time, and this is where I got to know Foucault.) Foucault died in June 1984 of an AIDs-related illness at the Salpêtrière Hospital in Paris at the age of 57.

To offer some very brief perspectives on Foucault's intellectual trajectory, his work is commonly divided into three phases. The first, during the 1960s, was his "archeology" phase of studies excavating the "epistemes" or discourse rules and conceptual frameworks underlying and ordering knowledge in various phases of the development of the human sciences. After excavating the conceptual substrates of both psychiatry (in *History of Madness* [2006], originally published in 1961) and general medicine in the hospital with its "medical gaze" (in *The Birth of the Clinic: An Archaeology of Medical Perception* [1973], originally published in 1963), he then made an ambitious attempt in

The Order of Things: An Archaeology of the Human Sciences (1966) to apply his archaeological methodology on a larger scale to the development of the "human sciences" (e.g., biology, psychology, economics, and linguistics, the sciences of life, labor, and language). He argues in this work that all the major scientific disciplines of a given era share a reliance on a common episteme or underlying conceptual-epistemological framework determining what makes sense as a claim or an acceptable explanation, and that a change in the episteme yields a conceptual discontinuity to the point where people across the divide may hardly be speaking the same language and may be incapable of understanding each other.

In his second "genealogy" phase in the 1970s, Foucault produced his two most influential histories, *Discipline and Punish* (1975) and *The History of Sexuality, Volume 1: An introduction* (1978; *HS1*; originally published in 1976 with the subtitle *The Will to Knowledge*). These works explore how social power has become internalized via the reconstitution of the modern subject by theories of man and regimes of power implicitly embedded in the knowledge of the human sciences. Here emerges the notion of power/knowledge in which scientific theory about human beings and social regulatory power are intertwined. It is the work of this second phase, and specifically Foucault's work on sexuality encompassing his 1975 lectures and *HS1*, that will be of primary relevance here.

The final phase, during the last years of his life in the early 1980s, is sometimes called Foucault's "ethical" phase, during which Foucault wrote three further volumes in his history of sexuality focused on ancient ethical disciplines of the body. Exploring the different ways we have understood and related to our pleasures and displaying possible alternatives to our current "deployment of sexuality" (see below), Foucault attempted to show how ancient and medieval practices regarding sexuality and pleasure were both radically different from but also evolved into our own practices. His focus moved from power to the constitution of the subject.

Foucault on Power/Knowledge

Foucault approaches the question of the incest theory's influence from his distinctive "power/knowledge" perspective. (Note that "power/

knowledge" has become the standard English scholarly translation of Foucault's original terminology, *savoir-pouvoir*, or "knowledge-power.") By "power," Foucault does not mean a power from above to impose control on others (which he dismisses as "sovereign" or "juridical" power). Rather, he takes a very broad approach to power that refers to the influences and constraints imposed by the structure of a web of social relationships, and most generally any way in which one individual's actions shape the actions of another: "For Foucault, power is not a *drive*; it is not something that springs from the individual or the body. Rather, it is a series of forces generated by differential social relations" (Grace, 2013, p. 239). As Foucault explains:

> What does it mean to exercise power? It does not mean picking up this tape recorder and throwing it on the ground. I have the capacity to do so…[b]ut I would not be exercising power if I did that. However, if I take this tape recorder and throw it on the ground—in order to make you mad or so that you can't repeat what I've said, or to put pressure on you so that you'll behave in such and such a way, or to intimidate you—Good, what I've done, by shaping your behavior through certain means, that is power…I'm not forcing you at all and I'm leaving you completely free—that's when I begin to exercise power. It's clear that power should not be defined as a constraining act of violence that represses individuals, forcing them to do something or preventing them from doing some other thing. But it takes place when there is a relation between two free subjects, and this relation is unbalanced, so that one can act upon the other, and the other is acted upon, or allows himself to be acted upon.
>
> (Foucault, 1980b, as quoted in Taylor, 2014, p. 5)

More succinctly, for Foucault the exercise of power is simply "to structure the possible field of action of others…[O]ne defines the exercise of power as a mode of action upon the actions of others" (1998, p. 341). Foucault explains that according to this broad notion of power, it is dispersed throughout human relationships and encompasses

> the methods and techniques used in different institutional contexts to act upon the behavior of individuals taken separately or in a group, so as to shape, direct, modify their way of conducting

themselves, to…fit it into overall strategies….These power relations characterize the manner in which men are 'governed' by one another.

(1998, p. 463)

This broad conception of power can be applied to the effects on action of the acceptance of scientific theories about human nature. Foucault observes that in the human sciences, acceptance of a scientific theory of human nature can change how people understand and react to each other, and thus change the nature of power in interpersonal relationships. *Power/knowledge* refers to the effects on power inherent in the acceptance of a scientific theory about human nature that, once accepted, reshapes how we understand and relate to each other and to ourselves. Especially in cases in which theories of human nature are widely accepted without adequate scientific evidence, their acceptance, Foucault argues, can often be explained in terms of their effects on social power relations. When such effects on power are congruent with the direction of changing social demands and values, this can make the theory implicitly appealing as a solution to social-structural challenges and explain why the theory is accepted.

Thus, Foucault intends something like the following by his question about the appeal of the incest theory: how did the theory fit with changing cultural values and evolving social and family relationships such that believing the incest theory was useful and appealing because of the new forms of power that its acceptance created? Foucault suggests that the theory's effects on power explain why the theory was selected and disseminated as a presumed truth.

Especially when it comes to nineteenth-century sexual theories, Foucault argues for the intimate relationship of knowledge and power:

One must not suppose that there exists a certain sphere of sexuality that would be the legitimate concern of a free and disinterested scientific inquiry were it not the object of mechanisms of prohibition brought to bear by the economic or ideological requirements of power. If sexuality was constituted as an area of investigation, this was only because relations of power had established it as a possible object…. Between techniques of knowledge and strategies of power, there is no exteriority, even if they have specific roles and are linked together.

(1978, p. 98)

On the other hand, he is clear that although evidential and power concerns become linked in theory acceptance, these are still two distinguishable considerations. He reassures us that "when I talk about power relations and games of truth, I am absolutely not saying that games of truth are just concealed power relations—that would be a horrible caricature" (Foucault, 1997, p. 296). He dismisses as absurd the idea that scientific theorizing is just the exercise of power:

> I know that, as far as the general public is concerned, I am the guy who said that knowledge merged with power, that it was no more than a thin mask thrown over the structures of domination and that those structures were always ones of oppression, confinement, and so on. The first point is so absurd as to be laughable. If I had said, or meant, that knowledge was power, I would have said so, and, having said so, I would have had nothing more to say, since, having made them identical, I don't see why I would have taken the trouble to show the different relations between them.
>
> (1988, pp. 264–265)

Foucault also frames his work as an analysis of subjectivity, in the sense of the ways that people experience and understand themselves and their deepest natures as a result of the theories they accept. Thus, he has undertaken

> to study the constitution of the subject as an object for himself: the formation of procedures by which the subject is led to observe himself, analyze himself, interpret himself, recognize himself as a domain of possible knowledge. In short, this concerns the history of 'subjectivity,' if what is meant by the term is the way in which the subject experiences himself in a game of truth where he relates to himself.
>
> (1998, p. 461)

Foucault's point is to understand the subtle ways that we are governed by and experience ourselves in terms of what we believe are the truths of the human sciences: "My objective has been to create a history of the different modes by which, in our culture, human beings are made subjects," especially "the way a human being turns him- or herself into a subject" (Foucault, 1983, p. 208).

What Foucault calls "games of truth" are "the rules according to which what a subject can say about certain things depends on the question of true and false ...; it is the history of 'veridictions,' understood as the forms according to which discourses capable of being declared true or false are articulated concerning a domain of things" (1998, p. 460). He thus focuses on the rules of the social process for arriving at what will be taken to be the truth as forms of power, rather than on truth and falsity in themselves. The emergence of such games of truth defining when truth is obtained at a given time and in a given context constitute a "historical a priori of a possible experience" (p. 460), and the excavation of the nature of the rules of such games of truth constitutes Foucault's "archaeology of knowledge": "In sum, the critical history of thought is...the history of 'veridictions,' understood as the forms according to which discourses capable of being declared true or false are articulated concerning a domain of things" (p. 463).

Regarding why he has expended so much energy on studying the relationship of knowledge and power specifically in the psychology of sexuality and related psychological and social sciences rather than the harder sciences, Foucault explains that, in endeavoring to address the relationship between power and knowledge, he reasoned (none too flatteringly with regard to psychiatry's scientific status!) as follows:

For me, it was a matter of saying this: if, concerning a science like theoretical physics or organic chemistry, one poses the problem of its relations with the political and economic structures of society, isn't one posing an excessively complicated question? Doesn't this set the threshold of possible explanations impossibly high? But on the other hand, if one takes a form of knowledge (*savoir*) like psychiatry, won't the question be much easier to resolve, since the epistemological profile of psychiatry is a low one and psychiatric practice is linked with a whole range of institutions, economic requirements and political issues of social regulation? Couldn't the

interweaving of effects of power and knowledge be grasped with
greater certainty in the case of a science as 'dubious' as psychiatry?

(1980a, p. 109)

That is, the evidence for theories of human nature is particularly weak
but these theories often become highly influential nonetheless. This is
where the likelihood is greatest that the theory finds favor because
belief in the theory alters how people think about and interact with
each other in a way that serves some useful social regulatory purpose.

Foucault argues that the acceptance of such "dubious" psychological or social theories for social regulatory purposes is not intentional
but can be explained through a process of social selection of theories
due to their being useful for structuring social power. They come to be
accepted because of the political and economic advantages they
confer, and in that sense their acceptance is explained by the social
functions they serve. The social selectionist process, which Foucault
writes about in somewhat mentalized goal-directed terms as having its
own aims, yields strategies of social power and constitutes a form of
power/knowledge that need not involve any explicit human choices
aimed at creating or selecting the mechanisms as forms of power:

We need to see how these mechanisms of power...have begun to
become economically advantageous and politically useful.... [W]hat
the bourgeoisie needed, or that in which its system discovered its real
interests, was not the exclusion of the mad or the surveillance and
prohibition of infantile masturbation...but rather, the techniques and
procedures themselves of such an exclusion. It is the mechanisms of
that exclusion that are necessary, the apparatuses of surveillance, the
medicalisation of sexuality, of madness, of delinquency, all the micro-
mechanisms of power, that came, from a certain moment in time, to
represent the interests of the bourgeoisie..... [I]t was not the bourgeoisie itself which thought that madness had to be excluded or
infantile sexuality repressed. What in fact happened instead was that
the mechanisms of the exclusion of madness, and of the surveillance of
infantile sexuality, began from a particular point in time, and for
reasons which need to be studied, to reveal their political usefulness
and to lend themselves to economic profit, and that as a natural
consequence, all of a sudden, they came to be colonised and

maintained by global mechanisms and the entire State system. It is only if we grasp these techniques of power and demonstrate the economic advantages or political utility that derives from them in a given context for specific reasons, that we can understand how these mechanisms come to be effectively incorporated into the social whole.

(1980a, p. 101)

This exercise of power is not an intentional action aimed at domination, but a change in socially sanctioned practices often inscribed in bodily dispositions:

[T]he analysis should not concern itself with power at the level of conscious intention or decision;...Instead, it is a case of studying power at the point where its intention, if it has one, is completely invested in its real and effective practices.... Let us not, therefore, ask why certain people want to dominate.... Let us ask, instead, how things work at the level of on-going subjugation, at the level of those continuous and uninterrupted processes which subject our bodies, govern our gestures, dictate our behaviours etc.

(1980a, p. 97)

The result is a self-organizing process of social change that cannot be attributed to the decisions of individuals: "you get a coherent, rational strategy, but one for which it is no longer possible to identify a person who conceived it" (1980a, p. 203);

[T]here is no power that is exercised without a series of aims and objectives. But this does not mean that it results from the choice or decision of an individual subject... [T]he rationality of power is characterized by tactics...which, becoming connected to one another, attracting and propagating one another..., end by forming comprehensive systems: the logic is perfectly clear, the aims decipherable, and yet it is often the case that no one is there to have invented them.

(1978, p. 95)

Such theories that are accepted because of the effects of their power/ knowledge can thus be said to have social functions that explain their continued acceptance. Consequently, commentators frequently classify Foucault as a social functionalist (e.g., Basaure, 2009). Foucault explains how his focus on sexuality fits within this overall framework:

> "One sees how the theme of a 'history of sexuality' can fit [Foucault's] general project. It is a matter of analyzing 'sexuality' as a historically singular mode of experience in which the subject is objectified for himself and for others through certain specific procedures of 'government.'"
>
> (1998, p. 465)

As noted, Foucault sees theories themselves as "truth games" or "discourses" or "discursive formations"—that is, as systems of rules for producing and applying statements of what is considered knowledge or truth. The rules that constitute a specific domain of scientific inquiry such as sexuality are thus themselves a form of power that shapes what can be said, what is considered a sensible hypothesis, and how a phenomenon can be explained within that domain. The analysis of power/knowledge examines these implicit rules that govern the "will to knowledge," for example, the attempt to formulate a truth about one's sexual nature:

> The central issue, then (at least in the first instance), is not to determine whether one says yes or no to sex, whether one formulates prohibitions or permissions, whether one asserts its importance or denies its effects...but to account for the fact that it is spoken about.... What is at issue, briefly, is the over-all "discursive fact," the way in which sex is "put into discourse." Hence, too, my main concern will be to locate the forms of power... entailing effects that may be those of refusal, blockage, and invalidation, but also incitement and intensification: in short, the "polymorphous techniques of power." And finally, the essential aim will not be to determine whether these discursive productions and these effects of power lead one to formulate the truth about sex, or on the contrary falsehoods designed to conceal that truth, but rather to bring out the "will to knowledge" that serves as both their support and their instrument.
>
> (1978, pp. 11–12)

Referring to the supposed Victorian silence about sex, Foucault illustrates the all-encompassing subtlety of the power in discursive rules so that even the lack of explicit discourse can be a form of discourse:

Take the secondary schools of the eighteenth century, for example. On the whole, one can have the impression that sex was hardly spoken of at all in these institutions. But one only has to glance over the architectural layout, the rules of discipline, and their whole internal organization: the question of sex was a constant preoccupation. The builders considered it explicitly. The organizers took it permanently into account. All who held a measure of authority were placed in a state of perpetual alert, which the fixtures, the precautions taken, the interplay of punishments and responsibilities, never ceased to reiterate. The space for classes, the shape of the tables, the planning of the recreation lessons, the distribution of the dormitories (with or without partitions, with or without curtains), the rules for monitoring bedtime and sleep periods—all this referred, in the most prolix manner, to the sexuality of children.

(1978, pp. 27–28)

Thus, the rules of discourse are operative both in what one says and what one refuses to say. Power/knowledge operates in both directions.

Although Foucault continued to emphasize the structure of discourse and its rules as prominent vehicles of power, he also came to focus on the social and bodily practices that accompanied the discursive formations and theories—practices such as confession, surveillance, and medicalization—as themselves incorporating new forms of power. For Foucault, power expressed itself directly in bodily practices by "exercising upon it a subtle coercion, of obtaining holds upon it at the level of the mechanism itself—movements, gestures, attitudes, rapidity: an infinitesimal power over the active body" (1975, pp. 136–137). Within a broader episteme, there would then be combinations of discourse rules and bodily practices together making up an overall "apparatus" of power:

This is what the apparatus consists in: strategies of relations of forces supporting, and supported by, types of knowledge ... .[W]hat I call an apparatus is a much more general case of the *episteme;* or rather, that the *episteme* is a specifically *discursive* apparatus, whereas the apparatus in its general form is both discursive and non-discursive, its elements being much more heterogeneous.

(1980a, pp. 196–197)

Foucault does not look for a "top-down" explanation along the lines, say, of the medical profession imposing on the population an understandable error or physicians yielding to economic self-interest by inflicting the masturbation crusade on a pliant general population. Nor, as we shall see in Chapter 3, does Foucault see the power involved in the deployment of sexuality as linked to political (or what he calls "sovereign" or "juridical") top-down power. His analysis is not at all a replay of Marxist or Marcuse's or Reich's arguments that the repression of eros is part and parcel of the apparatus of political repression by the ruling class in our society and thus that sexual liberation is a revolutionary political act that could well bring broader political liberation closer. Rather, he thinks that the focus on sexual liberation is itself part of an apparatus of social regulation that is bottom-up in the sense that it comes about by chance and then percolates through society when it is selected due to the functions it serves and not because of ruling-class desires or intentions. Instead of a top-down approach, Foucault postulates broader disparate social forces and changes that mutate and converge to create a variety of strategies of power without any intentionality behind them that form into larger regulatory structures:

Power comes from below; that is, there is no binary and all-encompassing opposition between rulers and ruled at the root of power relations.... One must suppose rather that the manifold relationships of force that take shape and come into play in the machinery of production, in families, limited groups, and institutions, are the basis for wide-ranging effects of cleavage that run through the social body as a whole.

(Foucault, 1978, p. 94)

As Leslie Thiele aptly explains,

Foucault's genius is evidenced...in illustrating that historical coherencies are formed from the confluence of multiple strategies and tactics of power and knowledge. History, he shows, is not the product of grand narratives with teleological movements but of diverse struggles that nonetheless become organized into coherent…patterns of domination, subjectification, and government.

(1991, p. 585)

Of course, one can choose to read Foucault without completely accepting at the outset the self-organizational and social-functional explanations he postulates, but rather as a description of the unexpected effects on power of the acceptance of certain theories, leaving open the question of whether those effects are their functions and fully explain their acceptance for further scrutiny.

Foucault on the Deployment of Sexuality and the Repression Hypothesis

My focus in this book is on understanding Foucault's analysis of the history of sexuality and its relation to psychoanalysis, and specifically his attempt to explain the success of Freud's Oedipal theory in terms of its relationship to the two-century "masturbation crusade" that preceded it. He sees these phenomena as parts of a larger power/knowledge phenomenon that he calls "the deployment of sexuality" (alternatively, "the apparatus of sexuality") in which medical and scientific theories of sexuality guide people to seek the truth about their sexual nature, all as part of a tactic of social regulation. Foucault proposes that the role the Oedipal theory plays in the deployment of sexuality resolves the puzzle of how to explain the influence the theory has enjoyed despite its weak scientific credentials.

Why the choice of sexuality as the topic for extended analysis? Foucault explains:

[T]he question of sex and sexuality appeared … to constitute not the only possible example, certainly, but at least a rather privileged case. Indeed, it was in this connection that … individuals were all called on to recognize themselves as subjects of pleasure, of desire, of lust, of temptation and were urged to deploy, by various means (self-examination, spiritual exercises, admission, confession), the game of true and false in regard to themselves and what constitutes the most secret, the most individual part of their subjectivity.

(Foucault, 1998, p. 461)

In other words, our culture is awash with theories of sexual identity, sexual desire, sexual gratification and fulfilment, and other theories of lurking sexual secrets that purport to determine the truth of who we *really are*. Sex and sexuality, Foucault observes, have become so closely connected with the question of identity, subjectivity, and selfhood that disciplines seeking a truth about sexuality, whether in our intimate relationships, in psychoanalysis, or in a quest for identity, appear inextricably attached to elements of social power. Foucault's central concern is how it came to be that the question of truth was posed in regard to sexuality: "what had to happen in the history of the West for the question of truth to be posed in regard to sexual pleasure? ... [W]hat I'm concerned with, what I'm talking about, is how it comes about that people are told that the secret of their truth lies in the region of their sex" (1980a, pp. 209, 214). Forrester explains the close link between this statement by Foucault of the basic question addressed in *HS1* and Foucault's understanding of psychoanalysis:

Foucault's initial problem is: Why, since the eighteenth century, have we talked so much about sex?... [Psychoanalysis] has given the purest expression to the notion, to which we all perhaps subscribe, that the subject's truth is to be found through a discourse on his or her sexuality. What is more intimate seems to be most important and precious.

(1980, p. 289)

Foucault's surprising answer is that the centrality of sexuality and sexual identity in our culture, rather than being a manifestation of our striving for and achieving liberation from social constraints and repression, is the very way that social regulation now works to serve social functioning. In *HS1*, Foucault examines the deployment of sexuality beginning with concerns about the dangers of sexuality during the masturbation crusade and reaching its zenith in Victorian theories of perversion and ultimately in the Oedipal theory. The central technique of this apparatus was medicalizing the confession of sexual pleasures, desires, and actions. At first, these confessional practices were direct and brutal, extorting the truth by "simply demanding that the subject tell his or her story" (1980a, p. 217), but eventually they culminated in the more indirect approach of the psychoanalytic session.

Foucault identifies four targets of medical-scientific sexual knowledge that served the deployment's purposes of power: the masturbating child; the hysterical woman; the perverse adult; and the reproducing ("Malthusian") couple that raised the issue of the regulation of populations. The strategies for regulating these forms of sexuality were applied within and by the family with medical guidance, and so had the effect of sexualizing family life. Foucault describes how these issues changed from matters of sin to social and medical concerns at the beginning of the nineteenth century:

> there emerged a completely new technology of sex ... truly independent of the thematics of sin. Through pedagogy, medicine, and economics, it made sex not only a secular concern but a concern of the state as well ... that required the social body as a whole, and virtually all of its individuals, to place themselves under surveillance.
>
> (1978, p. 116)

As will be explained in Chapter 3, the concern about the masturbating child turns out to have some doctrinal overlap with concerns about the Malthusian couple via the construction of "conjugal onanism." Of these targets of power/knowledge, my focus will be almost exclusively on the masturbating child.

Foucault argues that a basic social "mutation" occurred at the beginning of the nineteenth century:

> the sexual instinct was isolated as a separate biological and psychical instinct; a clinical analysis was made of all the forms of anomalies by which it could be afflicted; it was assigned a role of normalization or pathologization with respect to all behavior; and finally, a corrective technology was sought for these anomalies.
>
> (1978, p. 105)

This theoretical development "isolated a sexual 'instinct' capable of presenting constitutive anomalies, acquired derivations, infirmities, or pathological processes" (1978, p. 117).

For Foucault, the deployment of sexuality, in which the body is sexualized and then made a target of medical sexual knowledge, involves ever-expanding power structures that reshape how people define their self-identities:

> The deployment of sexuality has its reason for being ... in proliferating, innovating, annexing, creating, and penetrating bodies in an increasingly detailed way, and in controlling populations in an increasingly comprehensive way....[T]he arrangement that has sustained it is not governed by reproduction; it has been linked from the outset with an intensification of the body—with its exploitation as an object of knowledge and an element in relations of power.
>
> (1978, p. 107)

The deployment from the beginning involved sexual concerns about childhood masturbation and its potentially pathological harms, which, contrary to appearances, Foucault sees as intensifying the sexualization of the family to serve social ends of emotionally entangling and thus solidifying the emerging nuclear family:

> The restrictions on masturbation hardly start in Europe until the eighteenth century. Suddenly, a panic-theme appears: an appalling sickness develops in the Western world. Children masturbate.... [A] system of control of sexuality...is established over the bodies of children. But sexuality, through thus becoming an object of analysis and concern, surveillance and control, engenders at the same time an intensification of each individual's desire.
>
> (1980a, pp. 56–57)

Foucault's analysis of the deployment of sexuality upends the usual story about Victorian repression that Foucault labels the "repressive hypothesis":

> For a long time, the story goes, we supported a Victorian regime, and we continue to be dominated by...our restrained, mute, and

hypocritical sexuality. At the beginning of the seventeenth century a certain frankness was still common, it would seem. Sexual practices had little need of secrecy.... But twilight soon fell upon this bright day, followed by the monotonous nights of the Victorian bourgeoisie. Sexuality was carefully confined; it moved into the home. The conjugal family took custody of it and absorbed it into the serious function of reproduction. On the subject of sex, silence became the rule.... [T]he seventeenth century, then, was the beginning of an age of repression emblematic of what we call the bourgeois societies, an age which perhaps we still have not completely left behind.

(1978, pp. 3, 17).

This standard repressive hypothesis is rejected by Foucault on the grounds of an increase rather than decrease in talk about sex:

[S]ince the end of the sixteenth century, the 'putting into discourse of sex,' far from undergoing a process of restriction, on the contrary has been subjected to a mechanism of increasing incitement.... [A]round and apropos of sex, one sees a veritable discursive explosion...., an institutional incitement to speak about it, and to do so more and more.

(1978, pp. 12, 17)

He observes that the explosion of scientific sexual discourse went beyond general medicine to "psychiatry, when it set out to discover the etiology of mental illnesses, focusing its gaze first on 'excess,' then onanism, then frustration, then 'frauds against procreation,' but especially when it annexed the whole of the sexual perversions as its own province" (1978, p. 30). He thus offers the hypothesis that something other than repression was taking place. Given that books were filled with talk about sex—albeit often aimed at discouraging sex—Foucault argues that the repression hypothesis is disconfirmed:

Let us put forward a general working hypothesis. The society that emerged in the nineteenth century—bourgeois, capitalist, or industrial society, call it what you will—did not confront sex with a fundamental refusal of recognition. On the contrary, it put into operation an entire machinery for producing true discourses concerning it. Not only did it speak of sex and compel everyone to do so; it also set out to formulate the uniform truth of sex.

(1978, p. 69)

The repression hypothesis at the social level was the foundation for Freud's hypothesis that individuals then repressed their own sexual desires and such repressed sexuality is the cause of the psychoneuroses such as hysteria. Turning specifically to childhood sexuality and the masturbation crusade, Foucault argues that the repressive hypothesis that sex was repressed during the Victorian era is incorrect in light of the discursive explosion about sex in which it was endlessly discussed and examined and new sexual identities constructed, and correspondingly the idea that Freud liberated us from sexual silence is mistaken:

The situation was similar in the case of children's sex. It is often said that the classical period consigned it to an obscurity from which it scarcely emerged before the *Three Essays* or the beneficent anxieties of Little Hans. It is true that a longstanding "freedom" of language between children and adults, or pupils and teachers, may have disappeared.... And the boisterous laughter that had accompanied the precocious sexuality of children for so long—and in all social classes, it seems, was gradually stifled. But this was not a plain and simple imposition of silence. Rather, it was a new regime of discourses. Not any less was said about it; on the contrary. But things were said—in a different way; it was different people who said them, from different points of view, and in order to obtain different results.

(1978, p. 27)

Freud's method of "free association" directed to sexual history is a prime example of Foucault's notion of the discursive explosion of sexual talk camouflaged by the doctrine of repression and the supposed challenge of overcoming it. Indeed, according to Foucault, the supposed repression was accompanied by such a focus on sexuality that it actually created new and more intense sexual feelings:

It is customary to say that bourgeois society repressed infantile sexuality to the point where it refused even to speak of it or acknowledge its existence. It was necessary to wait until Freud for the discovery at last to be made that children have a sexuality. Now if you read all the books on pedagogy and child medicine ... you find that children's sex is spoken of constantly and in every possible context. One might argue that the purpose of these discourses was precisely to prevent children from having a sexuality. But their *effect* was to din it into parents' heads that their children's sex constituted a fundamental problem in terms of their parental educational responsibilities, and to din it into children's heads that their relationship with their own body and their own sex was to be a fundamental problem as far as *they* were concerned; and this had the consequence of sexually exciting the bodies of children while at the same time fixing the parental gaze and vigilance on the peril of infantile sexuality. The result was a sexualising of the infantile body, a sexualising of the bodily relationship between parent and child, a sexualising of the familial domain. 'Sexuality' is far more of a positive product of power than power was ever repression of sexuality.

(1980a, p. 120)

Foucault proceeds to examine the historical phenomena afresh, asking why the increase in sexual discourse occurred and what effects on power it had that led to such sustained discussion. He allows that some fields of knowledge are more scientifically well-founded than others, and observes that medical theories of sexuality were particularly scientifically weak:

When we compare these discourses on human sexuality with what was known at the time about the physiology of animal and plant reproduction, we are struck by the incongruity. Their feeble content from the standpoint of elementary rationality, not to mention scientificity, earns them a place apart in the history of knowledge. They form a strangely muddled zone.

(1978, p. 54)

Foucault also acknowledges that there are fundamental social prohibitions that structure social and family life, but he argues that these rules can mistakenly lead one to conclude that sex is or was repressed when in fact they do not constitute society's essential relation to sexuality over the past two centuries. In fact, he argues, we must abandon the hypothesis of an age of sexual repression given the proliferation of categories of sexual activities and perverse sexual desires. Rather than being a prudish society as the repression hypothesis portrays us, we are quite the opposite. Disputing our supposed sexual constriction, Foucault chides us: "It may well be that we talk about sex more than anything else; ... It is possible that where sex is concerned, the most long-winded, the most impatient of societies is our own" (1978, p. 33).

In disputing the repressive hypothesis, Foucault puts forward one of his most fundamental and distinctive theses, that power/knowledge is generally not an oppressive "negative" form of power in which one individual or group prohibits or controls or dominates over the actions of another. Rather, theories give rise to "positive" forms of power by constructing new ways of behaving, thinking, and categorizing oneself. These positive new constructs reshape people's sense of identity and cause individuals to self-regulate so that external coercive control is not needed.

Foucault's thesis is that positive mechanisms of power are a more fundamental part of the story of modern social power than repressive mechanisms. Such positive mechanisms deploy power/knowledge by producing discourse, inducing pleasure, and generating new forms of power. Foucault is thus suspicious of the notion of sexual liberation because he sees it as based on the mistake of seeing a natural sexuality as repressed, when in fact what comes to be "liberated" is itself a deployment-of-sexuality construct with its own form of power/knowledge. One is "liberating" an apparatus of power.

Perhaps having in mind Freud's theory of "component sexual instincts" that extends sexuality to many bodily zones (see Chapter 7), Foucault argues that the concept of sexuality is itself a positive construction out of "a great surface network in which the stimulation of bodies, the intensification of pleasures, the incitement to discourse, ... are linked to one another, in accordance with a few major strategies of knowledge and power" (1978, pp. 105–106). Sexuality thus emerges out of a variety of bodily pleasures and social interactions beyond the sexual organs for purposes of social-regulatory power. That is, where we can, we tend to categorize as sexuality whatever bodily pleasures or interpersonal interactions serve the social control functions of the sexuality construct. Thus, for example, various pleasures ranging from thumb sucking and cuddling with one's mother to a child's sleeping in its parents' bed are sexualized and become targets of regulation. This new categorization, Foucault argues, is generally not anchored in a scientific reality but is a positive construct that organizes power/knowledge in a socially useful way. He claims that our current positive construction of sexuality first emerged in the nineteenth century.

Why does the question with which Foucault starts his 1975 lecture on the incest theory refer specifically to its acceptance by the bourgeois family? Foucault was not a Marxist, but he does attend to class differences in the deployment of sexuality. He recognizes that major aspects of the deployment of sexuality initially occurred in and influenced primarily middle-class or bourgeois segments of society: "[W]hat I have just said is certainly not valid for society in general or for every type of family....[T]he crusade against masturbation addressed itself almost exclusively to the bourgeois family" (2003, p. 268). Thus, it is primarily the self-made educated urban middle class—such as the family of Little Hans, whose case will be discussed in Chapter 7—that was attuned to these developments and for whom the deployment of sexuality initially had its major functions: "this deployment does not operate in symmetrical fashion with respect to the social classes ... . [S]exuality is originally, historically bourgeois" (1978, p. 127). We shall see in Chapter 6 that the differentiation between the classes plays a role in Foucault's later account of the incest theory in *HS1*.

Foucault is not denying that sexual repression existed during the Victorian era, and he acknowledges that it is obvious that sex was indeed in some respects repressed: "The notion of repression ... does indeed appear to correspond so well with a whole range of phenomena which belong among the effects of power" (1980a, p. 118). However, repression served only to displace sexual focus onto processes of sexual examination aimed at detecting sexual activity—for example, the sexual examination of the child in the home and in the boarding school to be sure that boys were not masturbating. The entire process of supposed repression followed by a process of liberation and sexual self-discovery could then be channeled for social purposes.

Foucault on Confession as a Primary Tool of the Deployment of Sexuality

A central element of Foucault's account of the deployment of sexuality is the use of confession of one's sexual nature as a tool of power. By "confession" Foucault simply means "all those procedures by which the subject is incited to produce a discourse of truth about his sexuality which is capable of having effects on the subject himself" (1980a, pp. 215–216). Foucault sees confession as omnipresent in today's culture:

> We have become a singularly confessing society ... .[The confession] plays a part in justice, medicine, education, family relationships, and love relations, in the most ordinary affairs of everyday life, and in the most solemn rites: one confesses one's crimes, one's sins, one's thoughts and desires, one's illnesses and troubles; one goes about telling, with the greatest precision, whatever is most difficult to tell. ...One confesses—or is forced to confess.
>
> (1978, p. 59)

During the mid-nineteenth century there occurred a crucial transformation from moral to medical and scientific judgments about sexual confessions, according to Foucault: "It was a time when the most singular pleasures were called upon to pronounce a discourse of truth concerning themselves, a discourse...not of sin and salvation, but of bodies and life processes—the discourse of science" (1978, p. 64). He refers here to the surge of medical publications about sexual perversion that categorized sexual peculiarities as failures of the function of the sexual instinct and thus as a variety of mental disorders. Foucault suggests that this medicalization of not only masturbation and homosexuality but all manner of sexual deviations constitutes a true turning point in the deployment of sexuality, greatly expanding the domain of the confessions sought by the physician, so that "a great archive of the pleasures of sex was gradually constituted" (1978, p. 63).

Foucault argues that current modes of confession—particularly in psychoanalysis but also in the two centuries prior to Freud in confessions of sexual transgressions such as masturbation or perversion to a physician or a family member—are modeled on medieval religious confessional practices. He observes that the similarity of the medieval Catholic confessional concerned with penance to the psychoanalytic session concerned with uncovering sexual secrets is evidenced in the early confessional's discourse rules, in instructions such as the following:

> Examine diligently, therefore, all the faculties of your soul: memory, understanding, and will.... Examine, moreover, all your thoughts, every word you speak, and all your actions. Examine even unto your dreams, to know if, once awakened, you did not give them your consent. And finally, do not think that in so sensitive and perilous a matter as this, there is anything trivial or insignificant
> (Paolo Segneri, *L'Instruction du penitent*, French translation of 1695, as translated and quoted by Foucault, 1978, p. 19)

and "Tell everything, not only consummated acts, but sensual touchings, all impure gazes, all obscene remarks...all consenting thoughts" (Alfonso de' Liguori, *Preceptes sur Ie sixieme commandement*, French translation of 1835, as translated and quoted in Foucault, 1978, p. 21). The difference is, first, that the early confessional and the practice of penance was spiritual and moral in character whereas psychoanalysis conducts the confessional under the authority of medical science and with the assumption that confession is necessary for health. Second, psychoanalysis is based on the search for an Oedipal sexual secret that is the essence of one's identity, and the aim is to bring that identity to light and either liberate or reshape it.

As to psychoanalysis, Foucault thinks it sprung from a culturally idiosyncratic combination of the transformed confessional and the medicalization of sexuality:

> [P]sychoanalysis grew out of...confessional procedures which has been so characteristic of our civilisation.... [I]t forms part of that medicalisation of sexuality which is another strange phenomenon of the West.... [O]ne finds in the West a medicalisation of sexuality itself, as though it were an area of particular pathological fragility in human existence. All sexuality runs the risk at one and the same time of being in itself an illness and of inducing illnesses without

number. It cannot be denied that psychoanalysis is situated at the point where these two processes intersect.

(1980a, p. 191)

Foucault further argues that confessional practices, whether classic spiritual practices or contemporary psychoanalysis, are by nature intrinsically tied to power relations:

The confession is a ritual of discourse...that unfolds within a power relationship, for one does not confess without the presence (or virtual presence) of a partner who is not simply the interlocutor but the authority who requires the confession, prescribes and appreciates it, and intervenes in order to judge, punish, forgive, console, and reconcile; a ritual in which the truth is corroborated by the obstacles and resistances it has had to surmount in order to be formulated; and finally, a ritual in which the expression alone, independently of its external consequences, produces intrinsic modifications in the person who articulates it: it exonerates, redeems, and purifies him; it unburdens him of his wrongs, liberates him, and promises him salvation.

(1978, pp. 61–62)

The result of confession is thus considered central to the individual's fate—whether it be furtive self-touching, emission in bed at night, a longing for a perverse form of sexual gratification, or a repressed incestuous sexual desire from one's early family life.

Foucault rejects the possibility of attributing such far-reaching and long-lasting social changes to errors, moral posturing, and happenstance, as many accounts of the masturbation crusade attempt to do: "instead of adding up the errors, naivetes, and moralisms that plagued the nineteenth-century discourse of truth concerning sex, we would do better to locate the procedures... [that] caused the rituals of confession to function within the norms of scientific regularity" (1978, p. 65). Rather than critiquing the false beliefs of nineteenth-century physicians, Foucault asks how the ritual of confession became embedded within medicine: "how did this immense and traditional extortion of the sexual confession come to be constituted in scientific terms?" (1978, p. 65).

He theorizes that confession was transformed into scientific investigation of sexuality using five tactics: (1) embedding confession within clinical processes ranging from taking a personal history to free association; (2) attributing to sex an elusive and multifaceted causal power that could manifest itself in many ways, so that every imaginable malady, from the bad habits of childhood to the diseases of old age, could in some way involve sexual etiology, with the consequence that to trace sexuality's pathological influence the confession had to be extremely thorough and detailed; (3) the principle of latency, that the workings of sex within individuals are not necessarily known to the individuals themselves and require deep exploration to extract the hidden truth based on scientific principles despite the individual's possible denial; (4) The requirement that confessions must be interpreted and deciphered to be scientifically validated so that the confession must be presented to a listener who determines the truth in accordance with scientific discourse; (5) The medicalization of sexual truths revealed in the confession meant that "the sexual domain ... was placed under the rule of the normal and the pathological" so that "sexuality was defined as being 'by nature' a domain susceptible to pathological processes, and hence one calling for therapeutic or normalizing interventions" (1978, p. 68). As Forrester (1980) explains, this analysis, although framed by Foucault as a process starting much earlier, is clearly aimed at psychoanalysis as its prototypical target, for each of the five tactics plainly applies quite clearly to psychoanalysis:

So it is as if Foucault had read Freud and turned his account of the *science* of psychoanalysis on its head, turning it into a *historical* account of how we, all of us, are subject to this need, this compulsion, or perhaps, simply this *desire* to talk out the mystery of mysteries. In place of Freud describing what occurs in psychoanalysis, we have Foucault describing what goes on in our everyday discourse.

(Forrester, 1980, p. 293)

The critical dimension of Foucault's argument lies in his perception that the twin pillars of the 'deployment of sexuality'—the notion that the truth of the subject is to be found hidden in his sexuality, and the notion that repression is the model of models by which to describe power relations—these two pillars are a major support for whatever forms of domination presently exist.

(1980, p. 297)

Indeed, once the repression model is accepted, it is implied that something important is hidden, and that can easily be understood to be the essence or truth about the individual.

Stefan Zweig on the Incitement of Sexualization as an Effect of Sexual Repression

Foucault argues that the exercise of power that at first looks strictly sexually repressive in nature might have effects or use tactics that are "positive" in his sense of amplifying and structuring sexuality. Do these speculations about the hyper-sexualizing effects of apparent sexual repression reflect the reality of the late nineteenth century? In fact, these Foucauldian observations are consistent with the personal observations in some of the literature and memoirs of the time. As an illustration, I consider the gifted and internationally acclaimed writer Stefan Zweig's (2013; originally published in 1942) vivid autobiographical account of Victorian sexual attitudes when he was growing up in Vienna in the late 1890s and early 1900s in his book *The World of Yesterday*.

Chronicling the repressive attitudes of the Victorian era, he says that families, schools, and the entire culture were "remarkably insincere on...the subject of sexuality" and that they "wanted us, too, to dissimulate and cover up anything we did in that respect" (p. 89). In contrast to the more liberal attitudes in the 1940s when Zweig was writing his memoir, in Victorian bourgeois morality "the question of sexuality was anxiously avoided" (p. 90). Sexuality "must not move into the light of day, because any form of extramarital free love offended bourgeois 'decency'" (p. 90). Thus,

By tacit agreement, therefore, the whole difficult complex of problems was not to be mentioned in public, at school, or at home, and everything that could remind anyone of its existence was to be suppressed.... Wherever you look in the books of the period—philosophical, legal, even medical—you find that by common consent every mention of the subject is anxiously avoided.

(pp. 90–91)

Like Foucault, Zweig observes that Victorian sexual constraints, although impacting everyone, fell hardest on the bourgeois class: "What opportunities were open to a young man of the bourgeois world? In all other classes of society, including the so-called lower classes, the problem was not a problem at all" (p. 102).

Zweig was a Freudian who interpreted the practices of sexual repression and the changes he had seen through a Freudian lens:

We, who have known since Freud that those who try to suppress natural instincts from the conscious mind are not eradicating them but only, and dangerously, shifting them into the unconscious, find it easy to smile at the ignorance of that naive policy of keeping mum. But the entire nineteenth century suffered from the delusion that...if young people were not enlightened about the existence of their own sexuality they would forget it. In this deluded belief that you could moderate something by ignoring it, all the authorities agreed on a joint boycott imposed by means of hermetic silence.

(p. 91)

Before Freud, it was an accepted axiom that a woman had no physical desires until they were aroused in her by a man... However, as the air of Vienna in particular was full of dangerously infectious eroticism even in that age of morality, a girl of good family had to live in an entirely sterilised atmosphere from her birth to the day when she went to the bridal altar.

(pp. 98–99)

Despite his compelling description of Victorian sexual silencing, Zweig, presaging Foucault, observes that the effect of suppression was a pronounced amplification of sexuality. He captures the eroticism of the endless examination for violations of sexual decency that Foucault emphasizes: "The fact was that nothing increased and heightened our curiosity so much as this clumsy technique of concealment.... In all classes of society, this suppression of sexuality led to the stealthy overstimulation of young people" (p. 97); "What was suppressed found outlets everywhere.... So ultimately the generation that was prudishly denied any sexual enlightenment...was a thousand times more erotically obsessed than young people today, who have so much more freedom in love.... [T]he less the eyes saw and the ears heard the more minds dreamt" (p. 98). The result was increased sexual speech and action, albeit often in unlikely settings: "There was hardly a fence or a remote shed that was not scrawled with indecent words and graffiti, hardly a swimming pool where the wooden partition marking off the ladies' pool was not full of so-called knotholes through which a peeping Tom might look" (p. 97).

Discussing how Victorian female clothing hid the woman's body until her female form was entirely obscured (with the exception of the corset's accentuation of the woman's breasts), Zweig observes the inevitable amplifying effect of this attempt to hide sexuality:

> What strikes our uninhibited gaze today about those costumes, garments so desperately trying to cover every inch of bare skin and hide the natural figure, is not their moral propriety but its opposite, the way that those fashions, provocative to the point of embarrassment, emphasized the polarity of the sexes.... This unnatural tension separating them in their outward behaviour was bound to heighten the inner tension ... In its constant prudish anxiety, it was always sniffing out immorality in all aspects of life—literature, art and fashion—with a view to preventing any stimulation, with the result that it was in fact forced to keep dwelling on the immoral. As it was always studying what might be unsuitable, it found itself constantly on the alert; to the world of that time, 'decency' always appeared to be in deadly danger from every gesture, every word.
>
> (p. 95)

However, Zweig has none of Foucault's suspicion of the liberating nature of the change to more openness about sex. Of the shift from Victorian repressiveness to post-Victorian liberal attitudes, Zweig says, "Perhaps there has never been such a total transformation in any area of public life within a single human generation as here, in the relationship between the sexes" (p. 89). He cites several factors as having brought about this transformation, including Freudian psychoanalysis, the emancipation of women, and the general increase in independence among the young. Zweig was enraptured by what he saw as straightforward liberation. In contrast to the way that "covering up sexuality and keeping it quiet weighed down on us in our youth" (p. 92), Zweig says of the present: "What a great revolution in morality has taken place to the benefit of the young; how much freedom in life and love they have regained, and how much better they thrive both physically and mentally on this healthy new freedom!" (pp. 111–112).

In sum, in Zweig's description of the Victorian world of his youth we find the commonsense version of the repressive hypothesis portrayed as personally experienced in vivid detail. We also find the view that Freud (among others) liberated us from the Victorian social repression of sexuality. These are both instances of common wisdom that Foucault critiques. However, in Zweig's account we also find clear premonitions of the Foucauldian thesis that the net effect of the supposed Victorian silencing of sex was in fact an extraordinary amplification of sexual expression and sexual focus, in part through the process of constant examination for prohibited sexual expression. Both Foucault's description of the standard view of Victorian repression followed by Freudian liberation and his reversal of the standard view in arguing that the supposed repression served to greatly amplify sexuality are found in Zweig's articulate depiction of his personal experiences growing up in Victorian culture during the repressive era.

Foucault on Freud's Theory of Unconscious Mental Contents

One may think of Freud as putting forward four central theoretical innovations: the Oedipal theory; the theory of unconscious mental states; "infantilism," the theory that neurotic disorders and personality traits are generally shaped by childhood experiences rather than by hereditary weaknesses; and Freud's psychoanalytic model of treatment. Leaving his primary target of the Oedipal theory momentarily aside, in this and the following sections I review what Foucault has to say about each of the other three Freudian contributions in order to have a larger context of Foucault's view of psychoanalysis into which to fit the discussion of his views of the Oedipal theory. I start with Freud's postulation of unconscious meanings.

It seems fair to say that Foucault accepts the unconscious in something resembling Freud's sense, although he has some concerns about the way this notion can be used. Foucault himself occasionally uses the term "unconscious" or implies unconscious states when describing underlying structures such as epistemes—fundamental organizing epistemological, ontological, and explanatory principles—and discourse rules (e.g., he refers to the rules of which we are unaware that form an episteme as a "positive unconscious of knowledge" [Foucault, 1966, p. xi]). Foucault sometimes suggests that power is deployed in bodily dispositions and practices, but the subtle and sophisticated rules of evidence and truth that Foucault attributes to discourse rules must be cognitive and are clearly unconscious. We are not consciously aware of these rules and models but they nonetheless determine within a given domain of discourse what can be said, how something can be explained, and what can be considered true. Thus, unconscious contents are a useful and almost necessary construct for Foucault's project. However, it should be noted that Foucault tends to conceptualize the unconscious in terms different from Freud's and Sartre's representational cognitivism. He tends to describe the unconscious either in the existential-phenomenological terms of his teacher Merleau-Ponty while rejecting phenomenology as a general approach, or in structuralist terms as a set of cultural background practices and presuppositions of which we are not aware (e.g., "structuralism explores above all an unconscious" [Foucault, as quoted in Grace, 2013, p. 226]), while otherwise rejecting structuralism as an overall approach.

Beyond doctrinal specifics about the nature of the unconscious, above all Foucault wants to persuade us that it is not the sexual theory of the neuroses, but rather the theory of the unconscious (as well as rejection of hereditarian theories of mental disorder; see below), that is Freud's major advance. This allows him to isolate the sexual theory as a cardinal expression of power/knowledge while retaining the ability to attribute to power/knowledge various structures, meanings, and purposes of which we are not aware. As Grace (2013) puts it, along with many other French theorists of his era, Foucault shared an "attraction to the methodological potentials of the Freudian unconscious" and he thus "embraced the methodological elaboration of the unconscious," "redeploying it as trans-individual and cultural," but above all he wanted "to keep the unconscious baby but not the sexual bathwater" that went along with it in Freud (2013, pp. 226–227).

In *The Order of Things*, Foucault documents how varying epistemes underlie different periods in the history of science. He recognizes psychoanalysis (as well as ethnology, which psychoanalysis requires to provide relativization to local culturally variant unconscious meanings and discourse rules) as having a unique role in the human sciences because it directly grapples with the implicit unconscious background rules that shape and make possible our explicit conscious representational world:

> Psychoanalysis and ethnology occupy a privileged position in our knowledge.... In setting itself the task of making the discourse of the unconscious speak through consciousness, psychoanalysis is advancing in the direction of that fundamental region in which the relations of representation and finitude come to play.... Psychoanalysis advances and leaps over representation.
>
> (1970, pp. 394–395)

(Note that Foucault studied with Merleau-Ponty and tends to write about psychoanalysis in the existential-phenomenological manner in which he was trained.)

The source of Foucault's concerns about the unconscious is easy to understand. Foucault is wary of the obvious problem that the interpretation of unconscious meanings can easily be exploited as a tactic of power/knowledge in the deployment of sexuality: "the unconscious of the subject, the truth of the subject in the other who knows, the knowledge he holds unbeknown to him, all this found an opportunity to deploy itself in the discourse of sex" (1978, p. 70).

In contrast to Freud's focus on sexuality, Foucault maintains that the systematic development of the concept of unconscious rules and meanings, as exemplified in Freud's first great book, *Interpretation of Dreams*, is Freud's major contribution:

> The strength of psychoanalysis consists in its having opened out on to something quite different, namely the logic of the unconscious. And there sexuality is no longer what it was at the outset ... .In

other words, the important part is not the *Three Essays on the Theory of Sexuality* but *The Interpretation of Dreams*.... Not the theory of development, nor the sexual secret behind the neuroses or psychoses, but a logic of the unconscious.... Freud's originality was taking [Charcot's comment on sexuality] literally, and then erecting on its basis the *Interpretation of Dreams,* which is something other than a sexual aetiology of neuroses.

(1980a, pp. 212–213, 218)

Foucault thus accepts the value of Freud's theory of the unconscious. He must, for his signature theory of unconscious discourse rules that shape the acceptance of truths in a discipline requires unconscious rules or some equivalent form of "historical a priori." This is despite Foucault's occasional assertions that the notion of an interior self is a misleading construction. It is difficult to conceptualize how discourse rules that shape the logical nuances of what sentences can be stated, what can be said to exist, and how evidence is to be evaluated in a scientific discipline could work simply as bodily habits without internalized cognitions or their equivalent regulating the process.

Foucault on Freud's Repudiation of the Degenerescence Theory

Besides the unconscious, the primary accomplishment of Freud's that Foucault accepts as a legitimate advance is Freud's "infantilism" (as Freud called it at times)—that is, his argument that adult psychoneuroses generally have their origins in childhood experiences. Foucault observes that Freud "assumes an adversary position with respect to the theory of degenerescence" (1978, p. 130) and "turned the theory of degeneracy inside out, like a glove" (1980a, p. 212). Freud's infantilism was a direct challenge to the standard account at the time that the cause of mental disorders lies in faulty heredity and consequent constitutional degeneracy, which Foucault calls the "degenerescence" theory. This account was so widely accepted that it was formalized in diagnostic categories of various forms of "constitutional inferiority" in pre-DSM American psychiatric diagnostic manuals.

Freud argued that the constitutional-degeneracy approach was based on the fallacy of assuming that the causes of a pathological disposition that cannot be explained by current circumstances must lie in a faulty constitutional nature derived via heredity from past generations, when the causes might lie instead in the largely forgotten childhood experiences of the patients. This alteration, from focusing on the individual's hypothesized constitutional heredity to focusing on an individual's past for an explanation of current suffering, constituted a revolution that now determines our thinking about childhood and parental responsibilities, and shapes the heightened anxieties of today's parents.

Foucault explains that the degenerescence theory held that corrupt heredity could cause perversion and that perversion in turn could yield progeny with corrupt heredity, creating a motive to intervene in the overall population's sexuality and fertility. He also emphasizes how well-established this theory was when Freud took it on:

> let it not be imagined that this was nothing more than a medical theory which was scientifically lacking and improperly moralistic. Its application was widespread and its implantation went deep. Psychiatry, to be sure, but also jurisprudence, legal medicine, agencies of social control, the surveillance of dangerous or endangered children, all functioned for a long time on the basis of 'degenerescence' and the heredity-perversion system...[and] furnished this technology of sex with a formidable power and far-reaching consequences.
>
> (1978, p. 119)

Substituting childhood traumas for hereditary degenerescence in etiological theory was, Foucault holds, a historically important Freudian accomplishment that should—contrary to standard accounts—be seen as closer to the center of Freud's contribution:

> And the strange position of psychiatry at the end of the nineteenth century would be hard to comprehend if one did not see the rupture it brought about in the great system of degenerescence:... [O]f all those institutions that set out in the nineteenth century to medicalize sex, [psychoanalysis] was the one that, up to the decade of the

forties, rigorously opposed the political and institutional effects of the perversion-heredity-degenerescence system.

(1978, p. 119)

Psychoanalysis was established in opposition to ... the psychiatry of degeneracy, eugenics and heredity ... . Indeed, in relation to that psychiatry—which is still the psychiatry of today's psychiatrists— psychoanalysis played a liberating role.

(1980a, pp. 60–61)

Foucault thus grants Freud's rejection of the degeneracy theory the status as a genuinely discontinuous and liberating theoretical rupture that he denies to the Oedipal theory. To place the "rupture" issue that absorbs Foucault into a broader context, both Foucault and the American philosopher and historian of science Thomas Kuhn were influenced by the work of the French philosopher of science, Gaston Bachelard, known for postulating the discontinuous development of science through "epistemological ruptures" in which unconscious categories and assumptions that define a scientific era are overthrown and replaced by a new way of thinking. Kuhn (1962) famously translated this perspective into the notions of *paradigms* that dominate thinking in a scientific community and *scientific revolutions* that occur when a scientific community shifts to a new paradigm in ways that may be incommensurable—not rationally comparable—with the old one. Foucault, as explained above, developed the ideas of *epistemes* and *discourse rules* that regulate a scientific community's notions of what can be said to exist, what kinds of explanations are acceptable, and when one is considered to reach the truth, and for him a rupture is a change in these assumptions. However, whereas Kuhn's revolutions occur exclusively because of processes internal to the scientific discipline, such as the accumulation of scientific anomalies, Foucault expands what determines acceptance of scientific theories to include the social functions served by theories of human nature in the society at large. Foucault thus opens a route of influence between theory acceptance and social regulation. Ruptures for Foucault occur not only in the scientific theories themselves but also in the power/ knowledge that they generate. (I return to the centrality of the issue of rupture versus continuity in Foucault's analysis in Chapter 6.)

Note Foucault's astute suggestion that the degenerescence theory "is still the psychiatry of today's psychiatrists," that is, the current turn toward biological psychiatry emphasizing the genetic etiology of mental disorders is in effect a return to elements of the degenerescence approach. Foucault is quite aware that in arguing that the theory of the unconscious and the rejection of the degenerescence theory are major scientific advances whereas the sexual theory is not, he is attempting to transform how we see the importance of Freud's various contributions, acknowledging that this "isn't the usual way of situating the Freudian break as an event in terms of scientificity" (1980a, p. 212).

Foucault on the Psychoanalytic Session

Foucault is ambivalent about Freud's construction of the psycho-analytic clinical interaction. Although acknowledging that in some respects it is an advance from the asylum, he argues that it produces its own multiple forms of oppression. On the positive side, "Freud demystified all other asylum structures: he abolished silence and the gaze, and ... silenced the instances of condemnation" (2006, p. 510). In contrast to the asylum's ignoring of what the mad had to say, Freud took a positive and liberating step in listening to the mentally disordered. Psychoanalysis rejected a common conception of psychology as the study of reason and thereby "restored ... the possibility of a dialogue with the unreason to medical thought," revealing "an experience of unreason that psychology, in the modern world, was meant to disguise" (Foucault, 2006, p. 339). This listening "only really came about with Freud ... (and in that sense, psychoanalysis is indeed the great lifting of prohibitions that Freud himself defined)" (2006, p. 546). Thus, "[A]ll the psychiatry of the nineteenth century really does converge on Freud, who was the first to accept the seriousness of the reality of the doctor-patient couple" (p. 510).

The problem, according to Foucault, is that the interpretive stance of the psychoanalyst meant that the patient's speech "appeared as speech wrapped up in itself, saying, below everything that it says, something else" (2006, p. 547). The promising psychoanalytic interchange eroded into a monologue, according to Foucault, because the patient does all of the talking—or, more subtly, because the therapist does all of the interpreting that validates the meaning of the patient's talk. Moreover, the interaction takes place within the predefined framework of interpretation of the Oedipus complex, so treatment becomes a sexual confession. Psychoanalysis thus listens while not really listening in a straightforward way to what the mad have to say: "since Freud, Western madness has become a non-language because it has become a double language" (2006 pp. 546–547).

All of this is indicative of fundamental flaws in how Freud constructed the psychoanalytic session:

> he exploited the structure that enveloped the medical character: he amplified his virtues as worker of miracles, preparing an almost divine status for his omnipotence. He brought back to him, and to his simple presence, hidden behind the patient and above him, in an absence that was also a total presence, all the powers that had been shared out in the collective existence of the asylum.
>
> (2006, pp. 510–511)

Foucault's Disparagement of Freud's Sexual Theory of Hysteria

In order to emphasize that, unlike the unconscious and infantilism, the sexual theory was not one of Freud's distinctive scientific contributions, Foucault repeatedly demeans the originality of Freud's early sexual theory of hysteria by attributing the idea to a comment by Charcot. Foucault offers a sexualized interpretation of the hypnotically induced hysterical paroxysms Charcot induced in his patients, witnessed by Freud during his visit to Charcot's clinic. He argues that Freud simply took what he saw and heard there and elevated it into a formal theory. Foucault relies heavily in this argument on an offhand comment of Charcot's overheard by Freud, to the effect that hysteria comes down to sex:

> One must not speak of these 'genital causes': so went the phrase— muttered in a muted voice—which the most famous ears of our time overheard one day in 1886, from the mouth of Charcot.
>
> (1978, p. 112)

[I]n the usual histories one reads that sexuality was ignored by medicine, and above all by psychiatry, and that at last Freud discovered the sexual aetiology of neuroses. Now everyone knows that that isn't true, that the problem of sexuality was massively and manifestly inscribed in the medicine and psychiatry of the nineteenth century, and that basically Freud was only taking literally what he heard Charcot say one evening: it is indeed all a question of sexuality.

(1980a, pp. 212–213)

Freud doesn't need to go hunting for anything other than what he had seen *chez* Charcot. Sexuality was there before his eyes in manifest form, orchestrated by Charcot and his worthy aides.... Freud's great originality wasn't discovering the sexuality hidden beneath neurosis. The sexuality was already there, Charcot was already talking about it.

(1980a, p. 218)

Moreover, in *History of Madness* Foucault suggests that Freud, rather than discovering the sexual source of pathology, simply "discovered" the way our culture divides reason from unreason using sexuality as a measure, and then transformed this into the distinction between health and neurotic disorder:

[P]sychoanalysis understood that all forms of madness have roots in troubled sexuality; but to say that is to do little more than note that our culture...placed sexuality on the dividing line of unreason. Since time immemorial, and probably in all cultures, sexuality has been governed by systems of constraint; but it is a comparatively recent particularity of our own culture to have divided it so rigorously into Reason and Unreason. As a consequence and degradation of that, it was not long before it was also classified into healthy or sick, normal or abnormal.

(2006, pp. 88–89)

These are not substantive arguments and they offer no evidence of the link between Freud's theory and the masturbation crusade. Moreover, there is a difference between an offhand comment and a systematic theory. I leave these blanket claims of the nonoriginality and vacuousness of Freud's theory aside. Instead, I will closely examine in later chapters the evidence in Freud's text that is relevant to assessing Foucault's claims.

Foucault Versus Freud on the Interpretation of Sophocles's "Oedipus Rex"

Beyond attributing the sexual theory to Charcot, another way that Foucault attempts to deny Freud the high ground regarding the Oedipal theory is to dispute Freud's interpretation of Sophocles's play, *Oedipus the King*. Freud used Sophocles's play, in which Oedipus in ignorance of the identity of his parents kills his father and marries his mother, to argue for the plausibility of his theory, claiming that the play imparts a sense of dread in the audience because we all harbor the desires to do those very things to our mothers and fathers.

In considering the play, Foucault rejects Freud's interpretation and instead explores the implications of the Oedipus story for understanding the history of social and political power and the development of the way governing relates to truth through power/knowledge:

> I want to show how the tragedy of Oedipus, the one we read in Sophocles...is representative and in a sense the founding instance of a definite type of relation between power and knowledge...It seems to me that there really is an Oedipus complex in our civilization. But it does not involve our unconsciousness and our desire, nor the relations between desire and the unconscious. If there is an Oedipus complex, it operates not at the individual level but at the collective level; not in connection with desire and the unconscious but in connection with power and knowledge. That is the 'complex' I want to analyse.
>
> (Foucault, 2000, p. 17)

Foucault emphasizes the intertwining of the issues of truth and power as central to Oedipus's story. He rises to power through certain truths (e.g., his confrontation with the Sphinx and answering the Sphinx's riddle) and then loses his power due to a successful quest for further truth (e.g., the revelations that he killed his father, Laius, and he married his mother, Jocasta). Foucault argues that it is the topic of power, not sexuality or incest, that is central to the play:

> Oedipus is the man of power, the man who exercises a certain power. And it is characteristic that the title of Sophocles' play is not *Oedipus the Incestuous*, or *Oedipus the Killer of his Father*, but *Oedipus the King*. What does the kingship of Oedipus mean? We may note the importance of the thematic of power throughout the play. What is always in question, essentially, is the power of Oedipus, and that is why he feels threatened.
>
> (Foucault, 2000, p. 25)

Foucault focuses his interpretation on the relationship between power and knowledge in Oedipus's search for the truth about himself. He points to the techniques he uses in that search, in particular his reliance on first-hand witnesses, as opposed to traditional methods such as oracular or religious verification, the voice of the people, or imposition of arbitrary political will. To Foucault, this suggests that the play "is a way of shifting the enunciation of the truth from a prophetic and prescriptive type of discourse to a retrospective one that is no longer characterized by prophecy but, rather, by testimony" (Foucault, 2000, p. 23). Foucault argues that reliance on this sort of testimony represented a crucial shift in the relation between the governing and the governed that was occurring at about the time of the play, in which truth and power come together in a new way:

> In Sophocles' play Oedipus basically represents a certain type of what I would call knowledge-and-power, power-and-knowledge. It is because he exercises a certain tyrannical and solitary power, aloof from both the oracle of the gods - which he does not want to hear - and what the people say and want, that, in his craving to govern by discovering for himself, he finds, in the last instance, the evidence of those who have seen.
>
> (Foucault, 2000, p. 30)

In *Oedipus Rex*, Foucault claims, we find "a struggle between kinds of knowledge (*savoirs*) and kinds of power, a struggle between forms of power-knowledge" (Foucault, 2013, p. 256). In disputing Freud's interpretation of *Oedipus Rex* in terms of universal incestuous and patricidal impulses and arguing instead for an interpretation in terms of the evolution of power/knowledge, Foucault projects his dispute with Freud about Oedipal theory into the distant past and challenges a key evocative part of Freud's defense of his theory's universality. Nevertheless, Foucault at no point argues persuasively that his power/ knowledge interpretation of *Oedipus Rex* renders Freud's Oedipal theoretic interpretation false.

Foucault's Overall Attitude Toward Psychoanalysis

Foucault's *HS1* (1978) is often characterized as an all-out attack on Freudian (and perhaps Lacanian) psychoanalysis (Dorfman, 2010; Basaure, 2009; Whitebook, 1999; 2003). Whitebook, for example, asserts that Freud was Foucault's lifelong target and that in *HS1*, "Foucault claimed to have definitively refuted the basic claims of psychoanalysis" (2003, p. 312)—although there is no such sentence, and Foucault acknowledges that further evidence might show him wrong about his specific targets, the repressive hypothesis and the self's sexual essence. Whitebook further writes: "If we just think of the topics Foucault tackled – the normal and the pathological, rationality and irrationality, the modern subject, the human sciences, sexuality and techniques of self-transformation – we can see that he was challenging the good doctor from Vienna on his own theoretical turf" (p. 313). These topics are not distinctive to Freud, they are the "theoretical turf" that any eminent social or psychological theorist is likely to tackle. Yes, Foucault's relationship to psychoanalysis was complex. He productively grappled for decades with profound issues regarding psychoanalysis itself and the topics it addressed, and inevitably disagreed with Freud on many issues. Nonetheless, characterizing Foucault as engaged in a general campaign against Freud is at best an exaggeration.

In a less polarizing vein, Adrian Switzer (2014), noting that the content of Foucault's views of various facets of psychoanalysis change over time but the tone of his remarks "are always both positive and negative or critical," concludes that "'ambivalence' in the Freudian sense may serve as a guiding heuristic in reading Foucault's engagements with psychoanalysis" (2014, p. 411). Amy Allen (2018) agrees:

"to my mind the best interpretation of Foucault's own position on psychoanalysis deploys the psychoanalytic concept of ambivalence" (p. 170). She summarizes Foucault's views of various aspects of psychoanalysis:

> On the one hand, he credits psychoanalysis for its (not completely successful) attempt to establish a dialogue with unreason (*History of Madness* 497), describes it as a critical counter-science occupying a privileged place in relation to the human sciences (*Order of Things* 373–86), and praises Freud's rejection of the racialized hereditary theory of neurosis (*History of Sexuality* 117–19). On the other hand, he criticizes psychoanalysis for its normalizing and confessional tendencies with respect to sexuality, its adherence to the repressive hypothesis, and its reliance on an overly simplistic juridico-discursive model of power (*History of Sexuality*).
>
> (2018, p. 170)

Summarizing this as "ambivalence" toward a single object, psycho-analysis, seems to me to trivialize what is more accurately characterized as a carefully differentiated view of the many independent doctrines that comprise Freudian theory. Indeed, many branches of psychoanalysis reject some of the doctrines that Foucault rejects, yet maintain their psychoanalytic identity. Foucault is relatively clear on the aspects of Freud that he accepts as constructive—such as unconscious contents and rejection of the degenerescence theory—and those he rejects as sheer imposition of power/knowledge. Jacques Derrida asked, "Would Foucault's project have been possible without psychoanalysis?" (Derrida, 1998, p. 76), and Foucault seems to implicitly acknowledge that psychoanalysis is indeed one of several crucial developments making his project possible: "[T]he nineteenth century—and particu-larly Marx, Nietzsche, and Freud—have put us back into the presence of a new possibility of interpretation; they have founded once again the possibility of a hermeneutic" (1998, 271–272).

Deborah Cook (2014) offers a reasonably balanced judgment:

> Many commentators argue that Michel Foucault was anti-Freudian, even virulently so. And, to give these commentators their due, Foucault was critical of psychoanalysis. From *History of*

Madness to the first volume of *The History of Sexuality*, Foucault targeted a number of key Freudian theses including the Oedipus complex, the role of the analyst in therapy, and the repressive hypothesis. Nevertheless, Foucault's criticisms were always tempered by respect, even admiration, for the founder of psychoanalysis. Concerned that his criticisms of Freud had been misunderstood, Foucault denied that his attempts to situate Freud within the history of the modern age amounted to a repudiation of Freudian theory, an 'anti-psychoanalysis.' His critical histories explore the historical context in which Freudian theory developed—an exploration that, on Foucault's view, no more undermines the validity of psychoanalysis than his archaeology of biology compromises the validity of biology.

(2014, p. 148)

Foucault intended to return to the topic of psychoanalysis in later volumes of his history of sexuality: "How it was possible for psychoanalysis to take the form it did, at the time it did, is something I will try and establish in the later volumes" (1980a, p. 192). He did not live to bring his history of sexuality up to Freud's time, but was already anxious that his fuller account of psychoanalysis would be misinterpreted as "anti-psychoanalysis" in the way that he considered his earlier work on madness to have been misinterpreted as "anti-psychiatry" despite his protestations that he does not directly address the validity of current claims:

I am afraid that the same situation will arise with psychoanalysis as arose with psychiatry after I had written *Madness and Civilisation;* I had attempted to narrate there what took place up to the beginning of the nineteenth century, but psychiatrists took my analysis to be an attack on present-day psychiatry. I don't know what will happen with the psychoanalysts but I very much fear that they will take for an 'anti-psychoanalysis' what will merely be a genealogy. Why should an archaeology of psychiatry function as an 'anti-psychiatry', when an archaeology of biology does not function as an anti-biology? Is it because…psychiatry is not on good terms with its own history…?

(1980a, p. 192)

However, Foucault acknowledges the confusing complexity of his methodological stance in which he sets aside a discipline's claims to get a fresh perspective. He starts, he says, with "a systematic skepticism toward all anthropological universals" about human nature, but this "does not mean rejecting them all from the start, outright and once and for all"; rather, "everything...suggested to us as being universally valid must be tested and analyzed," which "does not imply that what these notions refer to is nothing, or that they are only chimeras invented for the sake of a dubious cause." In other words: "the first rule of method for this kind of work is this: Insofar as possible, circumvent the anthropological universals...in order to examine them as historical constructs" (1998, pp. 461–462). This methodological stance does not preclude bringing these concepts back into play once they are tested, or, as with Freud's sexual theories, rejecting them as exercises in power/knowledge and little more.

Conclusion: Foucault's Rejection of the Oedipal Theory

Foucault's complex way of positioning himself methodologically raises a question about my framing of this book. In light of the above passages in which Foucault denies that his analysis is an "anti-psychoanalysis," is "Foucault *Versus* Freud" a misleading way to frame his analysis?

Given the specific context of Freud's sexual theory of the neuroses and Oedipal theory, I think not. Foucault's sympathetic comments about other areas of Freud's thought cannot hide the fact that his defense of the doctrine of the deployment of sexuality from the alternative repression-liberation narrative requires rejection of the Oedipal theory—or at least the level of doubt that applies to the theories behind the masturbation crusade with which it is claimed to be continuous. Moreover, Foucault states his own view in the course of discussing Deleuze and Guattari's attack on the Oedipus complex in *Anti-Oedipus* (1972), a book for which Foucault provided a preface. He observes that since that book was published, the Oedipal theory has been seen differently:

Deleuze and Guattari try to show that the Oedipal father-mother-son triangle does not reveal an atemporal truth or a deeply historical truth of our desire.... In this conception, then, Oedipus is not a truth of nature, but an instrument of limitation and constraint that psychoanalysts, starting with Freud, use to contain desire and insert it within a family structure defined by our society at a particular moment. In other words, Oedipus, according to Deleuze and Guattari, is not the secret content of our unconscious, but the form of constraint which psychoanalysis, through the cure, tries to impose on our desire and our unconscious. Oedipus is an instrument of power, a certain manner by which medical and psychoanalytic power is brought to bear on desire and the unconscious.

(Foucault, 2000, p. 16)

After summarizing Deleuze and Guattari's position that Freud's Oedipal theory is "not a truth of nature, but…an instrument of power," Foucault equates his own position roughly with theirs: "everything that I'm trying to say…Deleuze and Guattari have shown with much more depth in *Anti-Oedipus*" (2000, p. 16). Later in the same essay, he directly states his position (as we saw above):

It seems to me that there really is an Oedipus complex in our civilization. But it does not involve our unconscious and our desire, nor the relations between desire and the unconscious. If there is an Oedipus complex, it operates not at the individual level but at the collective level; not in connection with desire and the unconscious but in connection with power and knowledge.

(p. 17)

Thus, despite the fact (as Basaure [2009] argues) that Foucault does not generally concern himself with scientific truth and falsity but only with function, in this case he plainly maintained that Freud's Oedipal theory is false. Although *in principle* a genealogical or power/knowledge analysis is independent of evidential status and need neither deny nor support the truth of a theory, some genealogical findings preclude the possibility of truth. In the context of Foucault's overall analysis of the deployment of sexuality, his analysis of the Oedipal theory involves a clear repudiation of Freud's theory.

In Auden's (1940) otherwise admiring poem in memory of Freud, he realistically acknowledged that Freud was often wrong, at times to an extreme of absurdity. One may take Foucault as arguing that, although Freud arguably did many things that were to some degree right or liberatory advances at the time, a major thing that he got wrong, perhaps to an absurd extent, is his sexual theory of the neuroses and in particular his Oedipal theory. That is the argument to be examined in subsequent chapters.

References

Allen, A. (2018). Foucault, psychoanalysis, and critique. *Angelaki, 23*(2), 170–186.

Auden, W. H. (1940). In memory of Sigmund Freud. *The Kenyon Review, 2*(1), 30–34.

Barrett, M. (1991). *The politics of truth: From Marx to Foucault.* Cambridge, UK: Cambridge University Press.

Basaure, M. (2009). Foucault and the 'Anti-Oedipus movement': Psychoanalysis as disciplinary power. *History of Psychiatry, 20*(3), 340–359.

Bowlby, J. (1982). *Attachment and loss (Vol. 1): Attachment* (Rev. ed.). New York, NY: Basic Books.

Breton, A. (1990). *Les pas perdus.* Paris: Gallimard. (Originally published 1924).

Cook, D. (2014). Foucault, Freud, and the repressive hypothesis. *Journal of the British Society for Phenomenology, 45*(2), 148–161.

De Liguori, A. (1835). *Preceptes sur le sixieme commandement* (French translation.). Paris.

Deleuze, G., & Guattari, F. (1972). *L'Anti-Oedipe.* Paris: Les Editions de Minuet.

Derrida, J. (1998). *Resistances of psychoanalysis.* Stanford, CA: Stanford University Press.

Dorfman, E. (2010). Foucault versus Freud: On sexuality and the unconscious. In E. Dorfman & J. De Vlemnick (Eds.), *Sexuality and psychoanalysis: Philosophical criticisms* (pp. 157–173). Leuven: Leuven University Press.

Eagle, M. (2018). *Core concepts in classical psychoanalysis: Clinical, research evidence and conceptual critiques.* Abingdon, UK: Routledge.

Forrester, J. (1980). Michel Foucault and the history of psychoanalysis. *History of Science, 18,* 286–303.

Foucault, M. (1966). *The order of things: An archaeology of the human sciences.* New York: Random House.

Foucault, M. (1973). *The birth of the clinic: An archaeology of medical perception.* New York: Pantheon Books.

Foucault, Michel (1975). *Discipline and punish: The birth of the prison.* New York: Random House.

Foucault, M. (1978). *History of sexuality Volume 1: An introduction* (R. Hurley, Trans.). New York, NY: Pantheon. (*HS1*)

Foucault, M. (1980a). *Power/knowledge: Selected interviews and other writings 1972–1977* (C. Gordon, Ed.). New York: Pantheon.

Foucault, M. (1980b). *Power, moral values, and the intellectual.* Caen, France: IMEC (Institut Mémoirs de l'Édition Contemporaine), Archival identification number FCL2 A02–06.

Foucault, M. (1983). The subject and power. In H. Dreyfus & P. Rabinow, *Michel Foucault: Beyond structuralism and hermeneutics* (2nd edition). Chicago: University of Chicago Press.

Foucault, M. (1988). *Politics, philosophy, culture: Interviews and other writings 1977–1984* (L. D. Kritzman, Ed.). New York: Routledge.

Foucault, M. (1997). *Ethics, subjectivity, and truth: Essential works of Foucault, 1954–1984, Volume 1* (P. Rabinow, Ed.). New York: The New Press.

Foucault, M. (1998). *Aesthetics, method, and epistemology: Essential works of Foucault, 1954–1984, Volume 2* (J. D. Faubion, Ed.). New York: The New Press.

Foucault, M. (2000). *Power: Essential works of Foucault, 1954–1984, Volume 3* (J. D. Faubion, Ed.). New York: The New Press.

Foucault, M. (2003). *Abnormal: Lectures at the College de France 1974–1975.* (G. Burchell, Trans.), V. Marchetti & A. Salomoni (Eds.). New York, NY: Picador.

Foucault, M. (2006). *History of madness* (J. Khalfa, Ed., J. Murphy, Trans.). New York: Routledge.

Foucault, M. (2013). *Lectures on the will to know: Lectures at the College de France, 1970–1971.* (D. Defert, Ed., G. Burchell, Trans.). New York: Palgrave Macmillan.

Freud, S. (1900). The interpretation of dreams (first part). *SE* 4.

Freud, S. (1905). Three essays on the theory of sexuality. *SE* 7, 123–246.

Freud, S. (1909). Analysis of a phobia in a five-year-old boy. *SE* 10, 1–150.

Freud, S. (1940). An outline of psycho-analysis. *SE* 23, 141–208.

Grace, W. (2013). Foucault and the Freudians. In C. Falzon, T. O'Leary & J. Sawicki (Eds.). *A companion to Foucault* (pp. 226–242). Oxford, UK: Blackwell Publishing Ltd.

Horney, K. (1939). *New ways in psychoanalysis.* New York: Norton.

Kohut, H. (1977). *The restoration of the self.* Madison, NY: International Universities Press.

Kuhn, T. S. (1962). *The structure of scientific revolutions.* Chicago: University of Chicago Press.

Lawrence, D. H. (1921). *Psychoanalysis and the unconscious.* New York: Thomas Seltzer.

Marcus, S. (1966). *The other Victorians: A study of sexuality and pornography in mid-nineteenth-century England.* (London: Weidenfeld and Nicolson).

Miller, J.-A. (1992). Michel Foucault and psychoanalysis. In T. J. Armstrong (Trans.), *Michel Foucault: Philosopher* (pp. 58–64). New York: Routledge.

Segneri, P. (1695). *L'Instruction du penitent* (French translation). Paris.

Switzer, A. (2014). Psychoanalysis. In L. Lawlor & J. Nale (Eds.), *The Cambridge Foucault lexicon* (pp. 411–418). Cambridge, UK: Cambridge University Press.

Taylor, D. (2014). *Michel Foucault: Key concepts*. New York: Taylor & Francis Group.

Thiele, L. P. (1991). Reading Nietzsche and Foucault: A hermeneutics of suspicion?: Reply to J. Scott Johnson. *American Political Science Review, 85*, 584–592.

Wakefield, J. C. (1992). Freud and cognitive psychology: The conceptual interface. In J. Barron, M. Eagle & D. Wolitzky (Eds.), *Interface pf psychoanalysis and psychology* (pp. 77–98). Washington, DC: American Psychological Association.

Wakefield, J. C. (2018). *Freud and philosophy of mind, Volume 1: Reconstructing the argument for unconscious mental states*. New York: Palgrave Macmillan.

Wakefield, J. C. (2023a). *Freud's argument for the Oedipus complex: A philosophy of science analysis of the case of Little Hans*. New York: Routledge.

Wakefield, J. C. (2023b). *Attachment, sexuality, power: Oedipal theory as regulator of family affection in Freud's case of Little Hans*. New York: Routledge.

Whitebook, J. (1999). Freud, Foucault and 'the dialogue with unreason'. *Philosophy & Social Criticism, 25*(6), 29–66.

Whitebook, J. (2003). Against interiority: Foucault's struggle with psychoanalysis. In G. Gutting (Ed.), *The Cambridge companion to Foucault* (2nd Edition) (pp. 312–347). Cambridge, UK: Cambridge University Press.

Zweig, S. (2013). *The world of yesterday* (A. Bell, Trans.). Lincoln, NE: University of Nebraska Press.

Chapter 2

The Appeal of the Oedipus Complex

For the many writers who claim there is no evidence to support Freud's Oedipal theory, the challenge is to explain why it became so influential not only in psychology, literature, and the humanities, but in our culture at large. This chapter reviews some of the proposed resolutions of this puzzle, including some by leading intellectual figures such as Ludwig Wittgenstein and D. H. Lawrence, and several by major Freud critics such as Frank Cioffi, Malcolm Macmillan, Mikkel Borch-Jacobsen, and Allan Esterson. This survey provides a context for considering Foucault's account of the Oedipal theory's success to be developed in the remainder of the book. The surveyed explanations range from the sexually liberating nature of Freud's theories to the purposeful and cynical historical manipulations and subterfuge of Freud's followers. I argue that despite these many proposals, Foucault may yet have something distinctive to contribute to this rich conversation when it comes specifically to the Oedipal theory.

The Puzzle of Freud's Success

Foucault's question posed in Chapter 1 about the appeal of Freud's Oedipal theory may seem odd, but it is not at all idiosyncratic. It is part of a large and ever-expanding literature that attempts to understand the remarkable success of Freudian theory given what is generally taken to be its evidential weakness. As noted in Chapter 1, critics of Freudian theory, especially the so-called "Freud bashers" in recent debates over the scientific status of psychoanalysis known as the

DOI: 10.4324/9781003480396-2

"Freud wars," argue that Freud's theory is based on manifestly weak reasoning and lacks any semblance of adequate scientific support. Such critics face the challenge of explaining why the theory enjoyed such enormous success and exerted such an outsized influence among intellectuals and middle-class Western families. The British philosopher Alasdair MacIntyre (1976) expressed the puzzle well: "I know of no other example of a system of unjustified beliefs which has propagated itself so successfully as Freudian theory. How was it done?" (p. 35). The French intellectual historian Mikkel Borch-Jacobsen similarly poses the challenge of explaining Freud's extraordinary success:

> In the interminable Freudian wars between opposing defenders and detractors of psychoanalysis, the former most often invoke its success and its long life: If Freud's theories are as false and absurd as you say, how do you explain that they have had such an impact on Western culture…We come back to the question…: how to explain the success of Freud's theories without seeing in it circularly the proof of their truth?
>
> (2019, p. 92)

In order to place Foucault's attempted explanation in context, it will be useful to have in mind some of the explanations offered by others. So, in this chapter I survey how some other critics of Freudian theory have attempted to rectify their negative judgments with the theory's influence.

For such critics, the acceptance and influence of Freud's theory is all the more puzzling because there has been no lack of challenges by capable critics. For example, John Forrester (1997), in the introduction to his book of essays on the Freud wars, observes both that "Freud's place in twentieth-century culture—scientific, philosophical, literary, cultural, and religious—is uncontested" and yet that "in the twenty-five years or so that I have been concerned with psychoanalysis,… there has never been a time when it was not contested or viewed with suspicion" (pp. 1–2). Similarly, Louis Menand (2017), in attempting to explain "why Freud survives," marvels that "He's been debunked again and again—and yet we still can't give him up." Menand's own speculation that "The principal reason psychoanalysis triumphed over alternative theories and was taken up in fields outside medicine, like literary criticism, is that it presented its findings as inductive" (Menand, 2017) is unpersuasive, both because anti-Freudian doctrines have also presented themselves as evidentially based and because even superficial scrutiny reveals Freud's claims of inductive support for the Oedipal theory to be questionable at best.

Note that the various accounts I will describe here of how to resolve the puzzle of Freud's success are not necessarily in conflict with the Foucauldian account to be developed in the remainder of the book. They could form parts of a larger explanation that includes elements of Foucault's account, although I will suggest reasons for being skeptical of some of them.

A major caveat is that, in contrast to this book's focus on the Oedipal theory, most of the views I review address Freud's theory in general without any special attention to the Oedipus complex. Yet, the Oedipal theory raises the intellectual puzzle of Freud's success more than any other aspect of Freud's legacy due to its combination of extreme evidential weakness (Wakefield, 2023a) and extraordinary cultural success. Freud surely made other influential theoretical contributions such as the study of unconscious meanings (Wakefield, 2018) and psychological defenses, but these hypotheses boast substantial evidential support. A global criticism of Freudian theory thus seems misconceived; Freud's various hypotheses must be considered individually. It is nonetheless worth reviewing some of the explanations that have been offered of why Freudian theory in general was appealing with an eye as to whether they might persuasively account for the success of the Oedipal theory.

Ernest Gellner on the Intellectual Enticements of Psychoanalysis

I start with Ernest Gellner (2003), a prolific British philosopher who devoted an entire book to addressing the "the problem...why [Freud's] system of ideas did not sink...why it conquered our language and to some extent our thoughts" (Gellner, 2003, pp. 1, 141). To those who said that Freudian theory was successful simply because it is true, Gellner replied with an analogy to the eighteenth-century British historian Edward Gibbon's (1952) famous study, *The Rise and*

Fall of the Roman Empire, that attempted to account for Christianity's remarkable success in the time of Rome. In response to those who argued that the reason for Christianity's rise was simply that it expressed the true religion, Gibbon replied:

> Our curiosity is naturally prompted to inquire by what means the Christian faith obtained so remarkable a victory over the established religions of the earth. To this inquiry an obvious but satisfactory answer may be returned; that it was owing to the convincing evidence of the doctrine itself, and to the ruling providence of its great Author. But as truth and reason seldom find so favourable a reception in the world..., we may still be permitted, though with becoming submission, to ask, not indeed what were the first, but what were the secondary causes of the rapid growth of the Christian church?
>
> (Gibbon, 1952, as cited in Gellner, 2003, p. 2)

Gellner (2003) observed: "The question which Gibbon asked about Christianity applies equally to psychoanalysis: by what means did the new vision obtain so remarkable a victory?" (p. 1).

Gellner's own answer is that Freud's theory addressed many intellectual issues that are profoundly important to people but that were not being adequately addressed elsewhere, and it did so in a way that resolved seeming conflicts: "He constructed a system which, were it valid, would dissolve many of the major, emotionally disturbing conceptual strains of our society, *and* solve some of the major problems of philosophy" (p. 182). Gellner argued that psychoanalysis was true to the "fleshy, realistic feel of human nature" (2003, p. 108), unlike increasingly mechanistic empiricist psychology. He further observed that the integration of humanistic and scientific elements in psychoanalysis via the fusion of causal/hydraulic/energic and intentional languages in the theory made it attractive:

> Is man to be handed over to impersonal scientific explanation or understood in his own terms and in his full individuality? Psychoanalysis ensures that the answer is both/and....[H]is system would never have possessed its great appeal, had it not been ambiguous or, if you like, ambivalent on this point....A purely

hermeneutic psychoanalysis would not sound like science, confer no power, and few men would turn to it in distress; a purely physicalist or biological psychoanalysis would have been too much like science, and no fun. But the plausible-sounding fusion of both is very different, and most attractive.

(2003, p. 184)

However, when applied specifically to the Oedipus complex, Gellner's analysis is not compelling. The Oedipal theory seems more likely to offend people's sensibilities than to reproduce people's preexisting "realistic feel of human nature." Moreover, there is no obvious metaphysical problem, cultural contradiction, or conceptual strain of the sort referred to by Gellner that is resolved by the postulation of the Oedipus complex.

Allen Esterson on Freud's Rhetorical Power

In contrast to Gellner's agnostic approach and attention to broad metaphysical themes, Allen Esterson, a prominent Freud critic, attempted to systematically demolish the logic of Freud's arguments in his book, *Seductive Mirage: An Exploration of the Work of Sigmund Freud* (1998). Toward the end of his book, he considers how, despite his critique of the cogency of Freud's arguments, Freud's theory was able to have so much influence: "The question which must now be addressed is how it came about that a theoretical system that rests largely on false claims and fallacious arguments could gain such widespread influence" (p. 205). His answer is, first, that even if the substance of Freud's theory lacks support, some of Freud's general framework concepts such as repression, resistance, and unconscious mental states have proven useful and have been adopted within contemporary psychology. This argument does not, however, apply to the Oedipus complex, which is neither a broad principle of that type nor one that has found wide acceptance among later non-psychoanalytic schools of clinical thinking.

Esterson's second and primary explanation is that Freud's success is due to his remarkable brilliance as a writer and specifically his ability as a propagandist to deploy multiple rhetorical devices to persuade the reader of his claims despite a lack of evidence. Freud is indeed a brilliant and endlessly engaging writer and rhetorician who presents the appearance of a scientist honestly confronting possible objections to his claims, and this can easily seduce the unwary reader. Nevertheless, Esterson's analysis is unpersuasive when it comes to understanding why the Oedipus complex in particular has had such great influence. The problem lies in the very success of Esterson's critique. Esterson establishes—perhaps with occasional overreach—that Freud's arguments, however compelling on first reading, are often quite weak or even inconsistent and unpersuasive when examined more carefully. Yet, given the ample and persistent criticism of psychoanalysis from the beginning, if initial impressions of the persuasiveness of Freud's arguments are dispelled by a careful reading, this undermines Esterson's explanation of Freud's success. The claim that Freud's Oedipal theory maintained its cultural predominance over much of a century due to the rhetorical power of Freud's prose makes no sense given the ease with which the spell of Freud's charmed prose is broken according to Esterson (for similar careful readings that reveal the deficiencies of Freud's arguments regarding the Oedipal theory, see Wakefield, 2023a; 2023b).

Moreover, rhetorical trickery cannot explain why the prima facie implausible and offensive Oedipal theory gained such acceptance within the general culture among people who never read Freud's work and therefore were never directly subjected to his rhetorical charms. One might argue that the general populace merely mechanically followed the lead of a gullible medical profession, but this explanation just pushes the problem back a step to the puzzle of why the medically educated did not immediately see through Freud's rhetoric as did Esterson.

Anthony Derksen on Freud's Seven Pseudo-Scientific Strategies

Anthony Derksen (2001) provides an analysis of Freud's success that is similar to Esterson's in its emphasis on rhetorical technique. In earlier articles, Derksen (1992, 1993) had argued that even the leading philosopher of science and Freud critic Adolf Grünbaum (1984) overestimated Freud by accepting that he is a sophisticated scientific methodologist who proposes a legitimate scientific hypothesis for evaluation, when in fact Freud's theory was a textbook case of pseudoscience. Derksen (2001) asks the obvious follow-up question: "[H]ow does Freud manage to fool many people, including such a sophisticated person as Grünbaum?" (p. 329). (For a full discussion of Grünbaum's analysis, see Wakefield, 2023a.)

Derksen's diagnosis attributes Freud's success to his use of several rhetorical techniques that pseudo-scientists often use to persuade people that they are legitimate scientists:

> My answer is that Freud is a sophisticated pseudo-scientist, using all Seven Strategies of the Sophisticated Pseudo-Scientist to keep up appearances, to wit, (1) the Humble Empiricist, (2) the Severe Self-criticism, (3) the Unbiased Me, (4) the Striking but Irrelevant Example, (5) the Proof Given Elsewhere, (6) the Favorable Compromise, and (7) the Display of Methodological Sophistication.
>
> (2001, p. 329)

According to Derksen, these strategies are commonly used by scientific writers and can indicate legitimate methodological awareness, so they are "not...disreputable in themselves." However, in Freud they "are used very cunningly so as to hide weaknesses in Freud's arguments" (2001, p. 329).

Having known and played interlocutor a couple of times for Grünbaum, I find the idea that superficial methodologically sophisti-cated talk would lure him into missing gross scientific malpractice to be hopelessly implausible. Recall that Grünbaum's analysis of Freud's sophistication ultimately rests on his identification of Freud's supposed "tally argument" for psychoanalysis based on therapeutic success, and Grünbaum's analysis of the tally argument is pursued based on rather minimal evidence in Freud's text and rather independently of Freud's various methodological pronouncements. If Grünbaum got it wrong on the tally argument (which I agree with Derksen that he did; see Wakefield, 2023a), that error in his analysis of Freud is not plausibly attributed to him being fooled by Freud's methodological pronounce-ments while other scientific methodologists can see through Freud's subterfuge.

Although Derksen (2001) claims that Freud's misleading presentation of himself as methodologically sophisticated is one of the techniques of the pseudo-scientist that convinces readers, he then goes on to list a great many passages from Freud that, he allows, illustrate that Freud was genuinely methodologically sophisticated. The passages express an understanding of the hypothetico-deductive method, a Popperian approach to theory evaluation, avoidance of ad hoc reasoning to immunize a theory against falsification, the theory ladenness of observation, and the value of controlled prospective scientific inquiry, among other insights. In effect, Derksen ends up agreeing with Grünbaum that Freud is in fact methodologically sophisticated. It is, Derksen seems to be claiming, Freud's very methodological sophistication that is misleading—but misleading how?

Derksen points to Freud's application of his methodological insights to specific scientific judgments as the place where the problem occurs: "Unfortunately, when it comes to Freud's actual scientific practice little remains of this sophistication. Hence I reach my final evaluation of Freud as a sophisticated pseudo-scientist" (2001, p. 347). (Note that I [Wakefield, 2023b] arrive at a similar distinction between Freud's methodological sophistication versus his inept specific judgments about case data as a core problem with his scientific claims.)

This analysis identifies what is wrong with Freud's claims, but fails to identify why they were so widely accepted. Oedipal theory in particular involves clinical application of Freud's theorizing in ways that are subject to the kinds of problems Derksen identifies with Freud's application of his theories to cases, yet the theory went on to be widely accepted and extraordinarily influential. Freud's methodological posturing would not influence those who did not carefully read his work, and it does not hide the fact that his concrete claims about cases do not in fact match the case data, so the methodological posturing fails to address the puzzle of the social acceptance of the Oedipal theory. Derksen's account fails to explain the outsized lure that led to widespread acceptance of Freud's Oedipal theory despite the fact that its flaws were not all that difficult to identify. If the intellectual flaws in Freud's application of methodological principles are manifest upon examination and were pointed out by critics from the start and yet the theory was accepted, then one might expect the allure to lie in some other domain.

Frank Cioffi on Freud's Liberation of Sexuality

Another possible suggestion is that Freud was so venerated that people accepted the Oedipal theory because of their prior faith in the solidity of Freud's ideas. However, the Oedipal theory was one of Freud's early contributions. Frank Cioffi (2007) points out that the "veneration" explanation begs the question because it does not explain why Freud's ideas came to prominence in the first place:

> I acknowledge, of course, that much of the veneration extended Freud is purely conventional....As the cynical adage has it, 'A dog's obeyed in office.' And though this explains why so many express veneration for Freud, nevertheless the intrinsic appeal of his views must also play a role—otherwise how did the dog get into office in the first place?
>
> (p. 110)

This brings me to Cioffi's own answer to the conundrum of the acceptance of Freud's theories. His claim is that Freud's ideas about sexuality had such a pronounced liberatory effect on sexual mores that people were ready to accept Freud's theory in order to protect these gains:

> What is this intrinsic appeal?... I have some suggestions as to the source of this general loyalty. Freud has become a symbol for so much that is liberating that it is almost impossible to criticize him without provoking passionate resentment on the part of people who would find it difficult to give any coherent account of what it is that he maintained....It was through its direct effect on sexual mores and attitudes...that Freud's ideas exerted a beneficial influence....It is in large measure due to its trafficking in images of penises and anuses and semen and nipples and vulvas—but in a distancing, scientific mode—that its prominence in our discursive transactions with mental life and cultural life in general is to be explained. The influence of Freud has been compared to that of Kinsey by Simon and Gagnon [1974]: 'When the Kinsey studies reported that very large numbers of people masturbated, other men

who had done so felt better.' The same thing goes for the range of perversities that Freud has naturalized.

(Cioffi, 2007, pp. 110–111)

According to Cioffi, Freud's ideas were appealing due to the spirit of acceptance of sexual deviance and the liberation of sexual desire from social constraints that Freud's theory cultivated: "Although we might have drawn on our Christian tradition for this tolerance ('Let he who is without sin,' et cetera), it seems that we got it from Freud" (Cioffi, 2007, p. 111).

Leaving aside here Foucault's theory-driven skepticism about Freudian sexual liberation considered in Chapter 1, it is doubtless true that Freud's theory, in naturalizing child and female sexuality, emphasizing the initial "polymorphous perverse" sexual nature of human beings, and blaming repressive sexual attitudes for neuroso-genesis, played a role in sexual liberation. The acceptance of sexual variation is indeed an appealing and profoundly influential aspect of Freud's thought that places him among a small group of intellectuals, such as Bertrand Russell, and scientists, such as Havelock Ellis, who are credited with triggering the "sexual revolution."

However, this explanation of Freud's appeal can hardly apply to the Oedipus complex! The Oedipus complex as a developmental hypothesis went well beyond the parts of Freud's theory, such as his theories of repression, component sexuality, and sexual theory of the neuroses, that supported sexual liberation. A son's developmentally inevitable and crucial incestuous sexual desire for his mother is one sexual peculiarity that emerged de novo from Freud's theory and was not an earlier recognized and oppressed sexual variation. Moreover, Freud's theory did not cause the expression of such desires to be accepted and liberated by our culture, although perhaps one might argue that some men felt relieved that they could more easily blame their sexual deviance on their mothers.

Moreover, as I showed in *Attachment, Sexuality, Power* (Wakefield, 2023b), Freud's application of the Oedipal theory in the Little Hans case history (which was Freud's major evidence for the existence of the Oedipus complex) is not at all liberatory for Hans or for his mother and led to less liberatory attitudes about their mother-son affection. For Hans, it yielded masturbatory prohibitions and Victorian physical restraints to prevent masturbation and thus prevent Oedipal fanta-sizing, as well as attempts to control even the simplest aspects of Hans's intimate relationship with his mother—such as his cuddling in bed with her in the morning—for fear of excessive sexual arousal. For the mother, it yielded corresponding interference in her ability to be intimate with Hans, as well as the suggestion that she is at fault for Hans's neurosis due to her overindulgence of Hans's sensual desires. As we shall see when I revisit the Hans case in Chapter 7, there is no plausible reading of the Hans case history according to which the Oedipal theory is used to liberate the sexuality of the child or the mother, and this is reflected in the broader cultural response as well—as manifested, for example, in our culture's uniquely harsh judgment about parent-child co-sleeping (Wakefield, 2023b). This is one "perversion" that may be "naturalized" but is not at all tolerated.

Cioffi (1998a) also sympathetically cites several authors who claim that Freud's theory is appealing simply because of the sexual titillation provided by his theory's content, referring to various forms of adult polymorphous perverse and symbolic sexual desires. Freud appears early on to have agreed that the sexual element appealed to people: "The sexual business attracts people who are all stunned and then go away won over after having exclaimed, 'No one has ever asked me about that before!'" (1893/1985, p. 57). However, this was long before the presentation of the Oedipal theory. Later in his career, Freud complained about the obstacle posed to his theory's success by people's resistance to its claims about the child's sexual desires. In any event, the Oedipus complex itself is not generally exploited as a source of such titillation, and incestuous sexual desire by a son for his mother has not become liberated due to the Oedipal theory.

Wittgenstein on Freud's Power of Overgeneralizing

In Cioffi's essay "Wittgenstein's Freud" (1998b), he presents a useful survey of Ludwig Wittgenstein's several explanations of Freud's appeal. For example, writing in *Zettel* (1970) of Freud's wish-fulfillment theory of dreams, Wittgenstein says: "It is the characteristic thing about such a theory that it looks at a special, clearly intuitive case and says: that shows how things are in every case. This case is the exemplar of all cases" (Wittgenstein, 1970, as cited in Cioffi, 1998b, p. 99). Similarly, in

Lectures and Conversations, Wittgenstein says that Freud's explanations are "not a matter of evidence" but rather "the sort of explanation we are inclined to accept...Some dreams obviously are wish fulfillments: such as the sexual dreams of adults for instance. But it seems muddled to say that all dreams are hallucinated wish-fulfillments" (Wittgenstein, 1972, as cited in Cioffi, 1998b, p. 99).

However, Wittgenstein's claim that Freud's explanations are appealing because they are overgeneralizations of intuitively true examples cannot be the explanation for the acceptance of the Oedipus complex. There are no prototypical pre-theoretical cases of normal human development in which it is intuitively obvious that development passes through a stage of incestuous desire for the mother. The Little Hans case (1909) might be considered Freud's attempt to provide such an example, but it is far from obvious or intuitive even there.

Another of Wittgenstein's suggestions, specifically in regard to the infantile sexual determination of adult character, is that psycho-analytic interpretations have "the attractiveness of a mythology" regarding fate: "explanations which say this is all a repetition of something which has happened before...[give] a sort of tragic pattern to one's life.... Like a tragic figure carrying out the decrees under which the Fates had placed him at birth" (Wittgenstein, 1972, p. 50). For example, who has not felt fated to repeat as an adult some flaw in a parent or a problem in one's childhood relationship to a parent? Such appeal surely exists at least for some individuals of a literary bent. For example, Cioffi (1998c) quotes a character in Italo Svevo's novel *The Confessions of Zeno* (1930):

> They have found out what was the matter with me. The diagnosis is exactly the same as the one Sophocles drew up long ago for poor Oedipus: I was in love with my mother and wanted to murder my father....I listened enraptured. It was a disease that exalted me to a place among the great ones of the earth; a disease so dignified that it could trace back its pedigree even to the mythological age.
>
> (Svevo, 1930, as cited in Cioffi, 1998c, p. 284)

However, although fascinating in a fictional character, it is unclear why the Oedipal theory of the nature of our fate—for example, that we will love someone who resembles a parent—would have widespread appeal among the middle class. The heroic sentiment expressed in Svevo's passage is not one that most people are likely to embrace.

Wittgenstein further observes that there is an inherent appeal of certain explanations in certain times and places: "The attraction of certain kinds of explanation is overwhelming.... If someone says 'Why do you say it is really this? Obviously it is not this at all,' it is in fact even difficult to see it as something else" (1972, p. 46). Perhaps this is an apt description of the seeming obviousness of Oedipal references during a lengthy period in our culture. However, it begs the central question: why was the Oedipal theory so appealing when it was put forward that it became a preferred explanatory schema? Wittgenstein's explanation is not persuasively anchored in the social processes at the time the Oedipal theory was initially proposed.

Nathan Hale Jr. on the Timing of Freud's Theory

Nathan Hale Jr. (1971) attempts to explain the puzzling fact of the exceptionally positive reception of psychoanalysis in the United States within just a few years of Freud's visit in 1909. This fact bewildered Freud himself, who had no love for America and famously asserted that "America is a mistake: a gigantic mistake, it is true, but nonetheless a mistake" (Jones, 1955, p. 60).

Hale argues that America's cultural readiness to embrace psychoanalysis was due to several factors. First, psychoanalysis appeared at a time when a physical approach to treatment of psychological problems was reaching a dead end within the American medical community and there was receptivity to a psychological approach. As well, psychoanalysis fit with broader American values, such as the belief in self-improvement and the ability to remake oneself. However, such sociological explanations have no specificity to the Oedipus complex and cannot explain why the Oedipus complex with its specific structure was accepted in Europe as well as America.

A further explanation offered by Hale is that psychoanalysis arrived just as the Victorian era of sexual repression was receding, and there was thus a crisis in the nature of sexual morality that could be filled by psychoanalysis's more open and positive attitude about sex. This fits with the common image of Freud's writings on psychoanalysis as a sexually liberating force, discussed above.

However, similar to Foucault's argument detailed in Chapter 1 that the repression of sex was itself a technique for amplifying the pleasurable discussion of sex, others have objected to Hale's depiction as overly simplistic. Demos (1978), for example, argues that the apparent liberation of sex was in fact a tactic in recalibrated sexual oppression:

> [C]ivilized morality was less attacked than readjusted during the same period; the cutting edge here was a new frankness about sex, in the service of suppressing its least attractive manifestations. So-called 'purity campaigns' were organized by leading progressives to oppose prostitution and reduce venereal disease, and increasingly their spokesmen deplored the polite façade of reticence that had veiled such problems from public scrutiny...[C]andor in sexual matters was advocated in the service of ever-greater 'purity'; except for a tiny minority of cultural radicals, American progressives reaffirmed the central core of traditional mores.
>
> (p. 26)

Moreover, even if Freud's thinking in general led to a degree of middle-class sexual liberation for which America was culturally ready, the question would remain whether the Oedipus complex's appeal is due to its being one of the features of Freud's theory responsible for its liberating influences.

John Demos on the Rise of the Oedipal Family

John Demos (1978), in an essay, "Oedipus and America," as well as subsequent reflections (Demos, 1996), attempts to understand "the long-standing enigma of the 'success' of psychoanalysis in the twentieth-century United States" (1996, p. 79). He argues that what he calls the "hothouse family" (or "Oedipal family") was an emerging pattern at the time that amplified the Oedipal dynamics in families and so prepared the way for psychoanalysis's reception. He holds that different family structures can amplify or decrease the expression of Oedipal dynamics, and argues that prior to Freud's theorizing the American family changed in ways that amplified such expression, allowing for a more ready acceptance of Freud's theory based on everyday experience.

Demos argues that as a result of the nineteenth-century movement of the population from rural agrarian culture to urban mass culture, there was a growing separation of the nuclear family from the community, and the family came to be seen as a self-contained refuge maintained by the wife to which the husband could retreat after the battles of the marketplace. This emerging family, Demos argues, was more differentiated and internally subdivided than families traditionally had been, including along lines of gender that included unprecedented levels of sex-role stereotyping, and along generations as well, with children increasingly differentiated from adults. All this led to a more self-conscious and anxious sense about child rearing, with child-rearing manuals concerned especially with the importance of the mother's every action in raising boys in particular. Women's roles as mothers became elevated as their prime responsibility and expression. All of these influences, according to Demos, led to "a massive intensification of the parent-child bond" (1978, p. 33), especially with respect to the mother-son relationship, with the father taking a less direct and authoritative role due to his working outside the home. In this hothouse family of the late nineteenth century "lay the social and cultural 'soil' in which psychoanalysis would subsequently take root" (Demos, 1996, p. 80). Demos speculates that, under these circumstances, the mother's suppressed sexuality was sublimated into her intense maternal role, yielding a quasi-Oedipal reality to her motherly behavior: "Is it too much to suppose that many nineteenth-century women—faced with overbearing cultural constraints on their sexuality in relation to sweethearts and husbands—proved to be rather 'seductive' in their maternal function?" (1978, p. 34).

Demos accepts the objective reality of the Oedipus complex, and to that extent he is different from the other writers surveyed in this chapter who are trying to explain how the theory could gain acceptance despite its falsity. He explains that he is not suggesting that the social situation created pseudo-Oedipal phenomena but rather that the Oedipus complex existed in the background and simply became more readily salient due to social conditions, facilitating the acceptance of Freud's theory:

[T]he Oedipus complex is a significant developmental potential in all persons, no matter what their location in time and space. However, particular patterns of historical and cultural circumstance have much to do with the way this potential is realized—whether it is highlighted, or muted, or neutralized, or whatever. Now the main line of historical change in the nineteenth century did, we suggest, create a situation in which oedipal issues become highly charged for many people. And among all the Western countries, this situation was most fully elaborated in the United States.

(p. 37)

Can one try to interpret Demos's argument more neutrally as claiming that social conditions created a family structure that made Oedipal-type eroticized family interactions more prominent and thus made the Oedipal theory seem to correspond to reality and thus appealing, whether or not it was true? From this perspective, Demos's argument is weak. His question above about whether women under the described conditions eroticized their parental relationships is sheer speculation, not evidence. This stretching of the evidence emerges as well in Demos's arbitrary sexual interpretation of Civil War–era ballads that sentimentalized mothers: "There is, of course, no overtly sexual reference in all this; Mother is sentimentalized, not erotized; but perhaps in the world of unconscious process the distance from sentiment to Eros was not so great after all" (1978, p. 34). He offers no evidence that the sentimentalization of motherhood is an expression of eroticism versus some other feeling, such as gratitude or attachment bonding—or a longing for home by young men being sacrificed on the battlefield. In other words, he reads into various features of family life an intensification of preexisting Oedipal-type dynamics, and on that basis explains the appeal of the Oedipal theory. Without independent evidence beyond his assumption that Oedipal dynamics are waiting to emerge, his argument lacks support.

My analyses of Freud's case of Little Hans (Wakefield, 2023a; 2023b) show that, at least in Hans's nuclear family in a European context, Demos's description is far from persuasive. The theory was imposed by Freud and Hans's father in the face of skepticism and resistance by the mother rather than recognition and acceptance. Rather than distinctive Oedipal dynamics first emerging and then being interpreted, Freud and Hans's father impose Oedipal interpretations on routine parent-child behavior that was not at all novel. It is also arguable that at the time of Freud's proposing the Oedipal theory, marriage was already moving beyond the Victorian model Demos describes and into a new era of emotional and sexual parental intimacy with a more separated child axis. Demos's thesis that the changing nature of the family and its growing emotional intensity at the turn of the nineteenth century made middle-class families more "Oedipal-like" and thus more receptive to Freud's theory remains unpersuasive. In reflecting on his thesis, Demos himself observes that his argument "could hardly achieve conclusiveness" because it was "long on speculation and short on evidence, schematic, spotty, oversimplified" (1996, p. 80).

Filip Buekens and Maarten Boudry on Psychoanalysis as Searlian Institutional Knowledge

Buekens and Boudry (2011; 2012) argue that Freudian theory's success despite lack of evidence is due to the formation of a tightly controlled society of believers in analytic institutes, whereby the claims of psychoanalysis became "institutional facts," in John Searle's (1995) sense in which a set of rules can constitute a form of social reality. That is, Freud's theories came to be true not as claims about the natural world independent of human intentions (even though Freud portrayed them as such truths) but rather due to their construction as part of a human system of rules of "truth" among a coordinated set of believers. Such claims as "dreams are wish fulfillments," "paranoia is caused by homosexual desire," or "boys want to have sex with their mothers and kill their fathers" are thus "true" by the conventions of the psychoanalytic interpretation game. This is analogous to the fact that someone swinging a wooden stick that fails to hit an approaching ball can "strike out" in a baseball game in virtue of the rules of the game that people mutually agree to accept, or that some otherwise worthless piece of paper can be money that has a value because of a system of valuation and exchange people have agreed to:

> What was not immediately transparent for Freud, and his intended audience, was the specific nature of the speech act he performed when he said that human phenomenon X is—or counts

as—psychoanalytic phenomenon Y. While he explicitly maintained that he was merely describing facts, he was, in fact, creating
new entities within an unfolding institutional framework.

(Buekens and Boudry, 2011, p. 45)

Buekens and Boudry support their argument for the institutional
character of psychoanalytic facts by citing the cultish and involuted
nature of the psychoanalytic community, its hierarchical internal
organization and religious-like dissemination of beliefs, the lack of
empirical evidence, and the careful monitoring of the supporting
beliefs held by community members: "Since no independent evidence
supports these beliefs...[f]aithful followers apply the central declaratives and 'find new confirmations'; committees ensure that the central
declaratives are not modified; dissident figures...must be renounced"
(2011, pp. 45–46). Note that this Searlian characterization of Freudian
theory also has a marked affinity to Foucault's notion of scientific
disciplines as "truth games" in which the ability to declare a claim as
true depends on an implicit set of rules of discourse that structure
what can and cannot be said.

However, the suggestion that psychoanalytic claims literally constitute a socially constructed institution with its own rules of discourse
implies that those who object to specific psychoanalytic hypotheses are
not disagreeing about the truth of human psychology but simply
refusing to play Freud's game, a construal that does not seem to reflect
the nature of the disputes about psychoanalysis. More troubling is the
broader implication of this approach. Buekens and Boudry deny that
their analysis implies a general social constructivism about science.
However, once dogma is construed not as irrationally held belief but a
language game outside of rationality and irrationality, the fact that
there are dogmatic periods in all sciences—which is considered an
adaptive feature in pursuing the truth by thinkers as diverse as Karl
Popper and Thomas Kuhn— threatens to take all of science out of the
literal truth game.

Buekens and Boudry's analysis of Freudian cultism at most
addresses why doctrinaire psychoanalysts generally held to Freud's
ideas. The question remains of what allowed these beliefs to be
interpreted and accepted by others as truth-claims about nature. The
cultish behavior of the psychoanalytic community provides no

explanation of why the population at large accepted or was influenced by the Oedipal theory. Bourgeois parents who were worried about over-arousing their children and writers and scholars in the humanities or social sciences using psychoanalytic ideas were not part of any cultishly controlled and institutionally defined semantic environment. For them, Oedipal doctrines were truth claims about reality which they accepted, and on which they acted in their families and their writings. The Oedipus complex thrived in the culture at large, outside of any cult that could control the institutional rules of truth.

Sarah Winter on Freud's Marketing Genius

The most ambitious recent attempt to understand the success of psychoanalysis as both a movement and a theory despite its apparent falsity is Sarah Winter's (1999) richly documented book-length assault on this problem in *Freud and the Institution of Psychoanalytic Knowledge*. Winter is motivated partly by the implausibility of Freud's gender-related views. One might object that the falsity of those doctrines may not have been obvious to educated readers at the time they were proposed, given the gender roles and constraints on women at the time. Consequently, it is not clear that there is a deep mystery about the acceptance of those specific psychoanalytic ideas that needs to be solved. However, Winter includes the Oedipus complex within the presumed-false gender-relevant doctrines she addresses, and casts a much wider net in her analysis than strictly gender claims, and so her work enters into the territory addressed here.

Winter attempts to explain the success of psychoanalysis primarily in terms of Freud's professional and intellectual political maneuvering and strategic posturing. She summarizes her overall analysis of Freud's moves to institutionalize psychoanalysis as follows:

> In speaking of 'the institutionalization of psychoanalytic knowl-edge,' then, I refer to the strategies Freud adopted in his writings and his professional life to ensure that psychoanalysis would prosper and expand as an autonomous profession and research project—ideally, as a science validated by scientists—and how he

attempted to orchestrate the broader social and international recognition of psychoanalysis....

I shall focus on three related institutionalizing strategies that Freud pursued to this end. The first involved incorporating into psychoanalytic theory generic elements of ancient Greek tragedy... so that tragedy could lend the 'universality' of its concerns and its embodiment of 'Necessity' to the psychoanalytic principles of unconscious determination and oedipal sexuality.....

The second major strategy was to define psychoanalysis as an independent profession, distinct from psychiatry and neurology,... with its own institutions of certification and training and its own diagnostic and therapeutic procedures...

A third important agenda involved Freud's endeavor to present psychoanalysis as a new scientific discipline in competition with the emerging disciplines of anthropology and sociology. Freud 'applies' psychoanalysis to the study of culture and society....

(Winter, 1999, pp. 8–9)

With the benefit of hindsight, Winter claims that everything Freud did to expand the explanatory domain of psychoanalysis—the links Freud forged to other disciplines, the references to myth, the links to popular culture—was simply part of a strategy by which Freud aimed to foist psychoanalysis upon the world. Although Freud no doubt had his desired scientific success in mind, Winter ignores the fact that these particular strategies were often intellectually relevant attempts at providing indirect evidence for the plausibility of psychoanalytic theory. The types of strategies Winter identifies are the sorts of things many large-scale psychological theorists—including those opposed to Freud—have attempted to do as part of the routine intellectual expansionism that characterizes most scientific theorizing. Freud's use of these intellectual strategies cannot explain the subsequent acceptance and cultural power of the Oedipus complex despite a lack of evidence.

Winter's main point specifically about the Oedipus complex is that Freud's use of the Oedipus myth and Sophocles's play as evidence for the theory allowed Freud to appropriate the prestige of the classical tradition with its universal themes as a selling point for psycho-analysis. It is of course true that Freud exploited the Oedipus myth to give his theory an air of plausibility. However, it seems doubtful that middle-class families were worried about their children's sexuality because of Freud's references to Sophocles. The Little Hans case (1909) is the original published Freudian case history in which the Oedipal theory is imposed on a middle-class family, and in the record of the family's interaction the words "Oedipus" and "Oedipal" are never mentioned, although Freud in his Discussion famously labels Hans a "little Oedipus." Instead, the case is about demonstrating that Hans has sexual feelings for his mother and murderous rage towards his father. These hypotheses are so incendiary and potent that the link to classical traditions via the use of the Oedipus myth seems more window dressing than deeply explanatory of why such a theory would be accepted. In the end, one cannot read the truth of Freud's theory off of the myth, nor can the appropriation of the myth explain why the theory was so successful among the bourgeois public at large in the early twentieth century in Europe and the United States.

Winter persuasively analyzes some of Freud's exploitations of intellectual politics to increase the chances of his theory's acceptance. However, such efforts by theoreticians are legion. She fails to elaborate the features of our culture that made Freud's efforts to sell his flawed product so extraordinarily and bewilderingly successful that we bought what Freud was selling. She fails to ask Foucault's question: what did the Oedipus complex do to us that might explain why it so strongly appealed to us?

D. H. Lawrence on the Inevitable Rational Appeal of the Incest Theory

The writer D. H. Lawrence was taken with Freud's Oedipal theory in his early years. He discussed it on his first date with his wife-to-be and interpreted his own family history in Oedipal terms in his letters, claiming to hate his father and to have an almost erotic love for his mother (Pierloot, 2000, p. 100). His novel, *Sons and Lovers* (1913), is generally considered a remarkably explicit "Oedipal" autobiographical account of his relationship to his parents.

However, Lawrence eventually came to reject the Oedipal theory—which he labeled the "incest theory"—declaring in 1916 that "The longer I live the less I like psychoanalysis" (Pierloot, 2000, p. 100).

Lawrence agreed with Jung's major criticism of Freud, namely, that Freud's pansexual theory of motivation rendered the very notion of sexual motivation meaningless: "when Freud makes sex accountable for everything he as good as makes it accountable for nothing" (Lawrence, 1922, p. 19).

Lawrence presented his analysis of what is wrong with the Oedipal theory in two nonfiction volumes (Lawrence, 2021; 2022), in which among other topics he attempts to explain why the incest theory is so appealing despite its falsity. Unlike most critics of Freud, Lawrence attempts to explain why people are drawn to the Oedipal theory independently of any manipulative tactics engaged in by Freud and his followers. Indeed, Lawrence makes a unique and quite clever attempt to explain how so many individuals could be brought to seemingly find their own Oedipus complexes and incestuous longings within themselves during psychoanalysis if the theory is false. Lawrence's explanation emphasizes what he calls the "passional self" that lies inside each of us and aspires to union and full satisfaction, and the inevitable frustrations and unfulfilled longings of that passional self in conventional marriage. This tension, he argues, is the origin of incest motives.

Lawrence's argument starts from Freud's assumption that the only source of neurotic psychopathology is repression of normal sexual components that then emerge in symptoms. The crucial point for Lawrence is that the Oedipus complex, including incestuous desire, is, for Freud, a normal developmental stage and not a neurotic symptom. The incest motive is not conceptualized by Freud as a displacement of some other normal sexual impulse that has been repressed and diverted, leading to a pathological desire. Rather, it is part of normal sexuality. Consequently, uncovering incestuous wishes and making the incestuous desires conscious does not lead to their dissipation. Rather, incest craving is a normal part of human sexual longing:

If a complex is not caused by the inhibition of some so-called normal sex-impulse, what on earth is it caused by?... You can remove all possible inhibitions of the normal sex desire, and still you cannot remove the complex. All you have done is to make conscious a desire which previously was unconscious. This is the moral dilemma of psychoanalysis. The analyst set out to cure neurotic humanity by removing the cause of the neurosis. He finds that the cause of neurosis lies in some unadmitted sex desire. After all he has said about inhibition of normal sex, he is brought at last to realize that at the root of almost every neurosis lies some incest-craving, and that this incest-craving is not the result of inhibition of normal sex-craving. Now see the dilemma—it is a fearful one. If the incest craving is not the outcome of any inhibition of normal desire, if it actually exists and refuses to give way before any criticism, what then? What remains but to accept it as part of the normal sex-manifestation?

(1921, pp. 19–20)

As noted above, when it comes to most sexual desires, Freud is rightfully seen as a liberationist, yet when it comes to Oedipal incestuous desires, he offers no liberatory solace whatsoever, as manifested in the case of Little Hans. In an earlier book (Wakefield, 2023b), I attributed this anomaly to Freud's belief in the "spoiling theory," that overly ample sexual gratification would increase rather than sate his desires.

Lawrence, confronting the same puzzle of Freud's restrictive attitude toward Oedipal gratification, arrives at a more incendiary conclusion. Given that Oedipal theory holds that incestuous desire is normal, and given psychoanalytic assumptions about the need to gratify normal sexual desires to avoid falling ill, the logical conclusion, Lawrence asserts, must be that incest should be allowed and even encouraged as the true expression of one's sexual passion:

Once, however, you accept the incest-craving as part of the normal sexuality of man, you must remove all repression of incest itself. In fact, you must admit incest as you now admit sexual marriage, as a duty even.... [N]eurosis is not the result of inhibition of so-called normal sex, but of inhibition of incest-craving.

Any inhibition must be wrong, since inevitably in the end it causes neurosis and insanity. Therefore the inhibition of incest-craving is wrong, and this wrong is the cause of practically all modern neurosis and insanity. Psychoanalysis will never openly state this conclusion. But it is to this conclusion that every analyst must, willy-nilly, consciously or unconsciously, bring his patient.

(1921, pp. 20–21)

Lawrence's own analysis of incestuous desire and how it emerges in psychoanalysis despite the falsity of Freud's theory depends on his ideational understanding of unconscious contents: "The question lies here: whether a repression is a primal impulse which has been deterred from fulfilment, or whether it is an *idea* which is refused enactment. Is a repression a repressed passional impulse, or is it an idea which we suppress...?" (1921, p. 27). Given his ideational understanding of the unconscious, Lawrence offers a unique explanation in terms of logical processing of how incestuous desires arrive in the unconscious via an entirely non-Freudian path, namely, a logical deduction that a man *should* have sex with his mother for complete fulfillment:

> Man...can proceed to deduce from his given emotional and passional premises conclusions which are not emotional or passional at all, but just logical, abstract, ideal. That is, a man finds it impossible to realize himself in marriage. He recognizes the fact that his emotional, even passional, regard for his mother is deeper than it ever could be for a wife. This makes him unhappy, for he knows that passional communion is not complete unless it be also sexual. He has a body of sexual passion which he cannot transfer to a wife. He has a profound love for his mother. Shut in between walls of tortured and increasing passion, he must find some escape or fall down the pit of insanity and death. What is the only possible escape? To seek in the arms of the mother the refuge which offers nowhere else. And so the incest motive is born. All the labored explanations of the psychoanalysts are unnecessary. The incest motive is a logical deduction of the human reason.
>
> (1921, pp. 28–29)

According to Lawrence, "the logical conclusion of incest...rouses the deepest instinctive opposition" (1921, p. 28) and is repressed and remains unconscious. However, this unconscious conclusion interacts with the mental system to produce unconscious incestuous longings that are also repressed, but may be uncovered in psychoanalysis even though they came about in a way wholly alien to Freud's Oedipal theory of natural childhood incestuous desire. The process of a logically deduced idea activating unconscious motives Lawrence labels "idealism":

> By idealism we understand the motivizing of the great affective sources by means of ideas mentally derived. As for example the incest motive, which is first and foremost a logical deduction made by the human reason, even if unconsciously made, and secondly is introduced into the affective, passional sphere, where it now proceeds to serve as a principle for action.
>
> (1921, pp. 29–30)

But why does the fact that one loves one's mother more than one's wife yield the conclusion that one must have sex with one's mother? Lawrence believes that our cultural ideal of the link between love and sex is so powerful that it has a determining influence on how we process such information:

> The identity of love with sex, the single necessity for fulfilment through love, these are our fixed ideals. We must fulfil these ideals in their extremity. And this brings us finally to incest, even incest-worship. We have no option, whilst our ideals stand. Why? Because incest is the logical conclusion of our ideals, when these ideals have to be carried into passional effect. And idealism has no escape from logic.
>
> (1921, p. 32)

Given this situation and the incest taboo, human beings must remain unsatisfied. Psychoanalysis, although mistaken in its doctrines, has nonetheless arrived at the motivational truth at the heart of our dissatisfaction. Lawrence thus holds that the Oedipal theory is appealing because it states something that is deeply true, namely, that we want to have sex with our parent and believe that would be the ultimate passional fulfillment, even if the theory's account of the genesis of this desire is false. However, at the core of Lawrence's construction there appear to be two tensions that are evaded only by begging the question. First, he argues that our cultural ideals unconsciously regulate desire and yield incestuous desire given the ideal of love and sex finding joint fruition at the most intense level. However, this ignores the fact that our cultural ideals that impact our ideational processing equally insist that any such joint expression of love and sex must be sought in extrafamilial love as the only legitimate outlet for erotic passion and are quite clear in condemning incestuous sex. Second, his account of how an idea that incest fulfills our cultural ideals transforms into actual incestuous desire is bewildering. As we know from everyday life, one can dwell endlessly on what one ought to desire according to some social standard without the desire coming into existence. Even if Lawrence were correct that we cannot help but formulate the unconscious idea that sex with the person we love most, namely, our parent, makes a certain logical sense, he provides no plausible reason to believe that this intellectual insight translates into the creation of actual incestuous desire.

Malcolm Macmillan on the Appeal of Psychoanalysis

Malcolm Macmillan (1991) ends his book's comprehensive and relentless critique of Freudian theory with a section titled "the appeal of psycho-analysis," noting that "criticism of psycho-analysis is not new and we should ask why Freud's theory continues to appeal" (p. 603). Macmillan offers "five main reasons" for psychoanalysis's appeal despite all the flaws he has identified. He does not specifically mention the Oedipus complex, and he apologizes ahead of time for "speculation" based on little hard data (p. 603).

The first reason is that the critiques of psychoanalysis are not widely known: "most lay people, as well as a large number of non-analyst professionals, think of psycho-analysis as beyond substantial criticism and as not much changed from the ideas put forward by Freud" (p. 603). Macmillan cites some of the major attacks on Freud's views, and argues that these attacks are "simply not known outside of psycho-analysis" (p. 603). Given the avalanche of critiques of psychoanalysis right from the beginning to recently widely reviewed attacks and even newspaper coverage of the "Freud wars," this argument lacks any credibility. In any event, why would one expect more widespread knowledge of Bowlby's or Kohut's criticisms of the Oedipus complex to end the theory's influence when even among scholars and analysts these developments did not have that effect?

Moreover, many of these critiques occurred half-a-century or more after the theory became predominant. The question is why, with inadequate evidential credentials right from the start, the Oedipus complex nevertheless grew to be a culturally central psychological construct for so long.

The second reason offered by Macmillan is psychoanalysis's "pseudo-explanatory power": "the understanding which psycho-analysis gives of the determinants of behaviour and personality seems to be especially extensive" (pp. 603–604). The problem here, Macmillan argues, is an "absence of rules for arriving at interpretations and evaluating explanations" so that "phenomena...can be interpreted in almost any way at all" (p. 604). However, Macmillan tries to explain the seeming power of psychoanalytic explanation as the reason for psychoanalysis's appeal while simultaneously denying that psychoanalysis does have real explanatory power. If psycho-analysis is in fact explanatorily vacuous, how was everybody fooled for 50 years into thinking it is highly explanatory?

Macmillan's third reason is the "appeal of the irrational": "there is the attraction of the irrational which appeals in and of itself" (p. 603). This begs the question. There are many proposed explanations of human irrationality, and the question is why psychoanalysis has been taken to be a correct theory for so long by so many people.

The fourth reason, echoing Cioffi's analysis, is "sexuality": "psycho-analysis concentrates upon precisely those things in which people have the greatest interest and about which no other discipline says anything very much" (p. 603). And fifth, there is "the appeal of therapy": "most people take it for granted that the effectiveness of psycho-analysis as a therapy for a wide range of disorders and problems is well established and certainly not a matter of dispute" (p. 603). It is true that illuminating sexuality and providing therapeutic help are appealing goals. However, as with irrationality, there were many competing theories in both these areas in Freud's day through to our own. Macmillan's hypotheses don't explain the unique power of psychoanalysis to dominate the explanatory landscape to the degree and for the length of time that it did. More importantly for present purposes, these proposed explanations are not specific to the Oedipal theory and address psychoanalysis in a broad impressionistic way rather than grappling with the influence of specific claims.

Mikkel Borch-Jacobsen on the Nonexistence of Psychoanalysis

A recent attempt to explain Freud's success is *The Freud Files* (2011) by intellectual historians Mikkel Borch-Jacobsen and Sonu Shamdasani, and a later related article by Borch-Jacobsen. The authors attempt to explain the remarkable success of psychoanalysis merely by Freud's manipulative efforts to gain acceptance for a spurious theory, as the book's front matter makes clear:

> How did psychoanalysis attain its prominent cultural position? How did it eclipse rival psychologies and psychotherapies, such that it became natural to bracket Freud with Copernicus and Darwin? Why did Freud 'triumph' to such a degree that we hardly remember his rivals? This book reconstructs the early controversies around psychoanalysis, and shows that rather than demonstrating its superiority, Freud and his followers rescripted history. This legend-making was not an incidental addition to psychoanalytic theory but formed its core.
> (Borch-Jacobsen, & Shamdasani, 2011, front matter)

Borch-Jacobsen and Shamdasani provide a relentless critique of Freud and psychoanalysis by combining quotations from critics with their own glosses that amplify the critics' complaints. They also present an impressive compendium of the ways Freud and his followers surreptitiously attempted to secure their success, often deviating from acceptable scientific standards:

> The censorship of Freud's correspondences, the sequestering of documents and reminiscences in sealed boxes in the Freud Archives, the compilation of the official Freud biography and the preparation of the *Standard Edition of the Complete Psychological Works of Sigmund Freud* was a systematic and concerted enterprise, intended to consolidate and disseminate the Freudian legend. The legend was now everywhere, massive and virtually unassailable. Texts available to researchers and the general public had been carefully filtered and reformatted to present the image of Freud and psychoanalysis that the Freudian establishment wanted to promote.... The success of

this propaganda mission rested on its invisibility...: cuts in letters weren't indicated, inconvenient facts were omitted, skeletons were hidden in closets, critics were silenced.

(2011, pp. 300–301)

I greatly admire Borch-Jacobsen's historical Freud scholarship, but I find the attempt to explain Freud's success wholly in terms of such manipulations unpersuasive. Borch-Jacobsen and Shamdasani offer no clear answer as to why these underhanded efforts were so successful in general or in the specific case of the Oedipus complex. Moreover, the many quotes they present from Freud's critics reveal that psychoanalysis's problems were publicly well-aired from the beginning, casting doubt on the book's thesis that the suppression of negative information that they document ensured psychoanalysis's success.

The authors also argue that psychoanalytic subterfuge had broader consequences for psychology because psychoanalysis's inflated image "effectively delegitimated the psychotherapies which psychoanalysis competed with in the mental health market place" (2011, pp. 301–302). Yet, aside from behavioral therapy that traces its lineage to Pavlov, Watson, and Skinner, the newer psychotherapies, ranging from rational-emotive and cognitive-behavioral to Gestalt and even some body therapies, were started by clinicians initially trained as psychoanalysts. Rather than an interloper that competitively squelched other approaches, psychoanalysis, despite itself, was a fruitful generator of new ideas and approaches that often thrived, albeit in opposition to the dominant Freudian doctrines. (But note that the history in France might better fit the authors' thesis than the American experience.)

The authors further argue that psychoanalytic manipulation yielded an image of psychoanalysis even more inflated than its actual success: "At the same time it led to the rescripting of the history of ideas in the twentieth century, giving psychoanalysis a prominence that it never properly had" (2011, p. 302). The claim that there was a spuriously inflated impression of psychoanalysis's prominence is difficult to defend. Prior to the late twentieth century, when biologicalism and psychopharmacology came to dominate American psychiatry, virtually every American psychiatry department in medical schools and major hospitals was chaired by a psychoanalyst and almost all the major psychiatry textbooks took a psychoanalytic perspective.

Freud was taught routinely even in undergraduate college psychology courses. Psychoanalysis's predominance was no manipulated illusion.

I turn now to a recent exchange in which Borch-Jacobsen responded to a critical review of *The Freud Files* by John Forrester, professor of the history and philosophy of science at the University of Cambridge. Forrester (2012) essentially argues that Borch-Jacobsen and Shamdasani's documentation of the many weaknesses and machinations of psychoanalysis do not explain how the theory succeeded even among scholars and intellectuals. Borch-Jacobsen's (2019) riposte to Forrester's critique distills and clarifies the book's most compelling points, so I focus on the article.

Forrester's basic and quite sensible point is that documenting Freud's failure to cite criticisms of his views and other such shenanigans is neither evidence for psychoanalysis's invalidity nor an explanation of psychoanalysis's success. There is nothing more common in intellectual and scientific life than for leading thinkers to forge ahead, aggressively building their contribution and reputation while avoiding spending their time grappling with endless criticism. Moreover, failure to attend to objections is an odd criticism of Freud, who does in fact spend an inordinate amount of time in his writings addressing criticisms that he thinks pose a threat to his views. For example, Freud recognized the suggestion objection as the major threat to his psychoanalytic method and he exerted considerable effort across multiple publications throughout his life in attempting to address this threat (Grünbaum, 1984; Wakefield, 2023a).

The sort of problem to which Forrester points might be illustrated by Borch-Jacobsen's comment: "In 1913, after eight years of furious controversy, psychoanalysis was solemnly condemned by the entire profession at the congress of the German Psychiatric Association organized in Breslau" (2019, p. 92). Borch-Jacobsen supposes that this vote revealed something about the scientific status of psychoanalysis that was ignored by Freudians, and perhaps it did. However, as he knows, this condemnation was cooked up beforehand by followers of Hoche and Kraepelin, with a letter going out prior to the conference asking the membership for reports of damage done by psychoanalysis—and only damage, not benefit. (One wonders what the results of such a one-sided survey would have been for Hoche's or Kraepelin's own patients treated with the medical interventions of the day.)

Yes, psychoanalysis surely overinterpreted meanings and over-emphasized sexuality, as the conference's subsequent report justifiably complained. However, psychoanalysis's real sin in the eyes of those participating in the 1913 Congress's "condemnation" was the assumption that there is a psychological component to the etiology and nature of mental disorders. This now-standard assumption opened the way to today's many psychological treatments that address the meanings and conflicts afflicting patients, and such treatments are often as effective as our still-crude psychopharmacological interventions. However, at the time, this idea was anathema to the Congress's attendees. The 1913 attack was primarily a tactical move in the grand battle that continues to this day between the Greisinger/Kraepelin view that the etiology of mental disorders always consists of brain lesions or other physically identifiable medical disorders versus the view that psychological meanings may interact to cause mental disorder (Wakefield, 2022). Given the primitive evidence of the day, there was no more scientific basis for the biologicalist doctrine embraced by the Congress's condemners of psychoanalysis than there was for the psychological presumptions of psychoanalysis. Borch-Jacobsen's portrayal of the 1913 Breslau Congress as expressing a scientifically privileged truth ignored by Freud thus distorts the nature of the exercise. It was an attempt to use the power of the dominant brain-disease Kraepelinian paradigm to suffocate in its cradle the growing challenge of psychological etiology and psychotherapeutic treatment.

Consistent with Forrester's complaints of negative bias, Borch-Jacobsen seems able to find failure in opposite Freudian practices. Thus, one major complaint is that Freud fails to take criticism into account and fails to amend his theory accordingly, in fact that Freud "deliberately erased from his historical summaries the many criticisms made of him at the time" (2019, p. 92). Yet, Borch-Jacobsen also takes Freud to task for adjusting his theory in response to the criticisms of others, albeit often without attribution, finding fault with Freud's "multiple theoretical reversals...by silently appropriating objections which were made to him by Fliess, Adler, Stekel, Jung, Rank and others" (p. 94). Freud often reports objections to his work by others in his writings and addresses them, but he also frequently revised his theories in response to criticisms without being explicit about it. None of this constitutes ignoring criticism.

I now turn from Forrester's critique to a major thread of Borch-Jacobsen's arguments in his 2019 response. Borch-Jacobsen suggests that the rapid dissemination of psychoanalytic ideas among the intellectual classes is the main phenomenon to be understood, and analogizes it to a "plague" or "infestation": "Faced with such phenomenon of contagion, the question is therefore not whether it is true or wrong, but only how it is spread and why" (2019, p. 94). So, he asks: "what were the conditions that favored the reception of psychoanalytic ideas, to the detriment of other ideas (other psychological theories, other psychotherapies) with which they were competing?" (p. 94).

Looking for the reason for psychoanalysis's contagious success, Borch-Jacobsen observes that the standard move is to say that despite its failures it still addressed our deepest longings:

> We will then say that psychoanalysis has responded (and still responds) to very deep needs: the need, for example, to find a substitute for the solid certainties of religion; the need to make sense of unhappiness and existential angst in a world deserted by God; the need for a theory justifying the liberation of sex at the time of the decline of the nuclear family, or the reverse. Conversely, the need to subject desire to symbolic law faced with the disintegration of paternal/male authority. We'll say that the rise of psychoanalysis at the beginning of the 20th century corresponded to the propagation of evolutionary theses, or that it provided an ideology to capitalist society and modern individualism, or that it served as refuge for those disappointed with Marxism when it collapsed.
>
> (p. 94)

Borch-Jacobsen takes the existence of such multiple hypotheses about fulfilled needs as a puzzle, and asserts that the real challenge is to explain "how psychoanalysis was able to meet such diverse and contradictory needs.... What is it in the psychoanalytic theory which enables it to prosper in so many of environments, to invade so many niches, to survive so many upheavals in the ecology of minds?" (p. 94). His answer is that it is a mistake to think about psychoanalysis as a coherent body of doctrine:

it is precisely because it is without any real theoretical consistency that psychoanalysis has been able to acclimatize to environments so different, mutating according to the circumstances and needs....In reality, it is a mutant, chameleonic theory, and as such supremely adaptable to the most refractory environments.

(p. 95)

He presents an impressive list of psychoanalysis's adaptations as evidence of the theory's vacuousness: "When the immigrants from Central Europe arrived in United States, they hastened to promote an ego psychology...compatible with the psychology of their new context. When Freud's biologism appeared obsolete and reductive, we saw the emergence in the UK of object relations theory, attentive to inter-personal relationships" (p. 95) and so on, encompassing hermeneutic, Marxist, narrativist, feminist, mindfulness, and neuropsychoanalytic offshoots.

Ignoring the possibility that psychoanalysis, whatever its many scientific failings, is simply a remarkably vital and tenacious discipline that attempts to address emerging challenges and objections with novel theoretical formulations, Borch-Jacobsen concludes instead that the very existence of these varieties shows, as it was put in *The Freud Files*, that psychoanalysis is so malleable that it "no longer exists –or rather, never did" (2011, p. 307). Yet, there are some continuities. These varieties often exist alongside the classic Freudian central claims, such as the Oedipus complex. In any event, simply adapting an absurd or vacuous theory to specific new circumstances with novel but equally absurd or vacuous theoretical doctrines need not make the theory acceptable and does not explain the theory's success. Borch-Jacobsen's conclusion that it is unsurprising that "psychoanalysis spreads everywhere" does not follow from his premises.

It is true that the Oedipal theory in Freud's original formulation has been twisted and turned to become many different things. Horney, Fromm, ego psychologists, and many others have reinterpreted the Oedipal theory and some, like Bowlby and Kohut, have rejected it outright. Yet such adaptations and innovative interpretations cannot explain how it survived for so long in its original form and how, in that form, it still influences us today. The sustained influence of Freud's postulation of universal childhood incestuous and patricidal desires cannot be explained by the alterations in subsequent offshoots of psychoanalytic theory.

The major limitation of Borch-Jacobsen's analysis is that, like other views examined above, it tries to explain the enormous success of a false theory by the clever manipulations—public relations, myth making, ignoring of criticism, suppression of embarrassing letters, inflated claims, and so on—of Freud and his followers. Yet, less successful theoretical groups have pushed no less hard, and psychoanalysis is surely one of the most publicly criticized theories in history despite its defensive manipulations. An answer to the question of why psychoanalysis—and particularly the Oedipal theory—was so widely accepted requires something more than simply pointing to the manipulative aspirations of psychoanalysts in pursuing success, because the question is why the still implausible and unsupported fruit of that manipulation was accepted. The central question—what was it about psychoanalysis, and specifically the Oedipal theory, that enabled it to succeed despite all of its amply publicized flaws?—remains at least partly unanswered.

Conclusion: Is There Room for Foucault's Account?

In light of the many theories reviewed above, one might ask: do we really need to examine *yet another* attempt to offer an account of how Freud's Oedipal theory could prove so influential among intellectuals and middle-class families despite its nonexistent evidential credentials? The above review suggests that, despite the already-crowded field of proposed explanations, there is room for another account that is more specific to the success of the Oedipus complex given its specific content. Most of the above explanations aim at psychoanalysis in general and do not offer a compelling answer to the specific question of why the Oedipus complex—with its uniquely provocative thesis that the son experiences an incestuous desire for sex with his mother—was so influential.

In particular, the above accounts leave room for an account that is fixed to the historical period, emphasizes the social functions that the theory fulfilled (rather than Freud's machinations to promote his theory), and, importantly, is anchored to actual case materials. In contrast to the above accounts, Foucault formulates an explanation that is specific to the Oedipal theory, is historically located, and explains the theory's success in terms of the social functions that it fulfilled. Moreover, I argue in later chapters that one can identify the specific evidence in Freud's writings on which Foucault likely relied. A reexamination of that evidence will provide surprising and often compelling evidence in support of Foucault's hypotheses about the Oedipal theory, though I will also suggest ways in which it is limited.

We saw that Hale's, Demos's, and Cioffi's accounts all link the social receptivity to Oedipal theory to ongoing social changes in sexuality and family dynamics that, like Foucault's account, provide a social function for the theory. However, those accounts fall into a common pattern of seeing the strength of Freudianism in its role as a liberatory theory that attacks the excessive constraints on sexuality that were inherited from the Victorian era. It is certainly true that Freud's theory, in naturalizing child and female sexuality and blaming repressive sexual attitudes for neurosogenesis, was part of the beginnings of what became the sexual revolution and did fulfill a social function of sexual liberation. However, it is not Freud's attempts to manipulate us, Foucault argues, but what his theory did to us that explains the theory's success—in a sense quite different from the standard "sexual liberation" explanation. Foucault's account is uniquely provocative in this regard because it rejects the standard narrative and offers a disorientingly contrary and novel interpretation of the same facts, locating Oedipal theory and the sexual revolution itself as a continuation of constraints at a more subtle level of power.

References

Borch-Jacobsen, M. (2019). Comment le virus du Freudisme s'est propagé. *Books, 100*, 92–96.

Borch-Jacobsen, M., & Shamdasani, S. (2011). *The Freud files: An inquiry into the history of psychoanalysis*. Cambridge, UK: Cambridge University Press.

Buekens, F., & Boudry, M. (2011). Freud's unintended institutional facts. In K. François, B. Löwe, T. Müller & B. van Kerkhove (Eds.), *Foundations of the formal sciences (Vol. 7, Studies in logic*, pp. 31–58). London, UK: King's College Publications.

Buekens, F., & Boudry, M. (2012). Psychoanalytic facts as unintended institutional facts. *Philosophy of the Social Sciences, 42*(2), 239–269.

Cioffi, F. (1998a). The myth of Freud's hostile reception. In *Freud and the question of pseudoscience* (pp. 161–181). Chicago, IL: Open Court Publishing.

Cioffi, F. (1998b). Wittgenstein's Freud. In *Freud and the question of pseudoscience* (pp. 93–114). Chicago, IL: Open Court Publishing.

Cioffi, F. (1998c). Bouveresse on Wittgenstein's Freud. In *Freud and the question of pseudoscience* (pp. 280–287). Chicago, IL: Open Court Publishing.

Cioffi, F. (2007). Freud and interpretation: Frank Cioffi and Allen Esterson discuss Freud's legacy. In T. Dufresne, *Against Freud: Critics talk back.* (pp. 88–112). Palo Alto, CA: Stanford University Press.

Demos, J. (1978). Oedipus and America: Historical perspectives on the reception of psychoanalysis in the United States. *Annual of Psychoanalysis, 6*, 23–39.

Demos, J. (1996). History and the psychosocial: Reflections on "Oedipus and America." In J. Pfister & N. Schnog (Eds.), *Inventing the psychological* (pp. 79–83). New Haven, CT: Yale University Press.

Derksen, A. A. (1992). Does the tally argument make Freud a sophisticated methodologist? Grünbaum's friendly attempt to save Freud as a methodologist. *Philosophy of Science, 59*, 75–101.

Derksen, A. A. (1993). The seven sins of pseudo-science. *Journal for General Philosophy of Science, 24*, 17–42.

Derksen, A. A. (2001). The seven strategies of the sophisticated pseudo-scientist: A look into Freud's rhetorical tool box. *Journal for General Philosophy of Science, 32*, 329–350.

Esterson, A. (1998). *Seductive mirage: An exploration of the work of Sigmund Freud.* Chicago, IL: Open Court Publishing.

Forrester, J. (1997). *Dispatches from the Freud wars: Psychoanalysis and its passions.* Cambridge, MA: Harvard University Press.

Forrester, J. (2012). *Books: The Freud files: An inquiry into the history of psychoanalysis. Times Higher Education, Issue 2043* (March 29, 2012), p. 56.

Freud, S. (1893/1985). Letter from Freud to Fliess, October 6, 1893. In J. M. Masson (Ed. and Trans.), *The complete letters of Sigmund Freud to Wilhelm Fliess, 1887–1904* (pp. 57–59). Cambridge, MA: Harvard University Press.

Gellner, E. (2003). *The psychoanalytic movement: The cunning of unreason.* Boston, MA: Blackwell Publishing.

Grünbaum, A. (1984). *The foundations of psychoanalysis: A philosophical critique.* Berkeley, CA: University of California Press.

Hale, N. G. Jr. (1971). *Freud and the Americans: The beginnings of psychoanalysis in the United States, 1876–1917.* New York, NY: Oxford University Press.

Jones, E. (1955). *The life and work of Sigmund Freud* (Vol. 2). New York, NY: Basic Books.

Lawrence, D. H. (1913). *Sons and lovers.* Hertfordshire: Wordsworth Classics.

Lawrence, D. H. (1921). *Psychoanalysis and the unconscious.* New York: Thomas Seltzer.

Lawrence, D. H. (1922). *Fantasia of the unconscious.* New York: Thomas Seltzer.

MacIntyre, A. (1976). Psychoanalysis: The future of an illusion. In *Against the self-images of the age* (pp. 27–37). London, UK: Duckworth.

Macmillan, M. (1991). *Freud evaluated: The completed arc.* Amsterdam: Elsevier.

Menand, L. (2017). Why Freud survives. *The New Yorker, 93*(25: August 28, 2017) Retrieved on July 7, 2020, at https://www.newyorker.com/magazine/2017/08/28/why-freud-survives.

Pierloot, R. A. (2000). D. H. Lawrence and the Freudian Oedipus complex. *Free Associations, 8,* 100–119.

Searle, J. R. (1995). *The construction of social reality.* New York, NY: The Free Press.

Svevo, I. (1930). *The Confessions of Zeno.* Santa Barbara, CA: Greenwood Publishing.

Wakefield, J. C. (2018). *Freud and philosophy of mind (Vol. 1): Reconstructing the argument for unconscious mental states.* New York, NY: Palgrave Macmillan.

Wakefield, J. C. (2022). Klerman's "credo" reconsidered: Neo-Kraepelinianism, Spitzer's views, and what we can learn from the past. *World Psychiatry, 21,* 4–25.

Wakefield, J. C. (2023a). *Freud's argument for the Oedipus complex: A philosophy of science analysis of the case of Little Hans.* New York: Routledge.

Wakefield, J. C. (2023b). *Attachment, sexuality, power: Oedipal theory as regulator of family affection in Freud's case of Little Hans.* New York: Routledge.

Winter, S. (1999). *Freud and the institution of psychoanalytic knowledge.* Palo Alto, CA: Stanford University Press.

Wittgenstein, L. (1970). *Zettel.* Berkeley, CA: University of California Press.

Wittgenstein, L. (1972). *Lectures and conversations on aesthetics, psychology and religious belief* (Cyril Barrett, Ed.). Berkeley, CA: University of California Press.

Chapter 3

The Masturbation Crusade

Foucault's hypothesis is that Freud's seemingly novel Oedipal theory (which he refers to as the "incest theory") is, in crucial respects, simply a continuous extension of the earlier two-century medical campaign against masturbation (or "masturbation crusade"), forming a continuous thread in the deployment of theories of sexuality for social control purposes. His interpretation of the Oedipal theory thus derives directly from his analysis of the earlier crusade. This chapter provides an introduction to the theories and doctrines underlying the masturbation crusade, its grip on medical theory, its spread to the United States by Benjamin Rush and Joseph Howe, its expansion in scope to concern about involuntary emissions ("wet dreams") by Claude-François Lallemand, and its application to interferences with natural conjugal sex ("conjugal onanism") by Louis François Étienne Bergeret. As an especially relevant context for Freud, close attention is also paid to the views on sexuality of the prototypical conservative English Victorian physician, William Acton.

The Masturbation Crusade and the Incest Theory

This book's ultimate focus is Foucault's power/knowledge account of the appeal of Freud's theory of the Oedipus complex presented in the tenth lecture he delivered in 1975 at the College de France (Foucault, 2003), and the further account he presented in *History of Sexuality, Volume 1* (*HS1*; Foucault, 1978). However, Foucault's interpretation of the Oedipal theory, or "incest theory," derives directly from his analysis of the earlier two-century medical campaign against

DOI: 10.4324/9781003480396-3

masturbation, or "masturbation crusade." Thus, before addressing Foucault's claims specifically about Freud and the Oedipus complex, this chapter provides a historical introduction to the masturbation crusade, and the following chapter reviews Foucault's analysis of the power/knowledge tactics deployed in the crusade as part of the larger historical phenomenon he labels the "deployment of sexuality."

This step-by-step development is necessary because Foucault's views of the masturbation crusade and the Oedipal theory are closely linked. Foucault's hypothesis is that Freud's seemingly novel Oedipal theory is simply an extension of the masturbation crusade insofar as power/knowledge functions are concerned, so that together they form a continuous thread in the deployment of sexuality. Consequently, in the tenth lecture, instead of developing a fresh analysis of the Oedipal theory, he mainly provides a series of replies to possible objections to understanding the Oedipus complex as a continuation of the mastur- bation crusade as he analyzed it in the previous lecture. Understanding Foucault's account of the tactics and functions of the masturbation crusade is therefore essential for evaluating his account of the Oedipal theory. And for that, it is essential to understand the remarkable and puzzling nature of the crusade itself.

Foucault (2003) observes, "[T]he crusade against masturbation... starts clamorously, first in England around 1710 with the publication of *Onania*, and then in Germany before being launched in France with Tissot's book around 1760" (p. 326). Accordingly, my review starts with *Onania* and Tissot and goes through to the late Victorian period, focusing on elements relevant to issues raised in later chapters.

In reviewing the doctrines of the masturbation crusade, I rely heavily on E. H. Hare's (1962) unparalleled historical survey as well as many other secondary sources. For key figures such as Tissot, Rush, Howe, Lallemand and Bergeret, I rely on original sources, mostly their books, and for other developments I go to publications in the leading medical journals of the day. When I finally come to developments during the Victorian era late in the nineteenth century just prior to Freud, in addition to medical journals, I rely heavily on William Acton's (1857/1875) medical text that was heavily cited and reprinted during the ensuing decades and is considered by scholars to be the most representative of the crusade's thinking at the time. Like Foucault, I document the crusade "without resorting to the more dubious or marginal texts of the crusade" (2003, p. 238), thus steering clear of the considerable lay and quack literature that make easy critical targets and were influential in swaying public opinion as they extracted the public's money, but are not representative of medical opinion. Instead, I rely on books and journal articles within the legitimate medical and scientific literature.

Note that there are two ways in which my review diverges from Foucault's coverage. First, Foucault cites mainly French writers who had pivotal roles in the crusade. I try to correct his locational bias by closely examining the works of some English and American writers as well, especially the English physician William Acton. Second, Foucault tends to focus on writings around the mid-century when he thinks decisive changes occurred in medical thinking, whereas I include more writings toward the end of the century that would have most directly influenced Freud.

The Enigma of the Masturbation Crusade

At the substantive core of the historical process that Foucault labels the "deployment of sexuality" (see Chapter 4) is the remarkable two-century sociohistorical phenomenon lasting from the early 1700s to the early 1900s of the intensive medical and lay concern about the pathogenic dangers of, and efforts to suppress, masturbation. As Foucault rightly notes, this medical campaign against masturbation remains a historical enigma. Without anything in the way of serious scientific evidence, the crusade was widely and enthusiastically embraced by the medical profession in Europe, England, and America and was largely accepted by a compliant bourgeois lay public.

What was distinctive about the masturbation crusade was not the moral disapproval of masturbation which it often expressed, for the Church had long condemned various nonprocreative sexual acts including masturbation as sins. Indeed, it has often been argued that medicalization was a sympathetic attempt to wrest the perceived problem of masturbation from the moral to the scientific domain and replace punishment by treatment (e.g., Zachar & Kendler, 2023). Rather, what was distinctive was the explicit, detailed, and widespread linking of masturbation to physical and mental medical disease by substantial parts of the medical profession who claimed either that it is a pathogenic process leading to disease or labeled masturbation itself as pathological. The result was a massive medically supported intrusion into family life:

> Parents eavesdropped at bedroom doors, tied their children to headboards, fastened night gloves on their hands, installed toothed rings over their genitals, and subjected them to stringent regimes of diet, exercise, and baths. Scientific opinion fully justified these measures: masturbation and spermatorrhoea were known to cause dozens of diseases and conditions including blindness, insanity, and death.
>
> (Miller, 2001, p. 222)

The masturbation crusade is sometimes referred to as the "masturbation panic." However, "panic" suggests something relatively delineated and brief in time with a sharply rising and then subsiding intensity. The masturbation crusade was anything but brief, and it maintained its remarkable intensity at a high pitch over a long period of time.

The crusade has been very extensively documented and analyzed by historians (e.g., Aspiz, 1987; Bullough, 1987; Comfort, 1969; Darby, 2005; Degler, 1974; Engelhardt Jr., 1974; Gilbert, 1975, 1980; Gullette, 1994; Hall, 1992, 2003; Hare, 1962; Holtzman, 1982; Laqueur, 2003; Macdonald, 1967; Mumford, 1992; Neuhaus, 2000; Neuman, 1975; Stengers & Van Neck, 2001; Stolberg, 2000, 2003). I will not attempt a general or balanced survey here, nor will I try to represent the great variety of opposed opinions that always existed within the contentious medical profession of the time on the details of various issues (as Mason notes, "for almost every point of view in the literature,...the antithesis may also be found" [1994, p. 177]). My aim is rather to briefly convey the frenzied nature of the crusade and to focus on a central and quite influential stream of opinion that I refer to as "conservative" Victorian medical opinion about masturbation and sexuality that supported the crusade.

These conservative opinions were not the most extreme, and in fact they commonly included condemnation of more extreme quacks and exaggerated fears. They represented a mainstream opinion about the harmful effects and the need for treatment of masturbation. Although often expressing religiously derived moral censure of non-procreative sexual practices, this was nonetheless by and large a medical literature that was attempting to be scientifically and professionally anchored, and these ideas were published regularly in leading mainstream medical journals. I will follow this literature in focusing primarily on male masturbation because it is most relevant to my later analysis of Freud, although female masturbation was certainly a target of the crusade and occasionally led to horrific interventions such as clitoridectomy.

The construal of masturbation as a disordered or disorder-causing condition that requires medical treatment is at the core of the masturbation crusade and poses its most perplexing historical puzzle. In his careful history of the masturbation crusade, E. M. Hare (1962) notes:

> [M]edical references to the harmfulness of masturbation are vanish-
> ingly rare before the 18th century....[F]rom the time of Hippocrates,
> physicians have recorded their belief that over-indulgence in sexual
> activity is harmful to health....However, none of the classical writers
> appears to make specific reference to the ill-effects of masturbation;...
> [A]lthough masturbation was perhaps included in the terms 'sexual
> activity' and 'loss of semen', yet there was no general belief before the
> eighteenth century that masturbation was specifically harmful to
> health or that it was more harmful than an equivalent indulgence in
> sexual intercourse.
>
> (pp. 1–2)

Nevertheless, Hare says, a major historical "sudden change in the climate of opinion" of the kind that "we can scarcely imagine" (1962, p. 2) occurred on this issue. (We saw in Chapter 1 that the marked discontinuity in the transition to the medical crusade against masturbation is a central datum in Foucault's analysis of the deployment of sexuality.)

Many other historians have observed that the masturbation crusade poses a historical conundrum. Peter Gay observes that "the persistent panic over masturbation is far easier to document than to explain. Heavily overdetermined, it was a cultural symptom laden with baffling meanings that reached across nineteenth-century society and down into the buried unconscious core of its most troubling preoccupations" (1984, p. 309). Hare wonders about the explanation for "the rise and fall of this idea and why it persisted for so long" (Hare, 1962, p. 1), and offers a variety of theories most of which blame fallacious medical reasoning. In a historical analysis, the psychoanalytic developmental psychologist Rene Spitz puzzles that "a medical practice as widespread as this and reaching so close to our own period might well tempt one to speculate on its origins and its consequences on the minds of people" (Spitz, 1952, p. 504). And, even a skeptical contemporary writer at the time of the height of the crusade, in an article on onanism in a prestigious medical encyclopedia, puzzles over Tissot's influence (discussed below): "we are hard put to explain the prodigious influence of this work not only on the public but still more on the physicians of his time" (Christian, 1881, as quoted in Hare, 1962, p. 2). Neuman (1975) puts the puzzle as follows:

> for two centuries before 1914 many of the best-informed and respected medical authorities (and, unfortunately, their patients) labored under the belief that masturbation, particularly among children and adolescents, caused myriad ills ranging from acne to homicidal insanity. In their efforts to prevent or to 'cure' what they called self-abuse and self-pollution, doctors and parents used a variety of chemical therapies, 'corrective surgery,' and mechanical devices that alternately astound and amuse the modern reader. How could parents and doctors dedicated to the healthy upbringing of children be so mistaken in their understanding of masturbation and so brutal in stamping it out?
>
> (p. 1)

A great variety of hypotheses have been suggested to answer these questions and explain the masturbation crusade, such as: logical errors in medical reasoning; a tendency to confuse perceived immorality or violations of religious prohibitions with pathogenicity; a misguided medical reaction to the rise of venereal diseases such as syphilis and gonorrhea in Europe; an adaptation to changing conceptions of childhood and adolescence; an attempt to address some consequences of the trend toward later puberty; an attempt by physicians to explain the continuing mystery of childhood mortality in the age of bacteriology's breakthroughs in understanding adult disease; the observation, in the growing use of asylums for the insane, of disinhibited psychotic individuals masturbating and a confusion of effect with cause; the general difficulty of refuting causal hypotheses in psychiatry once they are proposed and take hold; a revival or continuation of the paranoid social reactions underlying the witch-burning movement as the belief in witches waned; part of a general movement toward understanding mental disorders in terms of bodily processes with advances in pathological anatomy; a way to fill in gaps in explanation that frustratingly had not been illuminated by pathological anatomy; an increased moral strictness about sexuality with the rise of Puritanism in England and the bourgeoisie in France; a side effect of the "invention of childhood" as a vulnerable and pure period of life; a visible exercise of power and authority by physicians to support their increasing prestige and status; a hypothesized actual increase in masturbation at the beginning of the eighteenth century; an attempt by surgeons to use their new skills and prestige to create a domain of specialty that illustrated their expertise; social conservatives' fears of Western decadence that motivated the buttressing of traditional sexual values; concern by the rising middle class that their children would not be able to live up to the challenges of bourgeois progress and industrialization if in a weakened state; the shift into the medical field of various social anxieties during a time of social change; the motivation to look critically at excessive sexual behavior in light of the feminist purity movement attempting to decrease venereal diseases transmitted from men to their wives; as well as a variety of psychoanalytic explanations in terms of projection of repressed adult desires onto children and other forms of defenses, to mention a few.

The embarrassment of riches when it comes to proposed explanations of the masturbation crusade, combined with the lack of any serious evidential constraints that allow the rejection of most explanations, leads some authors to cite multiple contributory explanations as the most plausible approach:

T]he normal male sexual function—the production and emission of sperm—was categorised as a life-threatening disease which demanded drastic treatment. If all this sounds too incredible, we must remember that it was a time when the causes of most diseases were not understood, treatments were ineffective, and mortality (especially in children) was high; belief in witchcraft or spirits as causes of illness had been discredited by the Enlightenment, and masturbation at least offered a materialist explanation. At the same time, theologians and other public moralists were advocating increased sexual purity, a demand which grew more insistent in the nineteenth century and reached a crescendo in the syphilis scare of the early twentieth.

(Darby, 2003, pp. 749–750)

The broad social concern about masturbation grew out of a number of anxieties. Social conservatives feared that Western society was entering a period of decadence in which cherished institutions and values were under threat. Physicians worried that their social status (and income) would he undermined by the profession's failure to live up to the claims on which that status was grounded. Feminists associated with the purity movement were concerned that meaningful improvements to the status of women would never actually be realized. The middle class, which was asserting claims of dominance, worried that future generations would not live up to the challenges of industrialization and progress. Each of these anxieties was managed by focus on the evils of 'seminal weakness,' and by careful attention to the discipline needed to correct the problem.

(Miller, 2001, pp. 221, 223)

In regard to all of these explanations, whether single or combined, it seems fair to say that none has been accepted as entirely adequate to explain the puzzling specificity, great length, enormous scope, multiple locations, nature, and great social and medical influence of the anti-masturbation campaign. As we shall see in the next chapter, Foucault brings to this discussion a fresh focus on the tactics used in the crusade—primarily family surveillance and medical technology—to try to illuminate what social functions the crusade served that may have made it so appealing despite its lack of scientific credentials. I now turn to an overview of the masturbation crusade itself.

Onania and Tissot: Eighteenth-Century Origins of the Masturbation Crusade

There is a consensus that the medical masturbation crusade began in earnest early in the eighteenth century with the publication in London of an immensely popular but anonymously authored tract, *Onania, or the Heinous Sin of Self-Pollution*, first published about 1710. Hare (1962) observes that "the medical dangers of masturbation first became widely popularized throughout Europe" by *Onania*, and "that the book was very widely read we may presume from the fact that it had reached its 15th edition by 1730 and, at the time when Voltaire was writing about onanism in his *Dictionnaire Philosophique* (1764), it was in its 80th edition" (p. 2). For some time, each edition of *Onania* was larger than the last due to the added publication of letters from grateful sufferers in response to earlier editions, along with the author's responses—a sort of anti-masturbation "Dear Abby."

Onania has a religious tone and is concerned with moral deterioration and the sinful aspects of masturbation as much as it is with the medical consequences. Nevertheless, *Onania* claims that the consequences of masturbation include a great variety of medical problems such as insanity, epilepsy, consumption, impaired growth, fainting spells, and a variety of sexual problems including impotence, premature ejaculation, and nocturnal emissions, even including the possibility of death:

> In some it has been the Cause of fainting Fits and Epilepsies; in others of Consumptions; and many young Men, who were strong and lusty before they gave themselves over to this Vice, have been worn out by it, and by its robbing the Body of its balmy and vital Moisture, without Cough or Spitting, dry and emaciated, sent to their Grave. In others again, whom it has not kill'd, it has produc'd Nightly and excessive Seminal Emissions.
>
> (*Onania*, as quoted by Hodgson, 2005, p. 375)

The claim in this passage that masturbation leads to excessive and harmful loss of semen through nocturnal emissions presages the later popularization of the disease of spermatorrhea by Lallemand (1847; see below) in which such emissions cause semen loss to a medically harmful degree. Given these dire threats, the author of *Onania* offers what are, all considered, relatively benign recommendations for treatment. These include repentance and renunciation of the act followed by early marriage, cold baths, a milk diet, and possibly medicines to aid in the cure—the latter offered for sale by the author via identified shops.

The anonymous author of *Onania* (postulated by Laqueur [2003] to be John Marten, a surgeon who had previously published a book on venereal disease with a section cautioning about the harmful effects of masturbation, and whose work is heavily quoted in *Onania*) was highly influential in one terminological respect. *Onania* was instrumental in popularizing the enduring use of "onanism," with its negative Biblical reference to Onan, a man struck down by God, as a term for masturbation—this despite the fact that, as many scholars have noted, such a usage is not warranted by the Bible's story of Onan, on two counts. First, Onan was struck down by God after withdrawing during intercourse and ejaculating on the ground, an act of *coitus interruptus*, not masturbation. Second, Onan's crime was his refusal to obey the law of the levirate, according to which Onan was obligated to have a child with his slain brother's wife Tamar to give his dead brother an heir who would not be considered Onan's son. At the last moment, Onan refused to make this sacrifice, and God slew him for it. Masturbation had nothing to do with it, but for two centuries onanism came to mean masturbation.

If *Onania* was the tinder, then the match that caused the full ignition of the masturbation crusade was a book by the Swiss physician Samuel-Auguste Tissot (1728–1797), which was first published in Latin in 1758, translated into French in 1760, and soon translated into English as *Onanism, or a Treatise upon the Disorders produced by Masturbation* (1766). Like *Onania*, Tissot's book underwent many editions, and it was profoundly influential among physicians. Whether they fully agreed or partially disagreed with Tissot's conclusions (for few rejected his claims outright), physicians of the time generally acknowledged the book's influence and accepted its claims to some extent. Indeed, looking back, Havelock Ellis puts the primary blame for the masturbation crusade squarely on Tissot's book:

Tissot, combining with his reputation as a physician the fanaticism of a devout believer, raised masturbation to the position of a colossal bogy which during a hundred years has not only had an unfortunate influence on medical opinion in these matters, but has been productive of incalculable harm to ignorant youth and tender consciences.

(1900, p. 201)

Tissot adopts what in essence is a traditional humoral/hydraulic model according to which semen has a general vital power, perhaps suggested by the observation that sexual discharge is followed by lethargy. He follows others in asserting that semen forms part of the blood and circulates in rarified form throughout the body until it accumulates in condensed form in the testicles. He borrows from others the observation that orgasm is analogous to an epileptic seizure and therefore can have the power to harm the nervous system, and claims that semen's vital properties are implicated in the functions of all of the body's organs. Analogous to the ancient argument that semen must circulate throughout the body because only that would explain how the ejaculate can produce an offspring with features of the father (e.g., the father's nose shape or eye color) that are not proximate to the genitals, Tissot argues that semen must circulate because it causes local sex characteristics throughout the body during puberty, whereas eunuchs deprived of testicles and semen do not, for example, grow beards or have deep male voices. He calculates that the loss of one ounce of vital seminal fluid is as harmful as losing 40 ounces of blood: "the seminal fluid...has so much influence on the strength of the body...that physicians of every age have unanimously admitted, that the loss of one ounce of it, enfeebles more than forty ounces of blood" (1758/1832, p. v). This odd claim may have ancient roots: "Ancient Ayurvedic texts, for example, teach that it takes 40 meals to make one drop of blood, 40 drops of blood to make one drop of bone marrow and 40 drops of bone marrow to make one drop of semen" (Hodgson, 2005, p. 375). In any event, the notion that semen circulates had a strong hold on medical thinking for some time (e.g., "The spermatic fluid...is not...intended, like the urine, to be eliminated from the body; but, on the contrary (except during an occasional act of generation) to be received into the circulation, and thence distributed to every part of the system" [Smythe, 1841, p. 784]), and even has resonances with Freudian doctrines about the biological underpinnings of libido (see Chapters 5 and 7).

However, the harm caused by masturbation is not due only to the loss of semen, according to Tissot. Given that masturbation also harms prepubescent children, loss of semen could not possibly be the only explanation for masturbation's detrimental effects, so this was a theoretical paradox addressed by many of the crusade's authors, mostly following Tissot's general approach. The harm, Tissot holds, is also caused by the accumulation of blood in certain areas of the brain during arousal and, most importantly, the epileptic-like convulsions of sexual orgasm that, when repeated excessively, harm the brain. Because the brain regulates so many bodily functions, the brain damage from masturbation leads to severe harm of many kinds to various organ systems:

> When convulsions occur, the nervous system is in a state of excitement, or more properly in a degree of extraordinary action, which is necessarily followed by an extreme relaxation. Whenever the action of an organ is over-excited, depression succeeds; hence its functions are necessarily deranged, and as the nerves have an influence on all, every part is deranged when they are enfeebled....
>
> When we reflect on the effects of these two causes, the emission of the semen, and the convulsive motions, the disorders arising from them are easily explained.... The debility caused by these excesses, deranges the functions of all the organs.
>
> (Tissot, 1758/1832, p. 40)

However, this explanation poses a fundamental challenge to the assumptions underlying the masturbation crusade: why is it that other sexual activities, including sexual intercourse, are not equally harmful given that semen discharge and the nervous shock of orgasm may be equally experienced? As Foucault comments, "The target of this literature, then, is masturbation itself in its specificity....[T]here are texts that say there is a real difference between the nature of masturbation and that of normal, relational sexuality" (2003, p. 234). The question is how the difference is explained.

Tissot acknowledges the puzzle and initially suggests that it is the unnaturalness of masturbation that makes it especially harmful:

> If the dangerous consequences arising from the too abundant discharge of semen, depended only on the quantity, or were the same under different modes of evacuation, the quantities in each being equal, then it would be of little importance, physically speaking, in which it took place. But there is a difference; a too

great quantity of semen lost in the natural way, causes very serious symptoms, but these are much more serious when the same amount has been discharged by unnatural means. The diseases of those exhausted by natural connections, are terrible; but those produced by onanism, are much more so.

(1758/1832, p. vi)

Thus, "masturbation is more pernicious than excessive intercourse with females" (1758/1832, p. 45).

But, what explains the asymmetry between natural versus unnatural discharge? Tissot summarily rejects the theological explanation that masturbation is more harmful because, as in Onan's case, God is punishing the onanist for his sin. He insists on a naturalistic scientific explanation ("it can be explained very well, by the mechanism of the body; and by its union with the mind" [1758/1832, p. 45]). Tissot proceeds to offer a series of physiological and psychological answers to the puzzle of why masturbation is more harmful than sexual intercourse.

One reason is that masturbation is subject to excess (and thus excessive semen loss) in a way that intercourse is not because intercourse requires a willing partner and appropriate circumstances whereas masturbation is available at any moment when imagination or physical irritation brings one's attention to the possibility: "Numerous circumstances prevent illicit intercourse with females, but a solitary debauchee is confined by no limit and constrained by no obstacle" (1758/1832, p. 46). In this regard, Tissot quotes the seventeenth-century Italian physician Sanctorius's argument that the natural arousal from accumulated semen and the unnatural arousal by the lascivious imagination of the onanist have different consequences, analogizing it to hunger: "Hunger and thirst indicate the necessity for food and drink; if we take more than these sensations demand, the surplus is injurious to the body and debilitates it" (Sanctorius, as quoted by Tissot, 1758/1832, p. 46).

Another reason for the special harmfulness of masturbation is "the dominion it obtains over the senses" in the form of habitual lascivious ideas:

Nothing weakens so much as this continual excitement of a mind always intent on the same thing. A person addicted to this habit, experiences the same ill effects as does the literary man who fixes his attention wholly on one subject. This part of the brain, which is then in action, makes an effort which may be compared to that of a muscle which has been powerfully and for a long time extended; this is followed either by so much motion that the play of the part cannot be arrested, nor the mind diverted from this idea, (this is the case in those addicted to onanism); or by a perfect impotence. Finally exhausted by continual fatigue, these patients are affected with all the diseases of the brain, melancholy, catalepsy, epilepsy, imbecility, loss of sense, feebleness of the nervous system, and a multitude of other evils.

(Tissot, 1758/1832, p. 47)

Ultimately, Tissot medically endorses the romantic notion that the difference between those who have sexual intercourse and those who practice onanism is the element of erotic love that redeems sexual intercourse and renders it harmless but is lacking in masturbation (Woody Allen's famous quip that masturbation is "sex with someone you love" aside):

The exhilaration of the mind, which must be distinguished from that purely corporeal pleasure,...animates the circulation, favors all the functions, reestablishes the strength and sustains it. If they be connected with the pleasures of love, it contributes to restore that energy which otherwise might have been lost: this is proved by observation. Sanctorius has remarked that 'After excessive coition with a woman one loves and desires, we do not feel the lassitude which should result from this excess, because the exhilaration experienced in the mind, increases the strength of the heart, favors the functions and repairs what had been lost.'

(Tissot, 1758/1832, p. 51)

Later liberal critics of Tissot's views would deny the above theories and attribute any harm from masturbation exclusively to Tissot's final reason, namely, the guilt, shame, and anxiety experienced by masturbators due to the judgments of society and terrifying medical books like Tissot's. Note also that Tissot is concerned largely with post-pubertal masturbation. Like other pre-Freudian physicians, Tissot thinks that children are naturally nonsexual and that child masturbation is a pathological rarity: "We may remark here that masturbation is particularly injurious to children before the age of puberty; happily we find but few monsters of either sex who indulge in it before this period" (1758/1832, p. 46).

Tissot's theories were widely adopted, with myriad physicians repeating his claims and further amplifying the horrors of masturbation. By 1816, the French psychiatrist Jean-Étienne Dominique Esquirol was able to declare that "masturbation is recognized in all countries as a common cause of insanity" (Esquirol, 1816, as quoted in Hare, 1962, p. 4). One eminent nonphysician thinker who, perhaps surprisingly, was convinced by Tissot's semenic hydraulic model was the Enlightenment philosopher Voltaire (1694–1778), a proponent of various freedoms and critic of Catholicism. A couple of decades after Tissot's book was published, Voltaire propagated Tissot's views in an essay on onanism. Referring to masturbation as "a shameful and disastrous habit," Voltaire observed that Tissot's hydraulic model of semenic vitality, with danger lurking in any humoral imbalance of semen whether due to excessive loss in masturbation or excessive continence, placed individuals in a perplexing situation: "What then ought we to do with the precious liquor that nature has made for the propagation of the species? Released incautiously, it may kill you; retained, it may also kill you" (Voltaire, as quoted in Hare, 1962, p. 20 n. 7a). Voltaire's notion that both masturbation and continence are pathogenic, so that only discharge which is "just right" preserves health, encourages anxiety and surveillance. It is also a doctrine that, we shall see in later chapters, is resurrected by Freud in the novel guise of his libido theory and his theory of developmental fixation due to under- or over-gratification, as well as his theory of the actual neuroses as due to inadequate (e.g., *coitus interruptus*) or excessive (e.g., habitual masturbation) sexual discharge (see Chapter 5).

As we shall see, after Tissot the specifics of the diseases attributed to masturbation varied over time, and there were always those who objected to such attributions. However, there remained a prominent and often dominant thread of medical belief in the pathogenicity of masturbation in one way or another.

Rush and Howe: Exporting the Crusade to America

The masturbation crusade triggered by Tissot's work was quickly exported to America through the writings of the eminent physician, professor of medicine, and alienist, Benjamin Rush (1746–1813). A signer of the Declaration of Independence, Rush did early path-breaking work on a naturalistic approach to mental disorder as medical disease that led the American Psychiatric Association in 1965 to recognize him as the "father of American psychiatry." In *Medical Inquiries and Observations, upon the Diseases of the Mind* (1812), the first American textbook in psychiatry, Rush lists onanism as a cause of mental disorder, agreeing with Tissot's doctrine that masturbation is much more harmful than excessive sexual intercourse:

> Onanism. Four cases of madness occurred, in my practice, from this cause, between the years 1804 and 1807. It is induced more frequently by this cause in young men, than is commonly supposed by parents and physicians. The morbid effects of intemperance in a sexual intercourse with women are feeble, and of a transient nature, compared with the train of physical and moral evils which this solitary vice fixes upon the body and mind.
>
> (1812, p. 33)

In a section titled, "Of the Morbid State of the Sexual Appetite" (p. 347), Rush asserts that onanism "produces seminal weakness, impotence, dysury, tabes dorsalis, pulmonary consumption, dyspepsia, dimness of sight, vertigo, epilepsy, hypochondriasis, loss of memory, manalgia, fatuity, and death" (p. 347). Of three letters seeking his medical advice that Rush reproduces to illustrate the potential harms of excessive sexuality, two are cases of desperate patients seeking treatment for the pathogenic effects of masturbation from which they believe they are suffering. One patient, asserting that the cause of his many symptoms is onanism and consequent nocturnal emissions, says "I had rather be laid in the silent tomb…than remain in my present unhappy and degraded situation"; the physician of another patient, who "in consequence of indulging in the solitary vice of onanism" suffers from symptoms such as "prostration of strength, atrophy, and depression of spirits" (which seems very much like the symptoms of what would later be classified as neurasthenia) assures Rush that "Any plan you may suggest for the relief of this truly wretched being will be gratefully received" (pp. 349–350). Note that inviting Rush to try extreme treatments was risky; Rush was known for aggressive invasive treatment, including the routine use of such ample bloodletting that other physicians accused him of killing more patients than he cured.

Following in Rush's footsteps, subsequent prominent American physicians continued into the late 1800s to put forward standard crusade doctrines. For example, Joseph Howe (1843–1890), a professor of medicine at the University of the City of New York (which later became New York University) with broad medical interests, wrote one of the most prominent texts on the medical problems associated with immoderate sex, titled *Excessive venery, masturbation and continence: The etiology, pathology and treatment of the diseases resulting from venereal excesses, masturbation and continence* (Howe, 1883).

Like other crusaders, Howe argued for the greater harmfulness of masturbation than of sexual intercourse, and offered an explanation going back to Tissot in terms of the unnaturalness of the masturbatory act and the natural healing power of romantic attachment. Unlike the others, he derived as a corollary that when the positive features of intercourse are absent (perhaps due to lack of any higher attraction), intercourse may be more harmful:

The natural fulfillment of every function exerts a beneficial influence on the economy. Deleterious effects only manifest themselves when the bounds of moderation are passed. Even when an organ is overworked by natural means there is much less harm done the system than there is from excessive work in an unnatural direction. Men seldom suffer as much from inordinate sexual congress as they do from the same amount of self-pollution. The occurrence of seminal ejaculations three or four times a week from legitimate sexual congress will not be felt very much by a healthy man, while the same number of losses from masturbation or nocturnal pollutions will soon superinduce mental and physical debility. Indeed there are many persons in robust health who indulge in daily intercourse with impunity, while others with perhaps equal stamina, lose flesh from two or three weekly pollutions. The reasons for this are obvious. One act is performed in accordance with the dictates of nature—the other is subversive and degrading. During sexual intercourse the expenditure of nerve force is compensated by the magnetism of the partner...which prevents injury....Whenever sexual intercourse fails to produce its tonic effect, when, instead of exhilaration of spirits and clearness of intellect, there are depression, weakness, tremulousness, anxiety and diminished power of concentration, then the act is injurious and the intervals between each cohabitation should be lengthened. If these warnings of nature are disregarded, a disordered condition of mind and body similar to that which arises from onanism will soon appear.

(1883, pp. 76–77)

However, like some other crusade writers, including Lallemand and Acton (see below), Howe believes that childhood masturbation, while medically harmful, is not as serious as post-pubertal masturbation:

Onanism, developed after puberty in persons of sedentary habits, is more pernicious in its effect than when it is commenced in early childhood. The repeated nervous shocks which it occasions are stronger, and make a deeper impression on the system. The individual becomes more wedded to the vice, and is more likely to persist in his transgression than those younger patients who, with the first dawn of manhood, have been warned of the evil consequences of the habit which they commenced, before their reasoning faculties controlled them.

(1883, pp. 66–67)

Agreeing with other crusaders as to the variegated physical symptoms and diseases that can come about due to masturbation, Howe (1883) considers the extreme case of consumption and offers an explanation based on the nerve shock theory of how masturbation can yield consumption:

[T]hough consumption results from the transmitted weakness descending from parent to child, it is also developed directly in young men and women from long continued masturbation as well as from sexual excess. This fact was first brought prominently before my mind by an examination of fourteen young patients suffering from phthisis in Charity Hospital. Only two gave a positive history of hereditary predisposition to the disease. Ten of the number acknowledged that they had been addicted to onanism in their childhood and had practiced it for years.... One of the effects of excessive indulgence is a disarrangement, or, rather, an exhaustion of the nervous system or of the nervous force, from the successive shocks of the orgasm. Then follow indigestion, constipation, (which is only a result of indigestion) and lassitude, all tending to impoverish the blood, and the road is thus opened for the first bad cold to set up chronic inflammation in the lungs, or other forms of pulmonary consumption.

(pp. 94–95)

Lallemand: The Expansion of the Crusade to Spermatorrhea

The medical literature in the middle of the nineteenth century preserved much of Tissot's doctrines but saw several further developments in the masturbation crusade's medical theorizing and intervention. First, there was an increasing emphasis on the view that masturbation not only causes many physical and mental ills but that there are also distinctive and severe forms of dementia and psychotic insanity of which masturbation is the specific cause. Masturbatory insanity soon became a major topic in the leading medical journals and texts, with many articles and even series of articles devoted to it (e.g., Spitzka, 1887a; 1887b; 1887c; 1888a; 1888b). However, as Zachar and Kendler observe, given how common the practice is, "it would be incorrect to say that masturbation itself was considered a mental disorder" but rather only "excessive masturbation over which a person lost control and performed to the point of exhaustion... was hypothesized to be a causal factor in deteriorative illnesses" (2023, p. 1).

Second and of greater general influence, around mid-century, in an expression of the hydraulic-humoral model of semen as a vital fluid that must be kept at appropriate levels, a new disease entity, "spermatorrhea" (also spelled "spermatorrhoea"), involving potentially debilitating excessive involuntary discharge of semen—generally believed to result from earlier masturbation—became a focus of medical theory and practice. This was due largely to the influence of French physician and professor of medicine Claude-François Lallemand (1790–1853) of Montpellier. Between 1838 and 1842, Lallemand published a three-volume summary of his work on spermatorrhea (*Des Pertes Seminales Involontaires*) which was immediately discussed in English-language medical journals (e.g., Ranking, 1843) and rapidly translated into a condensed English edition (Lallemand, 1847). Lallemand's reports established spermatorrhea as an accepted disease category that became the subject of a vast medical literature, including extensive articles in leading medical journals (e.g., Milton, 1854a; 1854b; 1854c; 1854d; Phillips, 1843a; 1843b; 1843c; Wilson, 1856a; 1856b; 1856c; 1856d; 1857; "Sexual Disorders," 1870a; 1870b; 1870c; 1870d) and medical tracts through to the end of the century in Europe and America (e.g., King, 1897).

Lallemand's basic claim is stated in his book's first sentence: "During a period of fourteen years, I have collected more than one-hundred-and-fifty cases in which involuntary seminal discharges were sufficiently serious to disorder the health of patients considerably, and even sometimes, to cause death" (Lallemand, 1847, p. i). Lallemand's spermatorrhea diagnosis dramatically extended the reach of the masturbation crusade to cases in which there may be no recent masturbation but one can postulate unobvious semen discharge of which even the patient may be unaware. The involuntary seminal emissions occurred mainly through excessive nocturnal emissions ("wet dreams"), sometimes with erection and orgasm but also sometimes without arousal or pleasure, but in more severe cases leakage could occur during the day as well, especially in the presence of attractive women or due to lascivious thoughts.

Lallemand allowed that a modest frequency of nocturnal emissions in the continent individual may serve an adaptive function. However, masturbation often led to a pathological chronic irritation that caused involuntary emission of semen leading to depletion of vital fluids:

When [involuntary discharge of seminal fluid] occurs spontaneously during sleep in a healthy and continent individual, it doubtless exerts a beneficial influence on the economy by freeing it from a source of excitement, the prolonged accumulation of which might derange the animal functions.... But the discharge may become excessive...; then, like repeated nasal hemorrhage, it gives rise to inconveniences proportioned to its frequency, its quantity, and the constitution of the individual. Involuntary seminal emissions may be caused by too great excitement of the genital apparatus, following venereal excesses or masturbation. A state of irritation remains in the spermatic organs after such excitement, which induces an increased secretion and hurried discharge of the secreted fluid, without complete erection, and almost without sensation.

(1847, p. 1)

Diagnosis of spermatorrhea sometimes included examination of the urine with a microscope for evidence of sperm, but most commonly it was inferred from nocturnal emissions, the patient's symptoms, and a confession extracted from the patient of previous masturbation. Lallemand's signature treatment, which became standard across Europe, England, and the United States, was the use of silver nitrate or other caustic chemicals, introduced through a flexible catheter (bougie) into the urethra, to cauterize the mucus membranes near the neck of the bladder and thus to end the hypothesized irritation. The irritation was verified by the fact that the initial passage of the bougie often caused acute discomfort.

In his book, Lallemand reports the case of the patient who "was the first on whom I practised cauterization as a remedy for spermatorrhoea" (1847, p. 39). The 20-year-old male patient's symptoms, other than nocturnal discharges, were seemingly endless:

He complained however of violent pain in his head, pain in his bones, frequent spasmodic tremors in his limbs, and a constant agitation which prevented his enjoying an instant's sleep; of stunning sensations and vertigo, with ringing in his ears; of a sense of suffocation with palpitation of the heart, and of itching in the skin;....he complained of a fixed pain in the hypogastrium....was habitually costive...passed water very often, and complained of pain in the penis and bladder during micturition....there existed in his whole body, especially in his loins and joints, a sense of debility attended by obtuse pain...

(1847, p. 38)

and so on. This clinical picture is consistent with Foucault's observation that masturbatory disease was a total disease of every aspect of the body that could explain virtually any constellation of symptoms (see Chapter 4).

Lallemand eventually extracted from the patient the inevitable confession of masturbation:

> I suspected that he had been addicted to masturbation; he denied it obstinately, however, before the pupils, but told me privately, that he had practised it from the age of ten, even five or six times a day.... About fourteen, he again gave himself up to the vice almost madly.
>
> (1847, p. 38)

After all the standard treatments—exercise, diet, ice packs, enemas, various tonics and emollients, leeches ("Twelve leeches were ordered to the anus" [1847, p. 37])—had failed, Lallemand looked for a more targeted treatment:

> After about three weeks of these fruitless essays, I gave up general means altogether, and as I was convinced that the spermatorrhoea arose from a state of chronic inflammation of the prostatic mucous membrane, the irritation of which extended to the ejaculatory ducts and seminal vesicles, I considered that by removing this state of the membrane by means of cauterization, I should put an end to the irritation of the spermatic organs.
>
> (1847, p. 38)

Lallemand experimented by passing a catheter through the urethra toward the bladder, triggering severe spasms and pain in the patient, thus confirming his suspicions. He then "immediately applied the solid nitrate of silver to the prostatic portion of the urethra" (1847, p. 38). Initially, "the patient suffered much while passing urine," but this subsided rapidly, and the treatment was a success: "At the expiration of a month, his health was quite perfect, and he wished to resume his former occupation" (1847, p. 39). Lallemand attributes the origins of the condition to masturbation: "In the case I have just related...the excessive masturbation to which the patient had been addicted, even before puberty, must have contributed much to produce this unfortunate disease" (1847, p. 39).

Lallemand claimed that the many diverse symptoms of spermatorrhea were due to the loss of semen having an effect on the nervous system of general enervation:

> We must also admit that these discharges excite a powerful and rapid influence over the nervous system; hence they have always been justly considered enervating. We are thus able to explain the numerous and varied symptoms resulting from spermatorrhoea, as well as their resemblance to the symptoms produced by all other debilitating causes.
>
> (1847, p. 294)

Note that this description of enervation and weakness is markedly similar to the way that neurasthenia will be described a few decades later (see Chapter 5), and in writings later in the century spermatorrhea and neurasthenia were often diagnosed together (e.g., see King, 1897). Although often the identified masturbatory cause of spermatorrhea occurred deep in the past, it was also common for spermatorrhea to follow immediately upon or during the process of cessation of masturbation: "Of the fifty-two cases I have seen, with thirty-seven the spermatorrhea came on and continued without cessation while the patient was trying to stop the habit of masturbation, or immediately following its discontinuance" (King, 1897, p. 26). Three forms of spermatorrhea were eventually distinguished based on the nature and circumstances of excessive emission:

> A classification, which has become time-honored, is to divide spermatorrhea into three classes, namely: Nocturnal emissions, or emissions during the sleeping hours; diurnal pollutions, or those which take place abnormally during the waking hours [e.g., when interacting with a female]; and spermatorrhea proper, which is the unconscious flow of the semen from the urethra without erection or special sensations.
>
> (King, 1897, p. 1)

However, rather than these being seen as static variant forms of the disease, these are seen as stages of disease development that intermingle:

"the first symptoms which make their appearance are nocturnal emissions; and as the disease advances, diurnal pollutions and spermatorrhea proper follow in the order given...I...shall at the same time divide spermatorrhea into three stages...and describe the disease, when not arrested, as progressive" (King, 1897, p. 2).

However, if semenic discharge is the sole pathogenic etiology that causes the nervous system's enervation, Lallemand's theory is confronted with the same problem that faced Tissot, of how to understand the pathogenic effects of masturbation on women and children. Lallemand holds that children and women who masturbate manifest symptoms similar to adult male masturbators, so presumably they have the same disorder. Yet, children and women have no semen, so the cause cannot be excessive semenic discharge. Lallemand acknowledges the problem: "Masturbation is generally commenced before puberty, and the female sex is not exempt from it. In these cases, therefore, seminal emission cannot occur. Nevertheless, functional disorders of the spinal cord may arise, similar to those produced by passive discharges" (p. 273).

To address this anomaly, Lallemand follows Tissot in postulating shock to the nerves as an additional non-semenic pathway to symptoms of debility. However, Lallemand observes that skeptics argue that once the nerve shock theory is postulated to explain child and female masturbatory pathology, it is sufficient to cover all relevant instances of these disorders including adult males, thus rendering superfluous any need for the semenic discharge theory of enervation: "[S]ome authors... have attributed the debility which follows all abundant discharges of semen, to the nervous excitement and convulsive motions, which usually accompany the discharge" (1847, p. 131). He acknowledges that if nerve shock explains child and female masturbatory disease, then it must at least be part of the explanation of adult male etiology: "The accidents observed before puberty are evidently only due to the effects on the nervous system; and, the same sensation accompanying voluntary emissions after puberty, it is natural to suppose that the nervous system plays as active part then, as in childhood" (1847, p. 131). Nonetheless, based on his claim that even semenic emission unaccompanied by arousal and orgasm can prove pathogenic, he insists that the two processes of semenic discharge and nervous shock are both necessary to understand masturbatory disorder:

I willingly admit the importance of this nervous exhaustion in whatever manner it may be supposed to operate;...[but] this is no reason why the actual discharges should not be taken into account, seeing that they greatly modify the character and consequences of the nervous disturbance.... Every excessive loss of semen also, even when unaccompanied by sensation, is followed by debility, and this may be carried so far as to cause death; I have related several such cases in the beginning of this work. There exist then two distinct causes; nervous disturbance and debilitating discharges, and both these act at once, when seminal emissions are produced by the influence of the will. It is not to be wondered at, that both these causes should produce nearly the same symptoms, because they both weaken the economy.... It is very easy to confound these two causes when they act simultaneously.....

(1847, pp. 132–133)

Obviously stretching his explanatory logic to the limits of possibility, Lallemand supports his account by noting, first, that children and women are more reactive than men to nervous stimulation, so that this one cause can have an effect equal to both causes in the male. Moreover, their symptoms of masturbation revealingly include more nervous spasm: "In children, even at a very early age,...the spasmodic symptoms are generally more marked... This unfortunate passion produces exactly the same effects in the female sex at all ages... arising from the greater nervous susceptibility of the female" (1847, pp. 132, 294).

Second, Lallemand points to the fact that if children stop masturbating, their recovery is easier than in adults, which he explains by the fact that only one of the two causal pathways to symptoms is active. He notes that "Unfortunately matters do not follow so simple a course after puberty" when both causal pathways have been active. He adds: "What I have just said respecting children, applies equally to females; this is easily shown by examining the cases in which excision of the clitoris has been performed for the cure of nymphomania... [T]hey recovered very rapidly" (1847, pp. 132–133), due, he suggests, to nervous shock being muted.

The seeming counterexamples, Lallemand concludes, simply show that the debilities brought on by semen loss can be brought on by alternative causes of debility, of which genital stimulation irrespective of semen loss is a powerful one due to nervous shock:

> I am convinced that the effects produced by seminal discharges may be brought on by any other debilitating cause...and that of all such causes those which have their seat in the genital organs are the most enervating, and consequently the fittest to produce debility and functional disorder.
>
> (1847, pp. 294–295)

Theoretical complexities aside, Lallemand strongly emphasizes that child masturbation is serious and has been unjustly ignored:

> I shall lay particular stress on such as act before puberty, because they have, hitherto, attracted very little attention. The most anxious parents believe that there is no occasion to watch over the actions of their children with regard to their genital organs, previously to the epoch of puberty; and few, even of our own profession, are led to suspect bad habits before that period. This is a fatal error....In some children there is a kind of precocity of sexual instinct, which leads to very serious results.
>
> (1847, pp. 119–120)

This advice presages the sort of intrusive surveillance of children that Foucault describes (see Chapter 4).

To stop the child masturbation that caused the nervous shock leading to symptoms, Lallemand uses the catheter treatment in prepubescent boys but without cauterization, with the goal of creating sufficient pain to stop the masturbatory nervous stimulation. For example:

> In 1824 a woman brought her son, aged eight to the hospital St. Eloi: he had lost the use of his lower extremities for some months.... Masturbation, the cause of all these disorders, had only been discovered by his mother a few weeks before she placed him under my care, but she had used every means she could devise to prevent it without effect. After two or three trials I found that it was of no use trusting to the strait-waistcoats and other means usually employed, and accordingly I determined to pass a gum-elastic catheter into the

bladder, and to fix it so that the patient should be unable to withdraw it. The presence of the foreign body, excited inflammation of the urethra as I expected; when this occurred, I withdrew the instrument, but replaced it as soon as the inflammation had subsided. I kept up, in this manner, a constant state of inflammation for a fortnight, which rendered the parts so painful, that the child was unable to touch them. This treatment produced more decisive success than I had ventured to hope... In another fortnight he was able to run about the wards. I then sent him away threatening him with a return of the same treatment if he relapsed.

(1847, p. 131)

As we shall see, Lallemand influenced Acton's writing in England, and was also highly influential in America (e.g., Calhoun, 1856; Howe, 1883; King, 1897). Spermatorrhea is now generally considered a mythical disease category based on mistaken reification and theorization of various symptoms without a scientific basis in medical reality. However, to this day it is occasionally cited in medical journals (e.g., Nakajima et al., 2009; Wu, Hao, & Zhou, 2016).

Bergeret: The Expansion of the Crusade to Conjugal Onanism

Another development around the middle of the nineteenth century was a new focus on practices during sexual intercourse as potentially pathogenic. This appears to have been driven partly by the growing use of birth control techniques to control family size, which was driven in turn by personal family planning motives of the increasingly prosperous upper and middle classes. It also seems to have been motivated by fears awakened by the much-discussed book on the dangers of uncontrolled population growth by Thomas Malthus (1766–1834), *An Essay on the Principle of Population* (1798, with several greatly expanded subsequent editions). As well, unmarried couples having sex were increasingly availing themselves of techniques of birth control to avoid pregnancy, bringing attention to the details of deviations from "natural" intercourse.

Malthus argued that the exponential growth of humanity could not be matched by the arithmetical increase in the food supply and so population growth would lead to social catastrophe unless population growth was prevented. He listed moral restraint regarding sex as one of several "obstacles" that could provide a "preventive check" on population as opposed to the undesirable "positive checks" of war, disease, and famine. Malthus disapproved of birth control and meant for his analysis to promote abstinence and late marriage, but inevitably others argued that birth control is a moral duty. The increased use of birth control techniques such as condoms and *coitus interruptus*, even when used within marriage, triggered a moral and religious backlash that referenced Onan's punishment by God, as well as concerns about population decline. This disapproval was seemingly transformed into medical doctrine as "conjugal sin" or "conjugal onanism" that diagnosed and treated the medical harms resulting from interference with natural intercourse and the natural process of pregnancy that should follow (e.g., Gardner, 1870; McArdle, 1888; Wilder, 1870). Resonating with church doctrine, the category of conjugal onanism expanded from *coitus interruptus* to encompass virtually every possible deviation from intercourse in pursuit of reproduction. (In Chapter 5, we will see that Freud was caught in the related dilemma of believing in the desirability of family planning and imagining a world where it is readily available and safe, yet agreeing that "preventive obstacles" to natural sexual gratification are pathogenic.)

The first and most influential full-length medical book on conjugal onanism was by French forensic physician Louis François Étienne Bergeret (1814–1893). Published in French in 1868 titled *Des Fraudes dans l'Accomplissement des Fonctions Generatrices* ("frauds in the accomplishment of the generative functions"), it warranted three editions within a year and was rapidly translated into English with the expanded Malthus-referencing title, "The preventive obstacle; or, conjugal onanism: The dangers and inconveniences to the individual, to the family, and to society, of frauds in the accomplishment of the generative functions" (Bergeret, 1870). That Bergeret's book, in effect a diatribe against birth control, was controversial across the Channel is suggested by the fact that in 1874 the library committee of the Royal Medical and Chirurgical Society of London voted to place the book on a list of volumes that could circulate only with special permission of the Society's Council, but the Council overrode them and insisted that the book be destroyed altogether: "Council, however, took a sterner view and ordered its destruction, and there was a note in the minutes, 'The volume was therefore burnt at the library committee on December 7th'" (Wade, 1962, p. 630).

Bergeret explains that the phrase he uses, "conjugal onanism," is in fact misleadingly narrow because "this expression...is far from including all the varieties of frauds which are employed to corrupt and denaturalize sexual intercourse" (1870, p. 6). This is because "conjugal" appears to imply a concern only with marital sex but "fraudulent practices in coition are, however, even more common among those who are not married, and who, for that reason, are still less desirous of having children" (1870 p. 6). Moreover, "onanism" suggests a concern only with Onan's biblical act of *coitus interruptus*, whereas Bergeret addresses the medical harms from a great variety of nonprocreative sexual acts. Consequently, when writing of "frauds" committed during sexual intercourse in which conception is in principle possible, most commonly *coitus interruptus* but also, for example, use of a condom, Bergeret instead uses the term "genesiacal fraud" (i.e., fraud of Onan's kind in Genesis) or "direct fraud." All other frauds that replace sexual intercourse with some other method of gratification or that occur in a context in which procreation is impossible he refers to as "indirect" frauds:

[I]ndirect frauds...are practiced chiefly in two ways: Either the conjunction of the sexes is complete and normal, but from particular circumstances, such as the menopausis, irremediable sterility, etc., conception is impossible; Or sexual connection takes place through irregular channels, as the mouth, the anus; or by means of reciprocal manual pollution.

(1870, pp. 104–105)

He divides the harms from conjugal frauds into local harms to the sexual organs, covering every imaginable pathology from inflammation to cancer, versus general harms to the overall organism that encompass harms to the nervous system.

According to Bergeret, generally it is the husband that imposes fraudulent sex on his wife either for purposes of birth control or for perverse and intense pleasure, thus depriving her not only of natural and full sexual release but also blocking subsequent childbearing.

Bergeret attributes widespread use of conjugal frauds to a variety of motives beyond simply the weakening of religion, avoidance of responsibility for out-of-wedlock sex, or a Malthusian social conscience. These include increasing prosperity that relieves bourgeois individuals from anxiety about being taken care of by children in their old age and thus causes them to "prefer the selfish enjoyment of the present to the care of rearing a numerous family" (1870, p. 5). Also, some men are so possessed by pride in their accomplishments and wealth that they "cannot endure the idea of the sale and partition of their estates, and, to avert this anticipation, content themselves with one or two children" (1870, p. 5). Thus, a father wants his son to be the sole heir of his estate, "but being of very ardent passions, he has with his wife very frequent and fraudulent connections" that after several years give rise to intolerable physical symptoms (1870, p. 24).

Bergeret explains that, given the intense focus on the masturbation crusade, the topic of harmful deviations during interactive sex with a partner has not received the attention it deserves:

> Numerous authors have indicated the evils engendered by that deviation from the generative instinct which consists in individual masturbation...to which a certain number of persons addict themselves, to obtain an indirect and unnatural gratification of their desires. Still more pernicious, however, are the refinements of debauchery...between persons of different sex, who endeavor to avert the natural consequence of a junction of the sexes.
>
> (1870, p. 6)

Why are these frauds "more pernicious" than masturbation? Relying on the nerve shock theory, Bergeret observes that sex with a partner can often be more exciting and thus involve a more intense orgasm than masturbation, creating more chance for damage to the nervous system: "How much greater must be the exaltation of the nervous system, the concussion which results from the contact of two persons who mutually excite each other" (1870, p. 6). Note that this explanation, that sexual intercourse can be more exciting and thus more harmful than masturbation, goes in precisely the opposite direction of the traditional explanations of the greater risk from masturbation that held that intercourse with a loved partner is a protective factor against nerve shock.

Although Bergeret emphasizes the harm to the female partner of unnatural sexual practices, he insists that men are harmed as well: "Though genesiac frauds are far from having the same bad consequences for the man as for the woman,…it nevertheless happens frequently to him to be the victim of these fraudulent manoeuvres" (1870, p. 66). On both sides, the problem is with the impact of the practices not on spermatic discharge but on the nervous system: "the excesses I am combatting act principally upon the nervous centres, and produce the most painful neuroses" (p. 80). This is because such frauds create levels of excitement that the nervous system is not designed to withstand, and, among other possible consequences, this may lead to a chronic pathological hyperarousal: "The super-excitation of the nervous system by the practice of frauds, may be the cause of two dreadful diseases, Nymphomania and Satyriasis" (1870, p. 72).

Bergeret's cases illustrate that both the women who are stimulated in indirect sexual frauds and the men who experience sustained arousal from doing the stimulating can suffer dire medical consequences resulting from the prolonged high level of excitement. Indeed, he reports cases of men falling ill from simply being aroused by being near to desired partners. However, he focuses on the harm to the women, a harbinger of later Freudian and broader cultural concerns with female pleasure and lack of female gratification:

VULVAR COITION. Many husbands and lovers, for fear of pregnancy, content themselves with incomplete approaches, without penetrating.…But these manoeuvres…present most of the other inconveniences resulting from frauds with penetration. They super-excite deeply the nervous system and engender neuropathic disorders.
(1870, pp. 121–122)

RECIPROCAL USE OF THE MANUS STUPRUM [mutual manual stimulation]. Case CXII.—Woman aged thirty. Emaciated, gastralgic, and neuropathic. Married at nineteen; had a child in the beginning, though her husband was practising frauds and did not wish to have any children before a certain time. Attributing her unexpected pregnancy to the uncertainty of frauds, he was unwilling to employ them any longer; but, being of a very lubricious nature, he exercised upon his wife, with his fingers, such frequent and various manoeuvres that he determined in her a nervous erethism raised to the most painful general neuropathy. As to him, when he was super-excited by the sight of the venereal orgasm pushed in his wife to the last limit, he either satisfied himself, or obliged her to render him this ignoble service. This woman's health was very much impaired, and her sufferings were evidently caused by the practices of her husband; since, on his being obliged to absent himself in traveling for several months, she rapidly recovered.

(1870, pp. 123–124)

APPLICATION OF THE TONGUE AND LIPS. Instead of a manual pollution, certain men, with the view of provoking a very intense venereal orgasm in the woman, have recourse to an excitation determined by the application of the extremity of the tongue and lips. I have seen this kind of frauds produce great enervation in women.

Case CXIII.—Young woman aged eighteen. Married at sixteen, and having had a child immediately. She was of rare beauty…. Three years after her marriage, she grew pale, and withered…. She came to consult me, complaining of pains everywhere, but above all of gastralgia…. The same day I met one of her intimate friends and questioned her. She revealed to me that the husband had the fatal habit of applying the tongue and lips to his wife's genitals to provoke in her a venereal orgasm, which became so intense that this woman often told her friend: 'He enervates me too much; my health will not stand it.'

(1870, pp. 124–125)

Bergeret's concerns in some ways represent the opposite of twentieth-century sexual aspirations. He urges his readers to limit both the variety of kinds of sexual interaction and the length and intensity of excitement and orgasm to avoid nerve damage, and to keep in mind that reproduction is the ultimate natural goal of sex. Yet, he also presages some of the doctrines that will be adapted by Freud and influence twentieth-century marital sexuality. Chief amongst these is the focus on the need for female gratification rather than unrelieved excitement to avoid medical harm to the woman, and the implication that male lascivious needs should not dominate in the bedroom. In this respect, there is thus a nascent doctrine of sexual equality of natural and gratifying sex that he implies should hold sway. Bergeret's analysis of all the ways that sex can be unnatural is also part of what Foucault describes as another aspect in the deployment of sex, the focus on sexual perversion.

One might easily see the focus on conjugal Onanism as a resurgence of earlier Church doctrine. It is of course true that the Church had elaborate doctrines about acceptable sexual practices in marriage, the only place such practices were considered acceptable. As Rafael Domingo (2017) explains in an article on Thomas Sanchez, an eminent sixteenth-century Catholic writer on sexual morality,

> Sanchez's approach to sexual morality is based on...the goodness of sexual intercourse within marriage when it is ordered to its natural end....On the other hand, it is immoral to try to exercise the right in pursuit of pleasure alone.... Additionally, sperm is always ordered to generation, so a man may not ejaculate voluntarily outside of proper marital intercourse.
>
> (p. 254)

Both liberal and conservative medieval and renaissance theologians held that non-genital intercourse was a sin; they differed only on the details as to whether it is a mortal or venial sin and on whether it is still a sin when used only in nonejaculatory foreplay leading to a culminating act of genital copulation.

This history raises the question of whether Foucault is correct in seeing the masturbation crusade as a major cultural discontinuity. However, consistent with Hare's judgment of a major and puzzling historical discontinuity, Foucault observes that the attention to such earlier work on sexuality had waned and was largely moribund prior to the inauguration of the masturbation crusade in the eighteenth century. Moreover, the dramatic embracing of the crusade by medicine and the transformation of former sins into etiologies of disease was utterly novel in ways Foucault underscores:

> It may be the case that the intervention of the Church in conjugal sexuality and its rejection of 'frauds' against procreation had lost

much of their insistence over the previous two hundred years. But medicine made a forceful entry into the pleasures of the couple: it created an entire organic, functional, or mental pathology arising out of 'incomplete' sexual practices; it carefully classified all forms of related pleasures; it incorporated them into the notions of 'development' and instinctual 'disturbances'; and it undertook to manage them.

(*HS1*, p. 42)

Mid- to Late-Nineteenth-Century Shifts in the Masturbation Crusade

Although, like Foucault, I am surveying the overall history of the masturbation crusade, my greatest interest lies in developments during the height of the medical crusade against masturbation in the later decades of the nineteenth century, just prior to Freud's arrival on the scene—the time during which William Acton's views, to which I will shortly turn, dominated the literature. This is a medico-sexual literature with which Freud would have been well acquainted. A few words about this period will help to place Acton's views in context.

This was a distinctively frenetic period of change even for the crusade. Gilbert (1975) notes that "fears of masturbation reached new heights during the nineteenth century" (p. 224), with medical treatments evolving to address this challenge with a brutal intensity. Hare observes that in Britain "by the mid-nineteenth century...the hypothesis that masturbation caused insanity was taken one stage further before it finally collapsed towards the end of the century" (1962, p. 6), at which time these fears morphed into fears focused on neurosis. He also notes that, in contrast to the relatively benign and non-intrusive interventions (e.g., simply stopping masturbation, taking cold baths and fresh air, hydrotherapy, diet and exercise regimens) that predominated earlier, "by the second half of the nineteenth century the use of surgical and pharmacological methods of preventing masturbation was certainly widespread" (p. 10). Spitz (1952) notes "the innumerable, varied and subtle practices of refined cruelty" in the "extremely cruel persecution of the masturbator" during this period, and especially "the sudden rise of repressive and surgical measures in the treatment of masturbation beginning with 1850" (p. 505) that made this last gasp of the masturbation crusade particularly troubling:

> [B]etween 1850 and 1879 surgical treatment was recommended more frequently than any of the other measures. It is only in the second half of the nineteenth century that sadism becomes the foremost characteristic of the campaign against masturbation. This aspect is not limited to any one country..., [D]rastic measures (surgery, restraint, severe punishment, fright) constitute at least fifty percent of the measures recommended in all countries until 1925.... [T]hese sadistic practices found support among authoritative physicians.
>
> (Spitz, 1952, pp. 499, 505)

Of course, there existed diverse opinions about masturbation and sexuality in the late nineteenth century, with some sexologists and physicians arguing that the warnings and fear had gone too far. However, as Hall observes, "Victorian doctors, even if they did not subscribe completely to Acton's views on the subject, commonly were convinced of the physical as well as the moral evils of self-abuse" (1992, p. 367).

Makari (1998) underscores the point that during this time, even as some medical authorities became more critical of some of the outrageous excesses in theories about masturbation's pathogenic effects, they generally also remained convinced that masturbation was indeed related to the pathogenesis of multiple major diseases:

> By the 1870s, it had become common for medical authors to condemn the terrifying list of illnesses that...others had attached to masturbation in the first half of the nineteenth century.... Nonetheless, almost invariably these same authorities would then go on to list a wide array of urological, gastrointestinal, and nervous disorders that they believed *were* created by masturbation. In French- and English-language medical discourse after 1870, moral insanity, hysteria, epilepsy, and hypochondria headed the list of nervous illnesses to be feared.... [I]n the German-language medical literature masturbation continued to be an important etiology—being cited by some as a cause of epilepsy, tremor,

chorea,, and impotence. More commonly, it was thought to cause homosexuality, adult neurasthenia, and hysteria.

(pp. 645–646)

William Acton 1: The Victorian View of Masturbation

I now turn to William Acton (1813–1875), the English physician whose writings were most influential among conservative mid-to-late Victorian physicians regarding the dangers of masturbation. Acton's medical text, *The Functions and Disorders of the Reproductive Organs in Childhood, Youth, Adult Age, and Advanced Life, Considered in their Physiological, Social, and Moral Relations* (1875), after its initial publication in London in 1857, was republished in many English and American editions and it was frequently cited as authoritative by Acton's medical contemporaries. Acton's book has also become the "go to" standard reference for scholars studying the conservative Victorian physician's thinking about masturbation and related topics. Carl Degler (1974) observes that "Acton's book was undoubtedly one of the most widely quoted sexual-advice books in the English-speaking world" (p. 1467), Dominic Hodgson (2005) says that Acton is "perhaps the best-known 19th century British writer on sexual matters" (p. 377), and Lesley Hall (1992) notes that Acton's book "is often considered to be the definitive Victorian work on sexual functioning" (p. 366).

Acton strongly endorses the traditional theory of the vital nature of semen and its centrality to sexual desire and masturbatory disorder. This theory, he claims, is supported by ample medical treatment success:

[S]emen...is a highly organised fluid, requiring the expenditure of much vital force in its elaboration and in its expulsion. Even in the strongest adult, and much more in the youth or the weakly man, the whole of the functions connected with it are most vital and important.... [M]any of the most obstinate as well as obscure complaints which the medical man meets with arise from the loss of semen...[including] indigestion, debility, and nervous depression.... In such cases the best, and indeed the only treatment, is that which removes the cause, and is not confined to combating the symptoms. The best evidence of this cause and effect is, that such radical treatment alone relieves the symptoms when all other remedies have failed.

(Acton, 1875, pp. 97, 145–146)

Acton holds that the symptoms of masturbation that result from semen loss can be quite severe: "[M]y own belief is, that many cases of imbecility, insanity, and epileptic affections may be traced to previous abuses of the generative functions" (1875, p. 154). Acton's book has an entire section devoted to "insanity arising from masturbation," which begins with the bald assertion, "That insanity is a consequence of this habit is now beyond a doubt" (1875, p. 62).

Acton follows Lallemand, whom he quotes extensively, in extending the semenic theory of masturbatory disease to those who are not currently masturbating but due to earlier masturbation are having continued involuntary nocturnal (or diurnal) semenic emissions: "The condition or ailment which we here characterise as Spermatorrhoea... is a state of enervation produced, at least primarily, by the loss of semen" (1875, p. 146). As noted above, with enervation as its primary symptom, spermatorrhea is symptomatically the direct historical precursor of neurasthenia, a neurosis defined by nervous weakness (see Chapter 5). Acton acknowledges that spermatorrhea may also result from neurosis, but observes that the neurosis itself may be the result of masturbation: "Nervous affections are often the cause of spermatorrhoea; still I am not prepared to say that these nervous affections themselves may not be consequences of previous masturbation or venereal excesses" (1875, p. 148). Concerned about over-diagnosis of spermatorrhea in anxious or depressed patients ("Many a man has believed himself to be labouring under this affection when, in fact, entirely free from it" [1875, p. 146]), and aware that due to such misdiagnoses some physicians have "denied that such a disease exists at all" (1875, p. 145), Acton includes an entire section on "false spermatorrhoea" to help physicians and patients identify such cases. However, Acton is fully confident that the disease is real.

As we have seen, the semenic theory seems to imply that excessive sexual intercourse should be as harmful as excessive masturbation. So, like Tissot and Lallemand before him, Acton must explain his special medical concern with masturbation. Acton understands that sex is natural and essential for the propagation of the species and so there can be no blanket condemnation: "Not that this natural instinct is to be regarded with a Manichean philosophy as in itself bad. Far from it. That it is natural forbids such a theory. It has its own beneficent purpose; but that purpose is not early and sensual indulgence, but mature and lawful love" (1875, p. 50). Acton theorizes that intercourse, unlike masturbation, has built-in safeguards against pathogenic excess:

> A kind of natural safeguard is provided against the nervous exhaustion consequent on the excitement of coitus, by the rapid diminution of the sensation during successive acts. Indeed, in persons who repeat coitus frequently during the same night, the pleasurable sensation will diminish so rapidly that the act at last will not be attended with any.
>
> (p. 179)

In keeping with such natural guidance, moderation of the kind emphasized by Bergeret is advisable: "Duration of the Act.—It is, indeed, a wise provision that in the human being the act should last but a short time—some few minutes" (p. 180). Because no such safeguards exist for masturbation, it is more dangerous.

Rather than invoking the protective effects of love, Acton explains the greater danger of masturbation in purely pragmatic terms, as the ease of excessive abuse:

> [A] lavish expenditure of the vital fluid semen is most detrimental to a young man's constitution. Whether this arises from masturbation, sexual excesses, or very frequent nocturnal emissions, the effects will be very similar. If we here treat of masturbation, it is because this vice is one more readily and easily practised and repeated by young men, and to it, therefore, more frequently than to the other causes, it is that the evil consequences which we are now considering are due.
>
> (1875, p. 69).

Like his predecessors, Acton rejects the simple semenic depletion theory of masturbatory disease because semen accumulation and discharge do not occur in children or women and thus cannot explain the medical harms they too suffer from masturbation:

It has been generally supposed that the loss of semen was the sole cause of sexual debility in the male. That such is not the case is proved by the nervous depression coming on in young children from sexual excitement before they can be said to secrete semen. Similar exhausting nervous effects are noticed in women, who do not secrete any such fluid, but merely mucus, and yet may experience the nervous orgasm or spasm which acts as harmfully on them, when much indulged in, as on males.

(1875, p. 97)

Acton further asserts that although "no woman...loses semen, or anything analogous to it, during the sexual orgasm," nonetheless in women the "effect of long-continued, and often repeated sexual shocks" may include "epileptiform attacks, and various nervous affections, as well as local affections of the uterus" which are "direct consequences of sexual excesses" (1875, p. 97, note 1). Thus, "too much stress has been laid on mere loss of semen, and too little importance placed on the drain on the nervous system" (Acton, 1851, p. 82).

In sum, like his predecessors, Acton adopts a hybrid theory of masturbatory disorder that combines semenic loss with the more general impact of excessively frequent or intense arousal or orgasm on the nervous system:

I, in common with many modern writers, have come to the conclusion that there is a good deal of evidence now existing which shows that shocks constantly received and frequently repeated on the great ganglionic centres may produce irritation in them, and thus cause many of the obscure forms of disease to which we have hitherto failed in discovering a key. If there is any cause which is likely more than another to produce undue excitement of the ganglionic system, it is the too frequent repetition of acts involving this nervous orgasm.

(1875, pp. 97–98)

In keeping with the dual theory of masturbatory etiology, Acton lists "hard study" as a condition predisposing to spermatorrhea due to "over-exertion of the brain" (1875, p. 147), especially if it combines with semen loss due to sexual activity. Acton provides a case illustration of a patient who came to him complaining of "nearly all the symptoms which constitute spermatorrhoea":

> He stated that he had recently been studying hard at the University, and admitted also having had connection about four times in a month....I succeeded in convincing him that the only danger he had to dread arose from continuing venereal excess; that, if he remained continent, the temporary result of vigorous mental exertion would pass away, leaving him none the worse; but that the double strain on both the brain and the generative system...would most certainly deteriorate if not ruin both. I have become more and more convinced of the large proportion of students in all professions who suffer in a similar manner.
>
> (1875, p. 147)

(As we shall see in Chapter 5, Freud in a similar manner interprets hard intellectual work as throwing off the libidinal balance.)

Acton also endorses Bergeret's theory of conjugal onanism while resisting some of its more ambitious conclusions, with a dose of medical nationalism and claims of cultural differences thrown in:

> I cannot bring to a close this important chapter without directing the attention of the profession to the dangers that married couples incur in defrauding nature by practices that have been called conjugal onanism, and a M. Bergeret has...given a very succinct account of how it is that French parents determine (and carry out) that they shall only have one, or at most two children.... I am far from attributing, with the author of this treatise, so many of the local ill consequences which he traces in the female to the means pursued. On the contrary, I am fully convinced that the many ailments, such as simple affections of the uterus, which M. Bergeret considers to follow the practices adopted in France, attend— although, perhaps, in a less degree—married life in England, where, I am convinced, the practices are hardly known, and still less frequently resorted to. Still I raise a warning voice against either married or unmarried persons giving themselves up to ungratified sexual excitement.
>
> (Acton, 1875, pp. 140–141)

Although Acton emphasizes the danger of enervation from excessive discharge and advises a modest amount of sexual activity, influenced by Bergeret he nonetheless recognizes that undischarged sexual arousal is pathogenic:

UNGRATIFIED SEXUAL EXCITEMENT. Just in proportion to the degree of uneasiness caused by the presence of an excess of semen in the organs, is the relief experienced after its natural, or, so to speak, legitimate emission.... [T]he mere excitement of the sexual feelings when not followed by the result which it should produce, is...an unmitigated evil. I am becoming every day more and more convinced that much suffering and many ailments arise in great measure from the repeated and long-continued excitement of the sexual feelings unattended by subsequent sexual relations. I could mention many instances where I have traced serious affections and very great suffering to this cause.

(Acton, 1875, p. 138)

For Acton, as for Bergeret, the problem with unnatural sexual activity is that, first, it can yield an extremely intense orgasm that causes an excessively intense nervous shock; second, the orgasm or activity can be experienced more frequently without the requirements of natural intercourse; and third, the prolongation of pleasure prior to orgasm allows for excessively lengthy periods of extreme sexual excitement without satisfaction. Thus, if the sexual act is divorced from the natural outcome for which it is designed, medical harm and sexual dysfunction may ensue:

I have every reason to believe that if the co-ordinate performance of what constitutes the sexual act be repeatedly disturbed, the best medical treatment is not always efficacious in restoring sexual power. These ailments, I repeat, are not confined to the young. There are old men who marry young wives, and who pay the penalty by becoming martyrs to paralysis, softening of the brain, and drivelling idiocy.... [T]hese indulgences—which are thought so harmless—produce local mischief in the reproductive organs. Among the principal and primary evils they cause, is the weakening of that co-ordinate action which should connect the excitement of the organs and the complete performance of the sexual act.... [T]he excited nervous system, if it does not receive and reciprocate that shock which we have seen ought to attend ejaculation, suffers a longer and more severe strain, lasting often days or nights.... [T]he non-occurrence of emission after sexual excitement permits for a time the repetition of the excitement; but...after the preliminary excitement has occurred, and the control of the will shall have been able to prevent emission, the patient will very probably find that when he wishes it, emission will not follow erection. These practices, unnatural in the highest degree, cannot be carried on with impunity.... Under the head of impotence I have described...the case of an artist who had so schooled his will that he could look at the nude figure without excitement, yet when the time came for his marriage he felt himself unequal to the task.

(Acton, 1875, p. 140)

On the other hand, Acton recognizes that individual differences in constitution will matter to whether symptoms occur in response to sexual activity, much as Freud acknowledged that the ease of acquiring neurotic symptoms depends heavily on constitutional factors:

I have been consulted by some few persons...who never appear to suffer from the act, although excesses may be committed to a great extent. This tolerance of the orgasm—...which permits the frequent recurrence of the shock without any ill effect either at the time or later—must depend upon some constitutional difference of nervous system of which we are ignorant. We may, however, for the present, neglect...those who can commit almost satyrine excesses with apparent, though temporary, impunity. The question we have to consider is, what effect the act has upon ordinary men.

(1875, p. 95)

William Acton 2: Masturbation in Children and Women

I now turn to Acton's view of child and female sexuality. For Acton, the child is naturally sexually pure. Acton titles a chapter, "normal sexual condition in childhood" (1875, p. 1), but in fact he holds that there is no sexuality in the normal child, as he reiterates throughout his book: "Previously to the attainment of puberty the normal condition of a healthy child is one of entire freedom from sexual impressions" (1875, p. 1); "During...childhood, strictly so termed, the fitting condition is...absolute sexual quiescence" (1875, p. 8); "The child should know nothing of this trial, and ought never to be disturbed with one sexual feeling or thought" (1875, p. 49); "the proper condition of childhood" is "complete sexual quiescence" (1875, p. 203):

> In a state of health sexual impressions should never affect a child's mind or body. All its vital energy should be employed in constructing the growing frame.... [P]erfect freedom from, and indeed total ignorance of any sexual attraction is the rule. This state of purity and ignorant innocence in children are not in any way unnatural....It were well if the child's reproductive organs always remained in a quiescent state till puberty.
>
> (1875, pp. 17–18)

Despite this natural state, the child is capable of becoming prematurely sexualized. Acton holds that heredity plays a strong role in the disposition to such sexual pathology. However, any deviation from the natural nonsexual state, whether due to innate constitutional factors or outside influences, is unnatural and potentially pathogenic: "For prepubescent children, the premature development of the sexual inclination is...repugnant to all we associate with the term childhood" and "fraught with danger to his dawning manhood" (1875, p. 3);

> It were well if the child's reproductive organs always remained in a quiescent state till puberty. This is unfortunately not the case. Amongst the earliest disorders that we notice is sexual precocity....In many instances, either from hereditary predisposition, bad companionship, or other evil influences, sexual feelings become excited at a very early age, and this is always attended with injuries, often with the most deplorable consequences.
>
> (1875, p. 19)

The normal asexual childhood condition is easily perturbed by a variety of influences, according to Acton:

> Persons having the care of children cannot too constantly bear in mind that the tendency of all irritation or excitement of the generative system, either mental or physical, is to induce even the youngest child to stimulate the awakened appetite, and attempt to gratify the immature sexual desires which would otherwise have remained dormant for years to come.
>
> (1875, pp. 7–8)

These influences that can cause "an almost ungovernable disposition to touch or excite the sexual organs" include anything that irritates the genital area, such as worms and a tight foreskin:

> This most dangerous habit is not unfrequently, I believe, produced by irritation in the rectum arising from worms.... Irritation of the glans penis arising from an unusually long prepuce or the collection of secretion under it is another exciting cause which should not be neglected.... To the sensitive, excitable, civilized individual, the prepuce often becomes a source of serious mischief.... I am fully convinced that the excessive sensibility induced by a narrow foreskin...is often the cause of emissions, masturbation, or undue excitement of the sexual desires.
>
> (1875, pp. 4–5, 101)

Consequently, Acton and others often suggested circumcision as a treatment for masturbation.

Like early Freud, Acton also attributes the onset of childhood masturbation to adult seduction or initiation into sex by other children, possibly interacting with a constitutional tendency that leads to experimentation:

> In children too young to emit semen, friction of the organ is liable to produce that nervous spasm which is, in the adult, accompanied by ejaculation. This degrading practice in a young child may arise in a variety of ways. The most common is of course the bad example of other children. In other cases, vicious or foolish female servants suggest the idea. In such sexually disposed children as have been described above, the least hint is sufficient, or indeed they may, even without any suggestion from others, invent the habit for themselves.

This latter origin, however, is rare in very early life.... I have heard of a vile habit which some foreign nurses have (I hope it is confined to the Continent) of quieting children when they cry by tickling the sexual organs. I need hardly point out how very dangerous this is. There seems hardly any limit to the age at which a young child can be initiated into these abominations, or to the depth of degradation to which it may fall under such hideous teaching.

(Acton, 1875, p. 39)

As in Freud's vivid descriptions of the post-orgasmic look of satisfaction on the face of a baby who has just fed at the breast, Acton allows that childhood stimulation can produce an orgasm-like pleasurable crescendo, albeit without ejaculation.

Acton's discussion of children is not solely to shore up the holes in the semenic theory, but also because he believes that, in virtue of their supposed natural sexual purity, the consequences of masturbation are particularly dangerous.

The boy's health fails, he is troubled with indigestion, his intellectual powers are dimmed, he becomes pale, emaciated, and depressed in spirits; exercise he has no longer any taste for, and he seeks solitude.... If the struggle is severe for a youth to extricate himself from these vicious propensities, experience teaches me that it is very doubtful if...the physical frame will ever be wholly built up again; the haggard expression, the sunken eye, the long, cadaverous-looking countenance, the downcast expression, which seems to arise from the dread of looking a fellow-creature in the face, may be carried to the grave.

(1875, pp. 27, 59–60)

Acton emphasizes in vivid terms the degree to which masturbation prior to puberty has distinctive effects more severe than post-pubertal masturbation:

Effects of Abuses. — The effects produced by the different kinds of abuse of which I have been treating, vary according to the age.... The symptoms arising from masturbation in the child have been always hitherto confounded with those produced in the adult; they present certain distinctive characters, however, which require our consideration. However young they may be, children lose flesh, and become pale, irritable, morose and passionate; their sleep is short, disturbed, and broken. They fall into a state of marasm, and at length die, if not prevented from pursuing their courses.... Analogous symptoms are shown in the adult...but in infancy more or less severe nervous symptoms are superadded, which are not found in those who have commenced the practice after puberty.... Such are spasms and partial or general convulsions, eclampsia, epilepsy, and paralysis, accompanied with contraction of the limbs; these phenomena were present in all the children whose cases I have noticed, and numerous similar facts have been published by different authors.

(Acton, 1875, p. 130)

The responsibility for addressing the danger of such early mastur-bation lies squarely on the parents, according to Acton:

[I]t is my deliberate opinion that in many cases it would be true wisdom and true kindness for a parent openly and in plain language to lay before a boy the full extent of his danger, and impress upon him as urgently as possible, the fact that it is a danger, and that the consequences of yielding on his part will be most lamentable.... There may be the risk of tainting an ingenuous mind...; but, when it is needful, a father should in my opinion accept the grave responsibility and ought not to fall into the greater unknown ill of dismissing his child to the probability of contamination, without an attempt to save him.

(1875, p. 42)

However, Acton also indicates that the physician should be called upon to deal with these issues in the family when the parents do not succeed: "I would urge parents, if they feel themselves unequal to the responsi-bility, to transfer the duty to their medical adviser" (1875, p. 44).

Acton provides a dramatic—one might say melodramatic—comparison of continent and incontinent post-pubertal youths. The continent youth "evinces that elasticity of body and that happy control of himself and his feelings which are indicative of the robust health and absence of care which should accompany youth," he possesses "full vigour" and "His conscience is unburdened, his intellect clear, his address frank and candid, his memory good, his spirits are buoyant, his complexion is bright"; and "Every function of the body is well performed, and no fatigue is felt after moderate exertion" (1875, p. 15). The incontinent youth is the opposite in every way:

> [T]he outward signs of debasement are only too obvious. The frame is stunted and weak, the muscles undeveloped, the eye is sunken and heavy, the complexion is sallow, pasty, or covered with spots of acne, the hands are damp and cold, and the skin moist. The boy shuns the society of others, creeps about alone, joins with repugnance in the amusements of his schoolfellows. He cannot look any one in the face, and becomes careless in dress and uncleanly in person. His intellect becomes sluggish and enfeebled, and if his evil habits are persisted in, he may end in becoming a driveling idiot or a peevish valetudinarian.
>
> (1875, pp. 15–16)

Moreover, the incontinent youth's difficulties are just beginning. Acton believes that continued masturbation by the youth as he grows older can cause a variety of more serious physical and mental disorders including masturbatory insanity, dementia, tabes dorsalis (spinal degeneration, now known to be caused by syphilis), tuberculosis (phthisis, consumption), and heart disease. As always, early intervention is advised:

> Treatment.—In the earlier stages of this mental and bodily debility the services of the surgeon may be of great benefit. If a bougie be introduced into the urethra, and the [caustic] treatment...employed, the patient will find it much easier to exercise self-control (which is what is wanted).... It is in the earlier stages that advice should be sought.
>
> (1875, p. 62)

Acton's view of women's sexuality and the dangers to women of masturbation are similar to but somewhat more nuanced than his view of children. On the one hand, Acton admits to various obvious facts about women's sexual feelings. He acknowledges that women experience sexual pleasure in response to adequate stimulation during sexual intercourse: "That the erect penis should fill the vagina and distend it seems necessary to the full excitement of the female sexual feelings" (1875, p. 81); that women naturally differ in level of desire with some being highly desirous ("I admit that there are some few women who have sexual desires so strong that they surpass those of men, and shock public feeling by their consequences" [1875, p. 212]); that some women are good at pretending they are aroused ("the loose women of the London streets...who, if they have not sexual feeling, counterfeit it so well that the novice does not suspect but that it is genuine" [1875, p. 212]); and that some can suffer from the pathology of nymphomania ("I admit, of course, the existence of sexual excitement terminating even in nymphomania, a form of insanity" [1875, p. 212]). Acton suggests that, based on a misimpression derived from exceptional cases, men sometimes feel inadequate to perform their marital duties and "dread and avoid marriage" (1875, p. 213).

However, regarding female sexuality, Acton is most famous (or infamous) for his extraordinary denials of any general intense natural female sexual desire or pleasure and his male-centric view of sexuality and marriage, which may have fit Victorian ideals but have justly made him a target for feminist criticism. Here is a sampling of Acton's assertions regarding female sexual desire, which reveal much about the Victorian vision of an ideal marriage:

> [T]he majority of women (happily for society) [in earlier editions, this read "happily for them"!-JW] are not very much troubled with sexual feeling of any kind. What men are habitually, women are only exceptionally.... [T]here can be no doubt that sexual feeling in the female is in the majority of cases in abeyance, and that it requires positive and considerable excitement to be roused to all; and even if roused (which in many instances it never can be) it is very moderate compared with that of the male.... I am ready to maintain that there are many females who never feel any sexual excitement whatever.... Many of the best mothers, wives, and managers of households, know little of or are careless about sexual indulgences. Love of home, of children, and of domestic duties are

the only passions they feel. As a general rule, a modest woman seldom desires any sexual gratification for herself. She submits to her husband's embraces, but principally to gratify him; and, were it not for the desire of maternity, would far rather be relieved from his attentions.

(1875, pp. 212–213)

Acton's point here is not merely to analyze female sexual feelings but to reassure the anxious male that his virility will not be tested. This is the reverse of today's concern about inadequate male performance as a cause of anorgasia in the female. He concludes:

No nervous or feeble young man need, therefore, be deterred from marriage by any exaggerated notion of the arduous duties required from him. Let him be well assured, on my authority backed by the opinion of many, that the married woman has no wish to be placed on the footing of a mistress!

(1875, p. 213)

As to the source of female pleasure however slight it may be, presaging Freud's major theoretical error, Acton seems to discount clitoral orgasm and suggest that the source of female pleasure is in nerves in the vagina. He makes this comment in the course of discussing the accepted operation of clitoridectomy for nymphomania:

I shall probably have no other opportunity of noticing that, as excision of the clitoris has been recommended for the cure of this complaint, Kobelt thinks that it would not be necessary to remove the whole of the clitoris in nymphomania, the same results (that is destruction of venereal desire) would follow if the glans clitoridis had been alone removed, as it is now considered that it is the glans alone in which the sensitive nerves expand. This view I do not agree with, as I have already stated with regard to the analogous structure of the penis. I am fully convinced that in many women there is no special sexual sensation in the clitoris, and I am as positive that the special sensibility dependent on the erectile tissue exists in several portions of the vaginal canal.

(1875, p. 212)

Finally, Acton ventures into philosophical territory and expresses the conception of the ideal and prototypical relationship between man and woman in his Victorian milieu, anchored in his view of how men and women are biologically designed, in the following comment:

> During the last few years, and since the rights of women have been so much insisted upon,...numerous husbands have complained to me of the hardships under which they suffer by being married to women who regard themselves as martyrs when called upon to fulfil the duties of wives. This spirit of insubordination has become more intolerable—as the husbands assert—since it has been backed by the opinions of John Stuart Mill, who in his work on the 'Subjection of Women,' would induce the sex to believe that they are 'but personal body-servants of a despot.'.... As opposed to these doctrines, I would rather urge the sex to follow the example of those bright, cheerful, and happily constituted women, who, instead of exaggerating their supposed grievances, instinctively, as it were, become the soothers of man's woes, their greatest gratification apparently being to minister to his pleasures, seeing that woman was created for the purpose of being a help-meet to her husband.
>
> (1875, pp. 142–143)

Late-Nineteenth-Century-Trends in the Masturbation Crusade

In its evolution over the last years of the nineteenth and early twentieth centuries, the masturbation crusade underwent several gradual changes in focus. There was an increasing diversity of medical opinion as to whether masturbation is harmful at all, with some suggesting that the only harm was the fear and shame induced by medical writings. Among those who continued to assert the pathogenic effects of masturbation, there were two major changes. The first was a turn away from the emphasis we have seen in the crusade's writers from Tissot to Acton on the multiple severe physical disorders caused by masturbation. The idea that masturbation causes multiple severe physical disorders such as tuberculosis and epilepsy fell by the wayside in favor of an understanding of the physical pathogenic effects as more related to enervation and its psychosomatic disorders.

Of course, there may be local inflammation and its effects on the reproductive system, and to the degree that masturbation causes a neurasthenia-like nervous exhaustion the effects could include many somatic symptoms, but not the endless horrific often fatal diseases cited by the earlier writers.

The second change is the abandonment of the idea of masturbatory insanity or dementia as a distinctive psychotic or severe mental disorder caused by masturbation, which was much discussed in the leading medical journals into the 1880s (e.g., Spitzka, 1887a; 1887b; 1887c; 1888a; 1888b). Instead, there was a turn to neurotic disorders as the likely mental pathological outcome of masturbation. For example, the eminent English psychiatrist Henry Maudsley initially believed in masturbatory insanity, but by 1895 had recanted and retreated to the view that masturbation causes certain distinctive chronic neurotic disorders typically characterized by obsessional thoughts, compulsions, ruminations, pathological doubt and indecisiveness, and phobias, a view not that distant from Freud's view (see Chapter 5).

Hare (1962) describes this general shift to the masturbatory theory of neurosis:

During the last 15 years of the nineteenth century, there was a great decline in the belief that masturbation could cause insanity and epilepsy. The belief still lingered in the writings of some older psychiatrists...but these were vestiges, and by the beginning of the twentieth century the majority of writers had adopted the view of Kraepelin (1896) that insanity 'is never caused by onanism'. This decline, together with the renewed interest in the neuroses aroused by the writings of Beard, Charcot and Janet, raised into prominence the second aspect of the masturbatory hypothesis, the belief that masturbation was a common cause of neurotic disorders.

(1962, p. 9)

Once the endless variety of disorders supposedly consequent on masturbation were pruned of most physical disorders and of psychotic disorders and other forms of insanity, the types of conditions of bodily and mental enervation that were left as potential effects of masturbation resemble the increasingly salient disorder of neurasthenia. Eventually, these domains converged, and the theory of masturbatory pathogenesis became a theory of the etiology of neurasthenia in Freud's hands (see Chapter 5).

I have outlined the major doctrines about sexuality that formed the foundation for the masturbation crusade. In the next chapter, I examine Foucault's claims about the masturbation crusade and his account of the "deployment of sexuality," including an analysis of Foucault's account of the masturbation crusade's primary tactics and functions.

References

Acton, W. (1851). *A practical treatise on the diseases of the urinary and generative organs in both sexes* (2nd ed.). London: Churchill.

Acton, W. (1875). *The functions and disorders of the reproductive organs in childhood, youth, adult age, and advanced life considered in their physiological, social and moral relations.* Philadelphia, PA: Lindsay & Blakiston. (Original work published in 1857.)

Aspiz, H. (1987). Sexuality and the pseudo-sciences. In A. Wrobel (Ed.). *Pseudo-science and society in 19th-century America* (pp. 144–165). Lexington, KY: University Press of Kentucky.

Bergeret, L. F. E. (1870). *The preventive obstacle, or conjugal onanism: The dangers and inconveniences to the individual, to the family, and to society of frauds in the accomplishment of the generative functions* (P. De Marmon, Trans.). New York, NY: Turner & Mignard.

Bullough, V. L. (1987). Technology for the prevention of "les maladies produites par la masturbation". *Technology and Culture, 28*(4), 828–832.

Calhoun, G. R. (1856). *Report of the consulting surgeon on spermatorrhoea, or seminal weakness, impotence, the vice of onanism, masturbation, or self-abuse, and other diseases of the sexual organs.* Philadelphia, PA: Howard Association, printer.

Comfort, A. (1969). *The anxiety makers: Some curious preoccupations of the medical profession.* New York: Dell Publishing Company.

Darby, R. (2003). The masturbation taboo and the rise of routine male circumcision: A review of the historiography. *Journal of Social History, 36,* 737–757.

Darby, R. (2005). Pathologizing male sexuality: Lallemand, spermatorrhea, and the rise of circumcision. *Journal of the History of Medicine and Allied Sciences, 60*(3), 283–319.

Degler, C. N. (1974). What ought to be and what was: Women's sexuality in the nineteenth century. *The American Historical Review, 79*(5), 1467–1490.

Domingo, R. (2017). Thomas Sanchez. In J. Witte, Jr. & G. S. Hauk, *Christianity and family law: An introduction* (pp. 245–258). New York: Cambridge University Press.

Ellis, H. (1900). *Studies in the psychology of sex (Vol. 1): The evolution of modesty, the phenomena of sexual periodicity, auto-erotism.* Philadelphia, PA: F. A. Davis.

Engelhardt Jr., T. (1974). The disease of masturbation: Values and the concept of disease. *Bulletin of the History of Medicine, 48*(2), 234–248.

Foucault, M. (2003). *Abnormal: Lectures at the College de France 1974–1975.* (G. Burchell, Trans.), V. Marchetti & A. Salomoni (Eds.). New York, NY: Picador.

Foucault, M. (1978). *History of sexuality (Vol. 1): An introduction* (R. Hurley, Trans.). New York, NY: Pantheon. (*HS1*).

Gardner, A. K. (1870). *Conjugal sins against the laws of life and health, and their effects upon the father, mother, and child.* New York: J. S. Redfield.

Gay, P. (1984). *The bourgeois experience: Victoria to Freud (Vol. 1).* New York: Oxford.

Gilbert, A. N. (1975). Doctor, patient, and onanist diseases in the nineteenth century. *Journal of the History of Medicine and Allied Sciences, 30*(3), 213–234.

Gilbert, A. N. (1980). Masturbation and insanity: Henry Maudsley and the ideology of sexual repression. *Albion: A Quarterly Journal Concerned with British Studies, 12*(3), 268–282.

Gullette, M. M. (1994). Male midlife sexuality in a gerontocratic economy: The privileged stage of the long midlife in nineteenth-century age-ideology. *Journal of the History of Sexuality, 5*(1), 58–89.

Hall, L. A. (1992). Forbidden by God, despised by men: Masturbation, medical warnings, moral panic, and manhood in Great Britain, 1850–1950. *Journal of the History of Sexuality, 2*(3), 365–387.

Hall, L. A. (2003). "It was affecting the medical profession": The history of masturbatory insanity revisited. *Paedagogica Historica, 39*(6), 685–699.

Hare, E. H. (1962). Masturbatory insanity: The history of an idea. *Journal of Mental Science, 108*(452), 1–25.

Hodgson, D. (2005). Spermatomania—the English response to Lallemand's disease. *Journal of the Royal Society of Medicine, 98*, 375–379.

Holtzman, E. M. (1982). The pursuit of married love: Women's attitudes toward sexuality and marriage in Great Britain, 1918–1939. *Journal of Social History, 16*(2), 39–51.

Howe, J. W. (1883). *Excessive venery, masturbation and continence: The etiology, pathology and treatment of the diseases resulting from venereal excesses, masturbation and continence.* New York: Bermingham & Co.

King, W. H. (1897). *Treatise on spermatorrhea, impotence, and sterility.* New York: A. L. Chatterton & Co.

Laqueur, T. W. (2003). *Solitary sex: A cultural history of masturbation.* New York: Zone Books.

Lallemand C. A. (1847). *Practical treatise on the causes, symptoms, and treatment of spermatorrhoea* (H. J. McDougal, Trans.). London: Churchill.

Macdonald, R. H. (1967). The frightful consequences of onanism: Notes on the history of a delusion. *Journal of the History of Ideas, 28*(3), 423–431.

Makari, G. J. (1998). Between seduction and libido: Sigmund Freud's masturbation hypotheses and the realignment of his etiologic thinking, 1897–1905. *Bulletin of the History of Medicine, 72*(4), 638–662.

Malthus, T. R. (1798). *An essay on the principle of population, as it affects the future improvement of society.* London: J. Johnson.

Mason, M. (1994). *The making of Victorian sexuality.* New York, NY: Oxford University Press.

McArdle, T. E. (1888). The physical evils arising from the prevention of conception. In P. F. Munde (Ed.), *The American Journal of Obstetrics and Diseases of Women and Children,* (Vol. 21). New York: William Wood & Co.

Miller, G. P. (2001). Law, self-pollution, and the management of social anxiety. *Michigan Journal of Gender & Law, 7*(2), 221–290.

Milton, J. L. (1854a). On the nature and treatment of spermatorrhoea, part 1. *Lancet, 63 (1592: March 4),* 243–246.

Milton, J. L. (1854b). On the nature and treatment of spermatorrhoea, part 2. *Lancet, 63 (1593: March 11),* 269–270.

Milton, J. L. (1854c). On spermatorrhoea, part 1. *Lancet, 63 (1600: April 29),* 467–468.

Milton, J. L. (1854d). On spermatorrhoea, part 2. *Lancet, 63 (1605: June 3),* 595–596.

Mumford, K. J. (1992). "Lost Manhood" found: Male sexual impotence and Victorian culture in the United States. *Journal of the History of Sexuality, 3*(1), 33–57.

Nakajima, S., Uchida, H., Suzuki, T., Watanabe, K., & Kashima, H. (2009). Selective serotonin reuptake inhibitor-induced spermatorrhea in 2 patients. *Journal of Clinical Psychiatry, 70*(8), 1192–1993.

Neuhaus, J. (2000). The importance of being orgasmic: Sexuality, gender, and marital sex manuals in the United States, 1920–1963. *Journal of the History of Sexuality, 9*(4), 447–473.

Neuman, R. P. (1975). Masturbation, madness, and the modern concepts of childhood and adolescence. *Journal of Social History, 8*(3), 1–27.

Phillips, B. (1843a). Observations on seminal and other discharges from the urethra, with illustrative cases, part 1. *Boston Medical & Surgical Journal, 28*(2: 2/15/1843), 35–39.

Phillips, B. (1843b). Observations on seminal and other discharges from the urethra, with illustrative cases, part 2. *Boston Medical & Surgical Journal, 28*(5: 3/8/1843), 89–97.

Phillips, B. (1843c). Seminal and other discharges from the urethra. *Boston Medical & Surgical Journal, 28*(21: 6/28/1843), 413–415.

Ranking, W. H. (1843). Observations on spermatorrhoea: Or the involuntary discharge of the seminal fluid. *Provincial Medical Journal and Retrospect of the Medical Sciences, 7*(162), 93–95.

Rush, B. (1812). *Medical inquiries and observations, upon the diseases of the mind*. Philadelphia, PA: Kimber & Richardson.

Sexual disorders, part 1. (1870a). *The Lancet, 96* (2446; July 16, 1870), 89–90.

Sexual disorders, part 2. (1870b). *The Lancet, 96* (2447; July 23, 1870), 124–126.

Sexual disorders, part 3. (1870c). *The Lancet, 96* (2448; July 30, 1870), 159–160.

Sexual disorders, part 4. (1870d). *The Lancet, 96* (2450; August 13, 1870), 224–225.

Smythe, J. (1841). Miscellaneous contributions to pathology and therapeutics: Impotence and sterility. *Lancet*, 779–785.

Spitz, R. A. (1952). Authority and masturbation: Some remarks on a bibliographical investigation. *The Psychoanalytic Quarterly, 21*(4), 490–527.

Spitzka, E. C. (1887a). Cases of masturbation (masturbatic insanity), part1. *Journal of Mental Science, 33*(141), 57–73.

Spitzka, E. C. (1887b). Cases of masturbation (masturbatic insanity), part 2. *Journal of Mental Science, 33*(142), 238–254.

Spitzka, E. C., (1887c). Cases of masturbation (masturbatic insanity), part 3. *Journal of Mental Science, 33*(143), 395–401.

Spitzka, E. C., (1888a). Cases of masturbation (masturbatic insanity), part 4. *Journal of Mental Science, 34*(145), 52–61.

Spitzka, E. C., (1888b). Cases of masturbation (masturbatic insanity), part 5. *Journal of Mental Science, 34*(146), 216–225.

Stengers, J., & Van Neck, A. (2001). *Masturbation: The history of the great terror* (K. A. Hoffmann, Trans.). New York: Palgrave.

Stolberg, M. (2000). An unmanly vice: Self-pollution, anxiety, and the body in the eighteenth century. *Social History of Medicine, 13*(1), 1–22.

Stolberg, M. (2003). The crime of Onan and the laws of nature. Religious and medical discourses on masturbation in the late seventeenth and early eighteenth centuries. *Paedagogica Historica, 39*, 701–717.

Tissot, S. A. D. (1832). *Onanism: Or, a treatise upon the disorders produced by masturbation: Or the dangerous effects of secret and excessive venery*. New York, NY: Collins & Hannay. (Originally published in 1758.)

Wade, P. (1962). The history and development of the Library of the Royal Society of Medicine. *Proceedings of the Royal Society of Medicine, 55*(8), 627–636.

Wilder, A. (1870). Conjugal sins. *The American Eclectic Medical Review, 5*(11), 490–497.

Wilson, M. (1856a). Contributions to the physiology, pathology, and treatment of spermatorrhœa: part 1. *The Lancet, 68*(1721: August 23), 215–217.

Wilson, M. (1856b). Contributions to the physiology, pathology, and treatment of spermatorrhœa: part 2. *The Lancet, 68*(1724: September 13), 300–302.

Wilson, M. (1856c). Contributions to the physiology, pathology, and treatment of spermatorrhœa: part 3. *The Lancet, 68*(1731: November 1), 482–484.

Wilson, M. (1856d). Contributions to the physiology, pathology, and treatment of spermatorrhœa: part 4. *The Lancet, 68*(1737: December 13), 643–644.

Wilson, M. (1857). Contributions to the physiology, pathology, and treatment of spermatorrhœa: part 5. *The Lancet, 69*(1754: April 11), 376–377.

Wu, M., Hao, N., Zhou, D. (2016). Spermatorrhea and loss of libido induced by topiramate: First case report and review of literature. *Clinical Neuropharmacology, 39*, 325–326.

Zachar, P., & Kendler, K. S. (2023). Masturbatory insanity: The history of an idea, revisited. *Psychological Medicine*, May 29:1–6. doi:10.1017/S0033291 723001435. (Epub ahead of print.)

Chapter 4

Surveillance, Confession, Medicalization: Foucault on the Masturbation Crusade

In the last chapter, I detailed the doctrines of the infamous eighteenth- and nineteenth-centuries' medical anti-masturbation campaign, or "masturbation crusade." I now turn to Foucault's account of the crusade's tactics and functions, presented in the ninth lecture of his *Abnormal* series, titled "the problem of masturbation" (2003, p. 231), delivered on March 5, 1975.

This chapter's exposition of Foucault's analysis of the masturbation crusade involves a change of emphasis from the first chapter's account of theoretical doctrines regarding the deployment of sexuality. Foucault wants to show how medical power functioned during this period to bring about the pathologization of masturbation and the medicalization of sexuality in everyday family life. Consequently, he focuses not on broad theoretical doctrines but on specific techniques and the functions they might serve: "To account for this phenomenon we should examine the tactics rather than the themes of this campaign, or the crusade's themes as indicators of its tactics" (2003, p. 237). I will generally follow Foucault in this emphasis.

As we shall see, Foucault postulates that tactics such as surveillance of the child or adult suspected of masturbation, confession of masturbation to the doctor, use of restraints provided by physicians to prevent masturbation, and other such tactics that medicalized family life were at the core of the masturbation crusade's social impact and acceptance. These tactics, he argues, fulfilled its primary function of emotionally intensifying family life around the dangers of child sexuality to solidify the newly emerging nuclear family. As a secondary function, medicalization also provided an entry point into the family

DOI: 10.4324/9781003480396-4

by State power, and the focus on sexual pathology in children distracted parents from the State's takeover of children's education. In the course of presenting aspects of Foucault's analysis of crusade tactics, I add additional evidence for his claims about crusade tactics gleaned primarily from leading medical journals of the time, while also disputing some of his functional claims.

To place Foucault's lecture in perspective, the 1975 lecture course's topic was "the emergence of the abnormal individual in the nineteenth century" (Davidson, 2003, p. xvii). Foucault sees the social focus on the masturbator as the culmination of a three-step process of creating power/knowledge to regulate a normalized society—that is, a society run not by forceful exclusion of what is repugnant but by positively structuring life according to norms and ideals. Foucault sees here a reflection of the difference between the medical response to leprosy, which was exclusion, and the response to the plague, which was to restructure a town's life to control its spread. His overall discussion of the process of normalization covers a broad canvas, focusing in turn on the "monster" who commits incomprehensible crimes and is excluded, the "incorrigible" socially deviant individual who cannot be corrected, and finally the masturbator, as prototypical types to be regulated. This canvas stretches from the late Middle Ages through to psychoanalytic theory in the early twentieth century and details how theories of sexuality were used to justify the deployment of new techniques of power to be wielded by medical authorities.

This series of lectures occurred just as Foucault's signature book on power, *Discipline and Punish*, and his book-length account of the history of sexuality and critique of psychoanalysis, *The History of Sexuality*, *Vol. 1* (*HS1*), were being published initially in French (Foucault, 1975; 1976) and shortly thereafter in English (Foucault, 1977; 1978). The lectures thus represent a moment of extreme productivity and lucidity in Foucault's theorizing. Rather than the book entirely superseding the lectures, the lectures and *HS1* are complementary and mutually elucidating, and I will rely on both. In particular, the lectures contain more detailed analyses of the masturbation crusade and the Oedipal theory than appear in the book. As one reviewer put it, "some of Foucault's grand formulations in his better-known book publications qualify as condensations of arguments he developed more extensively in lectures like the ones published in *Abnormal*" (Puff, 2006, p. 252).

The Explanatory Riddle of the Masturbation Crusade

In Chapter 3, I noted the bewildering fact pointed to by Hare and others that, although there had been sporadic moral and religious censure of masturbation in earlier times (and Foucault, too, in lectures prior to the one on masturbation, considers earlier religious and confessional approaches to such acts), the eighteenth century saw a rather sudden and thoroughgoing transformation of anti-masturbation sentiment into a medical issue. Recall that Hare marveled at how such a "sudden change in the climate of opinion" of a magnitude that "we can scarcely imagine" (1962, p. 2) could occur without any evidence to support it. It is this remarkable phenomenon and how to explain it that Foucault poses as the core topic in his ninth lecture: "There is a problem then. How was it that such an extensive and indiscreet crusade broke out so suddenly in the middle of the eighteenth century?" (2003, p. 235).

We saw in Chapter 3 that Foucault is not alone in thinking that some explanation is needed. There are dozens of proposed explanations, but they remain unsatisfyingly nonspecific. Unlike some of the historians who have taken on this puzzle, Foucault understands that the challenge of proposing a new explanation for such a vast and complex historical phenomenon must be approached with appropriate humility: "I cannot guarantee that I will provide a solution to the problem. I can even say that in all likelihood I will only provide a very imperfect sketch of a solution. But we must try to make some progress" (2003, p. 237).

Foucault, as we shall see, provides a novel explanation of the appeal and influence of the anti-masturbation campaign in terms of the distinctive social functions the campaign performed in its historical period. Foucault sees the masturbation crusade as having two essential functions, the constitution of the nuclear family and the medicalization of family life. Paradoxically, one function is to close up the nuclear family by entangling its members with each other and distancing them from others, while the other function is to open up the nuclear family to the external influences of the medical profession and other State influences. Foucault argues that the "entangling" tactic also makes the family more amenable to State intrusion because parents who are urgently concerned about their children's possible sexual activities will be less concerned that the State is taking over educational functions and training their children to fulfill State needs. By emotionally cementing together members of the nuclear family and subjecting their relationships to outside authority, the crusade facilitated the momentous transformation occurring at the time from the extended family wholly responsible for its children to the nuclear family with the State taking responsibility for education. Foucault's functional explanation is aimed at making sense of why the crusade had the broad appeal and immense social influence that it did despite its lack of scientific foundation.

It is no objection to Foucault's functional analysis that other proposed explanations may have also played a role in acceptance of the crusade's assumptions. Indeed, Foucault seems to accept one such explanation, that the crusade offered a way to explain phenomena that were not explained by the recent advances in pathological anatomy, thus shoring up medical expertise and authority:

> In other words, at the end the eighteenth and the beginning of the nineteenth centuries, when pathological anatomy was identifying a causality of lesions in the body that founds nineteenth-century clinical and positive medicine, a campaign against masturbation brought to light around sexuality, or more precisely around autoeroticism and masturbation, a different medical causality, a different pathogenic causality, that plays both a supplementary and conditional role with regard to the organic causality being identified by the great clinicians and pathological anatomists of the nineteenth century. Sexuality enables everything that is otherwise inexplicable to be explained.
>
> (2003, p. 241)

However, this does not explain the specific nature of the crusade's doctrines and tactics, and it is not Foucault's basic account.

Foucault Versus the Marxists on the Masturbation Crusade

Foucault's initial challenge is to clear the ground by arguing persuasively against the then-dominant neo-Marxist explanation of the masturbation crusade, that the crusade's suppression of sexuality was aimed at redirecting the sexual energy of workers to the needs of the capitalist labor market. Commenting on Van Ussel's (1972) recently published book on the history of sexual repression that elaborates the Marxist position, Foucault says:

> [Van Ussel] gives considerable and, I think, just attention to the appearance of masturbation as a problem in the eighteenth century. Broadly speaking, Van Ussel's explanatory schema is hastily drawn from Marcuse. It consists in saying that with the development of capitalist society, the body, which until then Van Ussel says was an 'organ of pleasure,' becomes and must become an 'instrument of performance,' of the performance necessary for the requirements of production. Hence there is a split, a caesura in the body, which is repressed as an organ of pleasure and is codified and trained instead as an instrument of production and performance.
>
> (Foucault, 2003, pp. 235–236)

Foucault argues against Van Ussel's neo-Marxist explanation on several grounds. First, he claims that it is so vague that it cannot be falsified: "Such an analysis is not false and it cannot be false because it is so general" (2003, p. 236). However, Foucault goes on to argue rather persuasively that it is false, so it is not clear that he is on firm Popperian ground here. In any event, given Foucault's penchant for broad and evidentially elusive theoretical-historical claims of equal vagueness and generality, he appears to be throwing this stone from a glass house.

Foucault's second objection is that Van Ussel's (1972) analysis primarily invokes what Foucault considers "negative" concepts of power, that is, exercises of power that suppress desires or actions or enforce limitations on individuals—for example, the suppression of sexual desire and forcing the individual's body to be an "instrument of performance" for production. This emphasis appears to Foucault to have the problem that "they do not reveal the number of positive and constitutive effects produced in the history of society by campaigns like the crusade against masturbation" (2003, p. 236)—that is, they do not explain how the crusade created positive new forms of behavior and desire, such as surveillance of children and the reconceptualization of children as constantly at risk of disease due to premature sexual activity, that served purposes of social power. This notion of the positive workings of power is central to Foucault's perspective on how power works.

The problem with this riposte to Van Ussel is that, assuming that Foucault is correct about the positive workings of power, it is not clear that Van Ussel's analysis cannot encompass the systems of behavior and value modification that Foucault considers positive power structures. For example, Van Ussel might appropriate Marcuse's (1955; 1964) emphasis on "false consciousness"—the process of internalizing the value system of the ruling class in a manner that perpetuates and justifies one's own station—which would seem to be a positive structure in Foucault's sense. More generally, a common feature of Marxist-type critiques is that society is structured to cultivate desire and manage its satisfaction in order to maintain a class of reasonably satisfied workers, and this would fall under positive tactics of power. In taking as his target a simple top-down ruling-class repressive version of Marxism, Foucault sets up a purely negative-power straw man.

In any event, the prominence of positive structures of power is itself potentially at issue between Foucault and the Marxists, and cannot be assumed without potentially begging the question.

Foucault's main and most persuasive objection to Van Ussel's hypothesis is of a more traditional philosophy-of-science sort, namely, that as a theory it fails to adequately explain specific, salient features of the masturbation crusade: "However, I do not think it gets us very far in explaining the fine details of this campaign and crusade" (2003, p. 236). In particular, Foucault argues, both in the lecture and *HS1*, that the hypothesis fails to explain four crucial features of the crusade—its focus on masturbation, on children and adolescents, on the bourgeois class, and on idle women:

[T]he crusade essentially concerns children and adolescents from a bourgeois milieu....If it really was purely and simply a question of repressing the body of pleasure and celebrating the productive body, then one would normally expect to see a repression of sexuality in general and, more precisely, of the sexuality of the adult in work or, if you like, of the adult worker's sexuality. However, we are dealing with something different, not with the

questioning of sexuality but of masturbation, and of the masturbation of bourgeois children and adolescents. I think that we must try
to account for this phenomenon by a somewhat more detailed
analysis than that given by Van Ussel.

(Foucault, 2003, pp. 236–237)

If one writes the history of sexuality in terms of repression, relating
this repression to the utilization of labor capacity, one must suppose
that sexual controls were the more intense and meticulous as they
were directed at the poorer classes; one has to assume that they
followed the path of greatest domination and the most systematic
exploitation: the young adult man, possessing nothing more than
his life force, had to be the primary target of a subjugation destined
to shift the energy available for useless pleasure toward compulsory
labor. But this does not appear to be the way things actually
happened. On the contrary, the most rigorous techniques were
formed and, more particularly, applied first, with the greatest
intensity, in the economically privileged and politically dominant
classes....[I]t was in the 'bourgeois' or 'aristocratic' family that
the sexuality of children and adolescents was first problematized,
and feminine sexuality medicalized; it was the first to be alerted
to the potential pathology of sex, the urgent need to keep it under
close watch and to devise a rational technology of correction. It
was this family that first became a locus for the psychiatrization
of sex....

As for the adolescent wasting his future substance in secret
pleasures, the onanistic child who was of such concern to doctors
and educators from the end of the eighteenth century to the end of
the nineteenth, this was not the child of the people, the future
worker who had to be taught the disciplines of the body, but rather
the schoolboy, the child surrounded by domestic servants, tutors,
and governesses, who was in danger of compromising not so much
his physical strength as his intellectual capacity, his moral fiber, and
the obligation to preserve a healthy line of descent for his family
and his social class.

For their part, the working classes managed for a long time to
escape the deployment of 'sexuality.'

(1978, pp. 120–121)

Another line of analysis that Foucault wields against the neo-Marxist account is that the crusade was primarily about medical disease, not the morality of a proper devotion to work over pleasure: "When one forbids children to masturbate one threatens them with an adult life crippled by illness, rather than an adult life lost in debauchery and vice. That is to say, there is not so much a moralization as a somatization and pathologization of masturbation" (2003, p. 237). Foucault distinguishes three variations of the crusade's somatization: masturbation is considered a total illness that devastates an individual with every imaginable horrible symptom; it is identified as the etiology of a vast array of further disorders; and individuals can interpret whatever physical symptoms they have later as due to earlier masturbation. Foucault comments on the totality of the illness:

> We recognize here the portrait of the young masturbator with its fundamental characteristics: exhaustion, loss of substance, an inert, diaphanous, and dull body, a constant discharge, a disgusting oozing from within the body....The entire body is covered and invaded with not a square inch left unaffected. Finally, there is the presence of death, since the skeleton can already be seen in the loose teeth and cavernous eyes.
>
> (2003, p. 238)

He also notes the endless other diseases that physicians attribute to masturbation, including meningitis, encephalitis, myelitis, bone disease and degeneration, eye disease, heart disease, consumption, and madness: "we constantly find in this literature the idea that, for example, although masturbation has no specific symptomatology, any illness whatsoever can derive from it" (2003, p. 241).

This leads Foucault to emphasize that a further reason for doubting Van Ussel's neo-Marxist explanation is that it fails to explain the crusade's medicalization of sexuality:

> It would be inadequate, in fact, to see this campaign—in a perspective close to Reich that has inspired recent works by Van Ussel—as no more than a process of repression linked to the new requirements of industrialization.... It places sexuality, or at least the sexual use of one's own body, at the origin of an indefinite series

of physical disorders whose effects may be felt in every form and at every age of life. The unlimited etiological power of sexuality at the level of the body and illnesses is one of the most constant themes not only in the texts of this new medical ethics but also in the most serious works of pathology.

(2003, p. 327)

Foucault thus rejects the common view—reflective not only of neo-Marxists like Marcuse in *Eros and Civilization* (1955) and *One-dimensional Man* (1964) but also of Freud in *Civilization and Its Discontents* (1930)—that the demands of modern society require the suppression or redirection of sexuality which then causes neurotic symptoms:

In short, I would like to reject the linear progression that goes from the constitution of the conjugal family for economic reasons, to the interdiction of sexuality within this family, to the pathological return of this sexuality and neurosis due to the interdiction and finally to the consequent problematization of infantile sexuality. This is the schema that is usually accepted.

(2003, p. 265)

The "linear" schema that Foucault describes—essentially neo-Marxist with a Freudian spin—is that the nuclear family is formed and its sexuality is repressed to allow for its economic exploitation, with the result that repressed sexual longings reemerge in the form of neurotic symptoms. The "problematization" of childhood sexuality manifested in the masturbation crusade then occurs as a way to address the roots of the neuroses resulting from excessive sexual repression that are interfering with productivity.

In rejecting this analysis, Foucault is not merely arguing that a fuller account must attend to aspects of the campaign, noted above, that go unaddressed in that model. He is also saying that the causal structure of the neo-Marxist model is wrong. He proposes instead that the crusade, rather than being only a result of the constitution of the nuclear family and its economic exploitation, was also instrumental in the stable creation of the nuclear family and is a cause, not only a result:

[T]he hunting down of masturbation does not seem to me to be the result of the constitution of the restricted, cellular, substantial, and conjugal family. Far from being the result of the constitution of this new type of family, it seems to me that the hunting down of masturbation was rather the instrument of this constitution. It was through this crusade that the nuclear and substantial family was gradually constituted. The crusade, with all its practical instructions, was a means of compressing family relationships and closing up the central parent-child rectangle into a substantial, close-knit, and emotionally saturated unit. One way to coagulate the conjugal family was to make parents responsible for the children's bodies, for the life and death of their children, by means of an autoeroticism that had been rendered fantastically dangerous in and by medical discourse.

(2003, p. 264)

For Foucault, the fear of the child's masturbation played an integral role in creating, solidifying, and sustaining the intense intimacy of the nuclear family and thus was part of what made the emergence of the nuclear family possible. The crusade found ready acceptance because it fit well with the restructuring of relationships necessary for changed social circumstances and offered emotional compensation to its members for educational functions that were being increasingly annexed by the State.

I now turn to the detailed tactics by which Foucault thinks that the masturbation crusade, under the guise of medical concerns about sexuality, created novel positive structures for social regulation. In the discussion of tactics that follows, I will often add examples beyond those presented by Foucault to amplify and support his point or to illustrate the nature of the processes to which he refers. Although the two functions and their various tactics overlap and intertwine, I consider them separately, starting with surveillance and related processes.

Surveillance and Interrogation of the Suspected Masturbator by Parents and Schools

According to Foucault, the tactic most directly serving the function of constituting the nuclear family is the parents' relentless and intrusively intimate surveillance and interrogation of the child or adolescent to guard against masturbation, entangling them with the child. Moreover, the surveillance of the child is accompanied by precautionary vigilance regarding outsiders to guard the child against bad influences, unwanted knowledge, and above all seduction, and this also serves to strengthen the boundaries of the family. The tactic of medicalization (to be discussed below) supports surveillance because medical authority directs the family's surveillance, providing guidance in confronting the problem of masturbation and offering medical technology and intervention if needed. Because masturbation is autoerotic, solitary, and nonrelational and thus once commenced needs no external accomplices that might be observed, its control requires endless vigilance:

> [T]he sexuality of the child and adolescent is posed as a problem in the eighteenth century...in a nonrelational form, that is to say, it is the problem of autoeroticism and masturbation that is posed first of all: masturbation is hunted down and put forward as the major danger. From then on, bodies, actions, attitudes, appearance, facial features, beds, linens, stains, and so forth are brought under surveillance. Parents are required to hunt for odors, traces, and signs. I think that this represents the installation, the establishment of one of the new forms of relations between parents and children: a kind of extensive parent child physical clinch begins that does not seem to me to be characteristic of every family but only of a certain form of the family in the modern period.
>
> (2003, pp. 263–264)

Actually, the family space must be a space of continual surveillance. Children must be watched over when they are washing, going to bed, getting up, and while they sleep. Parents must keep a lookout all around their children, over their clothes and bodies. The child's body must be the object of their permanent attention. This is the adult's primary concern. Parents must read their child's body like a blazon or as the field of possible signs of masturbation. If the child has a pale complexion, if his face is wan, if his eyelids are bluish or purplish, if he has a certain languid look and has a tired or listless air about him when he leaves his bed, the reason is clear:

masturbation. If it is difficult to get him out of bed in the morning: masturbation. Hence it is necessary to be present at the important and dangerous moments of going to bed and getting up. Parents must also organize a series of traps that will enable them to catch the child at the very moment he is committing what is not so much a fault as the cause of all his illnesses.

(2003, pp. 245–246)

To underscore the point, Foucault quotes from the advice offered to parents by the physician Leopold Deslandes (1797–1852):

Keep your eye on a child who seeks out the dark and solitude, who remains alone for a long time without being able to give good reasons for his isolation. Direct your vigilance principally to the moments following going to bed and just before getting up; it is then above all that the masturbator can be caught in the act. His hands are never outside the bed and generally he likes to hide his head under the blankets. Scarcely has he lain down than he seems to be plunged into a deep sleep: this circumstance, always mistrusted by an experienced man, is one that contributes most to cause or nourish the parents' security…. When one uncovers the young man one suddenly finds his hands, if he has not had time to move them, on or nearby the organs he abuses. One may also find the penis erect or even traces of a recent emission: The latter may even be recognized by the special odor coming from the bed or with which his fingers are impregnated. Generally mistrust young people who, when they are in bed or while they sleep, often have their hands in the position I have just described.
(Deslandes, 1835, pp. 369–372, as quoted by Foucault, 2003, p. 246)

With regard to children, Foucault (1978) describes the masturbation-crusade period as one in which children were paradoxically considered naturally nonsexual and yet ever in danger of sexual self-abuse:

A pedagogization of children's sex: a double assertion that practically all children indulge or are prone to indulge in sexual activity; and that, being unwarranted, at the same time 'natural' and 'contrary to nature,' this sexual activity posed physical and moral, individual and collective dangers;…children were defined as 'pre-liminary' sexual beings, on this side of sex, yet within it, astride a dangerous dividing line. Parents, families, educators, doctors, and eventually psychologists would have to take charge, in a contin-uous way, of this precious and perilous, dangerous and endan-gered sexual potential: this pedagogization was especially evident in the war against onanism, which in the West lasted nearly two centuries.

(1978, p. 104)

Regarding youth, Foucault links the denial of the naturalness of masturbation to the view that, despite the development of sexual urges, the developmental trajectory of sexuality portends loftier functions. Indeed, it was a widespread Victorian view that retention of semen in adolescence is necessary for normal growth:

After all, purity (in the sense of continence) *is* of the first importance to boyhood. To prolong the period of continence in a boy's life is to prolong the period of *growth*…. To introduce sensual and sexual habits—and one of the worst of them is self-abuse—at an early age is to arrest growth, both physical and mental.

(Carpenter, 1899, pp. 487–488)

Consequently, surveillance not only of adolescents but also of pre-adolescents who might be initiating the harmful habit was particularly warranted:

[T]hose people who conducted this crusade frequently insisted that…masturbation did not have an endogenous causality. To be sure, the warming up of the humors with puberty, the development of the sexual organs, the accumulation of liquids, the tension of the walls, and the general irritability of the nervous system could all explain why the child masturbates, but the child's natural develop-ment must be exonerated of masturbation…. That is why when the doctors of the time raise the question of masturbation they insist on the fact that masturbation is not linked to natural development, to the natural thrust of puberty, and that the best proof of this is that it occurs before puberty. Starting in the end of the eighteenth century, we regularly find observations on masturbation in prepubescent children, and even in very young children.

(2003, p. 242)

As another expression of the surveillance mentality, Foucault quotes physician J. B. De Bourge: "Children should be supervised from the cradle" (1860, as quoted by Foucault, 2003, p. 243). Foucault comments:

[W]e see here the establishment of a whole family drama with which we are quite familiar and which is the great family drama of the nineteenth and twentieth centuries: the little theater of the family comedy and tragedy with its beds, its sheets, the night, the lamps, with its stealthy approaches, its odors, and the carefully inspected stains on the sheets; the little drama that brings the adult's curiosity ever closer to the child's body.

(Foucault, 2003, pp. 246–247)

Indeed, the crusade even encourages the parent to sleep with the child, not in order to soothe or comfort but to improve surveillance:

[O]ne comes across the instruction...of the immediate physical presence of the adult beside, alongside, almost on the child. If need be, say doctors such as Deslandes, one should sleep beside the young masturbator, in the same room and possibly in the same bed, in order to prevent him from masturbating.

(Foucault, 2003, p. 247).

By way of illustration, Foucault recounts a case reported by Rozier (1830) in which a caretaker suspected masturbation in a female charge and from that moment would "share her bed at night with the young patient" while "during the day she did not let her out of her sight for an instant" (pp. 229–230; as quoted in Foucault, 2003, p. 247).

The ever-present danger from outside negative sexual influences that might prematurely sexualize the child caused family life to be reorganized around the endless task of surveillance:

[I]t may be a deliberate stimulation, more perverse than careless, by nurses, for example, who want to get children to sleep. It may be pure and simple seduction by servants, private tutors, and teachers.... Servants, governesses, private tutors, uncles, aunts, and cousins will all come between the parents' virtue and the child's natural innocence and introduce a dimension of perversion.... What is required...is essentially a new organization, a new physics of the family space: the elimination of all intermediaries and the suppression, if possible, of domestics, or at least a very close supervision of domestics, the ideal solution being the infant alone in a sexually aseptic family space.

(Foucault, 2003, pp. 244–245)

One might be tempted to argue that once the nuclear family formed, the increased closeness gave rise to sexual awareness and surveillance of family members. Foucault defends the opposite thesis that it is the crusade's required sexual surveillance that helped to create and sustain the new more intimate nuclear form of family life:

Until the middle of the eighteenth century the aristocratic or bourgeois family (since the campaign is limited to these forms of the family) was above all a sort of relational system. It was a bundle of relations of ancestry, descent, collateral relations, cousinhood, primogeniture, and alliances corresponding to schemas for the transmission of kinship and the division and distribution of goods and social status. Sexual prohibitions effectively focused on these kinds of relations. What is now being constituted is a sort of restricted, close-knit, substantial, compact, corporeal, and affective family core: the cell family in place of the relational family.... In other words, I am not inclined to say that the child's sexuality that is tracked down and prohibited is in some way the consequence of the formation of the nuclear family, let us say of the conjugal or parental family of the nineteenth century. Rather, I would say that this sexuality is one of the constitutive elements of this family.... I would say that the small, affective, close-knit and substantial family that is characteristic of our society and that arose at the end of the eighteenth century was constituted... around the child's body. It is this...surveillance that was the basis of the modern family.

(Foucault, 2003, pp. 248–249)

It is the parents who are given the primary burden of surveillance, and this challenge restructures the family and its power relations both internally and in relation to external medical authorities. No matter what the immediate cause, the parents are to some extent blamed for the problem of masturbation because the cause is partly one of insufficient isolation and surveillance of the child by the parents:

> Parents are denounced as the real culprits for the child's 'abuse' of his sexuality: It is the absence of supervision, the neglect, and especially that lack of interest in the bodies and conduct of their children that leads parents to entrust their children to wet nurses, servants, and private tutors, that is to say, to all those intermediaries regularly denounced as initiators into debauchery (Freud will take his first 'seduction' theory from this).
>
> (Foucault, 2003, p. 327)

Family life is restructured, moving from the traditional extended family structure incorporating many outside helpers with permeable family boundaries to the nuclear family with its relatively closed boundaries, and becoming more child-focused:

> The need for a new relationship between parents and children and, more broadly, for a new system of relationships within the family emerges from this campaign: the solidification and intensification of father-mother-children relationships (at the expense of the multiple relationships that characterized the large 'household'); the reversal of the system of family obligations (which previously went from children to parents but now tend to make the child the primary and ceaseless object of parental duties that extend to their moral and medical responsibility for their descendants); the appearance of the principle of health as a fundamental law of family ties;...and finally, the need for an external medical control and knowledge to arbitrate and govern these new relationships...as a new apparatus of knowledge/power.... The small incestuous family that is characteristic of our societies, the tiny, sexually saturated family space in which we are raised and in which we live, was formed from this.
>
> (2003, pp. 327–328)

An examination of the crusade's medical literature attests to the reality of the extraordinary focus on surveillance described by Foucault. Although Tissot's treatments were relatively tame by later Victorian standards, involving mostly alterations in diet and exercise, he also inaugurated the crusade's signature intervention of surveillance. For example, he reports on the case of a prince whose health was declining. Once the physician discovered the cause, frequent masturbation, surveillance proved to be the only pathway to cure: "The habit was so strong, that the most pressing considerations forcibly stated to him could not eradicate it. The evil progressed, he lost strength daily, and was saved only by guarding him day and night for more than eight months" (Tissot, 1758/1832, p. 48).

Lallemand, too, emphasized surveillance as a preferred method, even with very young children:

The most anxious parents believe that there is no occasion to watch over the actions of their children with regard to their genital organs, previously to the epoch of puberty; and few even of our own profession, are led to suspect bad habits before that period. This is a fatal error against which it is necessary to be on our guard: numerous cases may give rise to abuses, at a much earlier period— infancy being hardly exempt from them.

(Lallemand, 1847, p. 94)

British psychiatrist Fielding Blandford's (1871) much reprinted textbook, *Insanity and Its Treatment*, asserts that the brain of the masturbator undergoes "permanent damage from the constant irritation to which it has been exposed by the habit" (p. 248) thus potentially yielding insanity or paralysis. Dismissing all standard remedies as inefficacious, Blandford concludes that "nothing but close personal watching will really stop it" (p. 248).

An article in the British Medical Association's magazine, *The Doctor*, reports that "in certain schools where the boys had nocturnal emissions, the night nurses prevented them laying on the back, and turned them on their side" (M. Verneuill on Spermatorrhoea, 1877, p. 115). The same article illustrates that surveillance and interruption alone are at times sufficient treatment for masturbation:

An Englishman or an American, among others, had at a specified time in the night erections followed by emission. M. Ricord had placed two servants near him, who awakened the patient as soon as erection took place. This was only required to be repeated a certain number of times for the patient to be cured, after all other therapeutic methods had proved fruitless.

(M. Verneuill on Spermatorrhoea, 1877, p. 115)

The close examination and interrogation of children until a confession is obtained was also a virtual obsession in boarding schools, especially schools for boys. Examination of students for hints of masturbation was carried out by school personnel, with potential dire consequences for boys suspected of the practice, as illustrated by this report in *The British Medical Journal* (forerunner of *The Lancet*):

Not long since, we had the opportunity of talking over this subject with the experienced head-master of one of our best smaller schools; and he told us of the excellent results obtained by direct and careful supervision of the boys under his charge. Wherever he happens to be during term-time, whether in the playground, or in the chapel, or in the class-room, his watchful eye is always on the look out;...If any lad droop in health and spirit without sufficient cause, if he mope or pine without actually being ill, the case is considered one for inquiry, and a careful investigation is made. Suppose an assistant-master comes to him, and says: 'I can't make out what is the matter with So-and-so; he has grown pale and listless, his memory is much worse than it used to be, and he seems to take no interest either in work or play. He says there is nothing the matter with him, but there is no doubt that he is quite a different boy from what he was six months ago.' This report is speedily followed by a summons to the head-master's study, who addresses the offender in something like the following terms. 'Mr. —— has mentioned to me that you are not doing so well as formerly, although that you are not specially ill; and I can perceive a change in your appearance within the last few weeks. Now, if you know of any reason for this, tell me at once, or think the matter over a little, and come back again tomorrow, when we can have another talk.' Usually the boy makes a clean breast of it at once; and, after a full and kindly explanation of the evil tendencies of his present course, promises an amendment, which is, in most cases, satisfactorily carried out. If, on the other hand, he decline to confess, and be slow to reform, he is very plainly told that such a contaminating influence can no longer be permitted to remain in the school; and this threat is duly carried out in the very rare cases where bad practices have obtained an ungovernable hold over the lad's moral nature.

(A grave social problem, 1881, pp. 904–905)

According to the unnamed medical correspondent, these concerns even caused some parents to wonder "whether the possibly exaggerated benefits of a public-school training may not impossibly be counterbalanced by the danger of acquiring habits, which may leave their permanent and disastrous impress on the mental and physical development of after-years" (A grave social problem, 1881, p. 905).

The view that surveillance is a critical intervention was sustained by the vestiges of the crusade into the early years of the twentieth century. Max Huhner, at the time the chief of the genitourinary department at Mt. Sinai Hospital in New York, held a moderate view that while "masturbation is the most widespread of sexual diseases" (1916, p. 1), nonetheless the consequences were at the neurotic level and "masturbation, no matter how severely indulged in, never leads to idiocy, insanity, or sexual perversion" (p. 2). Despite this moderate view, he still strongly endorsed the tradition of surveillance and in his popular textbook suggests a rather tricky interrogation technique to obtain a confession:

It is of no use to ask a boy directly if he masturbates, as in the vast majority of cases he will positively deny it, and it often requires the greatest tact on the part of the physician to get at the truth. The most important point in the diagnosis of this condition is: to bear in mind the possibility of such a disease in all cases of inexplicable nervousness or psychic symptoms.... The physician should not neglect an examination of the genitals in any suspicious case, and very often the local symptoms will tell the tale. In young boys, after an examination of the genitals by the physician, whether he finds anything there or not, it is often advisable for the physician, if he is reasonably sure of his ground from the general symptoms, to tell the boy immediately after the examination that he masturbates. The boy, being taken off his guard, if guilty, will imagine that the physician can tell by the examination, and will often admit the truth at once.

(Huhner, 1916, pp. 5–6)

William Acton, whose views were described in Chapter 3, strongly endorses this tradition of surveillance. As a preventive measure in the case of children, Acton promotes continuous watchful examination of the child along with stern warnings:

Preventive Treatment. — I cannot but think that much of this evil could be prevented, by wisely watching children in early life; and, where a sexual temperament, a suspicion of the practice having been only recently indulged in, or other circumstances render it desirable, by pointing out the dreadful evils that result from the practice, and kindly but solemnly warning them against it.... It is not to be denied, however, that there are great difficulties in the way of carrying out this protective method.... In addition to the instinctive shrinking which every right-minded person must feel from putting ideas of impurity into a child's innocent mind, a parent's pride leads him to hope that his boy would not indulge in any such mean and disgusting practices...I have myself no hesitation as to the advice I should give to parents in such matters. In all cases, I would tell them, the best preventive step to be taken is to watch their children.

(Acton, 1875, pp. 40–42)

For Acton, watchful prevention means that any sign of possible irritation to the genital area must be followed up:

Nothing of course can be more important than carefully to guard against unnecessary irritation from whatever cause...If, for instance, a child wets his bed—which is generally almost the first indication the parents have of the presence of irritation—the organ should be examined, and the boy's other habits watched.... The slightest symptom, however, of the existence of any such cause should never be neglected.

(Acton, 1875, p. 6)

Much like Freud, who (as we shall see in Chapter 5) implored physicians not to be fooled into misattributing masturbation-caused neurasthenia to other more obvious and easily ascertained causes, Acton prods physicians to be suspicious and worries that physicians will take nervous system, digestive, and other physical complaints as rooted in organic causes without exploring whether there is a sexual cause: "Abuse of the sexual feeling has often been the cause which has first produced the head symptoms, and it unfortunately too often happens that the primary cause of the complaint is ignored, while the subsequent symptoms are treated as if the brain had been primarily affected" (1875, p. 154).

Even in severe cases of supposed masturbatory insanity, the primary treatment was often surveillance and the use of various paraphernalia to prevent masturbation and thus reduce nocturnal emissions. For example, E. C. Spitzka, in a multi-part article concerning maturbatory insanity in the *Journal of Mental Science* (the forerunner of the *British Journal of Psychiatry*), presents a case of a 26-year-old single man to illustrate "a pure and typical case of insanity in a youth, resulting from self-abuse practiced in early years, and without any complicating factors, such as heredity, hebephrenia, or overwork" (1887, p. 64). The main treatment, other than some periods in the asylum, consists of intensive surveillance and prevention of emissions aided by the use of various instruments of medical technology—although in this case success was elusive:

[I]t was found necessary to place his hands in muffles to prevent his practising self-abuse.... [A]s the symptoms marking his relapses were usually noticed to be most marked in the morning, I had his bedding examined, and it was found, on every subsequent occasion, when his expression on rising was vacant, listless, and silly, or when causeless laughter occurred, that it presented the evidences of seminal emissions. Careful watching was resumed, and revealed that the patient still masturbated.... A jacket with endless sleeves had meanwhile been made.... For two months this device fulfilled all expectations; neither voluntary nor involuntary seminal discharges occurred. He continued improving.... After this period, it began to be noticed that he would frequently stand in one spot gazing at vacancy. Examination showed that he had succeeded in provoking the orgasm by femoral friction.

The knee-pieces which I had originally suggested, but which the local physician had delayed obtaining, were now applied. Unfortunately, they failed; the patient had become able to effect his purpose without any friction whatever. I then had him taken...to the nearest large city (St. Louis), where Dr. Bauer performed an operation on the prepuce, calculated to interfere with or to stop his vice.... During the past three years his physical condition, after a slight improvement, remained stationary.

(Spitzka, 1887, pp. 64–68)

Foucault is thus on safe ground in seeing a remarkable degree of intrusive, intimate, and seemingly obsessive surveillance of the child—and adults—as a core feature of the masturbation crusade. He is correct that this feature is so intensive in nature that an attempt at understanding its occurrence and its effects on the family is warranted. His account, that the effect of the surveillance was to entangle the family and thus to close and constitute the nuclear family, is at least consistent with the phenomenon. Whether this was indeed its effect, and whether, if so, this effect was its function and explains why it continued to occur, are hypotheses requiring more evidence. Foucault's larger claim that, in the parents' intently watching for evidence of movement of the sheets or stains in the bed that will reveal the child's self-touching, "it is around this suspect bed that the sexually irradiated and saturated and medically anxious modern family was born" (2003, p. 258), is evocative and intriguing but speculative.

The Medicalization of Sexuality

A second function of the masturbation crusade postulated by Foucault is the opening of family life to external State authority through the medicalization of sexuality. Once masturbation is framed in terms of medical consequences—as a "dangerous, inhuman, and monstrous X from which any illness may derive" (Foucault, 2003, p. 250)—the family dealing with it requires a link to medical authority.

[T]he internal parental control that fathers and mothers are required to exercise is necessarily plugged in to an external medical control. Internal parental control must model its forms, criteria, interventions, and decisions on medical reasons and knowledge. Parents are told that they must watch over their children because they will become ill, because this or that physiological, functional, and potentially even lesional problem will occur that doctors are familiar with. The parents-children relationship...must extend the doctor-patient relationship. The father or mother...must at the same time be...diagnosticians, therapists, and agents of health. But this also means that their control is subordinate, that it must be open to medical and hygienic intervention, and that they must call upon the external and scientific authority of the doctor at the first warning signs. In other words,... [the family's concern about illness] plugs it into a technology, into an external medical power and knowledge. The new substantial, affective, and sexual family is at the same time a medicalized family.

(2003, p. 250)

At the level of medical tactics, Foucault offers two examples of how the masturbation crusade systematically introduced medical power into the family: confession to the physician and the technology of the restraint of masturbation, both of which I review below. I am going to add a third medical tactic alluded to but not documented as fully by Foucault, the use of physically intrusive medical interventions, ranging from blistering of the penis and cauterization of the urethra to circumcision and, rarely, castration.

Confession to the Doctor

The first tactic of medicalization is requiring that the child confess to the doctor, not only to a priest or parent. From parents' surveillance of the child and their strongly worded suspicions and warnings, a confession may emerge, but it then must be given to the doctor who will treat the problem, introducing medical power into the family's system. So, surveillance goes hand-in-hand with the intrusion of medical authority into the family's life and "the endowment of [the family's] new space with a medical rationality":

Parents must watch over their children, spy on them, creep up on them, peer beneath their blankets, and sleep beside them. However, as soon as the sickness is discovered they must call in the doctor to cure it.

It will only be a genuine and effective cure if the patient accepts it and participates in it. The patient must acknowledge his illness, understand its consequences, and accept the treatment. In short, he must confess. As all the texts of the crusade say, the child cannot and must not confess to his parents. He can only confess to the doctor.

(2003, pp. 250–251)

When painful or intrusive treatment was involved, there was sometimes an almost inquisition-like pursuit of confession by the physician as a prelude to deciding whether to engage in or continue the treatment. One treatment commonly used to stop masturbation was the application of a chemical caustic substance to create a blister on the penis that would make it so painful to the touch that it would dissuade the child or youth from even touching the penis let alone masturbating. These blisters were often inflicted repeatedly over a period of time to prevent the recurrence of masturbation. The physician was then faced with the challenge of deciding when to end the blistering and thereby take a chance on the patient's self-control, of which many physicians were dubious. The cessation of the painful treatment and the gamble of reliance on the patient's self-control therefore depended on the physician's belief in the truthfulness and commitment of the patient, evidenced in the patient's confession, as this article in *The Lancet* explains:

Considerations of moral strength or weakness, and the presence or the want of truthfulness, must be the chief guides to the surgeon in determining how long the blisters or other applications should be continued. Many patients who earnestly desire to lay aside the practice of masturbation would be unable to do so if they were not aided by the soreness of the penis; and they will then be inclined to cling to this help after the habit is effectually broken. The only general rule that can be laid down is to err, if at all, in the direction of caution; and not to lay aside the blisters, unless entire reliance can be placed upon truthfulness of the patient, without first making arrangements for continued examination of the urine, so that any loss of semen may at once be detected and checked, if necessary, by returning to the applications.

(Sexual disorders, part 3, 1870, pp. 159–160)

This focus on the truthfulness and reliability of the patient's confession is illustrated by excerpts from cases of spermatorrhea reported in a three-part article by Dr. Benjamin Phillips (1843a; 1843b; 1843c) in the *Boston Medical & Surgical Journal* (later the *New England Journal of Medicine*). Phillips was a follower of Lallemand, and the paper is aimed at illustrating the success of Lallemand's major treatment technique, cauterization of the urethra, based on the theory that excessive irritation had occurred due to excess stimulation ("if you give any canal too much to do, you will ultimately develop irritation in it" [1843a, p. 36]), and "thus involuntary discharges, consequences of masturbation or excesses, are explained" (p. 36). His technique varied depending on whether the primary cause of the symptoms is voluntary masturbation, thus a matter of self-restraint ("Lunar caustic will be powerless unless the patient has sufficient determination to abstain from the practice" [p. 38]), or involuntary emissions, for which abstinence does not provide a cure and invasive intervention is required ("here a remedy must be found by the surgeon" [p. 38]).

The following are excerpts from two of Phillips's reported cases. The first is a 22-year-old man who had cardiac and digestive symptoms:

CASE 1.-...After examining the heart, which afforded no evidence of anything beyond functional disturbance, I was struck with the apparent languor, the downcast, unquiet look, and hypochondriacal expression of the patient, and my suspicion was at once awakened as to the cause of this state of things. I requested his mother, who accompanied him, to leave the room; when I told him at once that the cause of his present discomfort was the abuse of his sexual organs. At first he hesitated, but only for a moment, and then admitted that to a certain extent my impression was correct. When further pressed, he said that, living in the country, and being a good deal alone, about four years before he began to addict himself to masturbation; that the habit soon took such firm hold of him that scarcely a day occurred in which he did not recur to it at least twice.... I assured him that all his sufferings were owing to his indulgence in this baneful habit.

(1843b, pp. 90–91)

This case underscores the salient role of confession in these cases, often triggered by a firm accusation from the physician. When Phillips "told him at once that the cause of his present discomfort was the abuse of his sexual organs," the patient hesitated and then admitted to it, making treatment possible. Phillips mentions that the patient reported a previous consultation with another physician in which the patient had not confessed the magnitude of the problem, and so had simply been cautioned by the physician, leading to a worsening of his condition. Phillips treated this patient with cauterization, and when he was seen a week later, "his spirits were much improved;... with the exception of the fifth night no emission had taken place" (1843b, p. 91).

In another case, a man of 24 suffered from melancholy, lassitude, chronic abdominal pain, tinnitus, and impotence.

> Case III.—...I at once saw from the history of the case, and the cast of his countenance, that seminal discharges or excesses were at the bottom of his sufferings; but the probabilities were in favor of other modes of excitement than sexual intercourse. I charged him with masturbation, and, with a little hesitation, he confessed it. He had carried it to a very considerable extent, oftener twice than once a day.... He abstained lately from masturbation, but the frequency of the discharges was not lessened by it. By night and by day they still occurred, and, to use his own expression, 'life seemed leaking away.'... [T]he caustic was immediately applied.... I saw him at the end of four days from the application of the caustic, when his spirits were much improved.... I learned from Mr. Joseph that he rapidly recovered, and completely; and that he is at present quite free from any disorder of the sexual organs.
>
> (1843b, pp. 92–93)

The confessional process is quite explicit here. Phillips "charged him with masturbation, and, with a little hesitation, he confessed it" (1843b, p. 92). In both cases, the physician makes a firm judgment and accuses the patient. Given the widespread occurrence of masturbation, it is not surprising that under such conditions the patient is likely to confess. Phillips's assessment procedure is sure to lead to further accusations if success is not achieved: "If by the end of six weeks...*very decided amendment, or* a cure, be not produced, we may conclude either that an insufficient application of caustic has been made, or that the fatal habit is still persisted in" (1843a, p. 38).

These case excerpts suggest that Foucault is correct to emphasize not only the process of confession to the physician but also the remarkable list of infirmities and symptoms that were attributed to masturbation. Note that the core symptoms of general debility and nervous weakness as well as gaunt appearance are similar to conditions later labeled as neurasthenia, a point to which I will return in Chapter 5. It is also notable how the spermatorrhea diagnosis dramatically extended the domain of masturbation-crusade intervention, such that no actual masturbation, even for years prior to the consultation, was necessary to reach the diagnosis. For example, in Case III above, despite the patient abstaining from masturbation, "the frequency of the discharges was not lessened by it." Phillips also reports another case in which an addiction to masturbation in school days was conquered, but many years later "the irritation which had been set up continued, and induced nocturnal emissions" (1843b, p. 93).

The Medical Technology of Control

The second and quite troubling tactic identified by Foucault in the medicalization of family life is the extensive use of ingeniously designed paraphernalia of various kinds to prevent individuals, including children, from masturbating. For cases in which surveillance, interrogation, and warnings failed to deter the masturbator, and such treatments as vigorous exercise, cold baths, tonics, and moderate diets fail to work, the crusade's physicians provided an elaborate technology of masturbation control devices to parents who preferred to avoid more extreme remedies such as blistering, cauterization, or circumcision. These devices served to solidify the growing intrusion of medicine into family life:

The problem of instruments for preventing masturbation also shows how familial power is connected with medical power. To prevent masturbation the family must become an agency for transmitting medical knowledge. Essentially, the family must function merely as a relay or transmission belt between the child's body and the doctor's technique.

(2003, p. 251).

Foucault reviews in some detail the devices used in the masturbation crusade's inquisition of children and youths, emphasizing the way that this technology was linked to medical authority:

Children are made to sleep with their hands tied and attached by cords to the parent's hands, so that the adult will be awakened if the child moves his hands. There is the story, for example, of an adolescent who, of his own free will, was tied to a chair in the room of his elder brother. There were little bells on the chair and he slept like that. Whenever he moved during the night, wanting to masturbate, the bells rang and his brother woke up.... There are the famous nightshirts...with low drawstring hems and corsets and bindings. There is...a sort of metal corselet that was attached to the pelvic area with, for boys, a little metal tube lined with velvet and with a number of holes pierced at the end through which he could urinate. The device was closed, padlocked and opened only once a week in the presence of the parents so the child could be cleaned.... There are mechanical devices like Wender's cane,...a little cane that was split up to a certain point, hollowed out, placed on the boy's penis and tied up ... to keep voluptuous sensations at bay.

(2003, pp. 247, 252)

A distinctive American invention aimed at combatting nocturnal emissions and spermatorrhea—that became known in England as the "American cure"—consisted of a ring worn on the penis at night with spikes pointed inward that would stick into the penis if there was an erection during the night. It appears to have first been reported in the *Boston Medical & Surgical Journal* in 1853:

Treatment of Spermatorrhoea.—With the difficulties connected with the treatment of obstinate cases of this malady, most practitioners are familiar. Books without number have been written on the subject.... For several years past some of the very worst forms in which the disease presents itself, have been terminated in a short time, and the sufferer restored to permanent health, by a mechanical contrivance, which originated, it is believed, in Boston. The way to proceed is this: Take a piece of firm harness leather one inch wide, and make a ring or ferrule, which shall be one eighth of an inch greater in diameter than the penis. Thrust the points of four pins, equidistant from each other, through the walls of the ring, so that they will project through a little way on the inside, and then cut off the projecting part of the pins on the outside. On retiring for the night, slip the ring on the organ, midway, and insert cotton wool between the two, to keep the pins from pricking the flesh. An emission seldom occurs without a full distension of the penis. The theory of a cure, as well as the facts, are simply these. When an erection takes place, and even before, the uniform enlargement presses the cotton, which yields, causing the points of the pins to enter the flesh, and thus the patient is instantly awakened. This occurs as frequently as distension comes on, and the semen is therefore retained.... After interrupting the emission a few times in this way, the morbid tendency in many cases is removed, and the sickly, feeble youth rallies and regains his health.

(Treatment of Spermatorrhoea, June 1853a, pp. 445–446)

Yankee ingenuity being what it is, the same article reports a recent technological advance in the construction of such devices, with perhaps a promotional motive as well:

Last week an instrument was left on sale at Dr. Cheever's, under the Tremont Temple, in this city, that acts precisely like the leather ring. It is made of steel, however, clasping like a dog's collar, according to the size required, and having on its inner edge a row of sharp points. Within this steel ring is another, extremely delicate, which opens to receive the penis, and retains it exactly in the middle. When it begins to distend, the small ring allows the member to enlarge till it strikes the sharp points, and then the individual is awake and safe.

(Treatment of Spermatorrhoea, 1853a, p. 446)

The journal published several enthusiastic follow-up comments on the usefulness of the spermatorrhea rings, attesting to robust demand and continued innovation in design:

An article on spermatorrhoea, June 29th, was read with interest.
The next day a patient with that difficulty applied for relief. It was
decided to pursue the plan described in the article alluded to....
Cold water was to be applied to the thighs and back at bedtime, and
the ring put upon the offending member, the points of the tacks
being well protected with cotton. The patient informed me, a few
days after, that he had followed my directions, but was not careful
about a sufficient quantity of cotton around the points of the tacks;
yet the purpose was answered, for he was aroused by them, in the
midst of a lascivious dream, and then 'vowed to the saints and
blessed Virgin' ever after to follow the doctor's directions. The
patient presented himself to-day, and informed me that no emission
had troubled him since the first trial of the instrument.... The case
was of two years' standing, and had produced great despondency.

(Perry, 1853, pp. 16–17)

Treatment of Spermatorrhrea.—Since the first notice in this Journal
of spermatorrhrea rings, rapid improvements have followed in the
mechanism of the instrument by which the cure is effected. Dr.
Cheever...has had a demand for them that shows the estimation in
which they are held by sufferers. It is useless to attempt a cure in
these cases, with medicine. This mechanical contrivance, scarcely six
months old, is superior to any method heretofore proposed.... The
inner ring is covered with wash leather, and by means of a stud,
supporting it equidistantly from the outer side, when the teeth begin
to act, they are all brought into action at once. The material is
silver, neatly manufactured.

(Treatment of Spermatorrhoea, 1853b, p. 144)

Spermatorrhoea Rings.—Quite a revolution has been effected in
New England, in less than a year, by the use of a mechanical
invention, instead of medication, in the treatment of a formidable
malady.... It is a condition resulting, in most instances, from the
indulgence of a pernicious vice.... Some suffer intensely, and even
die, from excessive indulgence in this vice. Schools, too, and
colleges, are often the nurseries of this degrading habit, which
carries many young men to an early grave, often without the true
cause being suspected.... The rings, which this Journal was the first to

announce, are a sure remedy for involuntary forms of the disease....
Dr. Cheever has shown us another improvement of the instrument. It
is far lighter than the former patterns, and the middle ring is better
balanced in the centre of the large one. The simplicity of the
adjustment to any sized organ, makes it more economical, too, which
is a consideration not to be overlooked.

(Spermatorrhoea rings, 1853, pp. 209–210)

Despite the elegant design and popularity of spermatorrhea rings,
the American pragmatic spirit would not rest there. A sophisticated
improvement was soon developed for those hesitant about having
nails rend their penile flesh. This newer technology used a bell rather
than pain to perform surveillance and awaken the sleeper before any
emission could occur:

M. Moniere, a hospital student, had a brother who for the last
fourteen years, ever since the age of nineteen, had suffered from
spermatorrhea, with erections. The patient was almost rendered
sleepless, for as soon as sleep commenced the young man had
erections and seminal emissions. Several persons passed the night at
his bedside, with the injunction to awaken him so soon as erection
ensued; and his brother invented a very ingenious apparatus to
which he had given the name of electromedical alarm. A small, very
light ring was attached in front of the pubis by cords; two cords
make this ring communicate with the poles of a pile [i.e., a battery—
JW]; the penis is introduced into the ring so that contact takes place,
but no kind of pressure; on the contrary, as soon as the penis
becomes erect the smallest pressure makes the battery to work. In
order not to disturb neighbours, the bell is made very feeble; but
then it is necessary that an india-rubber tube should make the bell
communicate with the ear. Since the patient had used this instrument the spermatorrhea had almost altogether disappeared, gradually, and his general condition had greatly improved.

(M. Verneuill on Spermatorrhoea, 1877, p. 115)

As an aside, every invention no matter how well intended can be
misused. Regarding the electric erection alarm, in a case study I read
long ago it was used by a gentleman to wake him upon having an

erection, but, opposite of its intended function, to allow him to masturbate each time an erection occurred.

To prevent younger children from touching their genitals, constricting waist-coats, large gloves, shirts with endless sleeves, and other restraining devices were commonly used. As Gullette (1994) observes: "The younger the client, though, the tougher the regime could be. Some boys (and girls too) had their hands tied to the bed or were made to wear a night appliance that prevented them from touching their genitals" (p. 74). We shall see in a later chapter that Freud's Little Hans was subjected to such a device.

These medical technologies of restraint and control were an undeniably oppressive way of linking the family to medical authority:

[C]ontinuity is established between medicine and patient through what could be described as a widespread physical persecution of childhood and masturbation in the nineteenth century that, without having the same consequences, was almost as extensive as the persecution of witches in sixteenth and seventeenth centuries.... [B]y calling upon the doctor and by receiving, accepting, and when necessary applying the remedies he prescribed, the family linked sexuality with a medicine that previously had in practice related to sexuality only in a very distant and indirect way. The family itself became an agent of the medicalization of sexuality within its own space.... A medico-familial mesh organizes a field that is both ethical and pathological in which sexual conduct becomes an object of control, coercion, examination, judgment, and intervention. In short, the medicalized family functions as a source of normalization.... It is this family that reveals, and which from the first decades of the nineteenth century can reveal, the normal and the abnormal in the sexual domain. The family becomes not only the basis for the determination and distinction of sexuality but also for the rectification of the abnormal.

(2003, pp. 253–254)

Surgery, Castration, and Other Invasive Procedures

The deployment of medical power in the control of masturbation took many technical forms. Beyond the common treatments provided to families such as strait jackets, chastity devices, spiked penis rings, and other constraining devices, there was a more serious tier of medical treatments such as blistering of the penis, cauterization of the urethra, and passing needles through the prostate, done by the physician. Beyond these, there was the use of surgery in more difficult cases of masturbation and spermatorrhea.

The most common techniques, as we saw above, were blistering and cauterization of the urethra. John Milton, a leading medical expert on spermatorrhea, in one installment of a four-part article in *The Lancet* in 1854 "On the Nature and Treatment of Spermatorrhoea," reviewed typical interventions. Milton expresses strong reservations about standard remedies such as medications, aperients, sedatives, tonics, vigorous exercise, intensive study, and focused mental activity, suggesting that the latter might even have the opposite of the intended effect ("The most absorbing study will not suffice to quench entirely a natural passion" [1854, p. 245]). To address relatively mild cases of masturbation with nocturnal emission, where "physical weakness is the predominant symptom" along with "irritability, headache, and dyspepsia, with costiveness," Milton's preferred treatment is the use of a caustic chemical to cause blistering of the penis to make masturbation so painful that the individual will be forced to stop: "perhaps no remedy will act more quickly and surely than a blister" (1854, p. 245). For more severe cases, other than "a large opium plaster to the loins" (p. 246), Milton advises Lallemand's procedure of cauterization: "Along with blistering I have sometimes used injections of nitrate of silver to any part of the urethra which seemed diseased" (p. 246). Milton redesigned Lallemand's instrument for this purpose to make the application of the caustic more even and controlled, and, complaining that patients "bungle...every remedy put into their hands," he notes that cauterization has the great advantage that patients "have nothing to do; it is sufficiently powerful to keep the fingers quiet for a little time" (1854, p. 246).

Although not a first-line treatment, surgery was understood to be an acceptable potential treatment of severe masturbatory disease by authors publishing in the leading medical journals on both sides of the Atlantic, as an article in *The Lancet* in 1870 bluntly states: "In many cases the effects of masturbation will demand surgical treatment" (Sexual disorders, 1870, p. 160). Foucault only mentions a surgical technique in passing:

A surgeon, Lallemand, proposed inserting a permanent probe in the urethra....Lallemand used...the insertion of needles in the genital area....Napoleon's surgeon, Larrey,... proposed injecting a solution... that...caused lesions that took several days or weeks to heal during which time the boy did not masturbate. There was cauterization of the urethra and, for girls, cauterization and removal of the clitoris...'with a single slice of the lancet.'

(2003, p. 252)

A common surgical intervention for male masturbation was circumcision, and occasionally clitoridectomy for females. Lallemand (1847) had suggested circumcision as a treatment for spermatorrhea, and Acton (1875) strongly promoted the notion that irritation from a tight foreskin or from material accumulated under the foreskin was a major instigator of masturbation. This idea gained widespread attention and acceptance not only in Europe and England but in the U.S. as well (e.g., Hutchinson, 1890a, 1890b). For example, E. J. Spratling in the *Medical Record* wrote that in cases of masturbation, "circumcision is undoubtedly the physicians' closest friend and ally" as long as it was sufficiently thorough:

To obtain the best results one must cut away enough skin and mucous membrane to rather put it on a stretch when erections come later. There must be no play in the skin after the wound has thoroughly healed, but it must fit tightly over the penis, for should there be any play the patient will be found to readily resume his practice, not begrudging the time and extra energy required to produce the orgasm.

(1895, p. 442)

Given that masturbation was seen as potentially life-threatening, more dramatic surgical interventions were attempted in difficult cases using techniques too damaging to become common treatments. Severing of nerves to the penis to interfere with the functions of erection and pleasure was one such extreme surgical intervention reported in medical journals. Given the multiple nerves serving the penis, several approaches were tried. Spratling (1895) argued in the *Medical Record* that, for the treatment of masturbation among insane males, "complete section of the dorsal nerves of the penis is a rational procedure," although he acknowledged that, due to the enduring loss of function, this is "rather too radical for constant routine practice." For females, however, he thought that "nothing short of ovariotomy will be found to deserve even the term palliative" (1895, p. 442).

Clark and Clark (1899) took an alternative route to denying the masturbator penile functionality in an article in *The Lancet*. They justify their extreme intervention by noting that masturbation is "regarded as an incurable evil" because "in nineteen cases out of twenty moral suasion is utterly useless" and "mechanical means—some of them rather ingenious—have been tried, but the fury of the patient has torn to pieces all such restraints," thus "these cases have hitherto seemed hopeless" (1899, p. 838). However:

[I]t struck me...that only one means of cure was possible, viz.—a means that would not exercise mechanical restraint but would prevent sensation and therefore gratification. It occurred to me, when thinking out the nervous mechanism of the act, that by division of the afferent nerve of the reflex circuit not only would erection be impossible but sensation would be prevented.

(p. 838)

With this insight, and "having obtained the necessary consent," an operation to sever the pudental nerve was successfully performed on a 48-year-old man. The authors acknowledge that "It may be contended that this operation is not desirable in the majority of cases," and the patient did become "very much depressed." However, he gave up masturbation and his overall mental condition improved. The authors conclude that on balance it "is certain—that the mental result in this case justified the operation" (1899, p. 838).

Foucault briefly mentions the most extreme proposed surgical treatment of masturbation or spermatorrhea, castration—not as a Freudian fantasized threat but as a real surgical intervention (although surely the existence of the intervention and the use of the threat might have some relationship). Use of this extreme measure was of course controversial, and Foucault indicates that it was debated and defended:

The legitimacy of castrations or semicastrations was, of course, discussed in the nineteenth century. However, in 1835 the great theorist of masturbation, Deslandes, said that 'far from wounding the moral sense, such a decision is in keeping with the strictest requirements. We act as we do on other occasions when we amputate a limb; we sacrifice the secondary for the principal, the part for the whole'.

(Foucault, 2003, p. 253)

This was far from an abstract dispute. For example, Hamoway (1977) reports an instance in 1894 in which 11 boys in a Kansas mental institution were castrated, an action defended by many physicians and by the local paper on the basis that these boys were "confirmed masturbators" and thus a threat to the other boys in the institution's school. Leading medical journals published several cases in which removal of one or both testicles was undertaken to put an end to a patient's masturbation or spermatorrhea.

For example, in the first part of a five-part series in *The Lancet* on "Contributions to the Physiology, Pathology, and Treatment of Spermatorrhoea" (1856–1857), Marris Wilson, a leading spermatorrhea expert who attributed the condition to the practice of masturbation, reported a case of what one might label "treatment-resistant spermatorrhea." At the patient's insistence, removal of first one and then the other testicle was undertaken. Unhappily, this extreme measure was insufficient for cure. This outcome was in fact in accordance with Wilson's theory that the seminal vesicles could be the site of masturbatory irritation independent of the testicles, and he tells us that in treating his subsequent patients, "the correctness of my view has been fully confirmed" (1856–1857, p. 216).

Wilson's paper was not the first such report in a leading medical journal. Over a decade earlier, Josiah Crosby (1843) had published a case history in which bilateral castration was used to treat spermatorrhea, knowing that it would be highly controversial. The patient's condition was serious:

[The patient's] health had been declining for more than six years. He had secluded himself almost entirely from society, and even from his family....I found him pale, trembling and dejected—pulse frequent and feeble—appetite bad—digestion impaired, and rather emaciated....his family...fears that he would commit suicide.

(p. 10)

The history was typical:

About the age of 13 years he began to masturbate.... [H]e continued the habit more and more frequently, until he would perform the operation every day for several weeks in succession, and very often twice a day. At the age of 16 his health was so much impaired he was obliged to suspend all labor and active exercise.... After this time he says he did not practise masturbation much, but had been constantly troubled with involuntary discharges.

(p. 10)

Given the severity of the condition, the fact that the family was poor, and the many failed treatment attempts, Crosby reasoned: "[B]elieving the great constitutional disturbance to have been produced and kept up by the severe and often repeated shocks given to the brain and nervous system by the seminal emissions, and that removing the testicles would remove the great source of difficulty, I recommended castration" (1843, p. 11). The patient "was so miserable, and life itself had become such a burden to him, that he...urged me to perform it" (p. 11). Recovery was "very slow...until warm weather was established," and since then "he has improved rapidly" and now has "the appearance of good health" to the extent that he "is actively engaged in making arrangements to go into business" (pp. 10–11). Crosby acknowledges that "as to the propriety of this operation for the removal of such a disease, I admit there may be much doubt," but "the happy change produced in the patient, and the great relief afforded to the family, are abundant evidence of the propriety of the operation in this case" (pp. 10–11).

This case report engendered much controversy in the journal's pages, with commentary on both sides. Those disapproving of the operation had gone so far as to contact the patient and suggest to him that he had been mistreated so as to get him to publicly disavow the treatment. However, the patient's subsequent testimonial remained steadfastly positive. These events prompted a comment by A. McFarland (1844), who was familiar with the patient in question. He acknowledged that Crosby's procedure of removing the testicles is "undoubtedly unwarrantable as a general method of procedure in such cases" and appears cruel (pp. 177–178). He nonetheless defends Crosby's treatment partly on the grounds of the unusual intensity of the patient's attachment to his masturbatory habit: "[B]ut in the case before us, the patient labored under so strong an impulse…that though the discharge might be temporarily arrested, the detestable practice which laid the foundation of the evil would certainly continue, despite the best regulated treatment" (p. 178). His defense was ultimately based on the treatment's good outcome, which McFarland compares to an operation that gives a blind person his sight:

> From being an utter outcast from society, almost completely demented, and destined apparently to the life of a miserable recluse,… a complete metamorphosis has been effected both physically and mentally. Instead of being little better than a driveling idiot, as at the time of the operation…he is now actively engaged in mercantile pursuits, with mental vigor as well as physical capacity much above mediocrity.
>
> (p. 177)

The crucial point for McFarland is that Crosby has "restored to… society one of our species" and the patient "is raised to something more than a mere vegetable existence" (p. 178).

The Masturbation Crusade as Quid Pro Quo for Abandonment of the Child to Public Education

Toward the end of his lecture, Foucault returns for a final time to the question that motivated his investigation: "There is a question that requires an answer: Where did this campaign come from and what does it signify? What made masturbation emerge in this way as the major, or at least one of the major problems, in the relationship between parents and children?" (2003, p. 254). The two basic functions of the masturbation crusade—solidifying of the nuclear family and penetration of the family by medical authority—and the tactics that serve them have already been identified, but Foucault is here looking for a larger functional insight into the strategic importance and social functions of the crusade.

Foucault's answer is that the crusade's constitution of the nuclear family and introduction of medical regulation into the family represents, first, a process in which children's survival to become productive citizens is becoming more valued by the State:

Essentially, at the end of the eighteenth century the nuclear family… was called upon to take responsibility for the child's body…. Certainly, one of the reasons it was desirable to replace the loose, polymorphous, and complex apparatus of the large relational family with the limited, intense, and constant apparatus of the parental surveillance of children was the discovery of a political and economic interest in the child's survival…. The State demands from parents, and the new forms or relations of production require, that the costs entailed by the very existence of the family, by the parents and recently born children, are not squandered by the early death of children…. [T]his is certainly one of the reasons why parents are called upon to focus continuous and intense attention on the bodies of their children. This, I think, is the context in which we should set the crusade against masturbation.

(2003, pp. 254–259)

So, the idea is that a growing concern about children's health and survival in an increasingly complex society that requires trained workers expresses itself in an overwrought concern about masturbation. Foucault thus relates the masturbation crusade to concerns about the education of a skilled and capable workforce. This leads to a more surprising proposal that the underlying issue was a tension between "natural" family-mediated education with the advice of experts and State-provided education:

Really, it is only a chapter of a broader, well-known crusade for the natural education of children. What exactly is this idea of natural education…? It is the idea of an education that is first and foremost entrusted entirely, or in its essentials, to parents themselves as the natural educators of their children…. Natural education also means an education that conforms to a certain schema of rationality, to a number of rules for securing the survival of the children on the one hand and their training and normalized development on the other.

These rules and their rationality, like pedagogical and medical knowledge, belong to authorities like educators and doctors. In short, a series of technical authorities supervise and dominate the family itself. The call for natural education at the end of the eighteenth century is a call for an immediate contact between parents and children...and, at the same time, for the rationalization of parentchild relationships or their opening up to pedagogical or medical rationality and discipline.

(2003, pp. 255–256)

However, at the same time there were State aspirations to educate children outside of the family as they get older to prepare them for work. The implication is that families will thereby be giving up much of the traditional power and responsibility they had for the training of their children:

Now, and it is at this point that sexuality is encountered, what happens, at least at the level of the aristocracy and bourgeoisie, when parents are enjoined to take serious and direct responsibility for the physical existence of their children...and the possibility of their training? Parents are not only asked to train their children so that they will be useful to the State, but at the same time they are asked to cede back their children to the State and entrust, if not their basic education, then at least their instruction and technical training to an education directly or indirectly controlled by the State.... We need your children, it is said. Give them to us. We, like you, need these children to be normally formed. So entrust them to us so that we may form them according to certain norms.

(2003, p. 256)

The problem is how to wrest children out of the control of their families so that the State can prepare them effectively for their productive roles. Foucault proposes that this is accomplished via the masturbation crusade in the form of a subtle *quid pro quo* deal struck with families across developmental stages:

[A] process of exchange is called for: Take good care of your children's lives and health for us, of their physical strength, obedience, and ability, so that we can put them through the machine of the system of State education, instruction, and training over which you have no control.

I think that in this double request—'Concern yourselves with your children' and 'Let go of these children later'—the child's sexual body serves as the unit, so to speak, of exchange. Parents are told: There is something in the child's body that belongs imprescriptibly to you and that you will never have to give up because it will never abandon you: their sexuality.... However, when we create for you this field of power so total and complete, we ask you to give us in return your children's bodies, or, if you prefer, their abilities. We ask you to give us these children so that we can make of them something that we really need.... Thanks to their possession of the sexual body, however, parents will give up the child's other body of performance or ability.

(2003, pp. 256–257)

I said earlier that it seems paradoxical that one function of the crusade, entanglement, closes the family to external influences while another function, medicalization, opens it up to external influences. It can now be seen that for Foucault there is no paradox but rather a complementary relationship and a trade. The entanglement at an early age in some sense makes up to the family for the family's acquiescence to the State later having authority over education.

Foucault argues for this surprising claim about the relationship of the masturbation crusade to the rise of public education as follows:

The widespread demand for a State education, or for an education controlled by the State, is found precisely when the campaign against masturbation begins in France and Germany, that is to say, around 1760-1780.... In the same period, Basedow, in his *Philantropinum*, advances the idea that education for the more fortunate classes in society should take place in a State-controlled space of specialized institutions, rather than in the dubious space of the family.... [T]his is a period of the development of large educational establishments and schools throughout Europe.

(2003, p. 256)

Foucault thus argues that the sexualization of the child and the parental fear of masturbatory harm is integral to a new kind of compact between the family and the State. The State needs to socialize and educate children *en masse* for their roles in production. Yet, the family was the traditional locus of educational power. The masturbatory hysteria and the consequent intensification of sexual concern served, Foucault suggests, as a sort of sleight-of-hand by which parental attention was focused on one aspect of education, sexual hygiene, that was taken to be supremely important in its implications for health, whereas other aspects of education were then demoted and could be safely handed over to the State and to teachers in an implicit *quid pro quo*.

This view has interesting consequences for how one thinks about public education. Foucault observes that contemporary sexual education violates the original implicit compact between State and parent in which the child was "extracted" from the family by the State in return for ceding control over the child's sexual development:

> The child's sexuality is the trick by which the close-knit, affective, substantial, and cellular family was constituted and from whose shelter the child was extracted. The sexuality of children was a trap into which parents fell.... It was one of the instruments of exchange that allowed the child to be shifted from his family milieu to the institutionalized and normalized space of education. This worthless fictional element, this worthless money, was left in the parents' possession; worthless money to which, as you know, parents are enormously attached, since even in 1974, when the question arises of sexual education at school, parents who knew their history would have been justified in saying: We have been deceived for two centuries! For two centuries we have been told: Give us your children and you can take care of their sexuality; give us your children, but you will guarantee that their sexuality will develop in a family space controlled by you.... And now the psychoanalysts are saying: It's ours, the body of pleasure is ours! And the State, psychologists, psychopathologists, and others say: It's ours, this education is ours! This is the great deception in which parental power has been caught.

(2003, pp. 257–258)

In other words, according to Foucault, the transformation in the attitude toward the child's body as sexually dangerous created an intense closeness, and this along with the fear of external stimulation created a more closed, isolated family life of parent-child interaction. The reliance on medical authority then allowed medical power into the family and thus allowed the family's reshaping to be more open to authority, while the focus on masturbation allowed other aspects of the child's education to seem less urgent, thus easily displaced onto the State. The result is a more socially manipulatable family space and an implicit compact between the parent and the State that control of the child's sexuality is retained by the family whereas the child's education for economic productivity is given over to the State (although in fact the sphere given over to parents is a "fiction"). The result, Foucault avers, is the birth of the modern sexually and medically anxious enmeshed family.

Whether or not one accepts this story, one might argue that Foucault has at the very least pointed here to a great irony. The extraordinarily intense degree of anxiety of the modern bourgeois parent about correct educational and emotional childrearing so as not to inflict trauma on the child is matched only by the extraordinary extent to which such families hand over their children to State educational institutions, medical experts, and other State surrogates and experts for social training and preparation for economic and social life. The greater reliance on medical and other experts to guide intimate family life is essential for reducing the potentially unlimited anxiety created by the medical experts themselves about the possible harms inadequate emotional parenting might inflict. Today's parental concerns about controlling the child's environment so as to prevent various harms—such as low self-esteem, unruly temperament, self-indulgent mediocrity, lack of social acceptance, lack of preparation for the challenges of college and career, and so on—might be considered the modern equivalent of the intense concern about the feared masturbation of earlier times. Yet, despite these constant concerns, the actual control over the child's everyday life that is exercised by the distracted modern parent seems minimal relative to the control exercised by other institutions and agencies.

Commentary on Foucault's Analysis of the Masturbation Crusade

I have presented Foucault's masturbation-crusade analysis in some detail because it provides the background for his analysis of Freud's sexual theory of the neuroses and in particular the Oedipal theory, which he claims is an extension of the masturbation crusade. The presentation has been mainly expository. What is crucial to my analysis of Foucault's view of Freud is not so much whether Foucault's account of the masturbation crusade is entirely correct, but whether his ideas about the crusade are illuminating when applied to Freud's sexual theories and Oedipal theory. Nonetheless, I offer some brief evaluative comments before turning to other matters.

In making some initial judgments about the plausibility or implausibility of Foucault's masturbation-crusade analysis, we can take two cues from Foucault himself. The first is the degree of modesty he expressed about explaining such a vast and complex social phenomenon. Likely, the crusade has many strands of explanation.

Second, it seems appropriate to evaluate Foucault's claims in the same spirit and with the same evaluative strategy that Foucault himself deployed in his rather persuasive objections to Van Ussel's (1972) neo-Marxist account. Recall that Foucault's most evidentially sound tactic against Van Ussel was simply to show that Van Ussel's account did not possess adequate explanatory power to illuminate salient features of the crusade. Van Ussel's account, like Foucault's, is a functionalist account; they both argue that the crusade was maintained because it had certain social functions, although they differ on what those functions were. The enormous duration and scope of the masturbation crusade over so many countries and multiple centuries does suggest the possibility of functional reasons and not just a chance social event. Such proposed functional explanations can be challenged if the salient features of the structure do not appear to serve the proposed function. Thus, in response to Van Ussel's claim that the crusade had the function of suppressing sexual pleasures in favor of work performance, Foucault asked: Why, then, an initial concern with the upper and bourgeois classes rather than the working classes? Why a concern with masturbation rather than a concern with sexuality more generally? Why a prominent concern with children and adolescents rather than a focus on working adults? And, why medicalization rather than other, moral forms of social control? Van Ussel's view offered no direct answer, whereas Foucault's account, whatever its limits, does attempt to address these sorts of questions.

However, one can argue that Foucault's account also suffers from ample problems of explanatory inadequacy. From the perspective of evaluating Foucault's analysis, the run-of-the-mill masturbation-crusade medical journal cases presented above pose some questions. Contrary to the heart of Foucault's analysis, the crusade's medical literature was not primarily aimed at children or at the relationship between children and parents, although that is certainly one facet of the overall phenomenon and it may have been selectively left out of journals. Nonetheless, the primary target of the medical literature is adult men, not children and adolescents, and this is in *prima facie* conflict with Foucault's analysis. After all, the crusade's central semenic hypothesis of vital bodily fluids being lost during excessive masturbation did not even apply to prepubescent children and the crusade's doctrine was extended to nerve-shock theory to deal with the apparently anomalous cases of children and women. Children—at least, prepubescent children—were not the initial and primary domain of explanation of the crusade but rather an additional domain that had to be addressed by broadening the crusade's central doctrines. It is true that, given the increasing tendency at the time to delay marriage until economic viability, young men might have been more frequently living at home with parents (recall the physician above who reportedly sent one patient's mother out of the consulting room before bringing up the topic of masturbation). But even so, this would not necessarily fit Foucault's essential hypothesis that the crusade's target was specifically prepubescent and young adolescent children before the age of public schooling or during early schooling.

A glaring failure of perspicuity of Foucault's analysis is the remarkable fact that in a lecture analyzing the masturbation crusade and focusing on French sources Foucault does not mention sperma-torrhea even once, despite citing Lallemand (1847), whose most famous work was titled "Involuntary Seminal Losses" (*Les Pertes Seminales Involontaires*). As we saw, he notes Lallemand's influential treatments using urethral probes and needles, but fails to mention what Lallemand's treatments were for. Yet, the medical literature attests that spermatorrhea was at the core of the medicalization of masturbation throughout much of the later nineteenth century. This oversight is problematic because spermatorrhea—except in rare cases mentioned by some authors—cannot apply to prepubescent children. As the spermatorrhea craze underscores, the crusade's medical literature clearly locates the crusade's primary target not in early childhood but in youth and early adulthood.

Regarding Foucault's claim that the intensive surveillance of children served to entangle and close the family, one can safely say that such surveillance did occur, was recommended by physicians, and plausibly did have such effects. I will return below to the question of whether or not one can go further and accept the functional attributions that Foucault proposes.

As to the opening of the family to State influence through the medicalization of family life, looking at the details raises some doubts. There are two tactics that Foucault identifies as revealing the medicalization of family life: confession to the physician, and the introduction into the family of physician-prescribed technologies of restraint. Regarding Foucault's claim that confession of masturbation was reserved to the physician as a replacement for the priest, there is clearly some medicalization of confession, as we saw in the cases presented above. However, those were cases of adults. Contrary to Foucault's claims, when it comes to children and young adolescents, the confession was not specifically or even primarily reserved for the physician. It is clear in reading Acton's work that the surveillance and subsequent warnings when it comes to children and young adolescents are primarily intended to be handled by the parents themselves, and the physician is merely giving advice to parents on this matter rather than saying that the child must brought to the physician. Moreover, as we saw in passages quoted above, the massive surveillance in schools involves confessions that are not generally passed on to physicians but extracted and acted upon by the school's teachers and administrators. Granted, medical expertise in a more indirect way stands behind the parents' or schools' intrusive surveillance and obtaining of confessions. However, Foucault's claim that medicalization specifically and directly penetrates the family by the requirement that a confession must be presented to the physician appears incorrect (prior to psychoanalysis) in regard to the children, with which his analysis is primarily concerned.

Regarding technologies of restraint of children, Foucault is surely correct that this did create a conduit for medical authority to enter the home. However, Foucault further claims that the creation of this pathway of family medicalization was the function of the technology of restraint. The extended description I presented above of the literature on surgical interventions for masturbation and spermator-rhea poses a problem for Foucault's analysis—a problem of the same sort he poses against Van Ussel, namely, the lack of explanatory specificity. It is true that children, who live at home and are under the control of their parents, must be reached with medical restraints via the parents, and so in this instance there occurs a pathway from physician to family. But once the broader surgical interventions that were the main topic of relevant medical journal publications about the technology of the masturbation crusade are taken into account, Foucault's hypothesis is no longer tenable. The surgical interventions, from blistering and urethral cauterization to the extreme of castration, were not generally perpetrated on children and they were done directly by the physician and offered no pathway into the family, any more than any other surgical procedure. To single out certain waist-coats and gloves for children and claim that therefore the crusade's technology was aimed at medicalization of the family is like saying that the creation of aspirin is aimed at family medicalization because there is baby aspirin that must be given to the child by the parents upon medical advice. The phenomenon of medical control perpetrated on the population by the masturbation crusade is so much more general than the technologies applied to restrain children in the home that the hypothesis that the function of the crusade's medical technologies was family medicalization is implausible. The same point might be applied to surveillance and confession, for we saw above that adults with a history of masturbation were surveilled as intensively as children and that confession was applied to adults as readily as to children.

Finally, one must consider Foucault's claim that the ultimate function of the masturbation crusade was to facilitate the shift to State control over education. What is Foucault's evidence for this daring hypothesis? The reasoning that leads Foucault to this conclusion appears to involve a flimsy *post hoc ergo proper hoc* argument, that the masturbation crusade begins at about the same time that there is demand for State education.

Foucault claims that the ultimate function of the masturbation crusade is as a facilitator of the later separation of parents from their children for State-influenced training and schooling. It is true that over the period of the seventeenth to nineteenth century, schools gradually took over many educational functions that had been performed by the family. Indeed, we still see this process going on today in the controversies about the expansion of sexual education in schools. But the sheer fact that things were happening in two domains, medicine and education, at about the same time is not in itself persuasive evidence of the claimed causal relationship. To say that the demand for State-controlled education and the beginning of the masturbation crusade took place "precisely" (2003, p. 256) at the same time is an exaggeration concerning the relationship of the 200 year history of the crusade to the establishment of institutions for schooling throughout Europe, England, and America. More to the point, this hypothesis fails to explain why the crusade gained in influence and brutality and was more active than ever in the 1890s when extra-familial education had long been established as routine in the bourgeois classes. Nor does it posit any major correspondences between alterations in the crusade—for example, the elevation and then abandonment of the idea of masturbatory insanity, the advent of the spermatorrhea diagnosis, the addition of conjugal onanism, or even (according to Foucault) the extension of the crusade to Freud's theories—and alterations in the movement for State-controlled education. One would expect such correlations if the continuing *quid pro quo* Foucault describes is really in effect.

In correlating the initiation of the masturbation crusade with developments in education, Foucault is referring to the publication of Tissot's 1758 book published in French in 1760: "Soon after the publication of Tissot's book in France, the problem, the discourse, the immense jabbering about masturbation starts up and does not stop for a whole century" (2003, p. 233). However, at this point in its origins, at least, the crusade was not substantially about children—at least not about prepubescent children—thus denying Foucault one of his central claims about the targeting of young children. Tissot in fact argues that children are naturally nonsexual and that child masturbation is a pathological rarity: "We may remark here that masturbation is particularly injurious to children before the age of puberty; happily we find but few monsters of either sex who indulge in it before this period" (Tissot, 1758/1832, p. 46). This undercuts the significance of what Foucault hypothesizes as the crusade's driving *quid pro quo*, at least until a later time.

It is worth examining the timeline Foucault assumes in more detail. Foucault says that "Starting in the end of the eighteenth century, we regularly find observations on masturbation in prepubescent children, and even in very young children" (2003, p. 242). As evidence, Foucault cites five sources. The first three are anecdotes reported by Rozier (1830) in a book first published in 1806:

> Moreau de la Sarthe observed two little girls who were masturbating at seven years. In 1812, at the children's hospice on rue de Sevres, Rozier observed a seven-year-old imbecile who masturbated. Sabatier took statements from young girls who confessed that they had masturbated before they were six years old.
>
> (2003, pp. 242–243)

The fourth example is from a later book and concerns mentally disordered children: "In 1836, Cerise, in his *Medecin des salles d'asile*, says: 'In a ward, and elsewhere, we have seen children two and three years old carried away by completely automatic actions that would seem to suggest a special sensibility'" (2003, pp. 242–243). Consistent with Tissot's comment, these anecdotes identify a few observed cases as occurring in deviant individuals rather than claiming the regular occurrence of, or advocating for the need for routine attention to, child masturbation. Foucault offers only one example that involves a call to watch over prepubescent children due to a general danger, and that is from 1860, a full 100 years after Foucault claims the medicalization of child masturbation took place, in a passage noted above: "Finally, in 1860 in his *Memento du pere de famille*, De Bourge writes: 'Children should be supervised from the cradle'" (Foucault, 2003, p. 243). This, we saw in Chapter 3, is just after Lallemand argued that "Masturbation is generally commenced before puberty" (1847, p. 273). However, he also complained that prepubescent child masturbation happened in "numerous" cases (see above) and had until then been relatively ignored by the masturbation crusade: "I shall lay particular stress on such as act before puberty, because they have, hitherto, attracted very little attention" (1847, p. 119). This suggests that there was a turning point on this issue in the mid-nineteenth century.

However, if the early masturbation crusade prior to about the middle of the nineteenth century was not centrally aimed at pre-pubescents and was instead concerned primarily with adolescents and adults, then the timeline of Foucault's postulated exchange between the State and parents becomes problematic because it is in early to middle adolescence that schooling often begins. What, then, is supposed to be the period in a child's life that was "given" to the parents to intensively surveil in exchange for turning over the child to outside training that starts in adolescence? It seems that the coin of the exchange, for a period lasting over a century, was not only worthless but nonexistent.

Conclusion

Foucault attempts to make sense of what otherwise looks like an inexplicable two-century medical obsession with masturbation. Rather than invoking such standard explanations as misleading evidence, flawed reasoning, moral posturing, or physicians' cynical self-interest, Foucault provides a web of observations and interpretations to support his argument that the crusade is explained by the way that the tactics used in the crusade contributed to the solidification and regulation of the nuclear family. The problem is that Foucault has many degrees of explanatory freedom to construct something that looks sensible, but offers few tight arguments in support of his account.

His analysis is persuasive that in some broad sense there has been a "deployment of sexuality" that used certain "tactics" and had certain effects on the family. Perhaps these events fulfilled some broader social functions, as Foucault claims, but his arguments regarding such functions are weak and the explanatory functions, assuming they exist, remain obscure. However, even if we reject his inadequately supported claims about the relationship of the masturbation crusade to education, Foucault still offers persuasive observations of the pervasive use of surveillance, interrogation, confession, and medicalization—and, of course, the core concern about the potential pathogenic effects of masturbation—and the evidence, I have indicated, goes well beyond the primarily French sources that he cites. The family does become more open to outside medical authority, and the intimacy of family surveillance of children and the isolation from potential seducers and bad influences does yield the greater entanglement and closing of the family, as well.

How does Freud fit into this picture? Foucault claims that Freud's sexual theories are an extension of the masturbation crusade. Why did Foucault think that Freud's sexual theorizing had anything to do with the masturbation crusade, and on what evidence did he rest this presumption? In the next chapter, I evaluate Foucault's claim that early (pre–Oedipal-theory) Freudian sexual theory can be located smoothly and without rupture within the deployment-of-sexuality narrative and reproduces in substantial ways its concerns, tactics, and effects.

References

A grave social problem. (1881). *The British Medical Journal, 2*(1092), 904–905.

Acton, W. (1875). *The functions and disorders of the reproductive organs in childhood, youth, adult age, and advanced life considered in their physiological, social and moral relations.* Philadelphia, PA: Lindsay & Blakiston.

Blandford, G. F. (1871). *Insanity and its treatment.* Edinburgh: Arno Press.

Carpenter, E. (1999). Affection in education. *International Journal of Ethics, 9*(4), 482–494.

Clark, A. C., & Clark, H. E. (1899). Neurectomy, a preventive of masturbation. *Lancet, 154*(3969), 838.

Crosby, J. (1843). Seminal weakness—castration. *Boston Medical & Surgical Journal, 29*, 10–11.

Davidson, A. I. (2003). Introduction. In Foucault, M. (G. Burchell, Trans.), V. Marchetti & A. Salomoni (Eds.). *Abnormal: Lectures at the College de France 1974–1975* (pp. xvii–xxvi). New York, NY: Picador.

De Bourge, J. B. (1860). *Memento du pere de famille et de l'educateur de l'enfance, ou les conseils intimes sur les dangers de la masturbation (A father's and teacher's memento or intimate advice about the dangers of masturbation).* Paris.

Deslandes, L. (1835). *De l'onanisme et des autres abus vénériens considérés dans leurs rapports avec la santé.* Paris: A. Lelarge.

Foucault, M. (1975). *Surveiller et punir. Naissance de la prison.* Paris: Gallimard.

Foucault, M. (1976). *La volonté de savoir (Histoire de la sexualité, Vol. 1)*. Paris: Gallimard.

Foucault, M. (1977). *Discipline and punish: The birth of the prison*. (A. Sheridan, Trans.). New York: Pantheon.

Foucault, M. (1978). *History of sexuality* (Vol. 1): *An introduction*. (R. Hurley, Trans.). New York, NY: Pantheon. (*HS1*)

Foucault, M. (2003). *Abnormal: Lectures at the College de France 1974–1975*. (G. Burchell, Trans.), V. Marchetti & A. Salomoni (Eds.). New York, NY: Picador.

Freud, S. (1930). Civilization and its discontents. *SE* 21, 57–146.

Gullette, M. M. (1994). Male midlife sexuality in a gerontocratic economy: The privileged stage of the long midlife in nineteenth-century age-ideology. *Journal of the History of Sexuality*, *5*(1), 58–89.

Hamoway, R. (1977). Medicine and the crimination of sin: 'Self-abuse' in 19th century America. *Journal of Libertarian Studies*, *1*(3), 229–270.

Hare, E. H. (1962). Masturbatory insanity: The history of an idea. *Journal of Mental Science*, *108*(452), 1–25.

Huhner, M. A. (1916). *A practical treatise on disorders of the sexual function in the male and female*. Philadelphia, PA: F. A. Davis Co.

Hutchinson, J. (1890a). A plea for circumcision. *Archives of Surgery*, *2*, 15.

Hutchinson, J. (1890b). On circumcision as preventive of masturbation. *Archives of Surgery*, *2*, 267–269.

Lallemand C. A. (1847). *Practical treatise on the causes, symptoms, and treatment of spermatorrhoea*. (H. J. McDougal, Trans.). London: Churchill.

M. Verneuill on Spermatorrhoea. (1877). *The Doctor*, *7*, 115.

Marcuse, H. (1955). *Eros and civilization: A philosophical inquiry into Freud*. Boston: Beacon Press.

Marcuse, H. (1964). *One-dimensional man: Studies in the ideology of advanced industrial society*. Boston: Beacon Press.

McFarland, A. (1844). Result of an operation for the cure of spermatorrhoea. *Boston Medical & Surgical Journal*, *30*(9), 177–178.

Milton, J. L. (1854). On the nature and treatment of spermatorrhoea, part 1. *Lancet*, *63* (1592: March 4, 1854), 243–246.

Perry, I. (1853). Mechanical cure of spermatorrhoea. *Boston Medical & Surgical Journal*, *47*(53), 16–17.

Phillips, B. (1843a). Observations on seminal and other discharges from the urethra, with illustrative cases (part 1). *Boston Medical & Surgical Journal*, *28*(2), 35–39.

Phillips, B. (1843b) Observations on seminal and other discharges from the urethra, with illustrative cases (part 2). *Boston Medical & Surgical Journal*, *28*(5), 88–97.

Phillips, B. (1843c). Seminal and other discharges from the urethra. *Boston Medical & Surgical Journal*, *28*(21: 6/28/1843), 413–415.

Puff, H. (2006). Review of Michel Foucault, *Abnormal: Lectures at the Collège de France 1974–1975*. *Medical History*, *50*(2), 252–253.

Rozier, Le Docteur. (1830). *Des habitudes secrètes ou Des maladies produites par l'onanisme chez les femmes*. Paris: Audin, Librarie.

Sexual disorders, part 3. (1870). *The Lancet*, *96* (2448; July 30, 1870), 159–160.

Spermatorrhoea rings. (1853). *Boston Medical & Surgical Journal*, *47*(62), 209–210.

Spitzka, E. C. (1887). Cases of masturbation (masturbatic insanity). *Journal of Mental Science*, *33*(141), 57–73.

Spratling, E. J. (1895). Masturbation in the adult. *Medical Record*, *48*, 442–443.

Tissot, S. A. D. (1832). *Onanism: Or, a treatise upon the disorders produced by masturbation: Or the dangerous effects of secret and excessive venery*. New York, NY: Collins & Hannay. (Originally published in 1758.)

Treatment of Spermatorrhoea. (1853a). *Boston Medical & Surgical Journal*, *47*(48: June 29, 1853), 445–446.

Treatment of Spermatorrhoea. (1853b). *Boston Medical & Surgical Journal*, *47*(59: September 14, 1853), 144.

Van Ussel, J. (1972). *Histoire de la repression sexuelle (French translation)*. Paris: Laffont.

Wilson, M. (1856–1857). Contributions to the physiology, pathology, and treatment of spermatorrhœa. *The Lancet*, Part 1: August 23, pp. 215–217; Part 2: September 13, 1856, pp. 300–302; Part 3: November 1, 1856, pp. 482–484; Part 4: December 13, 1856, pp. 643–644; and Part 5: April 11, 1857, pp. 376–377.

Chapter 5

The Preservation of Victorianism: Freud's Early Theory as Extension of the Masturbation Crusade

Although Foucault focuses his critique on Freud's Oedipal theory (or "incest theory"), he also implies that Freud's sexual theories during his earlier "seduction theory" period were derived in important respects from the masturbation crusade. For example, in a remark noted in Chapter 4, Foucault states that, regarding the fear of seduction of young children, the crusade blamed parents who "entrust their children to wet nurses, servants, and private tutors, that is to say, to all those intermediaries regularly denounced as initiators into debauchery," and he adds the parenthetical remark, "Freud will take his first 'seduction' theory from this" (2003, p. 327). Moreover, there is a thread of continuity within Freud's thought that closely links the seduction theory to the Oedipal theory: the Oedipal theory was carefully formulated to address the failure of the seduction theory's claim that all psychoneuroses result from childhood sexual abuse while at the same time preserving Freud's broader sexual theory of the neuroses under-lying the seduction theory (Wakefield, 2023). If the Oedipal theory is indeed interestingly continuous with the masturbation crusade as Foucault claims, then one also would expect the seduction theory, the bridge between the two, to manifest such connections.

However, other than the remark about fears of child seducers, Foucault offers no systematic analysis of Freudian texts to support the claim that Freud's early theories are continuous with the masturbation crusade. In this chapter, I remedy this gap by asking: what evidence might have persuaded Foucault that, despite Freud's sexual-liberationist anti-Victorian reputation, his early theorizing should be located within the absurdities and oppressions of the masturbation

DOI: 10.4324/9781003480396-5

crusade and the deployment of sexuality? To answer this question, I closely examine early Freudian writings and identify the likely textual sources of Foucault's claim.

If Foucault is correct that, in important aspects and power/ knowledge, Freud's early theories are essentially part of the masturbation crusade, this would dramatically change how we understand Freud's sexual theorizing. Rather than being seen as releasing us from the socially and medically oppressive effects of the masturbation crusade era, Freud would have to be reconsidered as contributing a coda to that era—a coda that might still be influencing us today.

In reviewing aspects of Freud's early theorizing and its relation to the masturbation crusade, I rely primarily on Freud's theory papers from the 1890s through to his own summary of his theory's earlier development in his 1906 paper, "My Views on the Part Played by Sexuality in the Aetiology of the Neuroses." I also rely on a paper on masturbation that Freud presented to the Vienna Psychoanalytic Society (Freud, 1912) that is his most extensive discussion of the topic. Although this paper was presented after the introduction of the Oedipal theory, Freud is explicit that his views on masturbation have not recently changed and are continuous with his pre–Oedipal-theory views. I also include early aspects of the libido theory in this discussion, although the development of the libido theory stretched beyond the seduction theory period.

Freud and the Problem of Neurasthenia

A brief introduction to Freud's early views of the actual neuroses versus psychoneuroses and their causes and relationship to masturbation will be helpful as context for the discussion below. The term "neurosis," coined in the eighteenth century, was derived from the Greek for "disease of the nerves," and referred broadly and rather vaguely to a variety of psychiatric functional disorders with emotional and somatic symptoms that do not involve psychotic breaks with reality and for which no organic lesion-type cause can be identified. Freud remains historically the single most important systematizer and theoretician of the neuroses, much as Emil Kraepelin was the preeminent systematizer of the psychoses. Several of Freud's novel diagnostic categories—including obsessional neurosis and anxiety neurosis—have been retained in current psychiatric nosology, even though his etiological theories have been largely superseded and the generic term "neurosis" has largely been abandoned in favor of specific descriptive diagnostic categories in the DSM-5-TR and ICD-11. Indeed, it is precisely because of Freudian theory's strong association with the term "neurosis" that recent versions of these diagnostic manuals, attempting to be theory neutral and not biased in favor of psychoanalytic etiological assumptions, have eliminated the term's use.

Freud's primary concern with masturbation during his early theorizing was in regard to its hypothesized etiological relationship to what are known as the "actual neuroses." This label is derived from the German word *aktual* meaning "present day," reflecting that the postulated etiology of these conditions lay in the patient's ongoing current sexual practices.

Freud's theorizing about the neuroses initially concerned the actual neurosis of neurasthenia ("Originally my theory related only to the clinical pictures comprised under the term 'neurasthenia'" [1906, p. 271]), a category encompassing an enormous variety of non-psychotic emotional and somatic symptoms. Freud cites George Beard as the source of the neurasthenia diagnosis. Beard, a New York neurologist, published an early article on neurasthenia in a medical journal (Beard, 1869) and eventually followed up with two widely read books (Beard, 1880; 1881) among many other publications and talks (see Gosling, 1987, for an account of Beard's work).

Beard conceptualized neurasthenia as nervousness in the sense of nervous exhaustion—essentially, enervation—and defines it as "deficiency or lack of nerve-force" (1880, p. vi). Indeed, the term itself is simply Greek for "lack of nerve strength." Beard claimed that "nervous exhaustion (neurasthenia) is more common than any other form of nervous disease" (1880, p. v), but that its prevalence was not well recognized both because it was "of comparatively recent development" (1880, p. v) due to the demands of modern civilization and because it was labeled with a variety of vague terms such as "general debility," "nervous prostration," "nervous debility," "nervous asthenia," "spinal weakness," "spinal irritation," and "nervous dyspepsia." Consequently, he claimed that neurasthenia "is especially frequent and severe in the

Northern and Eastern portions of the United States" (1880, p. vi) due to the distinctively American demands and vices of modern urban living and the extreme competitiveness of American life. Beard even titled one of his books "American nervousness" and for a time it became known as the "American disease" and elixirs were advertised to overwrought businessmen and their anxious wives as cures for "Americanitis" (Daugherty, 2015; Marcus, 1998). However, the category was an extremely successful American export and quickly took root as a common diagnosis in Europe as well, but with revised views of causation focused more on sexual etiologies.

Neurasthenia was claimed to be manifested in general irritability and weakness of the nervous system with a remarkably diverse variety of potential symptoms. These symptoms encompassed an endless variety of bodily and psychological complaints, including fatigue, depression, headache, constipation, lack of concentration, indigestion, spinal sensitivity, bodily pains and tenderness of all kinds, feelings of numbness or hypersensitivity, nervous twitches and tingling sensations, pruritus, muscle spasms, tinnitus, and insomnia, as well as sexual symptoms such as impotence, premature ejaculation, loss of sexual desire, and nocturnal emissions. With regard to anxiety conditions, neurasthenia was thought to manifest in almost every imaginable symptom of anxiety such as sweaty hands, vertigo, palpitations, and all kinds of morbid fears and obsessions such as fears of lightning, certain places, being with other people, being alone, enclosed spaces, and contamination.

Given that both spermatorrhea and neurasthenia were explicitly conceptualized as states of nervous enervation, it is not surprising that the symptoms overlapped. It seems fair to say that in terms of symptomatology neurasthenia was the "new spermatorrhea," inheriting at least the milder part of the pathological territory that had been claimed by masturbatory disease and spermatorrhea. Freud rejected Beard's broad sociological etiological theory and returned to the crusade's conception, proposing a sexual theory of the actual neuroses including neurasthenia. Freud postulated that excessive masturbation is the specific cause of neurasthenia and that it is also a potential etiological factor in his other actual-neurosis category of anxiety neurosis.

Freud's Division of Neurasthenia into Neurasthenia Proper and Anxiety Neurosis

Freud set out to refine the sprawling diagnostic category of neurasthenia by dividing it into more homogeneous categories:

> It is difficult to make any statement of general validity about neurasthenia, so long as we use that name to cover all the things which Beard has included under it. In my opinion, it can be nothing but a gain to neuropathology if we make an attempt to separate from neurasthenia proper all those neurotic disturbances… which…exhibit essential differences in their aetiology and mechanism from the typical neurasthenic neurosis. If we accept this plan, we shall soon obtain a fairly uniform picture of neurasthenia.
>
> (1895a, p. 90)

Of the various kinds of neurasthenia, Freud "was particularly struck by two, which occasionally appear as pure types and which I described as 'neurasthenia proper' and 'anxiety neurosis'" (1906, p. 271). He thus split neurasthenia into these two categories:

> [O]n the one hand, we find cases in which certain complaints characteristic of neurasthenia (intracranial pressure, proneness to fatigue, dyspepsia, constipation, spinal irritation, etc.) are prominent; in other cases these signs play a minor part and the clinical picture is composed of other symptoms, all of which exhibit a relation to the nuclear symptom, that of anxiety (free anxiousness, unrest, expectant anxiety, complete, rudimentary or supplementary anxiety attacks, locomotor vertigo, agoraphobia, insomnia, increased sensitivity to pain, and so on). I have left the name of neurasthenia to the first type, but have distinguished the second type as 'anxiety neurosis'.
>
> (1898, p. 268)

As noted, the general somatic, digestive, and emotional symptoms and general enervation attributed by Freud to neurasthenia are quite similar in many respects to the symptoms attributed by the Victorian physicians such as Acton to the result of excessive masturbatory discharge or the excessive nocturnal emissions that they labeled "spermatorrhea":

> [M]any of the most obstinate as well as obscure complaints which the medical man meets with arises from the repeated loss of semen, and I am no less certain that hypochondriasis, the various forms of indigestion, debility, and nervous affection, with loss of sleep, are often only the effects of spermatorrhea.
>
> (Acton, 1875, p. 271)

Freud's distinction between neurasthenia proper and anxiety neurosis was an enduring nosological contribution. However, Freud's division was not without precedent in the masturbation crusade's distinctions. For one thing, there was already the crusade's humoral-like distinction between pathologies due to too little semen and those due to too much. Freud (as we shall see) translated this distinction into too little versus too much libido (i.e., sexual energy). More suggestive still is the crusade's condemnation of "conjugal onanism" as exemplified in Bergeret's work (see Chapter 3), named after Onan's act of *coitus interruptus* in the biblical tale—a condemnation that, we shall see, Freud also adopted, but on medical, not religious, grounds. Conjugal onanism during the crusade also covered a variety of other sexual deviations thought to be pathogenically unfulfilling (e.g., use of a condom), a category that Freud was to replicate in explaining anxiety neurosis as being due to a variety of acts yielding inadequate sexual gratification.

Although focusing on the danger of enervation from excessive discharge and recommending a modest amount of sexual activity to protect against overstimulation, Acton, too, we saw in Chapter 3, recognized that undischarged sexual arousal could lead to problems, although not specifically identifying the problem as anxiety symptoms as did Freud: "I raise a warning voice against either married or unmarried persons giving themselves up to ungratified sexual excitement" (Acton, 1875, p. 141);

> UNGRATIFIED SEXUAL EXCITEMENT [T]he mere excitement of the sexual feelings when not followed by the result which it should produce, is...an unmitigated evil. I am becoming every day

more and more convinced that much suffering and many ailments arise in great measure from the repeated and long-continued excitement of the sexual feelings unattended by subsequent sexual relations.

(Acton, 1875, p. 262)

Irrespective of this history, the creation of the new diagnostic category of anxiety neurosis was justified by Freud in quite modern terms. First, there was the syndromal co-occurrence of its symptoms: "The symptoms of this syndrome are clinically much more closely related to one another than to those of genuine neurasthenia (that is, they frequently appear together and they replace one another in the course of the illness)" (1895a, p. 91). Second, the various symptoms are all exclusively forms of anxiety: "I call this syndrome 'anxiety neurosis', because all its components can be grouped round the chief symptom of anxiety, because each one of them has a definite relationship to anxiety" (1895a, p. 91). And third, the new syndrome is characterized by a distinct etiology: the recategorized conditions "exhibit essential differences in their aetiology and mechanism from the typical neurasthenic neurosis" (1895a, p. 90) and "both the aetiology and the mechanism of this neurosis are fundamentally different from the aetiology and mechanism of genuine neurasthenia as it will be left after this separation has been effected" (1895a, p. 91).

In sharply distinguishing not only the clinical presentation but also the etiologies of the two actual neuroses, Freud explains that neurasthenia has a relatively straightforward presentation and a single specific etiology, excessive masturbation or nocturnal emissions:

Neurasthenia proper, if we detach anxiety neurosis from it, has a very monotonous clinical appearance: fatigue, intracranial pressure, flatulent dyspepsia, constipation, spinal paraesthesias, sexual weakness, etc. The only specific aetiology it allows of is (immoderate) masturbation or spontaneous emissions.

It is the prolonged and intense action of this pernicious sexual satisfaction which is enough on its own account to provoke a neurasthenic neurosis or which imposes on the subject the special neurasthenic stamp that is manifested later under the influence of an incidental accessory cause.

(1896, p. 150)

This sort of language is virtually identical to the language of the masturbation crusade. For example, in his chapter on "insanity arising from masturbation," Acton refers to masturbation as "the pernicious energy-sapping cause" (1875, p. 113). Freud even has an explanation for apparent counterexamples to his etiological hypothesis linking masturbation to neurasthenia that parallels remarks made by Acton, namely, that constitutional factors can occasionally mimic the enervating effects of masturbation:

I have also come across people presenting the indications of a neurasthenic constitution in whom I have not succeeded in bringing to light the aetiology I have mentioned; but I have at least shown that the sexual function has never developed to its normal level in these patients; they seemed to have been endowed by heredity with a sexual constitution analogous to what is brought about in a neurasthenic as a result of masturbation.

(Freud, 1896, p. 150)

In contrast, Freud observes, "anxiety neurosis exhibits a much richer clinical picture: irritability, states of anxious expectation, phobias, anxiety attacks,...tremors, sweating, congestion, dyspnoea, tachycardia, etc." (1896, p. 150). Whereas the cause of neurasthenia is too much sexual discharge via habitual masturbation, the cause of anxiety neurosis is essentially the opposite, lack of adequate discharge of sexual tension:

It is easily revealed as being the specific effect of various disorders of sexual life which possess a characteristic common to all of them. Enforced abstinence, unconsummated genital excitation (excitation which is not relieved by a sexual act), coition which is imperfect or interrupted (which does not end in gratification), sexual efforts which exceed the subject's psychical capacity, etc.—all these agents, which occur only too frequently in modern life,...prevent the psychical participation necessary in order to free the nervous economy from sexual tension.

(Freud, 1896, pp. 150–151)

Thus, Freud's overall sexual theory of the etiology of the neuroses remained intact despite the addition of the new "anxiety disorder" category:

The anxiety neurosis, too, has a sexual origin as far as I can see, but it does not attach itself to ideas taken from sexual life; properly speaking, it has no psychical mechanism [i.e., such as repression, which causes the psychoneuroses—JW]. Its specific cause is the accumulation of sexual tension, produced by abstinence or by unconsummated sexual excitation (using the term as a general formula for the effects of coitus reservatus, of relative impotence in the husband, of excitation without satisfaction in engaged couples, of enforced abstinence, etc.). It is under such conditions, extremely frequent in modern society, especially among women, that anxiety neurosis (of which phobias are a psychical manifestation) develops.

(Freud, 1894, pp. 80–81)

The Distinction between the Actual Neuroses and Psychoneuroses

Freud soon expanded his focus beyond the actual neuroses and divided all of the major neuroses recognized at his time into two overarching classes, the "actual neuroses"—consisting, as we have seen, of neurasthenia and anxiety neurosis—and the "psychoneuroses," which he also divided into two main diagnostic categories, hysteria and obsessional neurosis:

I have been engaged for years in researches into the aetiology of the major neuroses (functional nervous states analogous to hysteria)... I was obliged to begin my work with a nosographic innovation. I found reason to set alongside of hysteria the obsessional neurosis (*Zwangsneurose*) as a self-sufficient and independent disorder, although the majority of the authorities place obsessions among the syndromes constituting mental degeneracy or confuse them with neurasthenia.... Hysteria and obsessional neurosis form the first group of the major neuroses studied by me. The second contains Beard's neurasthenia, which I have divided up into two functional states separated by their aetiology as well as by their symptomatic appearance—neurasthenia proper and the anxiety neurosis (*Angstneurose*)....

(Freud, 1896, p. 146)

The division between actual neuroses and psychoneuroses, initially defined by their distinctive symptoms, was ultimately justified by Freud's theory of their distinctive etiologies. Freud claimed that all of the neuroses have etiologies that lie in disturbances of sexual life, but different kinds of disturbances lead to different neuroses. In the case of the actual neuroses, the etiology involves ongoing adult sexual practices that create current problems with sexual gratification that directly cause somatic complaints. In contrast, the etiology of the psychoneuroses involves repressed memories of childhood sexual experiences that are reawakened by current circumstances and then emerge as current symptoms. Combining cases of repressed sexual desire with cases of current excessive or inadequate sexual gratification yielded a unified sexual theory of the neuroses: "[I]n every case of neurosis there is a sexual aetiology; but in neurasthenia it is an aetiology of a present-day kind, whereas in the psychoneuroses the factors are of an infantile nature" (Freud, 1898, p. 268). He later summarized the etiological situation as follows:

By laying stress on the supposed aetiological factors it was possible at that time to draw a contrast between the common neuroses as disorders with a *contemporary* aetiology and psychoneuroses whose aetiology was chiefly to be looked for in the sexual experiences of the remote past. The theory culminated in this thesis: if the *vita sexualis* is normal, there can be no neurosis.... [T]he essence of these illnesses lies in disturbances of the sexual processes.

(Freud, 1906, pp. 273–274, 278)

Because the actual neuroses are caused by current sexual practices and not by a psychological defense against unconscious desires, they are distinguished from the psychoneuroses by the fact that they cannot be cured by the insights provided by psychoanalysis:

> [T]he 'actual neuroses'..., unlike psychoneurotic ones, cannot be analysed. That is to say, the constipation, headaches and fatigue of the so-called neurasthenic do not admit of being traced back historically or symbolically to operative experiences and cannot be understood as substitutes for sexual satisfaction or as compromises between opposing instinctual impulses, as is the case with psycho-neurotic symptoms.
>
> (Freud, 1912, p. 249)

For this reason, little was heard about the actual neuroses later in Freud's career, when his focus was on the use of psychoanalysis to cure the psychoneuroses. He did, however, eventually come to believe that analysis could help individuals suffering from neurasthenia or anxiety neurosis not via psychoanalytic insight but rather by supporting them in changing the current sexual practices that were causing their problems. In any event, given that my goal here is to explore the links between Freud and the masturbation crusade, and that masturbation as an etiology was linked by Freud to the actual neurosis of neurasthenia and not to the psychoneuroses, I will have little more to say in this chapter about the psychoneuroses.

Freud's Classification of Causes

Freud was well aware of the complexity of the causation of the neuroses. Although rejecting the "constitutional degeneracy" theory popular in his day, Freud understood that hereditary constitutional variation does play a major predisposing role in who becomes neurotic due to sexual vicissitudes. We saw in Chapter 3 that Acton also recognized the importance of the constitutional factor, observing that some individuals possess a "tolerance of the orgasm" that "permits the frequent recurrence of the shock without any ill effect either at the time or later" which "must depend upon some constitutional difference of nervous system of which we are ignorant" (Acton, 1875, p. 95). Freud, like Acton, also understood that neurotic conditions were obviously precipitated by a great variety of stressors, including physical illness, overwork, and psychological trauma. For example, he was familiar with the war neuroses and train-wreck neuroses in which a severe fright could trigger a neurosis. Yet, despite these seeming counterexamples, Freud insisted both in his early and late theories that all neuroses are ultimately caused by disturbances of sexuality. To make sense of these multiple known causal contributions and clarify the unique etiological role of sexuality, Freud put forward a typology of causes, organizing them into an overall etiological schema:

> I think we can arrive at a picture of the probably very complicated aetiological situation which prevails in the pathology of the neuroses if we postulate the following concepts: *(a) Precondition, (b) Specific Cause, (c) Concurrent Causes,* and, as a term which is not equivalent to the foregoing ones, *(d) Precipitating or Releasing Cause....* [W]e may characterize as the *precipitating* or releasing cause the one which makes its appearance last in the equation, so that it immediately precedes the emergence of the effect. It is this chronological factor alone which constitutes the essential nature of a precipitating cause.... The factors which may be described as *preconditions* are those in whose absence the effect would never come about, but which are incapable of producing the effect by themselves alone, no matter in what amount they may be present. For the specific cause is still lacking.
>
> The *specific cause* is the one which is never missing in any case in which the effect takes place, and which moreover suffices, if present in the required quantity or intensity, to achieve the effect, provided only that the preconditions are also fulfilled.
>
> As *concurrent causes* we may regard such factors as are not necessarily present every time, nor able, whatever their amount, to produce the effect by themselves alone, but which operate alongside of the preconditions and the specific cause in satisfying the aetiological equation.
>
> (Freud, 1895b, p. 137)

Freud identified several nonsexual precipitating conditions, ranging from traumatic emotions and intellectual overwork to physical illness, referring to these as "stock factors" to emphasize that they are not specific to any particular disorder:

> There are examples enough in which the final, releasing cause has not, in the face of critical analysis, maintained its position as the *causa efficiens*. One has only to think, for instance, of the relationship between trauma and gout.... [I]t is absurd to suppose that the trauma has 'caused' the gout instead of having merely provoked it.... [W]e come across aetiological factors of this sort—'stock' factors, as I should like to call them—in the aetiology of the most varied forms of illness. Emotion, fright, is also a stock factor of this kind. Fright can provoke chorea, apoplexy, paralysis agitans and many other things just as well as it can provoke anxiety neurosis.
>
> (1895b, p. 127)

For example, in the etiology of anxiety neurosis, Freud explains that heredity plays a role as a background precondition (a point still accepted today), and that a stock auxiliary or concurrent or precipitating cause (e.g., fright, physical exhaustion, overwork) may play a triggering role in this and many other disorders (also a point accepted today). In contrast, Freud understood the specific cause to be a cause that is always necessarily involved in the etiology of a given category of pathology. In anxiety neurosis, he claims, there is always a specific cause in the form of "a sexual factor, in the sense of a deflection of sexual tension away from the psychical field" (Freud, 1895b, p. 137) that is necessary for this specific form of disorder to come about. It is this distinctive necessity that distinguishes the specific cause from other causes:

> [H]ow do we distinguish between a precondition and a specific cause, since both are indispensable and yet neither suffices alone to act as a cause?...Among the *'necessary causes'* we find several which reappear in the aetiological equations concerned in many other effects....One of these causes, however, stands out in contrast to the rest from the fact that it is found in no other aetiological equation, or in very few; and this one has a right to be called the *specific* cause of the effect concerned.
>
> (1895b, p. 137)

In the case of neurasthenia, Freud claims that it is excessive masturbation (or its involuntary equivalent, excessive nocturnal emission) that provides such a necessary specific cause, and not the myriad stressors that were cited by others in his day. He takes the exclusive focus on masturbation as specific etiology to be his distinctive contribution. Freud's insistence on the exclusivity of masturbation as the specific cause of all cases of neurasthenia proper that involve enervation, with related sexual etiologies (such as *coitus interruptus*) as the specific cause of the anxiety-related forms of neurasthenia, stands in sharp contrast to Beard's view according to which neurasthenia results from an enormous variety of modern environmental circumstances, and places Freud more within the masturbation crusade's viewpoint on the primacy of sexual danger. Indeed, Freud's elaborate and well-organized typology of causes and his theory of the specific cause and its relationship to other causal contributions is used to provide what in effect is a sophisticated systematization and rationalization of the more chaotic system of beliefs that characterized the masturbation crusade.

In the light of Freud's early theory of the actual neuroses and his views of the crucial role of masturbation in neurasthenia's pathogenesis and sexual frustration in the etiology of anxiety neurosis, it is easy to understand how Foucault might have located Freud during his pre-Oedipal period with the Victorians and with the last gasps of the masturbation crusade. On the topic of masturbation, Freud certainly had more in common with the conservative Victorians than with his more modern-leaning and sexually liberal contemporaries who increasingly dismissed the notion that masturbation in itself is harmful. Instead, they tended to attribute any harm to the social disapproval and guilt masturbation might provoke, so that the bogus condemnation of masturbation as pathogenic was in fact the source of any pathogenicity it might possess. This tension about masturbation played out in meetings of the Vienna Psychoanalytic Society in disputes between Freud and his more etiologically liberal follower, Wilhelm Stekel—until Stekel was ejected from the movement shortly after the dispute over masturbation came to a head in 1912. Stekel's views are discussed by Freud in his 1912 paper, and considered below.

Freudian Libido Theory as Transformation of the Victorian "Semenic Economy"

There is also a broader way in which Freud's work reflected Victorian masturbation-crusade type views, namely, in the logic of his libido theory of sexual energy and its role in his overall schema of pathogenesis. Freud understood early on from his own clinical experience going back to *Studies on Hysteria* with Breuer and even to his witnessing Charcot's demonstrations of hysterical paroxysms that hysterical symptoms could appear anywhere in the body and interfere with a great variety of psychological or biological functions. In eventually conceptualizing hysterical symptoms as specifically sexual in etiological nature rather than more generally emotional, Freud was imputing to sexuality a presence throughout the body. He expressed this in his libido theory of mobile sexual energy.

As theoretical undergirding for his sexual theory of the neuroses, which required mobile energies the depletion or excess of which is pathogenic, Freud early on embraced a theory of transferable libido or sexual energy. However, it should be emphasized that this topic is not only or even mainly relevant to "early Freud," in the sense of the seduction theory period. Libido theory was much further developed along with the Oedipal theory and its theoretical accompaniments of component instincts (see Chapter 7) and psychosexual development, and expressed in mature form in Freud's *Three Essays on the Theory of Sexuality* (1905b). However, the libido theory is logically separable from Oedipal theory and in a preliminary form is often mentioned in Freud's early writings. To take just a few examples: "There are men...who produce an anxiety neurosis at the time of their decreasing potency and increasing libido" (1895a, pp. 101–102); "neurosis corresponds to a somatic sexual tension...which would otherwise have made itself felt as libido" (1895b, p. 126); "under the pressure of his prematurely awakened libido...he tried to repeat with the little girl exactly the same practices that he had learned from the adult woman" (1896, p. 208); "anxiety is always libido which has been deflected from its [normal] employment" (1898, p. 268); "neurotic anxiety is derived from sexual life and corresponds to libido which has been diverted from its purpose" [1900, p. 161]. These early references, we shall see, offer insights into Freud's masturbation-crusade–like view of sexuality prior to the Oedipal theory.

Libido for Freud was more specifically sexual than the broad "nervous energy" of the Victorian masturbation-crusade physicians, but decidedly more abstract than the literal "semenic economy" or "spermatic economy" (Barker-Benfield, 1972) that was represented in Victorian texts and that equated semen with a condensed form of life-giving blood that was considered the basis for normal growth into adulthood. The libido theory placed sexual energy potentially everywhere in the body and made libido close to an energic equivalent of a "vital fluid" analogous to the Victorians' view of semen. The proper shepherding of libido was considered by Freud to be the basis for healthy psychological development.

One might see the roots of both the semenic and libido theories in antiquity. Based on such observed facts as post-coital fatigue and of course the fact that semen interacting with female seed (often theorized in ancient times to be undischarged menstrual blood) gave rise to life, it had been commonly believed since antiquity that semen is literally a vital fluid that conferred life force and energy and was responsible for the general vitality and vigor of the organism. This sort of view endured and is reflected in Victorian medical texts that portray excessive masturbation as draining a boy of vitality, leaving him staring into space with sunken eyes and slouched demeanor, depriving the boy of life force literally to the point of illness and even death. As in ancient humoral theories that asserted that ill health came about due to either an excess or a lack of some substance needed by the body in a certain amount (e.g., depression and mania might be caused by an excess or lack of black bile, respectively), the Victorian idea was that either too much or too little semen in the body could cause disorder.

In adopting the libido theory of sexual energy, Freud was responding in part to an analog of an ancient puzzlement about the how parents managed to pass their various bodily features on to their offspring, given that semen was discharged from the genitals during intercourse but the features that were passed on were dispersed throughout the body. For example, the ancients puzzled over how a man's son could have his father's shape of nose if what the father passed on to contribute to the son's formation in the womb was only discharged from the father's genital region. The ancients, lacking genetics or information theory, came up with the theory that semen must be dispersed and circulate throughout the body thus carrying impressions of dispersed physical features. This semenic circulation was considered to be common to men and women in antiquity, with the female's ejaculation of semen occurring internally into the womb to mix with the man's semen. Alternatively, it was held that blood played the role of a thinner semen, so that it was blood circulation that allowed impressions of various bodily features to arrive at the genitals and interact with the semen. Either way, the semen could take and possess an impression of a man's nose and then communicate that impression to the offspring via fluid ejected into the female through the genitals.

Freud pondered three analogous puzzles about sexual energy. First, if sexuality is genitally centered, then how can there be sexual erotogenic zones spread throughout the body that give pleasure upon their stimulation—such as eyes aroused by a sexually stimulating sight, hands aroused by caressing a sexual partner, or mouth aroused by kissing? This seems to mean that libido and whatever biochemical process underlies its generation and discharge must be dispersed throughout the body as well and not just exist in the genitals.

Second, how does the stimulation of a distant erotogenic zone manage to perform not only its function of yielding pleasure in the zone itself but also its function of stimulating increased genital arousal and thus preparing the individual for the "specific action" (as Freud called it) of intercourse that yielded full discharge of sexual tension? Freud postulated that stimulation of an erotogenic zone must cause an alteration of some biochemical process that then circulates its products to communicate to centers linked to genital arousal:

> It may be supposed that, as a result of an appropriate stimulation of erotogenic zones, or in other circumstances that are accompanied by an onset of sexual excitation, some substance that is disseminated generally throughout the organism becomes decomposed and the products of its decomposition give rise to a specific stimulus which acts on the reproductive organs or upon a spinal centre related to them.
>
> (1905b, p. 215)

Third, if, as Freud held, hysterical symptoms are rooted in libidinal energy being converted to bodily symptoms, and if hysterical symptoms can occur almost anywhere in or on the surface of the body (e.g., hysterical blindness, paresthesia, or numbness), then how does the libido become present at such disparate locations? The answer again must be that libido, and the unknown biochemical processes on which it depends, are distributed throughout the body. In sum, Freud postulates that libido and the associated psychological tension and hysterical symptoms must be anchored in some as-yet-unknown chemical process that is the basis of sexual tension and pleasure throughout the body: "it is reasonable to suspect that we are still ignorant of the essential factors of sexuality...It must suffice us to hold firmly to what is essential in this view of the sexual processes: the assumption that substances of a peculiar kind arise from the sexual metabolism" (1905b, pp. 215–216).

Freud went beyond the Victorian focus on bodily fluids and in a sense "sublimated" Victorian sexual theory into something more ethereal and less testable than semenic imbalance. He fashioned a theory in which sexuality transcends a concrete focus on sexual discharge and sexual fluids per se but is nonetheless, in important structural respects, isomorphic to Victorian theories underlying the masturbation crusade that focus on the dangers of lack or excess of semen.

For example, reflecting the standard Victorian view, Freud accepts that the male phenomenology of sexual tension building in the genitals and relieved by sexual discharge is powerful *prima facie* evidence that semenic pressure is the source of libidinal sexual tension. Despite partially translating Victorian semenic doctrine into a more abstract theory of libidinal sexual energy, Freud acknowledges the appeal of this literal Victorian hydraulic hypothesis and how a combination of libido theory and semenic theory might offer novel explanatory possibilities:

PART PLAYED BY THE SEXUAL SUBSTANCES. Apart from the fact that normally it is only the discharge of the sexual substances that brings sexual excitation to an end, there are other points of contact between sexual tension and the sexual products. In the case of a man living a continent life, the sexual apparatus, at varying intervals,...discharges the sexual substances during the night, to the accompaniment of a pleasurable feeling and in the course of a dream which hallucinates a sexual act. And in regard to this process (nocturnal emission) it is difficult to avoid the conclusion that the sexual tension, which succeeds in making use of the short cut of hallucination as a substitute for the act itself, is a function of the accumulation of semen in the vesicles containing the sexual products. Our experience in connection with the exhaustibility of the sexual mechanism argues in the same sense. If the store of semen is exhausted, not only is it impossible to carry out the sexual act, but the susceptibility of the erotogenic zones to stimulus ceases, and their appropriate excitation no longer gives rise to any pleasure....

This would seem to lead to what is, if I am not mistaken, the fairly wide-spread hypothesis that the accumulation of the sexual substances creates and maintains sexual tension; the pressure of these products upon the walls of the vesicles containing them might be supposed to act as a stimulus upon a spinal centre, the condition of which would be perceived by higher centres and would then give rise in consciousness to the familiar sensation of tension. If the excitation of the erotogenic zones increases sexual tension, this could only come about on the supposition that the zones in question are in an anatomical connection that has already been laid down with these centres, that they increase the tonus of the excitation in them, and, if the sexual tension is sufficient, set the sexual act in motion.

(1905b, p. 213)

However, having explained why the semenic theory is so appealing, Freud goes on to explain why it cannot be completely correct given that children, women, and eunuchs can all experience sexual desire and pleasure and yet do not appear to have semenic pressures (at the time of the following passage in *Three Essays*, Freud had already postulated child sexuality):

The weakness of this theory...lies in the fact that, having been designed to account for the sexual activity of adult males, it takes too little account of three sets of conditions which it should also be able to explain. These are the conditions in children, in females and in castrated males. In none of these three cases can there be any question of an accumulation of sexual products in the same sense as in males, and this makes a smooth application of the theory difficult.

(1905, pp. 213–214)

Freud proposes instead what is in effect a double hydraulic model. He anchors the abstracted neo-hydraulics of the libido in an underlying literal hydraulics of sexual substances, at least provisionally or prototypically in men, while acknowledging that this may be only one surface indicator of a more essential underlying chemical process that more perspicuously explains sexual arousal in women, children, and castrated males. He observes that there must be more to the underlying physiological processes than is immediately apparent because his theory of erotogenic zones implies that sexual activity distant from the genitals—for example, in the eyes seeing, the hand stroking, or the lips kissing—can somehow communicate with and cause arousal in the genitals despite bypassing the seminal vesicles.

Excessive Versus Inadequate Libidinal Discharge in Neurosogenesis

Based on these proposed hydraulic processes, Freud's theory of anxiety neurosis is a straightforward "lack of adequate discharge" model in which the biologically designed "specific action" of intercourse is not adequately completed and there is a build-up of libido that expresses itself as anxiety:

> [T]he mechanism of anxiety neurosis is to be looked for in a deflection of somatic sexual excitation from the psychical sphere, and in a consequent abnormal employment of that excitation.... In the sexually mature male organism somatic sexual excitation is produced—probably continuously—and periodically becomes a stimulus to the psyche.... When this has happened, however, the group of sexual ideas which is present in the psyche becomes supplied with energy and there comes into being the psychical state of libidinal tension which brings with it an urge to remove that tension. A psychical unloading of this kind is only possible by means of what I shall call specific or adequate action. This adequate

action consists, for the male sexual instinct, in a complicated spinal reflex act which brings about the unloading of the nerve-endings, and in all the psychical preparations which have to be made in order to set off that reflex. Anything other than the adequate action would be fruitless, for once the somatic sexual excitation has reached threshold value it is turned continuously into psychical excitation, and something must positively take place which will free the nerve-endings from the load of pressure on them.

(1895a, pp. 108–109)

Indeed, during his early period of theorizing, Freud thought of anxiety as essentially a dissociated, desexualized bodily expression of sexual arousal:

The view here developed depicts the symptoms of anxiety neurosis as being in a sense surrogates of the omitted specific action following on sexual excitation. In further support of this view, I may point out that in normal copulation too the excitation expends itself, among other things, in accelerated breathing, palpitation, sweating, congestion, and so on. In the corresponding anxiety attacks of our neurosis we have before us the dyspnoea, palpitations, etc. of copulation in an isolated and exaggerated form

(1895a, p. 111);

"The dyspnoea and palpitations that occur in hysteria and anxiety neurosis are only detached fragments of the act of copulation" (1905a, p. 80).

Despite the origins of the hydraulic model in male fluids, Freud makes clear that he entirely rejects Victorian doctrine about the limited sexual needs of women. Like the Victorians, Freud rejects the ancient resolution of the puzzle of female desire that postulated that women possess a form of semen that is discharged with orgasm internally into the womb. However, unlike the Victorians, Freud makes clear that his libido theory, by replacing literal fluid with metaphorical energic fluid as the prime driver of sexual tension and relief, allows him to reject the notion that women are inherently nonsexual or less sexual than men, a mistaken doctrine that he attributes to social attitudes:

[I]n essentials this formula is applicable to women as well, in spite of the confusion introduced into the problem by all the artificial retarding and stunting of the female sexual instinct. In women too we must postulate a somatic sexual excitation and a state in which this excitation becomes a psychical stimulus:—libido—and provokes the urge to the specific action to which voluptuous feeling is attached.

(1895a, pp. 108–109)

It should be emphasized that Victorian doctrine recognized the possibility of both women and children becoming sexualized, but understood such conditions as pathological deviations from the natural state in the case of children, and pathological when overly intense in the case of women. In his early theorizing, Freud accepted this view of child sexuality. Only later did he conclude that such sexuality is natural, normal, and non-injurious.

Freud's postulation of the sexual needs of women had direct clinical implications in his account of the pathogenesis of female disorders in sexual practices. Freud thought that if a husband suffered from inadequate satisfaction due to lack of full intercourse, as in men who engaged in *coitus interruptus* or practiced *coitus reservatus* (using condoms) for birth control purposes, then his wife's lack of satisfaction might be collateral damage and she too might develop an anxiety neurosis. This is true as well in conditions of unconsummated excitation due to noncoital sexual interactions;

unconsummated excitation (e.g., during the period of engagement before marriage), or in those who (from fear of the consequences of sexual intercourse) content themselves with touching or looking at women...—which, incidentally, can be applied unaltered to the other sex (during engagements or relations in which sexual intercourse is avoided)—provides the purest cases of the neurosis.

(1895a, p. 101)

Such cases "depend simply on whether the woman obtains satisfaction in coitus or not. If not, the condition for the genesis of an anxiety neurosis is given" (1895a, p. 100). Thus, even under less-than-ideal circumstances of intercourse, the woman's problems can be avoided if full female satisfaction is reached:

On the other hand, she is saved from the neurosis if the husband who is afflicted with ejaculatio praecox is able immediately to repeat coitus with better success.... Coitus interruptus is nearly always a noxa. But for the wife it is only so if the husband practices it regardlessly—that is to say, if he breaks off intercourse as soon as *he* is near emission, without troubling himself about the course of the excitation in *her*. If, on the other hand, the husband waits for his wife's satisfaction, the coitus amounts to a normal one for *her*; but *he* will fall ill of an anxiety neurosis.

(1895a, p. 100)

However, what is good for the goose may not be good for the gander, for delay of gratification may in itself be problematic: "As has been said, coitus interruptus is injurious to the *woman* if it is practised without regard to her satisfaction; but it is injurious to the *man* if, in order to obtain satisfaction for her, he directs coitus voluntarily and postpones emission" (1895a, p. 101).

In sum, Freud attributed neurasthenia to excessive sexual discharge via masturbation or other sexual excesses and anxiety neurosis to lack of adequate discharge:

Neurasthenia develops whenever the adequate unloading (the adequate action) is replaced by a less adequate one—thus, when normal coition, carried out in the most favourable conditions, is replaced by masturbation or spontaneous emission. Anxiety neurosis, on the other hand, is the product of all those factors which prevent the somatic sexual excitation from being worked over psychically.

(1895a, p. 109)

Neurasthenia can always be traced back to a condition of the nervous system such as is acquired by excessive masturbation or arises spontaneously from frequent emissions; anxiety neurosis regularly discloses sexual influences which have in common the factor of reservation or of incomplete satisfaction—such as coitus interruptus, abstinence together with a lively libido, so-called unconsummated excitation, and so on.

(1898, p. 268)

In terms of reasons for inadequate discharge that can yield anxiety neurosis, Freud includes, for example, *coitus interruptus*, intentional abstinence, unconsummated excitation (e.g., during engagement before marriage), fear of pregnancy that causes a man to just touch or look at women, use of condoms, and senescent men who nonetheless have a surge of libido similar to the female climacteric. Freud continued to assert these views in his later summary of his theoretical development:

> It emerged that the form taken by the illness—neurasthenia or anxiety neurosis—bore a constant relation to the nature of the sexual noxa involved. In typical cases of neurasthenia a history of regular masturbation or persistent emissions was found; in anxiety neurosis factors appeared such as coitus interruptus, 'unconsummated excitation', and other conditions—in all of which there seemed to be the common element of an insufficient discharge of the libido that had been produced.
>
> (1906, p. 272)

The masturbation-crusade tone and content of these passages is manifest. Indeed, the specific claims about pathogenic sexual practices are identical to claims made by the crusade's physicians who focused on conjugal onanism and its sequelae. It would not have escaped Foucault that the crusade's features of surveillance and medicalization of conjugal onanism, as well as the implied confession in the psychoanalytic session, are salient in such passages.

Although the link between masturbation and neurasthenia due to excessive discharge was Freud's primary concern with masturbation, Freud also observed that many individuals manifested symptoms of both neurasthenia and anxiety neurosis. He theorized that masturbation could lead to anxiety neurosis as well as neurasthenia in a mixed-symptom actual neurosis:

> People who, as a result of practising masturbation, have become neurasthenics, fall victims to anxiety neurosis as soon as they give up their form of sexual satisfaction. Such people have made themselves particularly incapable of tolerating abstinence.... [I]t is very easy for

them to pass into a state of 'abstinence' after they have been accustomed for so long to discharging even the smallest quantity of somatic excitation, faulty though that discharge is.... For example, a woman with whom her husband practises coitus reservatus without regard to her satisfaction may find herself compelled to masturbate in order to put an end to the distressing excitation that follows such an act; as a result, she will produce, not an anxiety neurosis pure and simple, but an anxiety neurosis accompanied by symptoms of neurasthenia.

(1895a, pp. 102, 111, 113)

With continued masturbatory discharge and consequent neurasthenia, the individual becomes habituated to a chronically low level of libidinal tension and, if masturbation ceases, the surge of libidinal tension, even if modest, may overwhelm the individual and become anxiety. Thus, masturbation accompanied by lack of full coital satisfaction can yield neurasthenia and anxiety neurosis together.

Additionally, Freud acknowledges that the theoretical distinction between actual and psychoneuroses does not reflect the reality of neurotic conditions, which are frequently mixtures of the two. For example, masturbation might cause neurasthenia and simultaneously awaken repressed memories of, say, being masturbated by an adult as a child and thus trigger a related psychoneurosis. Indeed, Freud theorized that the symptoms of a psychoneurosis were in effect mini actual neuroses: "the two 'actual neuroses'— neurasthenia and anxiety neurosis...provide the psychoneuroses with the necessary 'somatic compliance', ...so that, speaking generally, the nucleus of the psycho-neurotic symptom—the grain of sand at the centre of the pearl—is formed of a somatic sexual manifestation" (1912, p. 248).

Masturbation in Early Freudian Theory

In discussions at the Vienna Psychoanalytic Society in 1912 (well into Freud's Oedipal theory period), Wilhelm Stekel disputed Freud's etiological distinction between actual neuroses caused by toxic products of inadequate or excessive sexual discharge and psycho-neuroses caused by repression, proposing instead that all neuroses are psychological. Stekel claimed, in a modern vein, that masturbation is harmless except for the guilt people felt about it. In responding to Stekel, Freud stood his ground and insisted on the pathogenicity of masturbation, consistent with his earlier views and with masturbation-crusade doctrine:

> On the question of the relation of masturbation and emissions to the causation of so-called 'neurasthenia', I find myself, like many of you, in opposition to Stekel, and... I maintain, as against him, my former views. I see nothing that could oblige us to abandon the distinction between 'actual neuroses' and psychoneuroses, and I cannot regard the genesis of the symptoms in the case of the former as anything but toxic. Here Stekel really seems to me greatly to overstretch psychogenicity.
>
> (1912, p. 248)

In his response to Stekel, Freud provides his most detailed discussion of the dangers of masturbation. Freud holds that in the adult there is damage from masturbation in virtue of its being an inadequate substitute for full coital engagement and discharge, imparting an almost mystical uniqueness to intercourse that is similar to masturbation-crusade doctrine:

> [D]o not forget that masturbation is not to be equated with sexual activity in general: it is sexual activity subjected to certain limiting conditions. Thus it also remains possible that it is precisely these peculiarities of masturbatory activity which are the vehicles of its pathogenic effects. We are therefore brought back once more from arguments to clinical observation, and we are warned by it not to strike out the heading 'Injurious Effects of Masturbation'. We are at all events confronted in the neuroses with cases in which masturbation has done damage.... Here we must take into account the considerations of excess and of inadequate satisfaction.
>
> (1912, p. 251)

Freud is not condemning early childhood masturbation but referring here strictly to post-pubertal masturbation, which extends the autoerotic activity proper to childhood inappropriately into adulthood. Freud holds that the problem with masturbation after puberty is that it does not provide full discharge of sexual tension due to lack of the unique stimulation of intercourse. Thus, he argues, masturbation cannot be equated with intercourse but "is sexual activity subjected to certain limiting conditions" and it is these "peculiarities of masturbatory activity which are the vehicles of its pathogenic effects." Freud also claims here to have clinical experience supporting his view that masturbation is dangerous, that the category of "injurious effects of masturbation" is real, and that the clinician is confronted "with cases in which masturbation has done damage" caused by either one of the two pathogenic poles of libidinal/semenic discharge, "considerations of excess and of inadequate satisfaction." Freud further speculates that masturbation's injurious effects generally are caused by "the characteristics of masturbation in so far as it represents a special manner and form of sexual satisfaction" interacting with "an individual's constitutional dispositions" (1912, p. 253).

Freud thus rejects Stekel's post-Victorian view that masturbation is harmless and that it is only our disapproval and guilt that makes it problematic. He instead clings to Victorian masturbation-crusade–type suspicions, at least in post-pubescents:

> I must confess that here again I am unable to share Stekel's point of view.... As he sees it, the injuriousness of masturbation amounts to no more than a senseless prejudice which, purely as a result of personal limitations, we are unwilling to cast off with sufficient thoroughness.... [T]o take up such a position contradicts our fundamental views on the aetiology of the neuroses. Masturbation corresponds essentially to infantile sexual activity and to its subsequent retention at a more mature age. We derive the neuroses from a conflict between a person's sexual urges and his other (ego) trends.
>
> (1912, pp. 250–251)

As we saw in Chapter 3, Victorian physicians, too, claimed on the basis of clinical evidence that masturbation must be the cause of the condition of spermatorrhea and that only by addressing that cause could the patient's enervation be reversed:

> In such cases the best, and indeed the only treatment, is that which removes the cause, and is not confined to combating the symptoms.

The best evidence of this cause and effect is, that such radical treatment alone relieves the symptoms when all other remedies have failed.

(Acton, 1875, p. 271)

Freud holds that habitual masturbation can enduringly reduce sexual potency. However, at one point he seems to suggest that such a condition, when it is mild, is perhaps not best conceptualized as a disorder because in the context of civilization a modest diminution of potency may be not injurious but beneficial in facilitating the satisfaction of social needs and values:

> On the basis of my medical experience, I cannot rule out a permanent reduction in potency as one among the results of masturbation.... This particular result of masturbation, however, cannot be classed unhesitatingly among the injurious ones. Some diminution of male potency and of the brutal aggressiveness involved in it is much to the purpose from the point of view of civilization. It facilitates the practice by civilized men of the virtues of sexual moderation and trustworthiness that are incumbent on them. Virtue accompanied by full potency is usually felt as a hard task.
>
> (1912, p. 252)

On the other hand, when contemplating the great harm that he thinks can be done by excessive masturbation, Freud is by no means consistent on this subtle point:

> [T]he prevention of masturbation in both sexes is a task that deserves more attention than it has hitherto received. When we reflect upon all the injuries, both the grosser and the finer ones, which proceed from neurasthenia—a disorder which we are told is growing more and more prevalent—we see that it is positively a matter of public interest that *men should enter upon sexual relations with full potency*.
>
> (1898, p. 278).

Freud here takes up the Victorian enthusiasm for surveillance and control of masturbation on which the crusade, as described by Foucault, similarly focused its attention.

Freud never lost his sense of the dangers of masturbation and nocturnal emissions. In his *An Autobiographical Study* (1925), at his most reflective and with his legacy in mind, he summarized the development of his view of masturbation as the etiology of neurasthenia and reaffirmed his belief in this theory:

> I now learned from my rapidly increasing experience that it was not any kind of emotional excitation that was in action behind the phenomena of neurosis but habitually one of a sexual nature, whether it was a current sexual conflict or the effect of earlier sexual experiences....
>
> Under the influence of my surprising discovery, I now took a momentous step. I went beyond the domain of hysteria and began to investigate the sexual life of the so-called neurasthenics who used to visit me in numbers during my consultation hours.... [I]t turned out that in all of these patients grave abuses of the sexual function were present.... Closer observation suggested to me that it was possible to pick out from the confused jumble of clinical pictures covered by the name of neurasthenia two fundamentally different types, which might appear in any degree of mixture but which were nevertheless to be observed in their pure forms. In the one type the central phenomenon was the anxiety attack with its equivalents, rudimentary forms and chronic substitutive symptoms; I consequently gave it the name of anxiety neurosis, and limited the term neurasthenia to the other type. Now it was easy to establish the fact that each of these types had a different abnormality of sexual life as its corresponding aetiological factor: in the former, coitus interruptus, unconsummated excitation and sexual abstinence, and in the latter, excessive masturbation and too numerous nocturnal emissions.... If it was possible to put an end to the abuse and allow its place to be taken by normal sexual activity, a striking improvement in the condition was the reward.
>
> I was thus led into regarding the neuroses as being without exception disturbances of the sexual function, the so-called 'actual neuroses' being the direct toxic expression of such disturbances and the psychoneuroses their mental expression. My medical conscience felt pleased at my having arrived at this conclusion. I hoped that

I had filled up a gap in medical science, which, in dealing with a function of such great biological importance, had failed to take into account any injuries beyond those caused by infection or by gross anatomical lesions. The medical aspect of the matter was, moreover, supported by the fact that sexuality was not something purely mental. It had a somatic side as well, and it was possible to assign special chemical processes to it and to attribute sexual excitation to the presence of some particular, though at present unknown, substances....

Since that time I have had no opportunity of returning to the investigation of the 'actual neuroses'; nor has this part of my work been continued by anyone else. If I look back to-day at my early findings,...on the whole they seem to me still to hold good....All that I am asserting is that the symptoms of these patients are not mentally determined or removable by analysis, but that they must be regarded as direct toxic consequences of disturbed sexual chemical processes.

(1925, pp. 23–26)

To the last, then, Freud maintained that both "excessive masturbation and too numerous nocturnal emissions" are pathogenic and cause nervous enervation taking the form of neurasthenia. He cites the success of treatment as evidence that he is correct ("If it was possible to put an end to the abuse and allow its place to be taken by normal sexual activity, a striking improvement in the condition was the reward"), just as Acton did before him in arguing for the ill effects of masturbation (see Chapter 3). Like earlier masturbation-crusade theorists who cited both the psychological effects of masturbation and its concomitant somatic effects on the nervous system, Freud notes that sexuality, due to whatever unknown substances underpin sexual desire, has its feet in both sides of the mind/body dichotomy.

Nor was Freud alone among psychoanalysts in his views of the prominent role of masturbation and *coitus interruptus* in neurosogenesis. In the discussions of 1912, most of his followers who were present sided with Freud over Stekel. For example, in his paper titled "A Modern Conception of the Psychoneuroses," Ernest Jones (1913) wrote matter-of-factly that "True neurasthenia—that is, a condition with pure fatigue, sense of pressure on the head, irritable spine, flatulent dyspepsia, and constipation...—will be found to depend on excessive onanism or involuntary seminal emissions" (p. 127).

In parallel to Freud's persistence in his view of the link between masturbation and neurasthenia, other analysts continued to repeat these views until the 1940s. To take one example, in 1930, New York psychoanalyst Adolph Stern published a paper in the *American Journal of Psychiatry* titled "Masturbation: Its Role in the Neuroses" (Stern, 1930), in which he asks, "What harm does masturbation do, physically, psychically?" (p. 1085). Stern follows Freud's post-Oedipal doctrine that masturbation is not generally harmful in childhood but can be harmful if continued after puberty: "The manifestations of masturbation go hand in hand with the individual's intellectual also affective development.... No doubt, however, exists that a pathological significance should be ascribed to masturbation under certain conditions" (p. 1085). Following Freud, Stern attributes the harm from masturbation over a long period to "the inadequate gratification accompanying the acts" (p. 1086). Stern summarizes the physical and psychological symptoms of masturbation: "A tired feeling on arising, lasting well into the day; heaviness of the lower extremities; sensitiveness to light and sound; indefinite gastric symptoms, paraesthesiae in the lumbar region, and tenderness to pressure along the large nerve trunks...diminished ability to concentrate, irritability, restlessness, some anxiety" (p. 1087). This, of course, is just to summarize the most characteristic symptoms of neurasthenia.

Other than the fact that these ideas were still publishable in 1930 in the leading American psychiatric journal, what is most interesting about Stern's paper is his summary of Sandor Ferenczi's attempted resolution of the puzzle going back to Tissot of why masturbation should be more harmful than sexual intercourse. It turns out that Ferenczi's answer is not all that distant from the answers provided by Tissot and Sanctorius:

Ferenczi has attempted an explanation of these phenomena in the following way. In a normal sexual act, between partners who fulfil for each other their physical and psychic requirements, at least for that particular act, the sexual fore-pleasure stimulating the genital organs into activity, is brought about by agencies other than the fantasy activity. In the normal act, fore-pleasure is aroused by looking, touching, stroking, fondling, hugging and kissing. With the consummation of the act, an explosion like discharge results, depleting these sensory and muscular pathways of all excitation, leading to a state of pleasant tiredness, followed by a feeling of being refreshed, with increase of energy. In the case of masturbation, or an unsatisfactory sexual act, fantasy plays the chief, if not the only role, as a stimulant to the genital organs, which alone then must serve as the discharge apparatus for the excitations aroused. According to Ferenczi, it is an insufficient discharging mechanism for the excitations aroused, and the reaction, physical and psychic, is unpleasant, inadequate.

(Stern, 1930, p. 1087)

Perhaps the most remarkable statement in Freud's above-quoted passage from *An Autobiographical Study* is his suggestion that he had corrected the failure of "medical science, which, in dealing with a function of such great biological importance, had failed to take into account any injuries beyond those caused by infection or by gross anatomical lesions." As was documented in Chapter 3, from Tissot to Acton, almost none of the theorists of the masturbation crusade had limited themselves to infection or gross anatomical lesions. Those had played a rather small part in etiological theories, with seminal discharge and nervous exhaustion playing the largest role. Freud thus offers a false and self-serving portrayal of the pre-Freudian literature on the pathogenic dangers of sexuality. In sum, insofar as the central characteristic of the masturbation crusade was the exaggerated fear of the pathogenic consequences of masturbation and nocturnal emissions, Foucault stands on solid ground in categorizing Freud as part of the crusade throughout his life.

By Freud's time, the masturbation crusade had largely pulled back from earlier views that masturbation caused myriad severe physical pathologies and psychotic mental illness in the form of "masturbatory insanity." The revised medical opinions fell into two camps. The first group, observing the near universality of masturbation—a point Freud acknowledged only for prepubertal childhood masturbation— questioned the justification for singling out masturbation from other sexual activities. For example, Havelock Ellis quotes Sir James Paget as asserting that "Masturbation does neither more or less harm than sexual intercourse practiced with the same frequency in the same conditions of general health and age and circumstances" (as quoted by Ellis, 1900, p. 185). These physicians tended to suggest that masturbation-specific harm was iatrogenic, caused by the guilt and shame inflicted on the masturbator by physicians' dire warnings. As we saw above, Stekel adopted the views of this liberal group, which led to his expulsion from Freud's circle. Ellis suggests that it was the German psychiatrist Wilhelm Griesinger who had initiated this "saner" more enlightened view: "Griesinger saw that it was not so much masturbation itself as the feelings aroused in sensitive minds by the social attitude toward masturbation which produced evil effects" (1900, p. 180).

However, even this liberal group often was ambivalent, expressing concern about sexual excess or masturbation in the young. For example, in his widely used medical textbook, Theodore Kellogg (1897) skeptically observed, "If it caused insanity as often as some claim, the whole race would long since have passed into masturbatic degeneracy of mind"—yet he goes on to state that "it is especially injurious in the very young and in all who have weak nervous systems" and attributes to habitual masturbators a physical look common to neurasthenics and neurotics (pp. 94–95).

The second group of late-nineteenth-century revisionist physicians, which includes Freud, were more conservative in tempering but not abandoning core crusade doctrines. While rejecting the notion that masturbation causes severe physical and mental disorders, they remained concerned about the enervating loss of vital fluids and the repeated shocks to the nervous system that could occur in habitual masturbation, and the many psychological and somatic symptoms that might result. They also retained the crusade's doctrine that masturbation possesses distinctive tendencies to pathogenicity beyond those of other sexual acts that is not reducible to social pressures and feelings of guilt.

Freud explicitly distinguishes himself from his contemporaries by his insistence on masturbation as the universal specific cause of neurasthenia proper. However, this distinction is not quite as straightforward as it may appear. It is true that, as Freud explains, others recognized many causes of nervous exhaustion other than masturbation, such as intellectual overwork and the pace of modern society. However, even when Acton identified intellectual overwork as the cause of symptoms, he expressed suspicion that it was the effects of that work interacting with sexual processes that triggered the disorder. Much like Acton, Freud acknowledges that other causes such as intellectual overwork can trigger neurasthenia but argues that this is only because the cited causes have pathogenic effects on the discharge of libido. In sum, Freud's account of masturbation as the pathogenesis of neurasthenia was not particularly radical.

The transition to masturbation as the cause of neurasthenia is a smooth one partly because virtually all of the relatively modest psychological and somatic symptoms attributed to neurasthenia had been attributed earlier to spermatorrhea. If one goes down the list of symptoms of masturbation and spermatorrhea of the Tissot through Acton tradition and eliminates extreme mental illness and the great variety of severe physical diseases, one is left with symptoms of mental and physical enervation that tend to converge on what came to be known as neurasthenia ("fatigue, intracranial pressure, flatulent dyspepsia, constipation, spinal paraesthesias, sexual weakness, etc." [Freud, 1896, p. 150]) and in Freud's hands came to be labeled neurasthenia proper, and the many anxieties that constitute its Freudian offshoot, anxiety neurosis. One might reasonably conclude that Freud's neurasthenia is essentially spermatorrhea in which the literal semenic theory of etiology is softened but not abandoned, including the belief that wet dreams are pathogenic: "The only specific aetiology it allows of is (immoderate) masturbation or spontaneous emissions" (Freud, 1896, p. 150); "Neurasthenia develops whenever the adequate unloading (the adequate action) is replaced by a less adequate one—thus, when normal coition, carried out in the most favourable conditions, is replaced by masturbation or spontaneous emission" (1895a, p. 109). Freud is thus very much a part of the larger medical masturbation-crusade perspective from Lallemand to Acton that saw seminal loss as both directly enervating and indirectly pathogenic through its shock to and weakening of the nervous system. Indeed, Freud if anything seems to have retrogressively relocated neurasthenia back into the strict sexual domain from whence its predecessor spermatorrhea had come, going against the drift by his contemporaries toward a more varied etiological theory, and he theoretically defends his view by abstracting both semen-depletion and nervous exhaustion into the more abstract libido-depletion.

Medical Regulation of the Family's Intimate Life

Freud's doctrines regarding masturbation, *coitus interruptus*, condom use, and other potentially pathogenic sexual practices manifest central Foucauldian characterizations of the masturbation crusade, including surveillance, confession, medicalization of family life, and intrusion into and manipulation of the sexual activities of the population. Despite initial skepticism, Freud did eventually come to believe that analysis could help those suffering from neurasthenia or anxiety neurosis despite these conditions not having psychogenic etiology:

> I will grant to-day what I was unable to believe formerly—that an analytic treatment can have an indirect curative effect on 'actual' symptoms. It can do so either by enabling the current noxae to be better tolerated, or by enabling the sick person to escape from the current noxae by making a change in his sexual régime. These would be desirable prospects from the point of view of our therapeutic interest.
>
> (1912, pp. 249–250)

What this meant in practice was that the therapist could help individuals to stop masturbating or stop practicing certain birth control techniques that interfered with sexual satisfaction.

Freud's particular interest in intervening to stop masturbation in youth was partly preventive and partly a social intervention:

> The main benefit which we obtain from it for neurasthenics lies in the sphere of prophylaxis. If masturbation is the cause of neurasthenia in youth, and if, later on, it acquires aetiological significance for anxiety neurosis as well, by reason of the reduction of potency which it brings about, then the prevention of masturbation in both sexes is a task that deserves more attention than it has hitherto received. When we reflect upon all the injuries, both the grosser and the finer ones, which proceed from neurasthenia—a disorder which we are told is growing more and more prevalent—we

see that it is positively a matter of public interest that *men should enter upon sexual relations with full potency*. In matters of prophylaxis, however, the individual is relatively helpless. The whole community must become interested in the matter and give their assent to the creation of generally acceptable regulations.

At present we are still far removed from such a state of affairs which would promise relief, and it is for this reason that we may with justice regard civilization, too, as responsible for the spread of neurasthenia. Much would have to be changed. The resistance of a generation of physicians who can no longer remember their own youth must be broken down; the pride of fathers, who are unwilling to descend to the level of humanity in their children's eyes, must be overcome; and the unreasonable prudery of mothers must be combatted—the mothers who at present look upon it as an incomprehensible and undeserved stroke of fate that 'their children should have been the ones to become neurotic'.

(Freud, 1898, p. 278)

Consistent with Victorian interventions to control masturbation and shape the population's sexual behavior, Freud's well-intentioned medical attitudes endorse direct medical advice about, and intervention to alter, intimate practices, even to the point of institutionalizing the masturbator:

To break the patient of the habit of masturbating is only one of the new therapeutic tasks which are imposed on the physician who takes the sexual aetiology of the neurosis into account; and it seems that precisely this task, like the cure of any other addiction, can only be carried out in an institution and under medical supervision. Left to himself, the masturbator is accustomed, whenever something happens that depresses him, to return to his convenient form of satisfaction. Medical treatment, in this instance, can have no other aim than to lead the neurasthenic, who has now recovered his strength, back to normal sexual intercourse.

(Freud, 1898, pp. 275–276).

The suggested control of sexuality extended not just to the encouragement of normal intercourse but also to the details of intercourse given the claimed relationship of such details to anxiety neurosis. Such interventions implied that the physician's authority took precedence over the couple's preferred complex tradeoffs between sex and birth control:

> Another task is set to the physician by the aetiology of anxiety neurosis. It consists in inducing the patient to give up all detrimental forms of sexual intercourse and to adopt normal sexual relations. This duty, it will be understood, falls primarily on the patient's trusted physician—his family doctor; and he will do his patient a serious injury if he regards himself as too respectable to intervene in this field.
>
> Since in these instances it is most often a question of a married couple, the physician's efforts at once encounter Malthusian plans for limiting the number of conceptions in marriage. There seems to me no doubt that such proposals are gaining ground more and more among our middle classes. I have come across some couples who have already begun practising methods for preventing conception as soon as they have had their first child, and others whose sexual intercourse was from their wedding-night designed to comply with that purpose.
>
> (1898, p. 276)

Freud's advice thus could lead to a failure of birth control and real consequences of the most important sort for the couple—especially because at the time pregnancy had significant dangers. Note that Freud's concern was strictly with preventing the pathogenic potential of sexual relations being realized. He was totally in sympathy with birth control, and he had a prescient understanding of the potentially revolutionary implications of the scientific discovery of reliable and safe birth control that did not interfere with sexual satisfaction:

> [I]t would be one of the greatest triumphs of humanity, one of the most tangible liberations from the constraints of nature to which mankind is subject, if we could succeed in raising the responsible act of procreating children to the level of a deliberate and intentional activity and in freeing it from its entanglement with the necessary satisfaction of a natural need....

This sets physicians a practical task to the solution of which they could bend their energies with rewarding results. Whoever fills in this lacuna in our medical technique will have preserved the enjoyment of life and maintained the health of numberless people; though, it is true, he will also have paved the way for a drastic change in our social conditions.

(1898, p. 277)

Yet, despite his appreciation of the challenge of birth control, given the high stakes in terms health and disorder that Freud attributes to the nature of the sexual act, he still places the responsibility for judging appropriate sexual practices in the hands of the physician, and he acknowledges that there is little among birth control techniques to choose from that is not pathogenic:

A perspicacious physician will therefore take it upon himself to decide under what conditions the use of measures for preventing conception are justified, and, among those measures, he will have to separate the harmful from the harmless ones. Everything is harmful that hinders the occurrence of satisfaction. But, as we know, we possess at present no method of preventing conception which fulfils every legitimate requirement—that is, which is certain and convenient, which does not diminish the sensation of pleasure during coitus and which does not wound the woman's sensibilities.

(Freud, 1898, p. 277)

The notion that "A perspicacious physician will therefore take it upon himself to decide under what conditions the use of measures for preventing conception are justified" illustrates the entry by medicine into the regulation of the family's intimate life that Foucault describes. Freud's concern about masturbation is expressed in a medical idiom but with an intensity reminiscent of the fervor of the Victorian masturbation crusade:

Masturbation is far commoner among grown-up girls and mature men than is generally supposed, and it has a harmful effect not only by producing neurasthenic symptoms, but also because it keeps the patients under the weight of what they feel to be a disgraceful secret.

Physicians who are not accustomed to translate neurasthenia into masturbation account for the patient's pathological state by referring it to some catchword like anaemia, under-nourishment, overwork, etc., and then expect to cure him by applying a therapy devised against those conditions.... If physicians knew that all the while the patient was struggling against his sexual habit and that he was in despair because he had once more been obliged to give way to it, if they understood how to win his secret from him, to make it less serious in his eyes and to support him in his fight against the habit, then the success of their therapeutic efforts might in this way well be assured.

(1898, p. 275)

Physicians, Freud says, must not take the patient's reports at face value or assume causes other than masturbation but must instead "win his secret from him" that the patient's problem is due to masturbation, thus reflecting Victorian notions of the need to elicit a confession. Statements such as this support Foucault's assertions that via a masturbation-crusade–like theory, Freud justified and encouraged a mode of intervention by which medical authority entered into and regulated the family. As Foucault puts it:

[M]edicine made a forceful entry into the pleasures of the couple: it created an entire organic, functional, or mental pathology arising out of 'incomplete' sexual practices; it carefully classified all forms of related pleasures; it incorporated them into the notions of 'development' and instinctual 'disturbances'; and it undertook to manage them.

(1978, p. 41)

Indeed, Freud's early "discoveries" of the sexual etiologies of the neuroses were probably facilitated by his Victorian zeal in relentlessly seeking to obtain a confession that reveals the patient's hypothesized sexual secrets irrespective of the patient's denials and resistance, as reflected in passages such as the following: "One only succeeds in awakening the psychical trace of a precocious sexual event under the most energetic pressure of the analytic procedure, and against an enormous resistance" (1896, p. 153);

Having diagnosed a case of neurasthenic neurosis with certainty and having classified its symptoms correctly, we are in a position to translate the symptomatology into aetiology; and we may then boldly demand confirmation of our suspicions from the patient. We must not be led astray by initial denials. If we keep firmly to what we have inferred, we shall in the end conquer every resistance by emphasizing the unshakeable nature of our convictions.

(1898, p. 269)

I was surprised to begin with at the frequency of gross disturbances in the *vita sexualis* of nervous patients; the more I set about looking for such disturbances—bearing in mind the fact that everyone hides the truth in matters of sex—and the more skillful I became at pursuing my enquiries in the face of a preliminary denial, the more regularly was I able to discover pathogenic factors in sexual life, till little seemed to stand in the way of my assuming their universal occurrence.

(1906, p. 271)

From Foucault's perspective, one can certainly see here masturbation-crusade–like "incitement to discourse" justified by the "repressive hypothesis"—concepts that we saw in Chapter 1 are central to Foucault's characterization of the masturbation crusade. There is also a similarity to Victorian techniques of masturbation interrogation, described in Chapter 3.

Another commonality between the masturbation crusade and Freud's early theory, pointed out by Foucault in a passage quoted above on "initiators into debauchery" ("Freud will take his first 'seduction' theory from this" [2003, p. 327]), concerns the dangers to the child from lascivious adults. Note that the discussion of the potential pathogenicity of masturbation above primarily concerns post-pubertal masturbation, not child masturbation. Both masturbation-crusade doctrine and Freud's early seduction theory postulated the inherent sexual innocence of children unless prematurely stimulated. Thus, both theories held that, except in unlikely scenarios (e.g., discovering pleasure when scratching a genital itch or experimentation due to a particularly lascivious constitution), seduction of a child by an adult or seduction of one child by another child who was already initiated into sex was generally the way a child was initiated into precocious sexual activity. The masturbation crusade tended to blame non-family household help for such seductions whereas Freud tended to blame family members, but both held "seduction theories" to account for childhood sexuality. Foucault argued that the masturbation-crusade doctrine that precocious child sexuality generally resulted from an adult prematurely stimulating and seducing a child created a pressure for close supervision by parents as guardians of their children's purity, and the same—but perhaps even more so, given the internal-to-the-family nature of the threat to the child—would seem to apply to Freud's theory.

Given the assumed intrinsically nonsexual natural state of the child, Freud argued that, rather than awakening precocious sexuality, seduction might be experienced as meaningless or puzzling at the time of occurrence. The event might then be repressed and the traumatic force might emerge only in a "delayed action" after puberty as the individual's new sexual experiences stirred up memories of the childhood act and the individual consciously or unconsciously reacted emotionally to the newly understood meaning of the event. Both of Freud's hypotheses about the effects of childhood sexual experience—the precocious sexualization of sexually stimulated prepubescents, and the notion of the delayed pathogenic action of prepubescent sexual activity until puberty—were put forward by his predecessors in the masturbation crusade, as we saw in Chapter 3. However, the crusade tended to see both the preciousness and the delayed effect as consisting of the onset of masturbation as the primary symptom, whereas Freud relocated the symptomatic effects into the psychological domain.

Freud and the Preservation of Victorianism

We saw earlier that Foucault suggests that Freud's pre-Oedipal work contains some elements of Victorian sexual ideology. The above review confirms the strong Victorian elements of Freud's early theory, well beyond the limited domain of protection from seduction identified by Foucault. Whether this early affinity leads to the inclusion of such elements in Freud's later Oedipal theory, as Foucault asserts, remains to be explored.

The quasi-Foucauldian position I have argued for regarding the relationship of Freud's early theory to the masturbation crusade yields a rather unsettling conclusion. Contrary to the common notion that Freud from the beginning challenged and reversed Victorian approaches to sexuality, in important respects early Freudian theory preserved and even amplified what I have argued to be the core thesis of Victorian sexual ideology, the belief in the special dangers of too much or too little sexual arousal and discharge. In Freud's transformation of Victorian sexual ideology, although challenging some doctrines such as certain views of female sexuality, he managed to preserve core tenets of Victorian medico-sexual ideology in a "sublimated" form by transforming claims about the pathogenicity of lack or excess of vital sexual fluids into claims about the pathogenicity of lack or excess of a more abstract sexual energy. The overall result supports Foucault's implied claim that Freud's theory was, at least at this early stage, understandable as an extension of the masturbation crusade.

In his early papers, Freud himself frequently acknowledges that his views are a systematic and universalized extension and amplification of the standard Victorian beliefs about the potential pathogenicity of variations of sexuality:

> What, then, are the specific causes of neuroses?... [T]hese functional pathological modifications have as their common source the subject's sexual life, whether they lie in a disorder of his contemporary sexual life or in important events in his past life.
>
> This, to tell the truth, is no new, unheard-of proposition. Sexual disorders have always been admitted among the causes of nervous illness, but they have been subordinated to heredity and coordinated with the other agents provocateurs; their aetiological influence has been restricted to a limited number of observed cases. Physicians had even fallen into the habit of not investigating them unless the patient brought them up himself. What gives its distinctive character to my line of approach is that I elevate these sexual influences to the rank of specific causes, that I recognize their action in every case of neurosis.
>
> (1896, p. 149)

Thus, Freud in effect doubled down on the masturbation crusade by making even more extreme and categorical claims about the role of sexuality in pathogenesis, arguing that the greater absoluteness of his claims about the pathogenic dangers of sexual lack and excess is how his contribution goes beyond what was already largely accepted. Similarly, Freud acknowledges that his focus on inadequate sexual discharge as pathogenic was a commonsense view in Victorian society:

> [T]he most significant causes of every case of neurotic illness are to be found in factors arising from sexual life. This theory is not entirely new.... A dim knowledge of the overwhelming importance of sexual factors in the production of neuroses (a knowledge which I am trying to capture afresh for science) seems never to have been lost in the consciousness of laymen. How often do we witness scenes like this: A married couple, one of whom is suffering from a neurosis, comes to us for consultation.... [W]e tell them that we suspect that the cause of the illness lies in the unnatural and detrimental form of sexual intercourse which they must have chosen since the wife's last confinement. We tell them that doctors do not as a rule concern themselves with such matters, but that that is reprehensible of them, even though the patients do not want to be told about things like that, etc. Thereupon one of the couple nudges the other and says: 'You see! I told you all along it would make me ill.' And the other answers: 'Well, I know, I thought so too; but what is one to do?'
>
> (1898, pp. 263, 265–266)

Looked at through the prism of Victorian sexual ideology based on a "semenic economy" in which the amount of semen might be pathogenic if it is too much or too little, Freud performed an astonishing service for Victorian sexual ideology. On the eve of these theories of the pathogenicity of semen imbalance being disproven by advances in science, Freud managed to save the essential conceptual apparatus by transforming the spermatic economy into the libidinal economy. By moving the empirically falsifiable spermatic economy into the less observable realm of the mind where science could not at that point easily disprove it, Freud made a scientific disconfirmation more difficult so that the tenets of Victorian sexual medicine were better able to survive increasing knowledge of sexual psychology. (Frank Cioffi [1998] made a similar point about Freud's move from the seduction theory, which concerns the occurrence of external events that at least in principle could be observed or measured and studied epidemiologically, to the Oedipal theory, which concerns internal repressed longings that are difficult to confirm or disconfirm.) Foucault alluded to the subtle continuity between Victorian sexual ideology and early Freudian theory, and that continuity, we can now see, consists of the fact that the structures of the two systems—the literally hydraulic semen system and the metaphorically hydraulic libidinal energy system—are in important ways isomorphic. Libido comes close to being a vital energy, so that its depletion via excessive masturbation yields exhaustion, lack of vigor, and ultimately the disorder of neurasthenia—parallel to Victorian beliefs about loss of semen.

Thus, the single most salient doctrine of Victorian sexual ideology is reproduced within Freud's early theory: sexual motivation and its arousal or non-arousal, its discharge or lack of discharge, are potentially dangerous and legitimate targets of medical intervention. It is arguable that Freud was the bridge via which echoes of this aspect of Victorianism and of the masturbation crusade were preserved to our time and reside to this day in our beliefs about the special dangerousness of sex. Given this affinity, it is not surprising that Foucault perceived in early Freudian theory a Victorian-like concern and an extension of Victorian techniques of control regarding masturbation and marital sexuality. Although repackaged in a radically altered theory that presents itself as more sex-friendly, Freud's early theory aligned in crucial respects with Victorian views on the dangerousness of sex and ushered in an era of continued medical attention to and intervention into people's intimate family life.

Conclusion

Foucault claims that Freud's early sexual theories were extensions of the masturbation crusade in terms of overlapping content and power/ knowledge implications. My review reveals ample evidence in Freud's texts that supports Foucault's claims, showing that Freud's early theorizing has core features that manifestly extend the framework and power/knowledge of the masturbation crusade. These include, for example:

the belief that masturbation can be pathogenic and drain a young person of vitality;

the belief that children are inherently nonsexual and generally become precociously sexual only when sexually seduced by an adult or another child;

the belief that all manner of phenomena from nocturnal emissions to overwork might interact with sexuality to have pathogenic influences on sexual vitality;

the belief that it is the responsibility of physicians to perform medical surveillance of patients' sexual lives not only to prevent masturbation but also to influence the intimate relations of spouses to prevent unnatural sexual relations;

the postulation of a sexual energic system (libido) that has the same functional properties as the masturbation crusade's "spermatic economy";

and, at a process level, Freud's assertive absorption in the relentless search for a confession by the patient of hidden sexual excesses parallel to the similar absorption of the Victorian medico-moralists of the masturbation crusade in obtaining confessions of sexual deeds.

Granting the persuasive power of this comparison, the question remains whether Foucault was justified in projecting the early Freud's affinity to the masturbation crusade into Freud's later Oedipal theory and thus also classifying the Oedipal theory as an extension of, and alternative means to achieve the power/knowledge goals of, the masturbation crusade. I will divide this question into two. First, in Chapter 6, I ask: what is Foucault's argument for rejecting the standard notion that the Oedipal theory was a liberating rupture that transcended the deployment of sexuality, and instead placing it within the deployment of sexuality, continuous with the masturbation crusade? And second, in Chapter 7, I ask: what in Freud's work was the evidential basis for Foucault's further claims about Freud? That is, what evidence might have suggested to Foucault that the Oedipal theory, which looks on its face so very different from both the masturbation crusade and early Freudian seduction theory, might in fact be an alternative strategy for extending the masturbation crusade's effects?

References

Acton, W. (1875). *The functions and disorders of the reproductive organs in childhood, youth, adult age, and advanced life considered in their physiological, social and moral relations.* Philadelphia, PA: Lindsay & Blakiston. (Original work published in 1857.)

Barker-Benfield, B. (1972). The spermatic economy: A nineteenth century view of sexuality. *Feminist Studies, 1*, 45–74.

Beard, G. M. (1869). Neurasthenia, or nervous exhaustion. *The Boston Medical & Surgical Journal, 80*(13), 217–221.

Beard, G. M. (1880). *A practical treatise on nervous exhaustion (neurasthenia): Its symptoms, nature, sequences, treatment.* New York, NY: W. Wood & Company.

Beard, G. M. (1881). *American nervousness: Its causes and consequences, a supplement to Nervous Exhaustion (Neurasthenia).* New York, NY: G. P. Putnam's Sons.

Cioffi, F. (1998). The Freud controversy: What is at issue? In M. S. Roth (Ed.). *Freud: Conflict and culture* (pp. 171–182). New York, NY: Vintage.

Daugherty, G. (2015). The brief history of "Americanitis." *Smithsonian*, March 25, 2015. Retrieved March 27, 2020 from https://www.smithsonianmag.com/history/brief-history-americanitis-180954739/.

Ellis, H. (1900). *Studies in the psychology of sex, volume 1: The evolution of modesty; the phenomena of sexual periodicity; auto-erotism.* Philadelphia, PA: F. A. Davis Company.

Foucault, M. (1978). *History of sexuality (Vol. 1): An introduction.* (R. Hurley, Trans.). New York, NY: Pantheon.

Foucault, M. (2003). *Abnormal: Lectures at the College de France 1974–1975.* (G. Burchell, Trans., V. Marchetti & A. Salomoni, Eds.). New York, NY: Picador.

Freud, S. (1894). Obsessions and phobias: Their psychical mechanism and their aetiology. *SE* 3, 69–82.

Freud, S. (1895a). On the grounds for detaching a particular syndrome from neurasthenia under the description 'anxiety neurosis'. *SE* 3, 85–115.

Freud, S. (1895b). A reply to criticisms of my paper on anxiety neurosis. *SE* 3, 119–139.

Freud, S. (1896). Heredity and the aetiology of the neuroses. *SE* 3, 141–156.

Freud, S. (1898). Sexuality in the aetiology of the neurosis. *SE* 3, 259–285.

Freud, S. (1905a). Fragment of an analysis of a case of hysteria. *SE* 7, 1–122.

Freud, S. (1905b). Three essays on the theory of sexuality. *SE* 7, 123–246.

Freud, S. (1906). My views on the part played by sexuality in the aetiology of the neuroses. *SE* 7, 269–279).

Freud, S. (1912). Contributions to a discussion on masturbation. *SE* 12, 239–254.

Freud, S. (1925). An autobiographical study. *SE* 20, 1–74.

Gosling, F. G. (1987). *Before Freud: Neurasthenia and the American medical community, 1870–1910*. Chicago, IL: University of Illinois Press.

Jones, E. (1913). A modern conception of the psychoneuroses. In E. Jones, *Papers on psycho-analysis* (pp. 122–133). New York, NY: William Wood & Co.

Kellogg, T. H. (1897). *A text-book of mental disease*. New York: William Wood & Co.

Marcus, G. (1998). One step back; Where are the elixirs of yesteryear when we hurt?". *The New York Times*, January 26, 1998, Section E, page 2. Retrieved March 27, 2020, from https://www.nytimes.com/1998/01/26/arts/one-step-back-where-are-the-elixirs-of-yesteryear-when-we-hurt.html.

Stekel, W. (1912). Uber Onanie. In B. Dattner, P. Federn, S. Ferenczi, et al., *Die Onanie: Vierzehn Beitrage zu einer Diskussionem der 'Wiener Psychoanalytischen Vereinigung' (Diskussionen der Wiener psychoanalytischen Vereinigung, vol. 2)* (pp. 29–45). Wiesbaden: J. F. Bergmann.

Stern, A. (1930). Masturbation: Its role in the neuroses. *American Journal of Psychiatry, 86*(6), 1081–1092.

Wakefield, J. C. (2023). *Freud's argument for the Oedipus complex: A philosophy of science analysis of the case of Little Hans*. New York: Routledge.

Chapter 6

Foucault on the Transition from the Masturbation Crusade to the Oedipal Theory

In this chapter, I reconstruct and critically evaluate Foucault's arguments for his daring thesis that Freud's Oedipal theory is in crucial respects continuous with the masturbation crusade. Foucault's thesis is in stark contrast to the standard view that the transition from Victorian doctrine to Freud's Oedipal theory represented a major theoretical rupture and a liberationist repudiation of oppressive crusade doctrines. The challenge for Foucault is to provide a plausible explanation of the nature and mechanics of the claimed continuity between these two seemingly very different theories and their associated practices. He must explain how parents' fear of the child's masturbation could shift to fear of the child's incestuous desire while preserving crucial tactics and functions of the masturbation crusade. He tackles this problem most explicitly in *Abnormal* (2003), and extends his analysis in *History of Sexuality, Volume 1* (*HS1*).

The Incest Theory as an Extension of the Masturbation Crusade

My goal is to understand Foucault's answer to his question: "What makes the psychoanalytic theory of incest acceptable to the bourgeois family?" (2003, p. 263)—that is, what allowed the incest theory (i.e., Freud's theory of the Oedipus complex), despite inadequate evidential credentials, to have such a remarkable level of influence on our culture, especially among middle- and upper-class families? Foucault's answer is that the incest theory, rather than being a major intellectual rupture with previous thought, was in important respects a continuous

DOI: 10.4324/9781003480396-6

extension of the two-century masturbation crusade that preceded it: "I think, then, that the functioning of the theme of incest should be situated in the century-old practice of the crusade against masturbation. In the end, it is an episode, or in any case a turning point, in this crusade" (2003, p. 268). As a "turning point" or what Foucault elsewhere calls a "mutation," there were of course significant theoretical changes: in the incest theory, childhood masturbation is no longer considered strictly autoerotic, child sexuality up to a point is considered developmentally natural, and so on. However, the incest theory, Foucault argues, is essentially the masturbation crusade in modified form, using novel theoretical means to achieve similar power/knowledge ends, and its acceptance can be understood in terms of that continuity. Like the crusade, the incest theory was accepted because, under the authoritative guise of a scientific-medical theory, it re-shaped family power relations in ways that were socio-culturally appealing.

Foucault is well aware that this "continuity" claim conflicts with the standard view that the Oedipal theory was a dramatic departure from and repudiation of the central doctrines of the masturbation crusade. Recall from Chapter 1 that Foucault says that the incest theory transformed the crusade's fear that "danger comes from the child's masturbation" into "danger comes from the child's desire [for the parent]" (2003, p. 263). He therefore must explain how parents' fear of the child's masturbation could shift to fear of the child's incestuous desire while preserving the crucial tactics and functions of the masturbation crusade.

Foucault's account of the incest theory in the tenth lecture of *Abnormal* is an attempt to provide such an explanation and demonstrate that the proposed continuity is more plausible than it seems.

In the next section, I offer some general comments on the nature of Foucault's continuity argument. After that, I turn to a close examination of Foucault's arguments in the tenth lecture and his further arguments in *HS1*.

Is the Oedipal Theory a Major Rupture in the Deployment of Sexuality?

Initially, Foucault's comments on the incest theory may seem peripheral to his vast argument about the two-century deployment of sexuality in his lectures and in his subsequent book, *HS1*. However, in the course of *HS1* it becomes apparent that Foucault's account of the incest theory is in fact pivotal to the credibility of his overall project. This is because the major challenge confronting Foucault's rejection of the "repressive hypothesis" (see Chapter 1) is the compelling power of the standard narrative that starting in the seventeenth century there was an era of sexual repression followed at the end of the nineteenth century by Freudian theory that largely reversed the repressive ideology, yielding the "sexual revolution" and our more sexually liberated era. Foucault's position on the incest theory directly challenges this standard narrative and thus opens the way for Foucault's overall analysis of a continuous deployment of sexual theories for social-control purposes lasting through Freud to our present time.

Foucault acknowledges that on the surface there appear to be some historical facts corresponding to the standard repression-liberation narrative with two "ruptures" in sexual medicine:

> The history of sexuality supposes two ruptures if one tries to center it on mechanisms of repression. The first, occurring in the course of the seventeenth century, was characterized by the advent of the great prohibitions, the exclusive promotion of adult marital sexuality, the imperatives of decency, the obligatory concealment of the body, the reduction to silence and mandatory reticences of language. The second, a twentieth-century phenomenon, was really less a rupture than an inflexion of the curve: this was the moment when the mechanisms of repression were seen as beginning to loosen their grip; one passed from insistent sexual taboos to a relative tolerance with regard to prenuptial or extramarital relations; the disqualification of 'perverts' diminished, their condemnation by the law was in part eliminated; a good many of the taboos that weighed on the sexuality of children were lifted.
>
> (1978, p. 115)

Foucault's goal is to dismantle this standard narrative by presenting a plausible alternative that denies Freud the role of revolutionary disruptor of the repressive regime: "[T]he mere fact that I've adopted this course undoubtedly excludes for me the possibility of Freud figuring as the radical break, on the basis of which everything else has to be rethought" (1980, p. 212). He must show that, to the contrary, Freud's incest theory is simply one more act in a continuing deployment-of-sexuality drama: "[A]round the eighteenth century there is installed, for economic reasons, historical reasons, and so forth, a general apparatus in which Freud will come to have his place" (1980, p. 212). In opposition to the "repression/rupture/liberation" narrative, Foucault offers an unsettling counter-narrative in which both the supposed sexual repression and the supposed sexual liberation are part of the same continuous social-regulatory process, with the two theories just different ways of delivering essentially the same social regulation

Of course, any two things are similar in some ways and dissimilar in others. Thus, in considering the magnitude of a theoretical rupture, it is important that the analysis be focused on the relevant domain. For example, Basaure (2009), noting that Foucault acknowledges some important ways that psychoanalysis diverges from earlier theory—for example, in rejecting the degenerescence theory—correctly observes: "According to Foucault, psychoanalysis was in the paradoxical situation of embodying both break and continuity with respect to traditional psychiatry" (2009, p. 341). However, Basaure is considering psychoanalysis overall. In the present context of evaluating Foucault's continuity claim about the incest theory, what is relevant is only whether there is predominantly continuity or a major rupture in regard to concerns about childhood masturbation and the associated tactics of power/knowledge, not the broader domain of psychoanalysis. It is in this domain that Foucault is unequivocal in postulating continuity.

If one accepts Foucault's notion of a two-century deployment of sexuality, then it might seem initially plausible that the Oedipal theory is a continuous extension of that deployment because temporally it directly follows the crusade, and in terms of content it too is about child sexuality. Moreover, for a concern about the prohibition of masturbation, it substitutes a concern about another sexual prohibition—the incest taboo.

However, this argument is ultimately based on a simple Gestalt impression of continuity in the timeline and sexual content from the incest theory to the masturbation crusade. Foucault's continuity claim calls for more rigorous evidence of specific lines of continuity in the mechanisms and tactics by which the transition was accomplished. In his 1975 lecture, Foucault attempts to provide just such evidence via a psychological account of how parents—and, presumably, theorists as well—might have easily moved from one theory to the other.

Foucault himself does not presume that, for example, if two temporally contiguous theories are about sexuality, a shift from one to the other cannot be a major rupture. In disputing the standard narrative of two centuries of sexual repression followed by Freudian liberation, Foucault argues that not only the eighteenth-century initial rupture in which confession, surveillance, and medicalization of sexuality were inaugurated, but also the surge in medical sexology and medicalization of perverse sexual acts in the mid-nineteenth century, which was a shift within the domain of sexual theory, were both major ruptures. Thus, he claims, during the nineteenth century a major rupture occurred in which both the earlier and later theories were within the deployment of sexuality. So, Foucault's own analysis precludes his relying on the simple Gestalt argument.

Foucault claims that the inauguration of the masturbation crusade marked a qualitatively much larger rupture to which Freud's theories cannot be compared:

> this transformation...seems to me enigmatic in a much profounder sense than that of psychoanalysis...: within the space of twenty years, throughout Europe, doctors and educators came to be exclusively obsessed with that incredible epidemic threatening the whole human race: child masturbation. Something that no one was supposed to have previously practiced!
>
> (1980, p. 217)

Freud, Foucault argues, is but an episode in a larger process defined by major ruptures:

> I'll say this, that for me the whole business of breaks and non-breaks is always at once a point of departure and a very relative thing.... I'm saying, let's try to shift the scenery and take as our starting point something else which is just as manifest as the 'break', provided one changes the reference points. One then finds this formidable mechanism emerging—the machinery of the confession, within which in fact psychoanalysis and Freud figure as episodes.
>
> (1980, p. 211)

Foucault claims that no similarly major rupture but only much smaller more routine ruptures occurred in the transition from late-nineteenth-century sexology to Freud's theories, comparable to many incremental changes in masturbation-crusade tactics over the previous two centuries:

> These multiple datings doubtless will not coincide with the great repressive cycle that is ordinarily situated between the seventeenth and the twentieth centuries... [T]hese techniques, with their mutations, their shifts, their continuities and ruptures, does not coincide with the hypothesis of a great repressive phase that was inaugurated in the course of the classical age and began to slowly decline in the twentieth. There was rather a perpetual inventiveness, a steady growth of methods and procedures, with two especially productive moments in this proliferating history: around the middle of the sixteenth century, the development of procedures of direction and examination of conscience; and at the beginning of the nineteenth century, the advent of medical technologies of sex.
>
> (1978, pp. 115, 119)

Psychoanalyst Jacques-Alain Miller (1992) attempts to defend Freud from Foucault's continuity claim by chiding Foucault for making a verbal continuity argument that has no substance. He explains that in *HS1*, Foucault "proceeds by means of inclusion," by using an arbitrary property common to the crusade and the incest theory—namely, talking about sex—to define a larger domain that includes both, creating the illusion that they have some unity:

> On the basis of psychoanalysis, he invents a vaster ensemble in which psychoanalysis is, in turn, situated. He calls this the 'apparatus of sexuality'. Next, we should consider how it is that, starting with psychoanalysis, Foucault obtains this apparatus of sexuality, in which he situates psychoanalysis as one composite part amongst others. In fact he does so by drawing on one key aspect, relevant for the purpose of inclusion in archaeology, which is summed up in the syntagma: 'talking about sex'. As soon as this key element has been isolated, all kinds of different forms of theoretical knowledge [*savoirs*], practices, institutions, forms of behavior, become apparent.

These might be considered to be contrary to psychoanalysis and yet, by virtue of this common trait, this attribute, they can be grouped alongside it to form an ensemble which, heterogeneous though it might be, can be given a name... That name is: 'the apparatus of sexuality'. Now that it has been situated in this new object, which has been created before our very eyes, psychoanalysis immediately loses the very uniqueness which psychoanalysts flatter themselves that it possesses. It can be seen as sharing common ground with the forms of discourse and practices which it called into question from the moment of its birth, yet which can now be seen as calling it into question.

(Miller, 1992, pp. 59–60)

In what Miller calls the "Foucault slide," he observes that Foucault finds that "talk about sex" is such a malleable criterion that it leads him even farther afield to yet earlier eras. And, when this is exhausted, Foucault further broadens his domain in later work by adding the property, "talking about the self."

These concerns—including the unpersuasiveness of the simple Gestalt argument, Miller's critique of the expansive "talking about sex" approach, and Foucault's confusing references to many smaller and larger ruptures of various sorts that are all judged very subjectively—demonstrate that Foucault's vague pronouncements about ruptures and continuities are evidentially insufficient by themselves to warrant his continuity claim. In his 1975 lecture, he takes on this challenge directly, offering a sustained argument for the ease and smoothness of the transition from the crusade to the incest theory due to their close and continuous psychological relationship.

Foucault on the Ease of Transition from the Masturbation Crusade's Autoeroticism to the Incest Theory's Relational Sexual Desires

Foucault begins his attempt to defend the plausibility of his account by acknowledging that his thesis seems unlikely. The pleasure of self-stimulated autoeroticism on which the masturbation campaign's conception of the child's precocious sexuality is based, and the conceptualization of the son as lusting for the mother on which the incest theory is based, appear strikingly different in content and implications. Consequently, it is not at all obvious how or why the incest theory should emerge from, or is even consistent with, the masturbation crusade's assumptions and associated practices, given the apparent conceptual gulf between the two theories

Recognizing this problem, Foucault attempts to rectify his account of the incest theory with the realities of the masturbation crusade and to show that such diverse concerns can be organic parts of a broader common power structure. He acknowledges that the shift from one to the other was difficult because of the gulf between child autoeroticism and adult-like object-related sexual desire. Yet, in another way it was easy, he suggests:

> [I]f we accept this schema that the problematization of the child's sexuality was originally connected to the contact established between the bodies of parents and children, to the folding of the parents' bodies over the children's bodies, you can see why the theme of incest assumed such intensity at the end of the nineteenth century, that is to say, why it was accepted both with such difficulty and so easily. It was difficult to accept precisely because, since the end of the eighteenth century, it had been said, explained, and profusely portrayed that the child's sexuality was first of all an autoerotic and consequently nonrelational sexuality that could not be superimposed on a sexual relationship between individuals. Moreover, this nonrelational sexuality entirely sealed off in the child's own body could not be superimposed on an adult type of sexuality. It was clearly very difficult to take up this sexuality and insert it in an incestuous relationship with adults and to bring child and adult sexuality back into contact or continuity with each other from the angle of incest, or of child-parent incestuous desire. It was difficult for parents to accept that they were beset and invested by their children's incestuous desire when they had been reassured for one hundred years [by the fact] that children's sexuality was entirely localized, sealed off, and locked up within autoeroticism.
>
> (2003, pp. 265–266)

According to Foucault, child sexuality had been presented by the masturbation theory as autoerotic and sealed up within the child, distinguishing it sharply from adult-like Oedipal sexuality aimed at an outside sexual object. (Note that I use "masturbation theory" as a shorthand to refer to the medical theories, reviewed in Chapter 3, that provided a framework and rationale for the crusade against masturbation.) To the degree that the theories are logically incommensurable, it would seem to be that much harder to locate them within the same power/knowledge structure or to expect them to manifest similar structures of surveillance. Foucault's discussion of the incest theory is largely an attempt to bridge this acknowledged gap between the two theories.

As an aside, in characterizing the masturbation crusade versus Oedipal accounts of masturbation, Foucault utilizes Freud's distinction between autoerotic sexuality not involving desire for an outside object versus Oedipal incestuous desire that has an object. However, the conceptual distinction between autoeroticism and object-oriented sexuality within Freud's thinking is more difficult to elucidate than it may seem, and it has puzzled many writers. For example, is early oral gratification when sucking at the breast autoerotic, or does the child's desire have the mother, or the breast, or milk, as an object? Other components of infantile sexuality, such as exhibitionism, sadism, and voyeurism seem to be potentially describable in terms that involve objects and relationships rather than sheer self-gratification via localized pleasure. Moreover, Freud occasionally says that sexuality is autoerotic until the reorganization of sexuality under the primacy of the genitals at puberty, thus bewilderingly—and presumably mistakenly—including the Oedipal period as autoerotic. I ignore these issues here and stick with Foucault's philosophically commonsense usage that distinguishes childhood masturbation driven by simple tension reduction and organ pleasure as autoerotic versus incestuous desire as object related. One might add that the difficulties of understanding the historical theoretical transition from autoeroticism to incestuous desire portrayed by Foucault have a parallel in the difficulties of understanding Freud's developmental theory, specifically in answering the question of how and why the child transitions from autoeroticism to object-oriented sexual desire (Eagle, 2011; Widlocher, 2002).

How, then, does Foucault account for the substantial influence of the counter-traditional incest theory among bourgeois families who were steeped in the masturbation crusade's ideology? In a glass-half-empty to glass-half-full Gestalt switch, Foucault suggests that the autoerotic sexualization of the child during the masturbation suppression campaign *eased* the way to the incest theory's acceptance by preparing the way on the issue of child sexuality more generally:

> However, from another angle, we could say that the crusade against masturbation in which this new fear of incest is inscribed to a certain extent made it easy for parents to accept the idea that their children desire them, and desire them incestuously. This easiness, alongside or intertwined with the difficulty, can be explained or accounted for fairly easily. From the middle of the eighteenth century, from around 1750-1760, what were parents told? Apply your bodies to the bodies of your children; observe your children; get close to your children; possibly get in bed with your children; slide between their sheets; observe, spy on, and surprise all the signs of your children's desire; come stealthily to their bed at night, lift up their sheets, see what they are doing, and put your hand there, at least to stop them. And now, after having been told this for one hundred years, they are told: This formidable desire you have uncovered—in the material sense of the word—is directed toward you. The most formidable thing about this desire is precisely that it concerns you.
>
> (2003, p. 266)

Foucault's argument here is that it is easier to reconceptualize an already-sexualized child's existing autoerotic "formidable desire" as a parent-directed desire than it is to invent the desire from scratch in a sexually innocent child. Thus, once the masturbation crusade paved the way for thinking of the child as possessing sexual desire in the autoerotic sense, it became easier to think about the child's sexuality in an object-related sense. Sexual danger is continuous, but it is shifted from the danger of family members seducing the child to the danger of family members arousing the child's own spontaneous desires. This degree of continuity allowed the easy transference of power/knowledge functions from one theory to the other, according to Foucault.

Note that there is also a suggestion in the above passages that perhaps the parents' intimate surveillance of the child aroused incestuous desires in the parents that they then found it easy to project onto the child. The idea that parents experienced such desires during their intimate surveillance of the child and felt guilty because of it is considered by Foucault, and is discussed below.

Problems with Foucault's "Ease of Redirection of Sexuality" Argument

Foucault argues that sexualizing the child was the larger challenge, and redirecting that sexuality at an incestuous object was easier once that had occurred. Can the ease of transition from the masturbation theory to the incest theory be "accounted for fairly easily" in the way Foucault suggests? This simple portrayal of the shift between theories ignores or sidesteps the problem that Foucault himself raises for the occurrence of such a transition. More importantly, it does not adequately take account of further differences in the logical structures and associated practices of the theories that pose obstacles to the ease of transitioning from one to the other within a constant power/knowledge framework.

Foucault suggests that the incest theory simply takes the already-sexualized child and directed the sexuality outward. This portrayal radically mischaracterizes the discontinuity involved. *In the relevant sense, the child was never really sexualized by the masturbation theory in the first place.* The challenge of creating a child that is inherently sexual was first undertaken by the incest theory and its associated (and at the time scandalous) theory of "infantile sexuality" and the libido theory.

The masturbation crusade prior to the Oedipal theory had no theory of *spontaneous normal* "formidable desire" at all. The masturbation crusade's vigilance was primarily *preventive*, and in most cases the point was to avoid ever uncovering a "formidable desire." It was directed at protecting the inherently *nonsexual* nature of the child from pathological influences that could prematurely awaken a sexual interest that properly emerges in puberty but can be precociously activated by earlier genital stimulation or constitutional disorder. Thus, when masturbation-crusade parents pulled back the covers on their sleeping child, what they expected to discover and did generally discover were not surreptitious expressions of autoerotic sexual desire but *no expression of sexual desire at all*, so there was nothing to be

easily redirected, at least nothing resembling the universal spontaneous incestuous sexual desire postulated by the incest theory. Thus,
the gulf between the masturbation and incest theories was much
greater than Foucault admits. The very thing that the masturbation
crusade urgently taught parents could be avoided by their actions, and
thus the point of the crusade and its surveillance—namely, the
sexualization of the child—was now claimed to occur as a matter of
developmental course no matter what the parents did. Surveillance
was helpless against a normal and inevitable developmental stage.

This basic point bears emphasis because it is a crucial omission
throughout Foucault's discussion. The Victorian campaign against
masturbation did *not* presume that the child is naturally an autoerotically sexual being. If that were so, it would be difficult to
understand why there was such urgency in the parents' struggle
against the child's sexuality. Rather, the masturbation theory, as put
forward in prominent conservative Victorian medical texts (e.g.,
Acton, 1875), postulates a naturally nonsexual child and attributes
any premature sexualizing of the child to pathogenic external sexual
influences (e.g., nannies, servants, relatives, wayward peers, and other
seducers), accidental discoveries by the child due to unusual circumstances (e.g., scratching a chronic genital itch due to worms), or to a
disorder yielding premature sexuality. Childhood sexuality within the
masturbation theory exists only in such pathological cases, and *any*
sexualization of the child is seen as potentially pathogenic. (We saw in
Chapter 5 that this was also Freud's early "seduction theory" view.)
What the parent was trying to accomplish through vigilance was the
prevention of the sexualization of the child to any degree and in any
way. Thus, there was no presupposed universal autoerotic desire into
which a universal incestuous object could easily be inserted.

In contrast, the incest theory is a theory of normal human development
that attributes sexuality to all children as a natural occurrence. Unlike the
masturbation theory, the incest theory does not in the first instance
portray childhood sexuality as a pathology of the few. It portrays a
universal, spontaneous, and normal sexual developmental stage essential
for healthy development. Pathology can occur if the stage goes wrong
and excessive sexual stimulation occurs. Nothing remotely like this sort
of routine and inevitable sexualization of the *normal* child—autoerotic or
otherwise—had been advanced during the masturbation crusade.

It is not true, therefore, as Foucault claims, that prior to the Oedipal theory parents had already taken the major step of seeing their children as sexual—not even autoerotically so—and the parents were merely required by the new incest theory to redirect the child's sexuality upon themselves. Rather, they had seen their children as naturally non-sexual and pure but as potentially subject to pathogenic influences that could prematurely awaken sexuality. These potential dangers could largely be banished from the home or prevented with adequate surveillance. Failing that, any manifestations of sexuality could be identified and extirpated using the severe remedies available. The sexual innocence of the child was still held as an ideal that could be attained.

The revolutionary step of seeing the child as naturally, inherently sexual is one taken by Freud. Indeed, Freud devotes a portion of the discussion section of the Hans case history to making the argument that Hans's manifest sexuality is typical of normal children. In the *Three Essays*, Freud himself differentiates his view from the traditional approach to childhood sexuality:

One feature of the popular view of the sexual instinct is that it is absent in childhood and only awakens in the period of life described as puberty....It is true that in the literature of the subject one occasionally comes across remarks upon precocious sexual activity in small children—upon erections, masturbation and even activities resembling coitus. But these are always quoted only as exceptional events, as oddities or as horrifying instances of precocious depravity. So far as I know, not a single author has clearly recognized the regular existence of a sexual instinct in childhood...
(1905, p. 173)

In a footnote to this passage, Freud underscores this point:

The assertion made in the text has since struck me myself as being so bold that I have undertaken the task of testing its validity by looking through the literature once more. The outcome of this is that I have allowed my statement to stand unaltered. The scientific examination of both the physical and mental phenomena of sexuality in childhood is still in its earliest beginnings.... Somatic sexual manifestations from the period before puberty have only attracted attention in connection with phenomena of degeneracy and as indications of degeneracy. In none of the accounts which I have read of the psychology of this period of life is a chapter to be found on the erotic life of children...

(1905, p. 173, n. 2)

Foucault tends to presume the "universality of child sexual deviance" (2003, p. 62) and even the "universal sexuality of children" (2003, p. 328) as assumptions of the masturbation crusade. However, the step to the incest theory required not merely, as Foucault would have it, the redirection of existing desire (because no such desire was assumed to exist in normal children), but rather the creation from scratch of a universal natural sexual desire in all children who were formerly seen as naturally innocent of any such desires. Nothing in the masturbation campaign prepared parents for this transforming revelation about normal child development—a revelation and conceptual leap much more basic and difficult to assimilate than the one Foucault postulates.

Rather than simply rotating the object of sexual desire 180 degrees from inside to outside, the Oedipal theory undermines all of the masturbation theory's most essential doctrines, including childhood innocence, the external triggering of any childhood sexual feeling, the uniformly pathological and dangerous nature of childhood sexuality, and the possibility of preventing any childhood sexuality through sufficiently vigorous surveillance. These conceptual gulfs undermine Foucault's portrayal of the ease of the transition.

Foucault's Three Further "Essential" Arguments for Why the Incest Theory Might be an Extension of the Masturbation Theory

Attempting to elaborate his general "ease of transition" argument (and perhaps aware that his general argument considered above is insufficient), Foucault proceeded to offer three supplementary "essential" answers to the question of why the psychoanalytic theory of incest was acceptable to the bourgeois family as the successor to the masturbation theory: "A number of consequences follow from this, three of which are, I think, essential" (2003, p. 266). As I consider these arguments, I evaluate their persuasiveness partly in light of divergence in logical structure and practical implications of the masturbation and incest theories described above.

Essential Argument 1: The Incest Theory Relieves the Parents of Guilt

Foucault postulates that the incest theory is acceptable because it relieves parents of guilt. The parents' guilt is, first, over their intrusions into their child's life in the attempt to prevent masturbation. But second, as indicated above, Foucault suggests, the parents feel guilty due to the fact that their observations of and focus on the child's intimate life inevitably arouses the parents' own incestuous sexual feelings toward the child:

> First, you can see that the relationship of incestuous indiscretion between parents and children that had been organized for more than a century is, as it were, inverted. For more than a century, parents had been told to get close to their children: A conduct of incestuous indiscretion had been dictated to them. Now, after a century, they are exonerated of precisely the guilt they may well have felt about actively discovering their children's desiring bodies. They are told: Do not be anxious, it is not you who is incestuous. The incest is not directed from you to them, from your indiscretion or curiosity about their bodies exposed by you. Rather, the incest goes from them to you, since it is they who have desired you from the start. Consequently, precisely at the point at which the incestuous child-parent relation is etiologically saturated, parents are morally exonerated of the moral indiscretion, approach, and closeness to which they had been constrained for more than a century. This, then, is the first moral benefit that makes the psychoanalytic theory of incest acceptable.
>
> (2003, pp. 266–267)

Foucault is claiming that when parents discovered that they themselves were the objects of their child's feared sexual desires, they felt exonerated from their guilt. The guilt that they felt was, first, about their intrusive surveillance of their child's sexuality, and second, about what Foucault hypothesizes to be their sexual feelings toward the child that the intimate surveillance aroused in the parents themselves.

It is difficult to give credence to this argument. Because the child's sexuality is now understood to exist spontaneously, perhaps it is true that Oedipal parents are exonerated from the guilt of thinking that they did something wrong, such as paying inadequate attention to visitors to the household or not adequately watching the child at bedtime, and thus failed to prevent the child's sexuality. However, the parents now know that it is their own presence and closeness to the child—including the intimacies of surveillance—that has stimulated the child's natural sexuality and could endanger the child's health, creating a new and potent form of guilt.

It is also arguable that the parents' intrusions were not generally guilt-inducing and needed no exonerating, for they were understood to be medically necessary to avoid potentially fatal illness. If we take the Little Hans case (Freud, 1909) as evidence for a family's reaction to the Oedipal theory, it would appear to support this view. The control of Hans's masturbation was one of the few things on which the parents firmly agreed and towards which they acted confidently and in concert, seemingly with no guilt at all—despite using extreme measures such as threats and physical restraints. The incest issue, on the other hand, was fraught with anxiety and dispute, not seeming to confer exoneration but rather an additional burden leading to accusations aimed at the mother for her inadvertently provoking Hans's incestuous desires (for further discussion, see Chapter 7).

Postulating a minimal natural pedophilic sexual arousal at parental sexual examinations of the child is not entirely implausible given empirical studies of sexual arousal. However, it is not clear why the incest theory would be comforting rather than alarming under such circumstances. Foucault suggests that the comforting inversion is that it is the boy, "not you" (the parent), who has the desire. But where does this "not you" come from? It seems interpolated by Foucault without warrant, given that he hypothesizes that such desires are causing guilt in the parent. The Oedipal parent, in Foucault's scenario, is most plausibly left with *both* the old guilt over arousal during surveillance *and* a new guilt over being the object of—and perhaps provoking to greater intensity—the child's Oedipal feelings. If one has inklings of pedophilic desire for one's child, the idea that the child "reciprocates" those feelings and is fantasizing you acting on those desires is more likely to produce disorientation, revulsion, and panic than comforting guilt-reduction in most bourgeois parents.

The key point from the perspective of social regulation and power/ knowledge is that the child's postulated natural incestuous desire poses a more pervasive and inherently guilt-inducing kind of problem than the prevention of masturbation, and thus requires new forms of family regulation. The parent's intrusion now becomes an occasion of potential overstimulation of the child, with the parent burdened by the unhappy thought that every act of well-intentioned affection may provoke the child to excessive sexual arousal, thus to potential disease. Thus, control not of the child but of such parental stimulation seems warranted. As Little Hans so sagely pointed out during his analysis, "wanting's not doing" (Freud, 1909, p. 30), and wanting is a much more elusive target of control. Unlike masturbation, the *desire* to have sex with one's parent, and the sexual arousal associated with the fantasies of doing so, are not controllable by physical restraints. However, they can perhaps be influenced to some extent by less intimate exposure to the exciting object and by the object's acting in a restrained way. With the incest theory comes an enormous new burden of moral responsibility from which, given the routine needs of family life, it is virtually impossible to fully exonerate oneself. The mother must perpetually live with guilt that her interactions with her child may overstep the proper boundaries and cause enduring psychological damage (Wakefield, 2023).

Because the incest theory conceives of a boy's sexuality as internally generated and thus more or less constant, the variability in the mother's indulgence of the son's erotic needs becomes the new center of attention for control purposes. Freud's doctrine of component sexual instincts (discussed in Chapter 7) and his emphasis on the hidden erotic nature of the usual affection between mother and son (i.e., his "sexualization of attachment" [Wakefield, 2023]) are combined in a toxic way with the incest theory to yield the conclusion that all mother/son affection is erotic. This leads to the scrutiny of every nook and cranny of mother-son interaction. When combined with the additional doctrine that over-gratification leads to "spoiling" (or pathological "fixation"), parental guilt is potentially enormously increased. That guilt becomes a primary means of control, with the parents' self-restraint in avoiding "seductive" actions that might amplify incestuous wishes replacing the child's physical restraint to prevent masturbation. Guilt is now omnipresent in a way it was not during the crusade.

Essential Argument 2: The Incest Theory as an Exchange for State Control of the Child

Foucault's next explanation of the ease of transition from the masturbation crusade to Oedipal theory is that the child's Oedipal desire is reassuring because it underscores the parents' deep possession of the child, even as the State is taking over the child's education:

> Second, you can see that parents are given a supplementary guarantee since they are not only told that the sexual body of their children belongs to them by right, that they are to watch over it, supervise it, control it, and surprise it, but they are also told that it belongs to them at an even deeper level since their children's desire is addressed to them. So not only is the child's body in some sense their material possession, but even more so they also control the child's desire, which is available to them because it is directed toward them. This supplementary guarantee given to parents may correspond to the family being further dispossessed of the child's body when the extension of schooling and procedures of disciplinary training at the end of the nineteenth century detaches children even more from the family milieu. All this should be examined more closely.
>
> (2003, p. 267)

The tentativeness of the last comments that the incest theory "may" correspond to greater State control of education and that "all this should be examined more closely" suggests that Foucault himself had doubts about this facile extension of his analysis of masturbation to the incest theory. The idea seems to be that more State schooling is offset by more sexual intensity within the family. The incest theory, it is claimed, offered parents a more profound sense of possession of their child in virtue of the child's sexual desire for the parents, thus reassuring the parents that the child was not really being lost to the

State and thereby allowing the parents to feel at ease relinquishing more of the child's education to the State.

However, having a child's sexual desire directed at oneself does not necessarily translate into a parent's reassuring feeling that the child "belongs" to the parent. This is, after all, a desire few parents could tolerate to embrace or exploit. Nor does it follow that the parents gain some leverage to "control the child's desire" just because it is directed at them—as the Hans case reveals. Indeed, desire being as ephemeral as it is, control over masturbation as a physical act is easier than control over desires of which the child himself may be unaware and which the child may be incapable of verbally expressing. Even if the child is now guaranteed to be "yours" in the incest theory's sense, what good is a guarantee that ensures a form of possession one finds aversive or even horrifying, and that has the primary result that you must vigorously disavow it and create distance between yourself and the child? As a result of this "possession" of the child's desire, the child in fact must belong to you even less than before because possession itself has become suspect, creating a gulf that can only exacerbate the problem of disengagement in other domains rather than offer an offsetting closeness.

If there is indeed any link between the incest theory and greater State control of the child, it must be for reasons opposite to the reasons congruent with the masturbation theory put forward by Foucault. The incest theory does not intensify sexual entanglement of the family, thus allowing for more distance on other issues. Rather, the parents must distance themselves from the child, and child care or greater educational control are more easily accepted, so that the child and parents can escape from the stifling Oedipal household and its anxieties. The State can best take control of the child if the parents are attached to each other but not too much to the child, a goal served if parents monitor themselves against being too intimate with their children.

One might argue that this distancing attitude has been gradually extended. In our day, even home schooling is commonly considered by metaphorical extension to be too "incestuous," trapping the child within the parents' intellectual and cultural limitations. Whereas the inheritance of guild membership was once a great advantage, now to push one's child into one's own vocation is viewed by many as tantamount to emotional abuse. To purposely attempt to reproduce oneself through one's child is seen as misguidedly selfish, like the horror of cloning, rather than as a desirable symbolic immortality. The reaction of horror to incestuous over-closeness has come to suffuse our most fundamental attitudes about the meaning of the parent-child relationship.

Essential Argument 3: Greater Penetration of Medical Power/Knowledge

Finally, Foucault argues that the incest theory brought parent-child relations more under the regimentation of medical theory and allowed greater penetration of the family by medical power, which was reassuring to parents:

> The third reason why, despite some difficulties, the theory of incest could, on the whole, be accepted was that by placing such a terrible offense at the very heart of the parent-child relationship, by making the absolute crime of incest the point of origin of every little abnormality, one strengthened the urgency of external intervention, of a kind of mediating element of analysis, control, and correction. In short, one strengthened the chances of medical technology getting a hold on the cluster of relationships within the family; the family was more effectively plugged in to medical power. Broadly speaking, the theory of incest that appeared at the end of the nineteenth century involved a kind of formidable gratification for parents who henceforth knew themselves to be the objects of a mad desire and who, at the same time, discovered through this theory that they themselves could be the subject of a rational knowledge concerning their relationships with their children: I no longer have to discover what the child desires by going to his bedroom at night and peering under his sheets like a dubious domestic. I know what he desires from a scientific knowledge that is authentic because it is a medical knowledge. I am therefore both a subject of this knowledge and the object of this mad desire. This enables us to see how—with psychoanalysis, from the beginning of the twentieth century—parents could become (and how willingly!) the zealous, excited, and delighted agents of a new wave in the medical normalization of the family.

(2003, pp. 267–268)

Much of what Foucault claims here is not persuasive when placed within the context of his broader account. Foucault is of course correct that Freud made Oedipal desire "the point of origin of every little abnormality" (e.g., "When, however, an adult neurotic patient comes to us for psycho-analytic treatment…, we find regularly that his neurosis has as its point of departure an infantile anxiety…taking its start from the conflicts of his childhood" [Freud, 1909, p. 143]). However, as we saw in Chapter 4, Foucault portrays the masturbation crusade in vivid terms as having attributed not just later psychological disorders but all manner of physical disorders as well to childhood masturbation. The incest theory did not in fact expand the domain of possible medical problems due to child sexuality that might require medical attention.

Foucault's claim that an effect of the incest theory was to "strengthen the urgency" of medical intervention seems dubious on its face. Perusing the rabid medical literature on masturbation (see Chapter 3), it would seem that the urgency could not get much greater, and the goal was clear and absolute. The masturbation crusade left no ambiguity about what needed to be prevented and how to prevent it; any genital stimulation of the child posed a great, even mortal, danger to the child and must be avoided. In contrast, given the Oedipal theory's ambiguity on the question of how much incestuous desire and parental affection is normal, the incest theory allowed a considerable role for parental judgment of how much was enough, making the target of intervention more elusive and the necessity of medical consultation less clear. One might consult a physician about the threshold of excessive physical affection and whether the child should be allowed to sleep in the parents' bed and the like, but unlike the masturbation crusade, there were few medically clear guidelines and the primary burden fell on the parents to monitor their interactions with the child and avoid encouragement of the child's desires. Unlike masturbation, there was no restraining apparatus sold by one's physician that would stop Oedipal fantasies, unless the fantasies were triggered or excessively amplified by masturbation (see Chapter 7).

One might think that Foucault is on solid ground in suggesting that Oedipal theory increased the opportunity for medical surveillance because the masturbation crusade was centered around occasional pathological child sexuality whereas the incest theory concerns a universal phenomenon, thus universalizing potential medical intervention. However, this notion does not fit the reality because during the crusade the fear that one's child might succumb to the nightmare of permanent abnormality from masturbation was universal and did cause a potentially universal medical intervention and medical guidance of parental actions, albeit aimed at universal *prevention* of a pathogenic occasional outcome rather than aimed at regulating a universal outcome from occasionally becoming pathogenic. Moreover, once incestuous fantasies were considered developmentally normal, it was clear that most of the time the Oedipal phase could be negotiated without external intervention, or with minimal medical advice such as separate sleeping arrangements for parents and children and restraint of cuddling. Given the medical penetration of the family during the masturbation crusade, the incest theory certainly does not seem like a turning point in this regard, nor does Foucault make any serious case that it is. In all, Foucault's suggestion that the incest theory increased medical penetration of the family from the already extreme levels of the crusade is questionable at best, although Foucault is correct that the incest theory at least maintained heavy medical guidance of family life.

What of Foucault's argument that Freud's incest theory "involved a kind of formidable gratification for parents who henceforth knew themselves to be the objects of a mad desire and who, at the same time, discovered through this theory that they themselves could be the subject of a rational knowledge concerning their relationships with their children"? I suppose one might accept Foucault's assumption that there is always some form of gratification in realizing that one is desired (but note how in this and some other of his speculative leaps Foucault relies on an informal understanding of "human nature" that he endlessly criticized). However, Foucault's claim that this presented parents with a "formidable gratification" seems difficult to square with his vivid characterization of the parents' reflexive horror of incest that he describes as "a terrible offense at the very heart of the parent-child relationship" and an "absolute crime" requiring "analysis, control, and correction." Moreover, the fact that parents "discovered through this theory that they themselves could be the subject of a rational knowledge concerning their relationships with their children" seems nothing new because the masturbation crusade also depended on scientific theories that placed the spotlight on parents and their relationships to and control of their children as well, albeit in different protective respects.

Is the parent really gratified by the notion that "I no longer have to discover what the child desires by going to his bedroom at night and peering under his sheets like a dubious domestic. I know what he desires from a scientific knowledge that is authentic because it is a medical knowledge"? This knowledge does no more for the parent than "I know what he may do if left alone in bed and what its outcome will be and what I must do to prevent it, from authentic medical scientific knowledge." The assumption of the scientific and medical nature of the knowledge of child sexuality was present in the masturbation crusade as much as in the Oedipal theory. Even the weaker claim that at least parents no longer had to examine their children because they could simply assume a fantasied incestuous desire—which would save the parent a monitoring trip to the child's bedroom—is not entirely correct because, as we will see in Chapter 7, under the incest theory's regime of power/knowledge as initially presented in Freud's Little Hans case history, a central role is preserved for the detection of masturbation as an indirect indicator of Oedipal over-arousal.

Despite these weaknesses, I believe that there is an illuminating insight into the incest theory's acceptance implicit in Foucault's comments on the third essential reason regarding penetration of medical power into the family. It remains implicit because Foucault is arguing for continuity of power/knowledge tactics across theories, whereas the insight concerns a dramatic difference in tactics. When Foucault says that "one strengthened the chances of medical technology getting a hold on the cluster of relationships within the family," what changes is not the magnitude of medical power but rather precisely which "cluster of relationships within the family" is targeted by that medical power to achieve "analysis, control, and correction." This change, ignored by Foucault, has reshaped family life through to today. The change was a shift from control of the child's behavior to control of the level of intimate physical affection between mother and son, especially in the bedroom with regard to sleeping and cuddling. What is momentous about the incest theory is that for the first time it made the parents not just the *controllers* of the child's desires (as Foucault's account of the masturbation crusade would have it) or the inadvertent *objects* of those desires (as Foucault's account of the incest theory would have it) but the *causes* of potentially pathological levels of the child's desires (as we shall see in Chapter 7), ushering in the era of parental anxiety that we still inhabit. It is true that the incest theory engulfed the parents within its theoretical medical domain, but the crucial effect was redirection of the theory away from the child and toward the mother as a locus of control efforts. This novel form of medical penetration of the family diverges radically from the masturbation crusade's forms of control. It is not any general increase in the urgency of medical regulation but rather the specific qualitative nature of the new forms of regulation involving the distancing of parents from children, I have argued (Wakefield, 2023), that is the key to understanding the acceptance of the Oedipal theory (for further discussion, see Chapters 7 and 8).

This completes my review of Foucault's arguments in his 1975 lecture aimed at explaining the acceptance of the incest theory. We have seen that in the lecture Foucault vigorously and systematically defends his central contention that the shift from the masturbation crusade to Freud's incest theory is relatively smooth and continuous and does not represent a major rupture in the deployment of sexuality's power/knowledge, a contention crucial to his overall argument against the repression-liberation narrative. However, the above examination yields the conclusion that Foucault's arguments in the lecture fail to convincingly support his continuity claim. I now move on to consider Foucault's quite different comments on the incest theory in his later book, *HS1*.

Oedipal Theory as Rectification of the Deployments of Sexuality and Alliance

Once Foucault solidified his story about the masturbation crusade as power/knowledge that causes intensification of family interaction in service of the formation and stabilization of the nuclear family (see Chapter 4) and argued that the Oedipus complex is an extension of the masturbation crusade, he had little more to say about the distinctive functions of the Oedipus complex in the 1975 lectures. However, he went considerably further in *HS1*.

Foucault in *HS1* retains the continuity argument of *Abnormal* but does not belabor it with the same sorts of argument about how parents might react. Instead, he moves to the level of the workings of power/knowledge and offers a much more substantive and multi-faceted analysis of the evolution of the tactics and functions of the incest theory. This analysis includes many dramatic claims, but it remains sketchy and lacking in regor, without any attempt at a systematic defense of explanatory claims of the kind presented in the 1975 lecture.

In the book's analysis, Foucault portrays a complex interaction between the deployment of sexuality and changing structures of family power. He refers to the latter as "the deployment of alliance," consisting of the rules that govern formal family relationships that establish patterns of family obligation, inheritance, kinship, and other such legally regulated commitments. However, changing sexual mores were inherently disruptive to alliance and its roles and constraints. The incest theory, Foucault argues, saves alliance by redeploying the development of sexuality within the family's own relationships in a way that solidifies the family in its nuclear form without disrupting the alliance. Thus, the Oedipal theory created mutual support between these two forms of power and "guaranteed that this deployment of sexuality... would not be able to escape from the grand and ancient system of alliance" (1978, 109–110).

Foucault emphasizes the very different workings of these two forms of power. Whereas the deployment of alliance has the function of maintaining society through reproduction regulated by law, the deployment of sexuality proliferates by penetrating bodies and con-trolling populations in increasingly detailed and comprehensive ways by influencing bodily sensations and the pursuit of pleasure. He portrays the relationship between the deployments of sexuality and alliance as shifting over time. Initially, the sexual deployment was part of the deployment of alliance. Referring to penance in the context of the confessional, Foucault notes that

historically it was around and on the basis of the deployment of alliance that the deployment of sexuality was constructed.... [T]he questions posed had to do with the commerce allowed or forbidden (adultery, extramarital relations, relations with a person

prohibited by blood or statute, the legitimate or illegitimate
character of the act...

(1978, p. 107)

However, during the nineteenth century, the family also became the
primary locus of an amplified deployment of sexuality:

[F]rom the mid-nineteenth century onward, the family engaged in
searching out the slightest traces of sexuality in its midst, wrenching
from itself the most difficult confessions, soliciting an audience with
everyone who might know something about the matter, and
opening itself unreservedly to endless examination....By virtue of
its permeability, and through that process of reflections to the
outside, it became one of the most valuable tactical components of
the deployment.

(1978, p. 111)

At the end of the nineteenth century, Foucault argues, psychoanalysis played a central role in continuing to forge a new relationship
between the two deployments that was begun by the masturbation
crusade. Whereas the masturbation crusade focused the family on
addressing sexuality within its midst, the incest theory went further
and incorporated the deployment of sexuality into the family alliance
itself by making incestuous desire aimed within the family the origin of
all sexual desire. Psychoanalysis thus played a role in saving the
deployment of alliance from challenges as changing social values
about sex outside of marriage seemed in danger of disengaging
sexuality from alliance and undermining the laws of alliance.

Foucault alludes to the fact that this view may seem paradoxical
because the standard complaint is that psychoanalysis encourages the
individual to be more individualistic and transcend family relationships and values. However, he argues, due to the incest theory,
psychoanalysis in fact props up the threatened alliance deployment
by reuniting sexuality with family. Indeed, despite psychoanalysis's
roots in the masturbation crusade (see Chapter 5), Foucault seems to
suggest that psychoanalysis at its beginnings did have the potential to
become a liberatory discipline that could negate some of the constric-
tions of the masturbation crusade, and that it was specifically the

Oedipal theory that instead cemented its support of the deployment of sexuality by placing the origin of all sexual desire within alliance:

> This was the context in which psychoanalysis set to work.... In the beginning it must have given rise to distrust and hostility, for...it undertook to examine the sexuality of individuals outside family control; it brought this sexuality to light without covering it over again with the neurological model; more serious still, it called family relations into question in the analysis it made of them. But despite everything, psychoanalysis, whose technical procedure seemed to place the confession of sexuality outside family jurisdiction, redis- covered the law of alliance, the involved workings of marriage and kinship, and incest at the heart of this sexuality, as the principle of its formation and the key to its intelligibility. The guarantee that one would find the parents-children relationship at the root of everyone's sexuality made it possible—even when everything seemed to point to the reverse process—to keep the deployment of sexuality coupled to the system of alliance.... Parents, do not be afraid to bring your children to analysis: it will teach them that in any case it is you whom they love. Children,...it is through [your parents] that you gain access to desire. Whence, after so many reticences, the enormous consumption of analysis in societies where the deployment of alliance and the family system needed strength- ening.... From the direction of conscience to psychoanalysis, the deployments of alliance and sexuality were involved in a slow process that had them turning about one another until, more than three centuries later, their positions were reversed;... with psycho- analysis, sexuality gave body and life to the rules of alliance by saturating them with desire.
>
> (1978, pp. 112–113)

Foucault is arguing that one function of the incest theory as a social phenomenon is to prop up the institution of the family. In early religious confession, alliance dominated and sexuality was confessed and surveilled merely as a way of preventing violation of alliance rules. Now, however, alliance itself is made coherent by the dominant role of incestuous desire in defining the family. Foucault's analysis suggests that, rather than being a rupture that liberates us from past repression, the incest theory puts a stop to the destruction of alliance in a freewheeling liberated sexuality, while continuing the masturbation crusade's process of intensifying the sexualization of family life and subjecting the family to ever more surveillance, confession, and medicalization. In sum, the Oedipal theory is "a mechanism for attaching sexuality to the system of alliance" (1978, p. 130).

Oedipal Theory as a Differentiator of the Bourgeois

Foucault additionally argues that the incest theory, when applied within psychoanalysis to its predominantly bourgeois clientele, served as a power/knowledge differentiator between the approaches to incestuous desire in the bourgeois and lower classes that served to maintain different forms of deployment-of-sexuality control exerted in the different classes:

> The history of the deployment of sexuality, as it has evolved since the classical age, can serve as an archaeology of psychoanalysis. We have seen in fact that psychoanalysis… functions as a differentiating factor in the general technology of sex. Around it the great requirement of confession that had taken form so long ago assumed the new meaning of an injunction to lift psychical repression. The task of truth was now linked to the challenging of taboos.
>
> (1978, pp. 129–130)

The argument here consists of three steps. The first step is the idea that the masturbation crusade and related deployments, such as concern about nervous or hysterical wives and sexually perverse men, were initially inflicted primarily on the bourgeois class and were a mark of its differentiation as a class with a special need to sacrifice its sexuality in order to achieve its rewards. However, this deployment of sexuality eventually percolated out to the other classes, losing its differentiating role. The stakes were then increased by attributing psychopathology to the bourgeois class's more severe repression of sexuality, thus the special need for psychoanalysis to address these problems.

This process of class differentiation was the origin of both the psychological and social theories of repression:

[O]ne has to admit that this [sexual] deployment does not operate in symmetrical fashion with respect to the social classes, and consequently, that it does not produce the same effects in them.... [A]t the end of the nineteenth century [the bourgeois] sought to redefine the specific character of its sexuality relative to that of others...It was here that the theory of repression...had its point of origin.... [T]he theory of repression would compensate for this general spread of the deployment of sexuality by its analysis of the differential interplay of taboos according to the social classes...[via] a discourse which said: 'Our sexuality, unlike that of others, is subjected to a regime of repression so intense as to present a constant danger; not only is sex a formidable secret..., not only must we search it out for the truth it conceals, but if it carries with it so many dangers, this is because...we have too long reduced it to silence.' Henceforth social differentiation would be affirmed...by the intensity of its repression.

(1978, pp. 127–129)

Given the development of a theory of repression that differentially affects the middle class, the second step in this explanation is the psychoanalytic idea that repression is directed especially at incestuous desire. Psychoanalysis, in accordance with the Oedipal theory, then became the way the bourgeois class could deal with the pathogenic effects of its incestuous desires that were more severely repressed than in other classes. This sharply differentiated it from the lower classes who came more under judicial constraints and official intrusion into the family by those concerned about child welfare:

Psychoanalysis comes in at this juncture...[as] a technique for relieving the effects of the [incest] taboo where its rigor makes it pathogenic.... [P]sychoanalysis gave itself the task of alleviating the effects of repression (for those who were in a position to resort to psychoanalysis) that this prohibition was capable of causing; it allowed individuals to express their incestuous desire in discourse. But during the same period, there was a systematic campaign being organized against the kinds of incestuous practices that existed in rural areas or in certain urban quarters inaccessible to psychiatry: an intensive administrative and judicial grid was laid out then to put an end to these practices. An entire politics for the protection of children or the placing of 'endangered' minors under guardianship had as its partial objective their withdrawal from families that were suspected—through lack of space, dubious proximity, a history of debauchery, antisocial 'primitiveness,' or degenerescence—of practicing incest. Whereas the deployment of sexuality had been intensifying affective relations and physical proximity since the eighteenth century, and although there had occurred a perpetual incitement to incest in the bourgeois family, the regime of sexuality applied to the lower classes on the contrary involved the exclusion of incestuous practices.... Psychoanalysis, as a limited therapeutic practice, thus played a differentiating role.

(1978, pp. 127–130)

Third, the theory of repression associated with the Oedipal theory was extended to blame repression of sexuality for social and political subjugation:

The task of truth was now linked to the challenging of taboos. This same development, moreover, opened up the possibility of a substantial shift in tactics, consisting in: reinterpreting the deployment of sexuality in terms of a generalized repression; tying this repression to general mechanisms of domination and exploitation; and linking together the processes that make it possible to free oneself both of repression and of domination and exploitation.

(1978, pp.130–131)

That is, the view that unconscious incestuous desires that form the core of one's nature are repressed for social purposes was transmuted by some thinkers into the view that if only the repression of sexuality could be relieved, more general social mechanisms of repression would be undermined and the self liberated. This view solidified the importance of endlessly seeking the truth about one's sexual nature as a way to liberation from political domination.

Foucault, of course, sees this joining of the theories of sexual and political repression as well as the entire "sexual revolution" as just another tactic in the deployment of sexuality, as evidenced by the lack of any political liberation accompanying sexual liberation:

The importance of this critique and its impact on reality were substantial. But the very possibility of its success was tied to the fact that it always unfolded within the deployment of sexuality, and not outside or against it. The fact that so many things were able to change in the sexual behavior of Western societies without any of the promises or political conditions...being realized is sufficient proof that this whole sexual 'revolution,' this whole 'antirepressive' struggle, represented nothing more, but nothing less—and its importance is undeniable—than a tactical shift and reversal in the great deployment of sexuality.

(1978, pp. 130–131)

This insistence that the sexual revolution was just another development in the deployment of sexuality supports Foucault's overall purpose of undermining the repression hypothesis and the associated view that the sexual revolution and Freud's sexual views constitute a rupture in longstanding repressive social responses to sexuality.

Comments on Foucault's Analysis of the Incest Theory in HS1

It is time to step back from Foucault's speculations and consider whether his claims about the acceptance of the incest theory in *HS1* are plausible enough to justify provisional acceptance or at least further consideration of his claims, and how one might advance the discussion. A direct evidential analysis of Foucault's complex historical claims is beyond the scope of this essay, so prima facie plausibility arguments—which is the level of Foucault's own presentation—will have to do.

In juxtaposing Foucault's discussions of the incest theory in the lectures and the subsequent book, it is important to keep in mind the distinction between the masturbation crusade itself, which was the initial and most salient and long-lasting feature of the deployment of sexuality, and the larger phenomenon of the deployment of sexuality that included other elements beyond the crusade (e.g., the scientific classification of perverse desires). We saw that, in the 1975 lecture on the incest theory, Foucault focused on how the incest theory might be a direct extension specifically of the masturbation crusade. He thus

attempted to show how the transition from a concern about masturbation to a concern about incestuous desire might occur in a relatively
smooth and continuous functional process that would be acceptable to
bourgeois parents, that retained much the same power/knowledge
implications, and that did not represent a radical rupture that might
be mistaken for sexual liberation.

In his analysis of the incest theory in *HS1* as described above,
Foucault takes a quite different approach, postulating novel functions
for the incest theory in the evolution of the larger deployment of
sexuality that are not directly linked to masturbation. Thus, the
lecture's micro-theoretical analysis of steps that could link the
masturbation crusade and the incest theory is abandoned for a
broader speculative historical account in which the acceptance of the
incest theory has little to do with an extension of the masturbation
crusade and more to do with larger social processes.

Foucault presents two perspectives on how the incest theory was a
continuous part of the historical development of the deployment of
sexuality. First, Foucault observes that there are in fact two great
deployments involved in social regulation, the deployment of sexuality
and the deployment of alliance, where the latter consists of the rules of
family relationships for everything from reproduction to inheritance,
and thus is the foundation of the maintenance and reproduction of
society itself. He claims that in earlier times the two deployments were
in harmony, with alliance dominant and the confession used to
regulate sexuality to stay within the bounds set by alliance (e.g.,
disapproval of reproduction and sexuality outside of marriage).

However, as the deployment of sexuality expanded its domain and
new sexual mores came into existence exerting very different forms of
social control via the notion of sexual liberation, the congruence
between alliance and sexuality weakened to the point that sexuality
became a threat to the continued integrity of alliance. In common terms,
sexual freedom threatened the traditional family. Foucault argues that
what made the incest theory appealing was that it relocated the
foundation of sexual development to inside the family in the powerful
sense that everyone's sexuality is initially aimed at and shaped by desire
for family members. In this way, alliance was cemented by family-
directed sexual desire—in contrast to the masturbation crusade in which
the family attempted to control the nondirected sexuality of one of its

members. By placing the foundation of sexual desires within the family, the incest theory performed a unifying function, Foucault argues, in which two diverging apparatuses of power, the deployment of sexuality and the deployment of alliance, were brought together again, thereby solidifying the nuclear family and protecting it from the changing sexual mores that presented a threat to the coherence of alliance. The strengthening of social regulation through a coherent resolution of the two deployments explains the incest theory's appeal.

Turning now to an assessment of the prima facie plausibility of this account, it is true that the incest theory locates sexual desire within and among family members in a novel way. There are historical timeline questions that I leave aside here, but one does have to ask whether the family was under siege in some special way around the end of the nineteenth century such that the discovery of Oedipal desires was needed at that time more than at other times to shore up family bonds. It is an evocative idea that the incest theory strengthens alliance and that this accounts for its appeal. Indeed, I agree with Foucault (and will later develop the point further) that the appeal of the incest theory lies in certain effects it had on family power.

However, it is difficult to see how one can take this idea seriously in the form in which it is put forward by Foucault. Foucault moves from the correct premise that incest is sexual desire within the family to the dubious conclusion that incestuous desire thereby strengthens the family bond and mitigates the challenge to the family of sexual promiscuity. He presents no cogent evidence that this provocative inference is sound. The opposite seems more likely; awareness of incestuous desires in their children, along with the inevitable moral condemnation of and aversion to those desires, causes parents to turn away from family intimacy.

At the heart of Foucault's argument appears to be an overly simplistic assumption that because the content of Oedipal theory concerns desires within the family, therefore perceiving children in this way or undergoing analysis and excavating these desires would lead to support of family values or greater engagement in the family. I can discern no evidence for this claim. The primary sexual threat to alliance was from adults who believed (whatever Foucault might say was really going on) that they were seizing their sexual freedom from the oppressive claims of the traditional rules of alliance. This threat was hardly neutralized by the incest theory. The influence of the incest theory peaked as the sexual revolution was also fully underway, and subsequent history underscores that the incest theory in no way saved the traditional family alliance. It is certainly difficult to see how the incest theory's impact addressed the problems afflicting the alliance from the sexual revolution, such as responsibility for children, sexual exclusivity, inheritance, and so on.

In a passing comment noted above, Foucault alludes to the fact that it is the general view and a common criticism that psychoanalysis alienates patients from their families. He dismisses this notion in favor of the view that Oedipal interpretations place the patient's sexual desires back into the family, thus solidifying the family bond. This ignores the fact that the point of Oedipal interpretations is the opposite, to liberate the patient from any remaining unresolved Oedipal desires that are interfering with the patient pursuing an erotic and assertive life independent of developmental resonances with the family. Recognizing how one's life has been limited by one's continued erotic and aggressive ties to one's family of origin generally motivates separation, not reunion.

Foucault argues in broad, imprecise terms that:

The guarantee that one would find the parents-children relationship at the root of everyone's sexuality made it possible...to keep the deployment of sexuality coupled to the system of alliance. There was no risk that sexuality would appear to be, by nature, alien to the law: it was constituted only through the law.

Oedipal sexual desire is not in fact "constituted only through the law" in Freud's incest theory. It does generally take place within the setting of the (social/family) law, but it is constituted by sexual feelings that would occur (according to the theory) inside or outside the law, as long as one has a parent to whom one is attached. More importantly, the original incestuous nature of early sexual feelings has little to do with the ultimate fate of sexual desire. Foucault's notion that there has been "enormous consumption of analysis in societies where the deployment of alliance and the family system needed strengthening" is unlikely on its face, as if a titrated dose of psychoanalysis is deployed in societies based on the strength of the family. Moreover, the weakening of the family as time went on was presumably occurring in all social classes and, one might argue, especially in the lower classes. Yet, the deployment of the Oedipal theory is described by Foucault, correctly, as being confined mainly to the bourgeoisie (see below), where the weakening of family bonds was presumably less, conflicting with his analysis.

Foucault's second perspective is that the Oedipal theory was accepted because psychoanalytic treatment aimed at the ill effects of the universal incest taboo differentiated the bourgeoisie from the lower classes. This became important as earlier class differentiations in deployment tactics, such as the sexualization of the child's body, intense repression of sexuality, and falling ill from the repression, became homogeneous across classes. According to Foucault, the incest theory functioned as an effective way of differentiating the deployment of sexuality in the bourgeois class versus lower classes by highlighting the bourgeoisie's sacrifice in allowing itself to be sexually repressed to the point of psychoneurotic disorder and also underscoring its urgent need of psychoanalysis to address its excessive self-abnegation. Foucault effectively argues for a differentiation by counterposing the genteel psychoanalytic grappling with incestuous wishes of the bourgeois class with the brutal intrusive child protection actions in the lower classes, who were treated for their incestuous desires not with psychoanalysis but with child removal and incarceration.

Although Foucault struggles valiantly to link class differentiation to the incest theory, his analysis falters because it has no power to explain specifically the acceptance of the Oedipal theory with its distinctive features. The "differentiation" claim is open to the obvious objection that whether it involves incestuous desire or is strictly ego psycholog-ical, psychoanalysis was and still is an expensive and time-consuming self-reflective bourgeois treatment that differentiates the bourgeois from the lower classes irrespective of its specific content, so the incest theory's acceptance has not been explained in any substantive way. Indeed, Foucault's conclusion that "Psychoanalysis, as a limited therapeutic practice, thus played a differentiating role with respect to other procedures, within a deployment of sexuality that had come into general use" (1978, p. 130) does not mention the Oedipal theory or its distinctive characteristics, let alone any relation to the mastur-bation crusade. Other expensive forms of treatment would do as well for the purpose of displaying the dire consequences of one's extreme self-repression.

Foucault also argues that the incest theory and the associated emphasis on repression led to the bourgeois view that repression of sexuality is a matter of subjugation and social oppression, which led in turn to distinctive bourgeois political views that were themselves part of the deployment of sexuality that saw the need for liberation from sexual repression as a political goal. This political activation, Foucault suggests, further explains the function of the incest theory.

These claims seem far-fetched and arbitrary. Freud himself, despite his analysis of the conflict between individual sexual desires and social requirements in *Civilization and its Discontents* and his belief that sex should be less constrained by social values, never suggested that political freedom depended on it and never suggested such a revolution. Foucault uses as his prime example the views of Wilhelm Reich ("Thus between the two world wars there was formed, around Reich, the historicopolitical critique of sexual repression" [1978, p. 131]). Reich focused primarily on non-Oedipal aspects of sexuality, especially the intensity of orgasm, and he eventually put forward a pseudoscientific theory of "orgone energy" as well as the useful theory of bodily defensive structures ("body armor"). His theory had no special focus on Freud's theory of incestuous Oedipal desire, and Reich is known for his intense disputes with Freud about the libido theory and for arguing that misery often sprang from real deprivation rather than Oedipal repressions. The links between the roots of the "sexual revolution" (a phrase coined by Reich) and related aspirations of political revolution to the incest theory are simply too ephemeral to form an explanation for why the incest theory thrived as it did.

Conclusion

Regarding *HS1*, I conclude that the account of the incest theory as deployment of sexuality that Foucault offers is unanchored in persuasive evidence and has an arbitrary and dubious "just-so" storytelling quality in its speculations about possible functions, such as differentiating between social classes and supporting family alliance. In his 1975 lecture, Foucault's argument is more focused and careful, but he argues on the basis of questionable speculations about how parents might respond to the incest theory and leaps to conclusions about power/knowledge continuities and a smooth transition between the crusade and the incest theory that are unwarranted.

The failure of Foucault's arguments to prove his point does not necessarily mean that his claim is false. It does indicate the need for further evidence to decide the issue. In Chapter 7, I will try to remedy this problem by engaging in my own examination of Freud's texts on the Oedipal theory, as I did in Chapter 5 for Freud's early seduction theory. Moreover, examining Freud's texts for relevant evidence could help to answer a related question: where did Foucault get his notion that the incest theory is essentially one with the masturbation crusade? To fairly evaluate Foucault's claim, we need to ask: what evidence made this prima facie implausible claim seem plausible to Foucault?

References

Acton, W. (1875). *The functions and disorders of the reproductive organs in childhood, youth, adult age, and advanced life, considered in their physiological, social, and moral relations* (6th ed.). London, UK: J. & A. Churchill.

Basaure, M. (2009). Foucault and the 'Anti-Oedipus movement': Psychoanalysis as disciplinary power. *History of Psychiatry, 20*(3), 340–359.

Eagle, M. N. (2011). *From classical to contemporary psychoanalysis: A critique and integration.* New York, NY: Routledge.

Foucault, M. (1978). *History of sexuality (Vol. 1): An introduction* (R. Hurley, Trans.). New York, NY: Pantheon. (*HS1*)

Foucault, M. (1980). *Power/knowledge: Selected interviews and other writings 1972–1977* (C. Gordon, Ed.). New York: Pantheon.

Foucault, M. (2003). *Abnormal: Lectures at the College de France 1974–1975.* (G. Burchell, Trans.), V. Marchetti & A. Salomoni (Eds.). New York, NY: Picador.

Freud, S. (1905). Three essays on the theory of sexuality. *SE* 7, 123–246).

Freud, S. (1909). Analysis of a phobia in a five-year-old boy. *SE* 10, 1–150

Miller, J.-A. (1992). Michel Foucault and psychoanalysis. In T. J. Armstrong (Trans.), *Michel Foucault: Philosopher* (pp. 58–64). New York: Routledge.

Wakefield, J. C. (2023). *Attachment, sexuality, power: Oedipal theory as regulator of family affection in Freud's case of Little Hans.* New York: Routledge.

Widlocher, D. (2002). *Infantile sexuality and attachment.* New York, NY: Other Press.

Chapter 7

The Dangers of Fantasy: Masturbation and Incestuous Desire in the Little Hans Case

In Chapter 6, I concluded that Foucault's arguments fail to persuasively support his claim that there are crucial continuities between the masturbation crusade and the Oedipal theory. In this chapter, I embark on my own evaluation of Foucault's thesis based on the evidence in Freud's texts, which Foucault fails to address. Although drawing on multiple texts, I identify Freud's (1909) "Little Hans" case history as the text that likely formed the primary basis for Foucault's notion of the close connection between control of masturbation and the Oedipal theory. This is because the two theories seem intertwined in the case report to a surprising degree. Investigating the case history as well as the structure of the Oedipal theory, I argue that, in ways that are generally unappreciated and are not identified by Foucault, and despite Freud's insistence that childhood masturbation is not only normal but necessary for health in light of Oedipal desires that require discharge, the Hans case reveals a dimension of Oedipal theory that is indeed reflective of a continued concern about and fear of masturbation's pathological potential, supporting Foucault's thesis.

Foucault's Incest Theory Hypothesis Reconsidered

In Chapter 5, I examined the evidence in Freud's early theorizing that supports Foucault's view of the close relationship between early Freudian theory and the theories behind the longstanding medical campaign against masturbation (or "masturbation crusade"). The striking overlap in doctrines between the two theories explains how Foucault could justifiably conclude that early Freud engaged in an

DOI: 10.4324/9781003480396-7

altered form of the masturbation crusade, and why Foucault could plausibly locate Freud's early theory within the larger "deployment of sexuality" he described.

However, Foucault's primary critique of Freud concerns not the roots of his early theory but Freud's later highly influential Oedipal theory (or "incest theory"), which Freud held to be his greatest discovery and is generally considered to be a radical innovation that renounced Victorian doctrine about masturbation. Foucault argues that despite this general impression, the Oedipal theory is also best understood as an extension of the masturbation crusade. He thus proposes that the incest theory gained its unusual degree of acceptance and influence not from any advance in scientific evidence but rather from extending certain of the doctrines, tactics, and effects on interpersonal power in the guise of a theory of human nature ("power/knowledge") of the masturbation crusade, and partaking of that theory's reasons for its two-century acceptance.

In Chapter 6, I examined Foucault's arguments in support of his claim of the continuity between the masturbation crusade and the incest theory and found his arguments to be forced and unpersuasive. That does not prove that the claim is false. It leaves us with the puzzle of why Foucault embraced it if the evidence was so flimsy, and whether he was right or wrong in his claim. This puzzle is not easily resolved because Foucault never reveals precisely what in Freud's theory convinced him of his thesis.

So, in this chapter, I engage in my own attempt to understand and evaluate Foucault's thesis about the continuity between the masturbation crusade and the incest theory. I again step outside of Foucault's own arguments, as I did in Chapter 5, and consider his thesis afresh. Specifically, I attempt to identify the evidence in Freud's work that might have led Foucault to justifiably draw his counter-intuitive conclusions about the relationship between the incest theory and the masturbation crusade.

Foucault's continuity thesis can be evaluated, and the incest theory compared to the masturbation crusade, along several dimensions. These include, for example, the content of the substantive doctrines (e.g., does masturbation still play a role in pathogenesis?), the tactics used (e.g., surveillance, interrogation, confession, and medicalization), and the ultimate power/knowledge functions served by the doctrines and tactics (e.g., in the case of the masturbation crusade, serving the purpose of emotionally entangling and intensifying the bond of the nuclear family, thus constituting the nuclear form of family life). All of these levels will be addressed in due course. However, this chapter will focus largely on generally unrecognized doctrinal and theoretical links between the masturbation crusade and the incest theory that are not widely appreciated because Freud did not emphasize them. The tactics will become apparent from the implications of the doctrines and from their heavy-handed application in the case history of Little Hans (Freud, 1909), a 5-year-old boy with a horse phobia treated by his father who was supervised by Freud, that I will be closely examining. This is the case in which Freud claimed to provide direct evidence of the Oedipal theory by observing the occurrence and pathogenic effects of a child's Oedipus complex as it occurred. Beyond basic doctrinal and tactical links to the masturbation crusade, further power/knowledge functions of the incest theory that facilitated its acceptance will be discussed toward the end of the chapter and in Chapter 8.

There are several pieces of Freud's theoretical construction as well as some background that have to be put in place before directly tackling how they come together to resolve the puzzle of the theoretical links between the incest theory and the masturbation crusade. Patience will be rewarded as several sections below lay the groundwork for fresh insight into the justification for Foucault's understanding of the Oedipal theory.

Makari on the Transition from the Seduction Theory to the Oedipal Theory

Before embarking on an examination of the evidence in Freud's writing on which Foucault's claims about the incest theory may have been based, it is worth underscoring the prominent role of masturbation-related theories in the period of Freud's theoretical brainstorming after the failure of the seduction theory and leading up to his arrival at the Oedipal theory. It turns out that Freud's theories during this period contain powerful clues to his later thinking. My comments will rely heavily on a paper by intellectual historian George Makari (1998), in which he traces Freud's evolving ideas during this between-theories period.

Makari documents that theoretical considerations about masturbation were surprisingly central to Freud's post–seduction-theory theorizing. He observes that standard histories portray Freud as taking a theoretical leap from the seduction theory to Oedipal theory, but in fact Freud was engaged in formulating hypotheses about masturbation for two years before arriving at the Oedipal theory. Moreover, Freud's provisional theorizing about masturbation was consistent with the standard Victorian medical theory of his day and provides a "missing link" between the seduction and Oedipal theories:

> [A] close examination of extant sources reveals a heretofore-neglected intermediary phase in [Freud's] theorizing that both situates his post-seduction hypothesis thinking in *fin de siècle* Viennese medicine, and can be seen as a 'missing link' between the differing sets of assumptions: those that guided the seduction hypothesis, and those that organized libido theory. For while Freud may indeed have been confused in this time period, he did not stop generating hypotheses about the etiology of neurosis, and those hypotheses often did not center on childhood seduction or libido. Instead, during this intermediary phase of theorizing, he was chiefly concerned with the causes and ramifications of childhood masturbation.
>
> (Makari, 1998, p. 640)

Indeed, as Makari notes, when Freud later explains what went wrong with the seduction theory, he attributes his error to his failure to recognize that his patients' seduction fantasies were in fact "attempts at fending off memories of the subject's own sexual activity (infantile masturbation)" (Freud, 1906, p. 274). That is, it was specifically *masturbatory* Oedipal fantasies that Freud thought were the origin of the reports he mistook as reports of actual seductions.

A focus on masturbation might be seen as an almost inevitable initial strategy on Freud's part after the seduction theory's failure. Once Freud ruled out seduction or other external traumas as well as constitutional sexual prematurity as the specific causes of repressed childhood sexual experiences that yield later psychoneuroses—and given that he was absolutely committed to retaining the sexual theory of the neuroses, so that the cause must be sexual in nature—it pretty much followed that it must be the child himself or herself who is spontaneously generating a pathogenic sexual experience. In the context of Victorian medicine, masturbation was the likely culprit.

A few strands of Makari's discussion are worth noting. During his seduction-theory period, Freud denied that childhood masturbation had an etiologic role to play in hysteria—noting it is too common to play such a role—and placed all the causal force on the early sexual trauma initiated by an adult or another already traumatized child. Masturbation often followed as a consequence of premature sexual arousal. However, once Freud abandoned the idea of traumatic seduction as the pathogen, he alluded vaguely to sexual experiences as leading to subsequent masturbation, and began emphasizing masturbation's possible etiologic role. The link here was the fantasy and longing resulting from the earlier sexual stimulation that then triggered masturbation to discharge the arousing fantasies resulting from the earlier experience. Freud held that masturbation could adequately discharge the fantasy-fed arousal, so, in keeping with his theory that repression underlies hysteria, it was only if the masturbation and associated fantasy was repressed that hysterical neurosis might eventuate.

These moves in Freud's adjustment to his seduction theory's failure placed both masturbation and fantasy into more central positions in neurosogenesis:

> Freud's new two-stage model—in which early nonspecific sexual stimulation, and then later masturbation (when repressed), accounted for hysteria—cohered with *fin de siècle* medical discourse in that, first, masturbation was a plausible etiology for hysteria, and second, childhood masturbation was seen by many to be caused by prior sexual experiences like seductions. But his new model also incorporated another element that was central to medical debates on masturbation: fantasy. Masturbatory fantasy was becoming, for some, the central pathogenic component of masturbation, for it answered this crucial and vexing question posed by skeptics such as Wilhelm Erb: why was masturbation more damaging than coitus? As Hermann Rohleder replied, the most important difference lay in the intense fantasy that the masturbator generated to satisfy his sexual urges. Similarly, for Albert von Schrenck-Notzing masturbation was

distinguished from coitus by its reliance on intense fantasy. He theorized that undifferentiated sexuality in children was molded by an early overstimulating sexual seduction, but a long-lasting pathology was created only if that experience was repeated again and again in masturbatory fantasy.

(Makari, 1998, p. 649)

Thus, the distinctive intensity of masturbatory fantasy and the dangers of such intense fantasy came to be a dominant Victorian answer to the puzzle that had absorbed masturbation crusaders from Tissot onward of why masturbation is more harmful than other forms of sexual discharge. Makari observes that by late 1897, Freud, too, was heavily focused on the interaction between masturbation and fantasy in his etiologic theorizing:

fantasy had now taken on more etiologic import. For while fantasy might cover prior overstimulating sexual experiences, fantasies also drove masturbation, which was etiologically crucial. Wishful fantasy was now both the result of prior sexual stimulation, and in part the cause of continued stimulation via masturbation. Hysteria developed only when such fantasies and the attendant masturbation were repressed.

(1998, p. 650)

Around the same time, Freud wrote in a letter: "The insight has dawned on me that masturbation is the one major habit, the 'primary addiction.'"... The role played by this addiction in hysteria is enormous" (as quoted by Makari, p. 651). In sum, rejecting constitutional degeneracy and traumatic seduction theories, at this transitional point Freud took most seriously the hypothesis that "unspecific early sexual experiences led to longing, fantasies, and later masturbation, which when repressed made for hysteria" (Makari, 1998, p. 651).

Makari's analysis of Freud's focus on masturbation as central to his theorizing fits quite well with Foucault's claim and with the position that I will ultimately take here, with one crucial difference. Despite his various revelations about Freud's focus on masturbation between his major theories, Makari accepts the standard wisdom that the Oedipal theory discarded any important role of childhood masturbation in the pathogenesis of hysteria. He accepts the common view that as Oedipal wishes became dominant factors in Freud's theory of neurosogenesis, the etiological involvement of masturbation waned and it became an epiphenomenon of Oedipal fantasy: "as wishful fantasy took on the power to drive masturbation, inner psychical life became essential to neurosogenesis" (pp. 660–661). By 1905, Makari says, Freud's understanding of childhood masturbation shifted "from a fragile state of immature sexuality that might be traumatized by stimulation, into a normal set of spontaneous…drives that manifested themselves normally in masturbatory actions." The result was that "masturbation as a traumatic etiology of hysteria and neurosis had apparently disappeared. Masturbation had shifted from a cause to an effect, from an etiologic agent to a marker of childhood psychosexuality" (1998, pp. 661–662). Masturbation, conceived as a mere means to reducing Oedipal tension, receded into the theoretical background, Makari suggests. Consequently, Makari's analysis offers no direct support for Foucault's position that features of the masturbation crusade remained central to the Oedipal theory.

However, as we shall see, Freud's Little Hans case study—the place where Freud most decisively develops his argument for the Oedipus complex—tells a more complex story. What Makari misses and his paper fails to adequately address, I will argue, is an unrecognized continued and quite fundamental role that masturbation plays in the application of the Oedipal theory's account of both normal child sexuality and neurosogenesis.

The "Little Hans" Case as Providing the Evidence for Foucault's Account of the Incest Theory

I propose that the evidence that most likely suggested to Foucault the close relationship between the Oedipal theory (or "incest theory") and the masturbation crusade was the Little Hans case record (Freud, 1909). As noted, this case provides Freud's most explicit evidential argument for the incest theory and so it is undoubtedly a case that Foucault studied carefully. We know that Foucault was familiar with the Hans case because he mentions it in *History of Sexuality, Volume 1* (1978; *HS1*) as a frequently cited example of the emergence of talk of child sexuality after the supposed Victorian suppression of such talk started to lift: "The situation was similar in the case of children's sex. It is often said that the classical period consigned it to an obscurity from which it scarcely emerged before the *Three Essays* or the beneficent anxieties of Little Hans" (*HS1*, p. 27). As well, Foucault would have been aware that Jacques Lacan, a leading psychoanalyst with whom Foucault frequently grappled, devoted much of his celebrated 1957 lecture course to Little Hans (Lacan, 1994).

Given this hint, other authors have found in the Hans case an evidential foundation for some of Foucault's most daring and well-known hypotheses:

> What Foucault calls the 'incitement to discourse', the imperative to speak about sex which defines sexuality as the named-as-hidden core of the modern subject, is exemplified in the relations between Hans and his analysts. And the diagnosis of an Oedipal complex centering on the study of Little Hans exemplifies what Foucault calls the 'repressive hypothesis.'
>
> (Driscoll, Garland, & Hickey-Moody, 2011, p. 118)

Indeed, the Hans case history exemplifies many of Foucault's signature issues. Foucault rejects what he calls the "repressive hypothesis" both in its broad social version, that talk about sexuality was socially suppressed during the Victorian era, and its narrower Freudian version that psychological repression of sexual desire is at the heart of an individual's character and neurotic conditions. He argues instead that there was an "incitement to discourse" about sexuality during that period, manifested in an explosion of talk and writing about sex and the scientific study of sexuality, a focus actually encouraged by the myth of the repression of sexual discourse against which it could be seen as a liberating reaction. Corresponding to this schema, in the Hans case one can clearly see illustrated, first, the assumption that sex is socially repressed, which motivates Freud to agree with Hans's parents that, as a liberationist intervention, Hans would be raised as free of such constraints as possible ("His parents...had agreed that in bringing up their first child they would use no more coercion than might be absolutely necessary for maintaining good behaviour....[T]he experiment of letting him grow up and express himself without being intimidated went on satisfactorily" [p. 6]). Nonetheless, the apparent social repression emerges in the "castration threat" when Hans's mother threatens to have the doctor cut off Hans's penis if he keeps touching it. At the psychological level, the repressive hypothesis frames the case as Freud insists that Hans's symptoms are due to his repressing his incestuous desires for his mother. However, all of this apparent repression is accompanied by an insistent "incitement to discourse" about sex by Hans's father who interrogates him ceaselessly and is devoted to uncovering his hidden sexual desires.

Foucault also argues that psychoanalysis's attempt to obtain a confession of the individual's repressed sexual secret, although framed as curative and liberating, is in fact a form of social control in which not just overt actions but thoughts, desires, and even dreams and fantasies are considered and evaluated, analogous to the medieval Catholic confessional. Correspondingly, Hans's interrogation delves not only into his behavior but also into his dreams and fantasies (e.g., the giraffe [Wakefield, 2007], policeman [Wakefield, 2008], chemise, and plumber fantasies) and unacted-upon desires (e.g., when Hans reports that he has finally stopped masturbating, his father justifies further intervention by the fact that he still wants to).

Foucault further argues that in the process of supposed liberation, the individual internalizes a set of norms and a conception of self that is experienced as liberating and finding one's true nature but in fact is the construction of an identity that embodies a subtle form of internalized social power exerted by the individual over himself or herself. Correspondingly, in the Hans case record, one watches as Hans internalizes many of the lessons given by adults, such as the masturbation prohibition—although he struggles with other internal-izations, such as the prohibition against cuddling with his mother. Foucault also argues that the masturbation crusade functioned to allow further intrusion of medical authority into the regulation of intimate family life, and such intrusion is manifest in Freud's supervision of the father's analysis of Hans. In these and other ways, Hans's case vividly illustrates many Foucauldian themes that characterize the deployment of sexuality.

One might object that all of these Foucauldian elements are available throughout Freud's clinical reports and so it is not clear why the Hans case should provide a distinctively compelling evidential basis for Foucault's claim that the Oedipal theory is a new version of the masturbation crusade. The answer is that the Hans case is unique in its intertwining of masturbatory and Oedipal issues. It is a veritable clinical demonstration that control of Oedipal longings and control of masturbation can (almost) come to one and the same thing. Although Freud's goal in the case history is to present direct childhood evidence for the Oedipus complex, the Hans case history also displays all the excesses of the Victorian masturbation crusade detailed in Chapter 3. In ways shocking to modern sensibilities, Hans's parents persistently attempt to control Hans's masturbation using the crusade's stock techniques ranging from scolding and threats to physical restraints.

This is not just a matter of the mother's early castration threat to stop Hans from touching his "widdler": "When he was three and a half his mother found him with his hand on his penis. She threatened him in these words: 'If you do that, I shall send for Dr. A. to cut off your widdler" (1909, pp. 7–8). For example, it is remarkable and cannot have escaped Foucault's eye that in the first recorded child psychoanalytic case and moreover the one that was specifically and explicitly aimed at demonstrating the Oedipus complex, the analysis by the child's father includes placing the child/patient in a sack at night when he sleeps to prevent him from masturbating, to everyone's—including the child's—evident relief:

[Hans's father] said to Hans: 'You know, if you don't put your hand to your widdler any more, this nonsense of yours'll soon get better....To prevent your wanting to, this evening you're going to have a bag to sleep in.' ... [H]is spirits were visibly raised by the prospect of having his struggles made easier for him, and he said: 'Oh, if I have a bag to sleep in my nonsense'll have gone tomorrow'.

(Freud, 1909, pp. 30–31)

Moreover, Freud, in his advice to Hans's parents, seems to endorse or at least acquiesce in the attempt to limit Hans's masturbation as part of the therapy: "I arranged with Hans's father that he should tell the boy...that it was not right to be so very much preoccupied with widdlers, even with his own" (1909, p. 28); "It was at this point that the first piece of therapy was interposed. His parents represented to him that his anxiety was the result of masturbation, and encouraged him to break himself of the habit" (1909, p. 119). Throughout the case, the masturbation and Oedipal aspects appear to be not merely accidental parallel contents but intricately related, with Oedipal concerns forming a novel rationale for control of Hans's masturbation. The complex interrelationship in the Hans case between the persecution of masturbation and the demonstration of the existence of the Oedipus complex could well have encouraged Foucault's view that the two power/knowledge structures were in fact one. I further explore this link below.

Freud's Argument for the Normality of Child Sexuality in the Hans Case

The persecution of masturbation in the Hans case is deeply puzzling because the Hans case is one of the places that Freud argues for the normality of child sexuality and masturbation. Indeed, the possibility of demonstrating that children are naturally sexual as he had claimed in *Three Essays* was the primary reason why Freud asked his followers, including Hans's parents, to keep diaries of their children's sexual development ("I have set out these hypotheses in my *Three Essays on the Theory of Sexuality*.... [E]ven a psycho-analyst may confess to the wish for a more direct and less roundabout proof of these fundamental theorems.... With this end in view I have for many years been urging my pupils and my friends to collect observations of the sexual life of children" [1909, p. 6]). Only when Hans unexpectedly developed a horse phobia did the diary of normal development turn into a case report aimed at demonstrating the Oedipal roots of neurosogenesis.

Freud got his proof of child sexuality, at least in terms of Hans's curiosity about sexual matters and phallic pleasures. As Freud notes,

> the first trait in little Hans which can be regarded as part of his sexual life was a quite peculiarly lively interest in his 'widdler' [in German, '*wiwimacher*']—an organ deriving its name from that one of its two functions which, scarcely the less important of the two, is not to be eluded in the nursery.
>
> (1909, p. 106)

Moreover, "this interest aroused in him the spirit of enquiry" (1909, p. 106), yielding an endless curiosity about widdlers. This led him to ask his mother, "Mummy, have you got a widdler too?" (1909, p. 7) and to comment when he saw a cow being milked, "there's milk coming out of its widdler!", on which Freud comments that "much, if not most, of what little Hans shows us will turn out to be typical of the sexual development of children in general" (1909, p. 7).

The first evidence that Hans is masturbating (i.e., touching his genitals for pleasure; the precise nature of the activity is never described) occurs soon after, and as we saw, Hans's mother deals harshly with it, threatening to have the doctor cut off Hans's penis. However, Freud considered Hans's sexual development, including his self-touching as well as his many curious comments about the widdlers of everything from lions and giraffes to his parents to be not only normal but typical: "The reason for his mother's intervention had been that he used to like giving himself feelings of pleasure by touching his member: the little boy had begun to practice the commonest—and most normal—form of auto-erotic sexual activity" (1909, p. 106).

After the castration threat, the next report implying Hans's self-stimulation occurs over a year later—although we shall see that Freud assumes that the self-touching continued throughout the intervening period—and qualifies in Freud's view as an attempt at Oedipal seduction:

Hans, four and a quarter. This morning Hans was given his usual daily bath by his mother and afterwards dried and powdered. As his mother was powdering round his penis and taking care not to touch it, Hans said: 'Why don't you put your finger there?'

Mother:	'Because that'd be piggish.'
Hans:	'What's that? Piggish? Why?'
Mother:	'Because it's not proper.'
Hans (laughing):	'But it's great fun.'

(1909, p. 19)

Hans's self-touching or implication of self-touching is thus plentiful throughout the early part of the case record, amply demonstrating sexual feelings, although whether those feelings are truly Oedipal or closer to autoerotic is unclear. In any event, they are a form of childhood sexual expression, and Freud persistently accepts such feelings and actions as normal.

Freud's tolerant attitude about masturbation obviously was not shared by Hans's parents, who, despite their Freudian sympathies, remain mired in the masturbation crusade's fears. Hans's mother's harsh threat of castration to stop Hans from touching his penis was likely triggered in part by fear of harm to her child based on standard Victorian views of a direct causal link between masturbation and the pathogenesis of mental disorder. Perhaps she felt her fears were vindicated when Hans subsequently developed a neurosis. Thus far, we have seen that the Hans case plainly illustrates masturbation-crusade fears, but on the part of the parents, not Freud, despite Freud endorsing or accepting the attempts to stop Hans from masturbating.

Masturbation as Part of Normal Child Sexual Development

The Hans case illustrates a crucial difference between Freudian and Victorian views that goes to the heart of the incest theory's apparent divergence from the masturbation crusade's ideology. (However, we shall see below that this divergence ultimately reveals a deep connection between the two theories.) Once Freud abandoned the seduction theory's postulation of a trauma prematurely triggering sexual feelings in a child as the cause of hysteria and put forward the Oedipal theory of spontaneous childhood incestuous sexual desire, he was forced to consider early childhood ("infantile") sexual feelings, including masturbation, as part of normal and spontaneous psychosexual development. Freud's Oedipal theory of infantile sexuality was radical in asserting the routine inherent normality of childhood sexuality as opposed to the masturbation crusade's belief in its occasional pathological emergence due to premature external stimulation. In terms of Makari's account of the development of Freud's thought after the failure of the seduction theory, the mysterious "unspecific early sexual experiences" that "led to longing, fantasies, and later masturbation" was eventually understood to be none other than the sexual longings of the Oedipus complex. Oedipal desire was the explanation for child masturbation, and the repression of masturbation thus became the repression of Oedipal fantasy.

Notably, despite embracing the normality of childhood masturbation, Freud refused to give up his belief that post-pubertal continuation of masturbation could cause neurasthenia. Instead, perplexingly, Freud insisted that the meaning and potential pathogenicity of masturbation varied by age. As we saw in Chapter 3, in the Victorian medical literature, masturbation at various ages, from early childhood through adulthood, tended to be lumped together as equally undesirable and pathogenic for similar reasons, with differences occasionally noted in treatability and a greater emphasis on nervous system effects in childhood since the loss of semen was not an issue. Freud argued to the contrary that this generalization obscured important developmental differences in the implications of early childhood, prepubertal, and post-pubertal masturbation: "full justice has not quite been done to this temporal division. The ostensible unity of masturbation, which is fostered by the customary medical terminology, has given rise to some generalizations where a differentiation according to the three periods of life would have been better justified" (1912, p. 247). He considered childhood (prepubertal) masturbation to follow regularly as a common extension of even earlier "infantile" self-touching of the genitals ("infantile" meaning the first few years of life, encompassing the early Oedipal period), although generally to be abandoned during latency. Freud considered infantile and prepubertal childhood masturbation to have similarly benign implications, so I will combine these as "childhood" masturbation. Similarly, Freud treated all post-pubertal and adult masturbation as a dangerous continuation of the habit with potentially pathogenic implications, so I lump them together as "adult" masturbation.

When it came to childhood masturbation, Freud thought that children started very early to touch themselves with pleasure and that this continued from the earliest years into later childhood. Not only is this nonpathological according to Freud, it is helpful and even necessary because it has the biological function of releasing Oedipal sexual energy. In the initial editions of his *Three Essays*, Freud expressed the view that masturbation is a universally evolved inclination with the biological function of establishing the centrality of genital pleasure over other component pleasures: "it is difficult to overlook Nature's purpose of establishing the future primacy over sexual activity exercised by this erotogenic zone by means of early infantile masturbation, which scarcely a single individual escapes" (1905, p. 188, n. 1). Freud later succumbed to criticism that he was over-teleologizing masturbation without adequate evidence, and expressed his intention to eliminate his reference to "Nature's purpose": "I will renounce my attempt at guessing the purposes of Nature and will content myself with describing the facts" (1912, p. 247). He carried out this promise in the 1915 edition of *Three Essays*, but retained the same essential idea of the ubiquity, harmlessness, and benefit of childhood masturbation reframed non-teleologically in causal terms: "it is scarcely possible to avoid the conclusion that the foundations for the future primacy over sexual activity exercised by this erotogenic zone are established by early infantile masturbation, which scarcely a single individual escapes" (1905, p. 188).

Although accepting the doctrine of the pathogenic nature of adult masturbation, Freud thus directly challenged the central Victorian notion that childhood genital self-touching is necessarily pathogenic. To the contrary, he held that interference with natural child self-touching is pathogenic. For example, in the "Wolf man" case, Freud suggested that suppression of childhood masturbation created pathological-like sexual deviations in the patient focused on component zones:

> He said that he gave up masturbating very soon after his Nanya's refusal and threat. His sexual life, therefore, which was beginning to come under the sway of the genital zone, gave way before an external obstacle, and was thrown back by its influence into an earlier phase of pregenital organization. As a result of the suppression of his masturbation, the boy's sexual life took on a sadistic-anal character. He became irritable and a tormentor.
>
> (1918, pp. 25–26)

We shall see below that a similar view of suppressed masturbation as pathogenic emerged in Freud's comments on the Hans case.

Freud's distinction between harmless childhood masturbation versus pathogenic post-pubertal masturbation has a weak parallel in Victorian ideology. Although holding that masturbation is intrinsically harmful at both ages, some Victorian physicians held that childhood masturbation, if stopped before puberty, was less harmful and had a better prognosis than later masturbation because it does not pathologically influence the body's crucial period of intensive physical and psychological development during puberty: "PROGNOSIS.-Evil as the effects are, even in early childhood, the prognosis of the ailment is not, in children, unfavorable.... not so, however, when masturbation occurs after puberty" (Acton, 1875, p. 27).

Freud's thesis that child masturbation is harmless leaves us with the twin puzzles, to be confronted as we proceed. The first is Freud's insistence on the normality of child masturbation given his continued view of the pathogenicity of adult masturbation. The second is the seeming conflict between the crusade-like control exerted over Hans's masturbation as described in the last section with the endorsement of the normality and beneficiality of childhood masturbation documented in this section.

Freud's Rejection of a Causal Link between Hans's Masturbation and His Anxiety Disorder

At the outbreak of Hans's phobia, consistent with standard Victorian views, his mother immediately identified Hans's masturbation as the likely cause of his anxiety:

> On January 8th my wife decided to go out with him herself, so as to see what was wrong with him....On the same day his mother asked: 'Do you put your hand to your widdler?' and he answered: 'Yes. Every evening, when I'm in bed.' The next day, January 9th, he was warned, before his afternoon sleep, not to put his hand to his widdler. When he woke up he was asked about it, and said he had put it there for a short while all the same.
>
> (1909, p. 24)

This view by the parents—that in one way or another, Hans's phobic anxiety must be due to or exacerbated by his masturbation—persisted in different forms throughout the case. For example, the father later declares: "On March 13th in the morning I said to Hans: 'You know, if you don't put your hand to your widdler any more, this nonsense of yours'll soon get better'" (1909, p. 30). It turns out that Hans himself had come to believe in this link: "*He:* 'Oh no, it's so bad because I still put my hand to my widdler every night'" (p. 30).

Freud's commentary on the case takes a different path. Freud repeatedly underscores that Hans's self-touching is normal and not a manifestation of degeneracy or disorder. Freud was undoubtedly sincere in these statements, but such assertions also served Freud's interest in using the Hans case to defend the existence of a universal Oedipus complex. If Hans's masturbation is part of normal development, that blocks the possible objection that Hans's masturbation reveals that he is suffering from a pathology that is responsible for any sexual feelings he has for his mother and thus that his case offers no support for Freud's Oedipal theory of *normal* development: "it is also our belief that [these sexual developmental vicissitudes] are the common property of all men, a part of the human constitution" (1909, p. 6).

After detailing the beginning of Hans's phobia in January 1908, Freud addresses the further question of whether Hans's anxiety problem should be attributed to his masturbation, which he takes to be the standard medical view. Freud considers and rejects the notion that masturbation is the pathogen:

> Hans admitted that every night before going to sleep he amused himself with playing with his penis. 'Ah!' the family doctor will be inclined to say, 'now we have it. The child masturbated: hence his pathological anxiety.' But gently. That the child was getting pleasure for himself by masturbating does not by any means explain his anxiety; on the contrary, it makes it more problematical than ever. States of anxiety are not produced by masturbation or by getting satisfaction in any shape. Moreover, we may presume that Hans, who was now four and three-quarters, had been indulging in this pleasure every evening for at least a year. And we shall find that at this moment he was actually engaged in a struggle to break himself of the habit—a state of things which fits in much better with repression and the generation of anxiety.
>
> (Freud 1909, p. 27)

So, despite allowing Hans's parents to try to stop Hans's masturbation as part of treatment, Freud sticks to his theory that, contrary to the standard medical view, it is not childhood masturbation but repression of childhood masturbation that is pathogenic. In claiming that Hans had been masturbating for over a year, Freud infers that

Hans's self-stimulation in all likelihood occurred throughout the year from the first report of his self-touching that provoked his mother's castration threat to the discussion of Hans's masturbation at the outbreak of the phobia. This inference allows Freud to cast doubt on the hypothesis that masturbation itself was the direct cause of the recent onset of the phobic symptoms and thus to support his benign view of child masturbation. Freud also relies here on his theory, reviewed in Chapter 5, that masturbation is not responsible for anxiety states because the latter are caused by excessively pent-up libido, whereas masturbation leads to lessened or depleted libido. Note that in his early theorizing, in arguing for repression rather than actual sexual practices as the cause of the psychoneuroses, Freud already rejected the notion that masturbation in childhood may be a direct pathogenic agent in causing hysteria:

Active masturbation must be excluded from my list of the sexual noxae in early childhood which are pathogenic for hysteria. Although it is found so very often side by side with hysteria, this is due to the circumstance that masturbation itself is a much more frequent consequence of abuse or seduction than is supposed.

(Freud, 1896, p. 164)

Of course, after the abandonment of the seduction theory, abuse and seduction can no longer be the relevant causes of masturbation. Another, more common cause must be identified—and this will be Oedipal sexual feelings. Moreover, any problem linked to masturbation must lie elsewhere than in its direct pathogenic effect. Freud provocatively argues that the real problem is the suppression of masturbation, which blocks the harmless discharge of Oedipal sexual energy and creates an excessive build-up of such energy that transforms into anxiety. It is this suppressed sexual desire, Freud argues, that explains the appearance of Hans's phobia. Although Freud never comes out and says so, his position implies that the mother's attempt to prevent disorder by suppressing Hans's self-touching had the opposite effect; suppression triggered repression, which in turn, Freud implies, caused Hans to fall ill. (For a detailed critical assessment of Freud's repression-of-masturbation argument for his Oedipal theory in the Hans case, see Wakefield, 2023a.)

Component Sexual Instincts

Freud's theory of component sexual instincts that accompanied his development of the Oedipal theory must be briefly reviewed because certain of its features play a role in resolving the paradoxes regarding masturbation in the Hans case. In Freud's brilliant analysis of the complex structure and development of sexuality from infantile to adult sexuality, he observes that adult genital sexual excitation is increased by excitation in other zones of pleasure (e.g., the eyes seeing, the lips kissing, the musculature grasping, the hands fondling the sexual object) that prepare the adult for intercourse. He argues that the prepubertal child experiences these and many other pleasures (e.g., urinary and excretory functions, being seen, skin contact, sucking, and so on) as independent sources of sexual pleasure in "component sexual instincts" in the relevant parts of the body. Freud's theory of component sexual instincts corrected the classical view of sexuality as a simple genital "itch" and provided explanations of such diverse phenomena as sexual foreplay and sexual perversion.

A key property of these autoerotic components during childhood is that they provide a degree of pleasure and sexual tension release without entailing additional genital tension that the child would be incapable of discharging. Only in the post-pubertal "genital stage" of sexual development does the adult's foreplay simultaneously provide component pleasure and increase genital arousal. The one partial exception is that directed Oedipal desire and stimulation is felt in the boy's penis, but here too local tension relief from masturbation is possible without the adult's semenic discharge.

Freud includes among the component instincts the boy's penis in its pregenital "phallic" status, prior to intercourse being a possibility—and this, Freud tells us, is the primary source of Hans's sexual feelings in childhood. I ignore other sites of component sexuality here and focus on the phallic aspects of Hans's sexual development. As Rene Spitz observes, at least penile masturbation is unambiguously sexual: "Masturbation is a sexual activity observed from earliest infancy. It is the only infantile autoerotic activity which is recognizable as such even to the lay public" (1952, p. 491). Indeed, Freud himself makes this very point to evade the common objection that he is overinterpreting other childhood pleasures as sexual:

[T]he sexual life of children is already free from all these doubts from the third year of life onwards: at about that time the genitals already begin to stir, a period of infantile masturbation—of genital satisfaction, therefore—sets in, regularly perhaps.

(1917, p. 325)

To explain the extraordinary diversity of hysterical symptoms while preserving his cherished sexual theory of the neuroses, Freud required an equally diverse sexual instinct. His component instinct theory unites diverse pleasures as sexual phenomena, making sexuality present everywhere in the body. Unsurprisingly, Foucault interprets the component instinct theory's imbuing all parts of the child's body with sexuality as an expansion of the domain of the masturbation crusade's sexualization of the child and thus an extension of the reach of Oedipal power/knowledge. In the name of regulation of sexuality, one might now be concerned about the child's thumb-sucking, what the child sees, the child's interest in excretory functions, and other such manifestations of component sexual instincts. The component instinct theory also illustrates Foucault's notion that sexuality itself has been constructed from disparate bodily pleasures. The theory also incorporates another feature that Foucault emphasizes as a positive manifestation of the deployment of sexuality, the identification of a variety of sexual perversions and thus the construction of a set of deviant sexual natures and their sexual secrets to be confessed, ultimately in the discourse of psychoanalysis: "these were the years that saw the...opening up of the great medicopsychological domain of the 'perversions,' which was destined to take over from the old moral categories of debauchery and excess" (1978, p. 118).

Why Hans's Masturbation is Frustrating Rather than Satisfying

I return now to the central puzzle raised above of explaining why Freud, despite paying lip service to the normality of child masturbation, goes along supportively with the rather extreme suppression of Hans's masturbation by his parents—a point no doubt noticed by Foucault. One must ask: just what kind of supposed liberation from Victorian sexual doctrine do we have here, with Hans tied in a sack at night to prevent him from masturbating? This approach is in accordance with the most conservative Victorian doctrine: "If the practice of masturbation be ascertained to exist, steps must be at once taken to check it. In young infants the habit may be corrected by the ordinary mode of muffling the hands or applying a sort of strait-waistcoat" (Acton, 1875, p. 36). Why would Freud declare Hans's defiant masturbation not only normal but blameless regarding pathogenesis, and then conspire with Hans's father in the persecution of this blameless activity? And, there is the more theoretical question: if Hans's masturbation decreases the build-up of Oedipal excitation, then why prior to ending his masturbation does Hans experience anxiety? These sorts of puzzles explain why Freud observes that the benign view of Hans's masturbation makes the source of Hans's anxiety "more problematical than ever" (1909, p. 27).

Before answering these questions, a brief return to the component instinct theory will be useful to clarify how childhood masturbation without orgasmic release can be satisfying rather than frustrating in the first place. The answer lies in the theory of how child component sexual instincts work. Freud (1905) suggests that quasi–orgasm-like satisfaction is reached when a child's component instincts are adequately stimulated. Adult arousal of a sexual zone during foreplay causes both satisfaction in the zone and an increase in genital tension that motivates genital sexual activity until semenic discharge occurs, whereas in the child the components are not yet integrated into the genital system and so component pleasures occur without increased genital tension and in the absence of semenic discharge. This yields a potential sexual "free lunch" of component pleasure without additional tension, a possibility available to the child but largely lost in adulthood. For example, the baby experiences a pleasurable satisfaction in sucking, evidenced in the blissful post-orgasm–type look on the baby's face after sucking at the breast, and this process does not increase genital tension in the way that, say, kissing does in the adult (although baby boys do get random transient erections). Oedipal-age phallic excitation is conceived of by Freud as pregenital in this sense, obeying the laws of children's component instincts and being inherently satisfying, not frustrating, for the child. So, an Oedipal child's masturbation without semenic discharge can be pleasurable and not frustrating within Freud's theory due to the disconnect, so to speak, between the phallic and genital stages of penile sexual development. Freud makes clear that the child's Oedipal arousal is itself primarily phallic (this is the basis for the child's reasoning that castration will be the punishment), although contrary to the theory of independent zones there is clearly some phallic arousal due to the pleasures in other zones (e.g., from the skin contact when cuddling in bed), and so phallic masturbation even without discharge can normally relieve this tension when it remains within the usual range. Although the ultimate inchoate desire for penetration is insatiable for the child, the primary phallic-zone component arousal is satiable via masturbation.

Returning now to the puzzle of how intrinsically tension-relieving phallic masturbation can be frustrating and anxiety-provoking, the answer can only be, as Freud often emphasized, a matter of libidinal quantities. That is, it is a matter of the balance between tension-decreasing and tension-increasing aspects of Hans's masturbation. The problem must be that the magnitude of the decrease is exceeded by the magnitude of a parallel increase in excitation that Hans is experiencing. So, the question becomes, where is this excessive excitation that outruns masturbatory tension discharge coming from?

Freud casts around for a solution to this puzzle. Perhaps, he suggests, the anxiety came about "as a result of his mother's rejection of his advances" (1909, p. 28), and Freud cites in this connection her statement "that'd be piggish" (see above), thus limiting his tension reduction. However, this proposal does not fit the case history's timeline, for the incident in question occurred just *after* the outbreak of anxiety. Or, perhaps the repression actually started before any anxiety: "we shall find that at this moment [of the anxiety's onset] he was actually engaged in a struggle to break himself of the habit—a state of things which fits in much better with repression and the generation of anxiety" (1909, p. 27). However, this claim, too, does not fit the facts of the case record. As late as March 2, two months after the phobia's onset, Hans admits "I still put my hand to my widdler every night" (p. 30).

Freud further speculates that perhaps "the scales were turned by the child's *intellectual* inability to solve the difficult problem of the begetting of children and to cope with the aggressive impulses that were liberated by his approaching its solution" (p. 136). However, even Freud seems to think that an intellectual puzzle, even about reproduction, is an unlikely trigger for a psychoneurosis. Finally, Freud wonders "whether the effect was produced by a *somatic* incapacity, a constitutional intolerance of the masturbatory gratification in which he regularly indulged (whether, that is, the mere persistence of sexual excitement at such a high pitch of intensity was bound to bring about a revulsion)" (p. 136). That is, it might be that Hans was constitutionally incapable of handling the level of tension that resulted from his Oedipal longings and thus the libido was transformed into anxiety. This is surely a possible part of the solution, but it fails to explain why despite the masturbatory outlet the Oedipal tension reached that extreme level. Freud finally gives up on identifying a specific triggering cause and returns to the basic point that there is excess despite masturbation: "The fact remains that his sexual excitement suddenly changed into anxiety" (1909, p. 119).

Although Freud says no more about the specific trigger of Hans's desire transforming into neurosis, at a more general level he is clear that the source of Hans's problem is an unusual intensity of Oedipal desire. Freud speculates that Hans's sexual desire for his mother greatly increased in the six months before the phobia's outbreak in January. This began during the summer holiday, when Hans's father often traveled on business during the week and Hans was consequently alone with his mother at their summer house in Gmunden outside Vienna (the father says, "In the summer I used to be constantly leaving Gmunden for Vienna on business, and he was then the father" [1909, p. 45]). During this time, Hans often cuddled with his mother in bed (to his father's question, "Did you often get into bed with Mummy at Gmunden?", Hans answers "Yes" [1909, p. 90]). Freud sees this summer period of intimacy as the occasion for intensified Oedipal feelings: "Hans's desires for his mother had consequently been awakened to an unusual degree: Hans really was a little Oedipus who wanted to...be alone with his beautiful mother and sleep with her" (p. 111). Freud reiterates this claim that Hans's desire for his mother was awakened "to an unusual degree" many times. According to Freud, Hans's "increased affection for his mother" (p. 25) caused him to experience "enormously intensified" (p. 25) affection at "such a high pitch of intensity" (p. 110) that his "state of intensified sexual excitement" (p. 118) and the "intensity of the child's emotions" (p. 25) grew "greater than he could control" (p. 25) and thus Hans "was overwhelmed by an intensification of his libido" (p. 25) and by an "intensified erotic excitability" (p. 133). This intensification of incestuous desire, Freud asserts, "was the fundamental phenomenon in his condition" (p. 24) during this pre-phobic period.

According to Freud, Hans's intensified desire became ripe for repression when Hans's sources of erotic gratification became grossly inadequate to the level of his desires: "his erotic needs became intensified, while at the same time they began to obtain insufficient satisfaction" (1909, p. 132). Freud offers several reasons for the development of the marked disparity between desire and gratification. First, the Graf family had moved to a new apartment shortly before the summer holiday, so when they returned to Vienna Hans was in a new environment and had few playmates or other acquaintances nearby, so all of his needs were now focused on his mother: "His affection had moved from his mother on to other objects of love, but at a time when there was a scarcity of these it returned to her, only to break down in a neurosis" (p. 110). Second, at the new apartment, Hans, whose bed had previously been in his parents' bedroom, was now for the first time moved into a bedroom of his own: "He had meanwhile suffered another privation, having been exiled from his parents' bedroom" (pp.132–133). The result of these various changes, Freud claims, caused Hans's heightened sexual feelings to be deprived of former outlets, increasing the disparity between longing and gratification.

Yet, according to Freud, the outlet of masturbation was available to discharge these tensions:

> During the preceding summer Hans had…the advantage of being taken by his mother into her bed. We may assume that since then Hans had been in a state of intensified sexual excitement, the object of which was his mother….he found an incidental channel of discharge for it by masturbating every evening and in that way obtaining gratification.
>
> (1909, pp.118–119)

The perspective here is that Hans was *primarily* experiencing "intensified sexual excitement, the object of which was his mother," and Hans's masturbation is interpreted as initially being merely a beneficial "incidental channel of discharge for" that excitement and not in any way pathogenic.

However, as masturbation becomes linked to Oedipal fantasizing, it transforms intrinsically harmless masturbatory activities into dangerous Oedipal pursuits. Recall that after being informed by this father of the difference between men's and women's genitals, Hans has a vivid dream or masturbatory fantasy of his mother's genitals being exposed by her short chemise: "I put my finger to my widdler just a very little. I saw Mummy quite naked in her chemise, and she let me see her widdler" (1909, p. 32). Although there is some ambiguity, Freud insists: "This was none of it a dream, but a masturbatory phantasy" (p. 32). The link between masturbation and Oedipal fantasy has been forged to the extent that masturbation, rather than only being triggered as a way to address prior Oedipal tension, has itself become a source of more elaborated and arousing Oedipal sexual fantasies, even when done only "just a very little."

Hans, plainly anxious about his self-stimulation at this point given his parents' prohibitions, defensively mentions that he touched himself only a little. Taking him at his word, the subsequent description reveals the potential disproportion between the amount of masturbation and the intensity and elaborateness of the accompanying fantasy. In the masturbation crusade, the harm was expectably roughly proportional to the amount of masturbation. With the advent of the Oedipal theory, the quantity of masturbation is no longer an indicator of the amount of danger. Any masturbation at all can have extreme implications if it triggers an intense fantasy that amplifies arousal.

From a Foucauldian perspective, it is notable that with the advent of the Oedipal construal of masturbatory danger, even "just a very little" masturbation is no longer entirely safe. Because masturbation is transformed by the incest theory into a sign of something quite different and libidinally potentially much bigger, the degree of masturbation itself is no longer the only issue. Under the right circumstances, even a little bit of masturbation can trigger intense and potentially pathogenic Oedipal fantasies. This is what makes masturbation dangerous in the Oedipal era.

The extraordinary intensity of Hans's Oedipal masturbatory fantasies provides a resolution of the clinical puzzle about Freud's acquiescence in the parents' masturbation prohibition. Although masturbation generally functions to discharge Oedipal desire and to that extent is usually beneficial, Freud's acquiescence in the control of

Hans's masturbation implies that Freud believed that it was, overall, increasing Hans's levels of excitation to harmful levels. This internally generated masturbatory increase in tension occurs *despite* rather than *because of* the intrinsic nature of masturbation; it involves something that is added to the normal masturbatory process. What is added can be nothing other than arousing Oedipal fantasizing during masturbation that floods Hans with additional intense desire that goes beyond the initial general Oedipal tension that he experiences. The problem with Hans's masturbation and the reason why Freud is willing to go along with its suppression is that, instead of simply being an outlet for independently generated Oedipal arousal, masturbation has become linked to intense Oedipal fantasizing that itself generates increased and even more intense Oedipal excitation during masturbation, and this increase in excitement outpaces the intrinsic tension reduction from masturbation. Such triggering of unusually intense fantasy that amplifies arousal to harmful levels is, we saw, precisely what some Victorian masturbation crusaders considered to be the distinctive pathogenic danger lurking in masturbation. Accompanied by intense Oedipal fantasies that can never be realized—which Freud suggests include inchoate fantasies of penetration—masturbation is checkmated in its usual role as a safety valve to reduce Oedipal excitation. Masturbation cannot fully discharge the insatiable Oedipal sexual desire that it generates, yielding a net increase rather than decrease in sexual tension and thereby creating the conditions ripe for an anxiety neurosis.

Freud and Hans's father believe that by foreclosing the possibility of masturbation, the associated intense incestuous fantasies and desires will also subside. Thus, the father says to Hans that "if you don't put your hand to your widdler any more, this nonsense of yours'll soon get better" because it will "prevent your wanting to" (1909, p. 31). And, what Hans wants to do—that is, the content of his fantasies—is not just to masturbate but to be intimate with his mother. The attention to masturbation is a pragmatic necessity because there is, after all, little that one can directly do about Oedipal desire or fantasy, except prevent what increases it.

The two puzzles—the theoretical puzzle about the source of the quantitative imbalance during masturbation, and the clinical puzzle about Freud's acceptance of the attempt to stop Hans's masturbation—thus have the same solution, namely, that unusually intense masturbatory fantasies cause masturbation to generate more additional tension than it discharges. As noted, this fear of the intensity of masturbatory fantasy was at the heart of the nineteenth-century's masturbation crusade's answer to the question of why masturbation is so distinctively pathogenic relative to other sexual acts. The idea that it is not masturbation in itself but rather the fantasies it arouses in the context of a given boy's constitution and circumstances that is pathogenic also calls to mind Tissot's and others' earlier masturbation-crusade view that it is the endless stimulatory resources of the imagination that explains masturbation's special harmfulness (see Chapter 3). The Hans case's focus on Hans's masturbation as a trigger of fantasy to this extent fits well with crusade doctrine.

Freud's hypothesized link between incestuous desire and child masturbation as its outlet—and the consequent association of masturbation with Oedipal fantasy, leading to the fear that incestuous masturbatory fantasy might spin pathogenically out of control—provides a novel rationale for the control of masturbation. It also provides a compelling justification for Foucault's reading of the incest theory as, in crucial power/knowledge respects, an extension of the masturbation crusade. It is in answering the two puzzles arising from the Hans case—the clinical puzzle of why the Hans case involves control of Hans's masturbation, and the quantitative puzzle of the source of the intensity of Hans's desires given that he is discharging Oedipal feelings through masturbation—that Foucault's claim that the suppression of masturbation and the incest theory are so intimately linked that one can move smoothly from one to the other gains its greatest traction.

This solution fits well with the hint that Foucault provides as to why he thinks that the incest theory extends the masturbation crusade. As noted in earlier chapters, at the beginning of his 1975 lecture on the incest theory, Foucault (2003) offers a brief parenthetical "spoiler" that the answer is that "danger comes from the child's desire" (p. 263). The danger must be medical to continue the crusade's approach, and, according to Freud, Oedipal desires are medically dangerous to the child only when they cannot be discharged adequately by masturbation due to Oedipal masturbatory fantasy. It is indeed the child's desire, amplified in fantasy, that is the danger.

The construal of masturbation as a vehicle for discharge of intense Oedipal desires was a doctrine Freud embraced beyond the confines of the Hans case. For example, in a paper on forms of love published shortly after the Hans case, Freud (1910) described how, when a boy first comes to understand sex, this simultaneously revives Oedipal desire and intensifies masturbation:

> He begins to desire his mother herself in the sense with which he has recently become acquainted... [H]e comes, as we say, under the dominance of the Oedipus complex. He does not forgive his mother for having granted the favour of sexual intercourse not to himself but to his father, and he regards it as an act of unfaithfulness. If these impulses do not quickly pass, there is no outlet for them other than to run their course in phantasies which have as their subject his mother's sexual activities under the most diverse circumstances; and the consequent tension leads particularly readily to his finding relief in masturbation.
>
> (1910, pp. 170–171)

Freud continued in his later years to endorse this close link between childhood masturbation and relief of Oedipal fantasy:

> [M]asturbation by no means represents the whole of his sexual life. As can be clearly shown, he stands in the Oedipus attitude to his parents; his masturbation is only a genital discharge of the sexual excitation belonging to the complex, and throughout his later years will owe its importance to that relationship.
>
> (Freud, 1924, p. 176)

The intimate link between the Oedipus complex and masturbatory fantasy continues to be a common theme in subsequent psychoanalytic writing. For example, the eminent developmental psychologist Rene Spitz explains: "Masturbatory fantasies shape the Oedipus complex; they are the enemy against which defenses are organized in the course of the liquidation of the Oedipus complex; they are determinants of the structure of character, of the conflicts of puberty, and of eventual sexual adjustment" (1952, p. 491).

From Freud's perspective, then, masturbation causes increased immersion in unsatisfiable Oedipal fantasies, potentially triggering repression. From Foucault's perspective, confronted by the belief that masturbation in itself is harmless, the Victorian masturbation crusade was extended by an ingenious Oedipal theory that justifies continued vigilance about and occasional control of masturbation despite its postulated normality because of the fear that it might lead to pathogenic-level fantasy. This theory justified control not only of the child's actions but also his thoughts.

Masturbation and Incestuous Fantasy in Freud's Abandonment of the Seduction Theory: Was Freud Inconsistent?

The understanding put forward in this chapter of the intertwined nature of masturbation and Oedipal arousal in Freud's theory can help to illuminate what otherwise might seem like an inconsistency in Freud's assertions. Allan Esterson (1998) has argued that Freud was inconsistent in characterizing his patients' reports that led him to switch from the seduction to the incest theory:

> Incidentally, the widely held view that he abandoned the seduction theory because he came to realize that most of his seduction theory patients had been reporting oedipal fantasies is manifestly erroneous. In his 1914 report he claimed that he had made the 'discovery' that the alleged fantasies were produced to cover up the shameful memories of infantile masturbation. The oedipal fantasy explanation of the 1896 claims didn't surface until 1925, some thirty years after the episode.
>
> (1998, p. 94)

Esterson claims that the following two passages of Freud's are in such obvious and irremediable conflict that Freud's description must be "manifestly erroneous":

> I was at that period unable to distinguish with certainty between falsifications made by hysterics in their memories of childhood and traces of real events. Since then I have learned to explain a number of phantasies of seduction as attempts at fending off memories of the subject's own sexual activity (infantile masturbation).
>
> (Freud, 1906, p. 274)

When, however, I was at last obliged to recognize that these scenes of seduction had never taken place,... I was for some time completely at a loss.... When I had pulled myself together, I was able to draw the right conclusions from my discovery: namely, that the neurotic symptoms were not related directly to actual events but to wishful phantasies, and that as far as the neurosis was concerned psychical reality was of more importance than material reality.

(Freud, 1925, p. 34)

In one passage, Freud says that his patients produced their seduction scenes to hide instances of infantile masturbation, and in the other he says they were hiding Oedipal fantasies rather than actual seductions. The above analysis of Freud's postulation of the close relationship between masturbation and incestuous fantasy shows that there is no contradiction between these passages. The seduction fantasies were, Freud is claiming, defensive in nature, covering over the truth of having masturbated while having masturbatory Oedipal fantasies of being seduced or seducing. The fact that Freud uses two different descriptions focusing on two different aspects of a single postulated reality is not a contradiction. The recall of the masturbatory episodes is also the recall of the Oedipal fantasies that accompanied them. None of this is to deny that Freud in other respects may contradict himself in attempting to explain the seduction theory episode, nor is it to deny that other aspects of Esterson's often brilliant critique of Freud hit the mark. But in this instance, it is Esterson's criticism of Freud that is "manifestly erroneous"—or at least highly uncharitable and unpersuasive. Moreover, one might say that Esterson's error in failing to see the close relationship between Oedipal fantasy and masturbation is precisely the error that Foucault's critique seeks to correct.

Doing and Wanting in Oedipal Confession

The fact that within the incest theory the danger now comes from excessive desire and fantasy associated with masturbation rather than from the physical act of masturbation emerges in a poignant interchange between Hans and his father. On March 13, Hans's father reassures him that "if you don't put your hand to your widdler any more, this nonsense of yours'll soon get better," and Hans retorts "But

I don't put my hand to my widdler any more," to which his father replies "But you still want to." Hans, faced with the realization that his father's aspirations for control in his treatment go beyond action to desire, sagely answers, "Yes, I do. But wanting's not doing, and doing's not wanting." Nonetheless, he will still be constrained, his father says, "to prevent your wanting to" (pp. 30–31).

Hans is surely correct that wanting is not the same as doing. (He is also likely wondering how putting him in a sack will prevent his wanting.) Hans's observation of the doing/wanting distinction points to a deeper current in the Oedipal-theoretic analysis. Doing—that is, the act of masturbation—was the exhaustive target of the masturbation crusade, for there was nothing else to autoerotic activity other than the doing of it and the attendant pleasure. The transformation wrought by the incest theory is that wanting masturbation is no longer simply considered to be the desire to masturbate. Wanting to masturbate now includes the desire to experience an incestuous fantasy so that the doing of masturbation is now linked to Oedipal wanting. This Oedipal desire now becomes the target of control by controlling masturbation. Wanting has superseded doing as the primary target of intervention just as, Foucault reminds us, the Catholic confessional holds the individual responsible for unfulfilled desire.

Hans's objection that wanting is not doing would have been an adequate defense during the masturbation crusade. But, in Freud's theory, what Hans (inchoately) wants is not what he does or even is capable of doing. The unfulfilled wanting is the danger and through it the vast intimate terrain of the child's meaning system becomes the target of interrogation. From Foucault's perspective, the Oedipal theory extended the masturbation crusade from the physical act of touching the penis into the dimension of desire and thus into the mind.

On the Transition from the Masturbation Crusade to the Oedipal Theory

We saw in Chapters 1 and 6 that Foucault asserts that Freud's Oedipal theory is another "episode" in the masturbation crusade, but a "turning point" in the form taken by the crusade. The explorations above suggest that Foucault's description is apt. We saw in Makari's work a documentation of how in the interval between the failure of the seduction theory and the announcement of the Oedipal theory, in working out his new approach, Freud was preoccupied with thinking about how childhood masturbation might be pathological and what might cause children to masturbate. Freud's solution was that Oedipal desire causes children to masturbate, and when the Oedipal fantasies associated with masturbation become too intense, masturbation can become pathogenic. Freud's postulation of masturbation as a normal sexual outlet is certainly a "turning point" in the crusade, but his theory that it is an outlet that can fail and yield pathogenic levels of fantasy and arousal offers a new episode in the masturbation crusade's concerns about the dangers of masturbation.

One puzzle raised above that has still not been addressed is the oddity of Freud's view, apparently maintained throughout his life, that adult masturbation is harmful but childhood masturbation is not harmful, a view that seems paradoxical today. The solution to the puzzle lies in Freud's absolute commitment to protecting his sexual theory of the neuroses. Freud continued to insist on the harmfulness of adult masturbation even as this idea became increasingly scientifically implausible because he had no adequate replacement for his theory that excessive sexual discharge in masturbation is the etiology of neurasthenia, thus no other way to protect his sexual theory of the actual neuroses.

Why, then, hold the contrary position that childhood masturbation is not harmful? The answer is the same. The sexual theory of the psychoneuroses required a repressed sexual experience in childhood, but some of the scenes of childhood sexual seduction by a parent "recalled" by his early patients that Freud had used to support the seduction theory turned out never to have actually occurred. So, he needed to identify a repressed sexual experience, and—with seduction no longer a plausible explanation—he needed to explain why supposedly sexually innocent children would have a sexual experience in the first place. And, for good measure, he needed to explain the seduction scenes produced by his patients to avoid the "suggestion" accusation that he had forced these supposed memories on his clients. His answer was that child sexuality is natural and is provoked by Oedipal desire, masturbation is a natural and necessary outlet to discharge Oedipal sexual energies, the seduction memories were memories of intense Oedipal fantasies of seduction during masturbation, and overly intense masturbatory fantasies were repressed and pathogenic. Thus, in terms of Freud's theorizing, masturbation and the Oedipus complex became inseparable.

It follows that that there are several ways things could go pathogenically wrong, yielding lack of libidinal balance between Oedipal desire and masturbation. Constitutional variation that makes desire overwhelming is one such possibility mentioned by Freud. Another is if the child is prevented from masturbating and Oedipal tension builds to untenable levels. However, in Hans's case the immediate problem—and the reason he was stopped from masturbating—was a further factor, that his masturbation fantasies had become so intense that the phallic discharge from masturbation was not able to lower libido enough to keep Oedipal tension from rising to pathogenic levels. Thus, masturbation becomes the new vehicle of the Victorian "semenic economy." If there is too little, the child falls ill of Oedipal desires undischarged. If there is too much, it is an indicator of pathogenically intense accompanying sexual fantasy. The shadow side of the Oedipal theory is a new if submerged focus on and surveillance of— and if problems are perceived, regulation of— the act of masturbation.

What Foucault Missed about the Changing Functions of the Deployment of Sexuality

What, then, explains the acceptance of the Oedipal theory? In asserting the Oedipal theory's continuity with important elements of masturbation-crusade doctrine and with major tactical features of the deployment of sexuality which had been accepted for over a century due to their sociosyntonic effects and functions, Foucault assumed that similar power/knowledge structures and functions, and thus similar inclinations to accept the theory based on its appealing effects, would carry over from one theory to another. He thus assumed that once continuity was established, the acceptance of the Oedipal theory would be explained along the same lines as the acceptance of the masturbation crusade.

The analysis above does display some doctrinal and tactical commonalities between the incest theory and the masturbation crusade. Nonetheless, I believe that assuming continuity in acceptance due to power/knowledge, Foucault missed some basic features of the shift in theories and practices. Specifically, he failed to adequately attend to some dramatic differences in the function of the Oedipal theory relative to functions of earlier theories, and thus missed a shift in the reasons why the new theory was so acceptable. These changes at a social level are reflected by and echo changes in the family already evident in the Hans case history in which, with the excuse of preventing Oedipal overstimulation to Hans, the parents take full control of the marital bed and limit mother-son affection. I briefly elaborate here what I explain in detail in *Attachment, Sexuality, Power* (Wakefield, 2023b) about what Foucault missed regarding the incest theory's acceptance from his power/knowledge perspective.

I noted above that one can examine Foucault's "extension" hypothesis at various levels, including the concrete level of masturbation concern and control, the power/knowledge level of specific tactics (e.g., surveillance, confession, and medicalization), and the more abstract level of the functions of applying power/knowledge to the family. For Foucault, the primary functions of the crusade were, first, the constitution of the emerging nuclear family by saturating it with sexual-emotional intensity and entangling parents and children with increasing surveillance of children; second, the penetration of the family by medical authority to allow the State more access; and third, distracting parents by sexual concerns as the State took a greater part in child education.

My analysis supports Foucault's "continuity" thesis at the levels of concrete concerns and most tactics. However, the function of Oedipal power/knowledge and the target of surveillance changed in important ways. The changes reflect a changing social context. They are thus consistent with Foucault's insistence that the question in elucidating a specific type of historically and locationally situated discourse on sex is what is "the most immediate, the most local power relations at work?" (1978, p. 97) and what "advantages derive from them in a given context for specific reasons" (1980, p. 101).

Freud's context included rapidly changing values around marriage, sexuality, and sexual equality at the beginning of the twentieth century. The nuclear family as well as medicalization of family problems and State control of child education were all well-established at that time, so further entangling and intensifying family emotional relationships to solidify the family was no longer needed. Indeed, the opposite was appealing.

What Foucault missed is that, although it was still true under the Oedipal theory that "danger came from the child's desire," the primary effect of accepting the theory—and what made it appealing—is that for the first time, danger came from a mother's affection for her child. There was little one could do to stop the child from having desires, but one could try to prevent excessive provocation of those desires by motherly affection that might trigger pathogenically excessive masturbatory fantasies. That is precisely what was going on in Hans's family prior to the outbreak of his horse phobia. Hans's father, a follower of Freud, who was influenced by his knowledge of Freud's Oedipal theory, began preventing Hans's mother from cuddling with Hans for fear of the mother's affection amplifying Oedipal arousal to pathogenic levels. (Ironically, this preventive interference in Hans's attachment relationship with his mother is likely what brought about Hans's anxiety disorder [Wakefield, 2023b].) The primary target of surveillance and restraint thus turned from the child to the mother. For this reason, the Oedipus complex represents a "turning point" in the deployment of sexuality in which the power/knowledge function of surveillance and medicalization is turned from the child to the parent and to the parent's demonstration of affection to the child. The deployment is consequently transformed from a *centripetal* force entangling family members and thereby solidifying the bond between members of the emerging nuclear family (as Foucault suggests), into a *centrifugal* force separating the parental axis from the child axis and making physical intimacy between parent and child something to be feared or anxious about and regulated. It is the precise opposite of the intimate "parent child physical clinch" (2003, p. 264) that Foucault describes as a function of the masturbation crusade—indeed, it is aimed at preventing that clinch.

For example, we saw in Chapter 4 that during the masturbation crusade, sleeping in the same bed with one's child offered optimal surveillance and thus was deemed useful for masturbation prevention, and was sometimes prescribed for this purpose. In sharp contrast, as I documented in *Attachment, Sexuality, Power* (2023b), our entire culture's sleeping arrangements were influenced to create distance early in life out of fear of excessive sexual stimulation to the Oedipally desiring child. Rather than the incest theory solidifying and preserving alliance, it distances the family's parental axis from its child axis and opens the way for children to be more independent minded about family ties.

This new family allows for physical intimacy in the marital bed without distraction from children, who are early exiled to their own bedroom. It is more malleable for the educational system and more useful as a two-worker unit. This centrifugal separation encouraged by the Oedipal theory is close to what the bourgeois nuclear family experiences today, from the very early ages at which children are separated from parents at bedtime—a practice virtually unknown and often thought to be cruel in other cultures—to the fear of too much physical intimacy, such as cuddling with a child in bed or washing a child in the bath, as potentially overstimulating. Rather than intensified entanglement, the Oedipal theory created fear of physical intimacy and affection between parent and child. For boys, this means that it is the mother who becomes the target of surveillance and control, because her well-intentioned affection is now seen as the primary danger in triggering the boy's incestuous fantasies. Thus, danger now comes from the mother's affection, and Oedipal power/knowledge is aimed at keeping a distance between mother and son.

Oedipal theory thus has the opposite function of the masturbation crusade. It disentangles the parental and child family axes, serving the sexual and emotional needs of the parents as they find themselves alone in the protected marital bed free of children and able to pursue the modern ideal of egalitarian marital sexual and emotional intimacy. This is, I believe, the appeal of the Oedipal theory, and it is what allowed the Oedipal theory to gain widespread acceptance despite its disturbing content and lack of scientific foundation.

Conclusion: Oedipal Theory as Both Episode and Turning Point in the Masturbation Crusade

The analysis in this chapter provides an account, which Foucault failed to offer, of the precise theoretical mechanisms by which a substantial degree of continuity was maintained between the masturbation crusade and the Oedipal theory. The account was prompted by a central puzzle regarding the Hans case, namely, how to explain the seeming paradox of Freud's simultaneous acceptance of the normality of childhood masturbation and extreme efforts to control Hans's masturbation. These efforts to control masturbation include all of the crusade's tactical features of surveillance, interrogation, confession, medicalization, and use of restraints. They were undoubtedly noticed by Foucault and taken by him as evidence that the Oedipal theory somehow extended crucial aspects of the masturbation crusade.

The continuity between the masturbation crusade and Oedipal theory, I argued, lies in the theoretical link Freud forged between control of Hans's masturbation and control of potentially pathogenically arousing Oedipal masturbatory fantasies. The normal process of relieving childhood Oedipal desire via masturbation in certain circumstances can yield a feedback loop in which masturbation amplifies rather than reduces Oedipal fantasy, yielding a pathogenic process in which intense Oedipal fantasies cause greater tension than can be tolerated or discharged, thus triggering repression and transformation of excess libido into anxiety. Thus, Foucault correctly perceives that despite Freud's anti-crusade thesis that masturbation is a normal channel for release of phallic component-instinct tension in children, the Oedipal theory offers a theory-driven rationale for a continuation of the masturbation crusade's concern about the dangers of child self-stimulation and encourages the medicalization and surveillance of family life. This analysis both explains Foucault's construal of the incest theory as an extension of the masturbation crusade, and supports his construal with textual evidence.

References

Acton, W. (1875). *The functions and disorders of the reproductive organs in childhood, youth, adult age, and advanced life considered in their physiological, social and moral relations*. Philadelphia, PA: Lindsay & Blakiston. (Original work published in 1857.)

Driscoll, C., Garland, C., & Hickey-Moody, A. (2011). (Hetero)sexing the child: Hans, Alice, and the repressive hypothesis. In F. Beckman (Ed.), *Deleuze and sex* (pp. 117–134). Edinburgh, UK: Edinburgh University Press.

Esterson, A. (1998). *Seductive mirage: An exploration of the work of Sigmund Freud*. Chicago, IL: Open Court Publishing.

Foucault, M. (1978). *History of sexuality* (Vol. 1): *An introduction* (R. Hurley, Trans.). New York, NY: Pantheon. (*HS1*)

Foucault, M. (1980). *Power/knowledge: Selected interviews and other writings 1972–1977* (C. Gordon, Ed.). New York: Pantheon.

Foucault, M. (2003). *Abnormal: Lectures at the College de France 1974–1975*. (G. Burchell, Trans., V. Marchetti & A. Salomoni, Eds.). New York, NY: Picador.

Freud, S. (1896). Further remarks on the neuro-psychoses of defence. SE 3, 157–185.

Freud, S. (1905). Three essays on the theory of sexuality. SE 7, 123–246.

Freud, S. (1906). My views on the part played by sexuality in the aetiology of the neuroses. SE 7, 269–279.

Freud, S. (1909). Analysis of a phobia in a five-year-old boy. SE 10, 1–150.

Freud, S. (1910). A special type of choice of object made by men (contributions to the psychology of love 1). SE 11, 163–176.

Freud, S. (1912). Contributions to a discussion on masturbation. SE 12, 239–254.

Freud, S. (1917). Introductory lectures on psycho-analysis, part 3. SE 16.

Freud, S. (1918). From the history of an infantile neurosis. SE 17, 1–124.

Freud, S. (1924). The dissolution of the Oedipus complex. SE 19, 171–180.

Freud, S. (1925). An autobiographical study. SE 20, 1–74.

Lacan, J. (1994). *Le séminaire, Livre IV: La relation d'objet et les structures freudiennes*. Paris, FR: Seuil. (Original lectures 1957.)

Makari, G. J. (1998). Between seduction and libido: Sigmund Freud's masturbation hypotheses and the realignment of his etiologic thinking, 1897–1905. *Bulletin of the History of Medicine, 72*(4), 638–662.

Spitz, R. A. (1952). Authority and masturbation: Some remarks on a bibliographical investigation. *The Psychoanalytic Quarterly, 21*(4), 490–527.

Wakefield, J. C. (2007). Attachment and sibling rivalry in Little Hans: The 'phantasy of the two giraffes' reconsidered. *Journal of the American Psychoanalytic Association, 55*, 821–849.

Wakefield, J. (2008). Little Hans and the thought police: The "Policeman Fantasies" as the first supervisory transference fantasies. *International Journal of Psychoanalysis, 89*, 71–88.

Wakefield, J. C. (2023a). *Freud's argument for the Oedipus complex: A philosophy of science analysis of the case of Little Hans*. New York: Routledge.

Wakefield, J. C. (2023b). *Attachment, sexuality, power: Oedipal theory as regulator of family affection in Freud's case of Little Hans*. New York: Routledge.

Chapter 8

Foucault's Critique of Freud's Oedipal Theory: Conclusions and Implications

---

In this final chapter, I briefly summarize the findings of this book and comment on the implications of my analysis for the future of psychoanalysis. I argue that the Oedipal theory was not only iatrogenically harmful to children by making parents suspicious of physical affection (as argued in Chapter 7), but was also harmful to psychoanalysis itself in associating it in the public mind with a Victorian-derived sexual theory, undermining the field's credibility. Yet, psychoanalysis remains a valuable discipline, emphasizing a focus on meaning within an overly biologicalized psychiatry. It is best defended with a clear-headed understanding and acknowledgment of past errors. Foucault helps us to see that one of the most serious of those errors was the Oedipal theory.

With Apologies to Foucault

According to Wendy Grace (citing David Halperin [1995]):

> After being told that a student had just finished writing a dissertation on his critique of 'humanism,' an embarrassed Foucault responded, in all seriousness, that the man should not have wasted energy talking about him, and, instead, should 'do what he was doing, namely, write genealogies.'
>
> (Grace, 2010, p. 365)

If this anecdote is true, then I suppose that I should preface my conclusions by apologizing to Foucault for writing this book that tries

DOI: 10.4324/9781003480396-8

to understand and evaluate his analysis of Freud's Oedipal theory. Indeed, as this completes a trilogy of volumes, I seem to owe him a triple apology (Wakefield, 2023a; 2023b).

My only defense is that I was not really trying to understand Foucault—that was a means to an end—I was trying to understand how to think about Freud. Moreover, frustrated by Foucault's lack of evidence for his claims, I did undertake my own analysis of Freud to test Foucault's claims. In attempting to better understand Freud in the light of Foucault's claims, I have tried to wend my way safely through the intellectual minefield produced by a clash between the ideas of two brilliant but monomaniacal theorists, one claiming the omnipresence of sexuality, the other the omnipresence of power. In this regard, note that in concluding that Foucault is largely correct in his dismissal of the Oedipal theory as one more expression of the two centuries of medico-scientific sexual obsession that preceded it and an imposition of spurious medical power on the family, I do not take a stand on or endorse Foucault's broader emphatically power-oriented analysis of human relationships in general.

In these concluding comments, I recapitulate some of the central elements of my argument. I then end with a brief allusion to the broader hopes I have for this analysis.

Summary of Findings

In an earlier book, *Freud's Argument for the Oedipus Complex* (Wakefield, 2023a), I emphasized that Freud created the Oedipal theory as a carefully tailored solution to the problems posed to his theoretical program by the devastating falsification of his seduction theory. Impressively, the Oedipal theory managed to explain his earlier misleading seduction-theory "data" in a way that vindicated his psychoanalytic method. Together with the libido theory with its broad and fluid conceptualization of sexuality that could thus sexually explain the endless variety of hysterical symptoms, the Oedipal theory preserved Freud's treasured sexual theory of the neuroses.

In this book, I have grappled with the question, how was this Oedipal theory that lacked serious evidence and was so obviously shaped by the idiosyncratic internal needs of Freud's unlikely sexual-etiology research program, able to enduringly command so much influence and achieve so much acceptance in both the clinical sciences and in the culture at large? Among many others, Michel Foucault attempted to explain this puzzling fact. Unlike classic philosophy of the social sciences, Foucault's power/knowledge account of the acceptance of scientific theories about human nature focuses not on the evidence for or against a theory that should ideally determine theory acceptance, but rather on the effects that acceptance of a theory of human nature has on how people think about themselves and others and thus the effects of theory acceptance on social and family power relationships. These effects may appealingly and helpfully fit with evolving social values and practices, encouraging the perception of the theory as reasonable and correct although in fact the theory functions primarily as an instrument of social power.

Many scholars have grappled with the question of what made Freud's Oedipal theory (or "incest theory") so appealing; some of their proposed answers were reviewed in Chapter 2. In evaluating Foucault's novel attempt to answer this question, I asked: Is Foucault correct that the right way to see Freud's sexual theories is not as a major liberatory theoretical rupture in sexual theory as usually assumed, but rather primarily as a relatively minor mutation—one more episode or extension—in a two-century continuous phenomenon of oppressively applied sexual theorizing that comprises what Foucault calls the "deployment of sexuality"? Specifically, can Freud be seen as extending the most outrageous and oppressive element of the deployment, namely, the relentless medical campaign (the "masturbation crusade") that elevated masturbation into a major health threat?

I accepted as a framework Foucault's admittedly vague notion of continuity versus rupture in scientific theorizing, which surprisingly turned out to be pivotal to Foucault's argument for the deployment of sexuality. By demonstrating important continuities between the masturbation crusade and the incest theory, Foucault can persuasively reject the standard "repression-liberation" narrative according to which Victorian repression of sexuality was relieved by the liberatory theoretical rupture provided by psychoanalysis. That opens the way for his view that not repression but positive constructs of power/knowledge have been continuously deployed as theories supporting the power/knowledge of the masturbation crusade.

One might question which is the dog and which the tail. Does psychoanalytic discontinuity threaten Foucault's history of sexuality agenda, or is the entire point of that agenda to undermine psychoanalysis's claim to discontinuity along with its claims to ahistorical truths about sexuality? Whatever the answer, the incest theory's continuity versus rupture status is not peripheral but cuts to the core of Foucault's project. So, I focused on the question of whether an argument can be made for significant doctrinal, tactical, and functional continuity between the crusade and the incest theory.

A major challenge was the lack of analytic rigor in Foucault's arguments for his claims. When I attempted to evaluate Foucault's striking contention that Freud's Oedipal theory is in fact an episode of the masturbation crusade and was appealing because it partook of the masturbation crusade's power/knowledge in intensifying and rearranging family life, I found that Foucault provides weak arguments and virtually no textual evidence for this claim. (Foucault's "discourse rules" in arriving at a claimed truth appear to be quite different from mine!) He offers no conceptual, theoretical, or empirical analyses of Freud's claims, a point that has earned him many complaints from commentators. Instead, he seems to assume that his hypothesis gains support simply from his ability to describe Freud's theory in a way that fits into his overall power/knowledge framework and that postulates a possible social function that it might serve. He is reticent about precisely what evidence supports his claims, and offers no detailed engagement with Freud's text or with the structure of Freud's theorizing.

Concocting possible social functions for the incest theory without providing independent evidence is a Foucauldian version of the "just so" stories about functions that long undermined the credibility of medical and psychological evolutionary theorizing until independent scientific evidence could be brought to bear (Wakefield, 2023c). Foucault's analyses of the potential power/knowledge appeal of theories that lack persuasive evidence is a useful cautionary lesson for the human sciences—but it is a lesson that applies as well to Foucault's own functionalist hypotheses. Some of Foucault's evidential laxity may of course have been due to Foucault's expectation that he would later write a more detailed analysis, which unfortunately was never to happen.

So, I undertook my own examination of Freud's texts in an attempt to evaluate Foucault's claim. First, in Chapters 3 and 4, I provided examinations of the masturbation crusade's doctrines and Foucault's analysis of the power tactics employed in the crusade and their functions. This clarified the "deployment" baseline against which Freud's theory could be compared. I then examined Freud's texts and identified evidence that plausibly supported or conflicted with Foucault's continuity claims. To my knowledge, no similar examination to assess Foucault's claims about Freud by the evidence of Freud's texts has previously been undertaken.

I first asked whether there is evidence that Freud's earliest sexual theorizing was already embedded within the masturbation crusade's framework, as Foucault at one point suggests. An initial careful look at early Freudian theory (in Chapter 5) robustly confirmed Foucault's perspective, clearly locating the central doctrines of Freud's early theory as variations on masturbation crusade themes. I documented the many basic features that Freud's early theorizing shares with the crusade, especially the key theoretical claim that either excessive or inadequate sexual discharge is pathogenic—although for Freud the quantity in question refers to sexual libidinal energy rather than semenic fluid. Also, Freud's early theorizing included the view that masturbation as well as restrictive practices during intercourse such as coitus interruptus—practices that the crusade condemned as "conjugal onanism"—should be discouraged by the physician. The crusade's preoccupations with confession, surveillance, and medicalization of sexuality can all be seen in the early Freudian papers—including, as Foucault points out, a suspicion of people who enter the household as potential child seducers. Although different in detail and thus a "mutation" (as Foucault describes minor changes in detail or function) in the deployment of sexuality, I concluded that Freud's early sexual theories are quite rightly seen by Foucault as being in important respects a direct extension of the masturbation crusade's doctrines and tactics, thus a reflection of Victorian sexual nonsense.

I then turned to Foucault's central target, Freud's Oedipal theory, and his claim that the Oedipal theory extends elements of the two-century masturbation crusade in altered form, and thus likely derives its appeal from the same sources as the crusade. First, in Chapter 6, I considered Foucault's main argument that the incest theory is best understood as a continuous extension of the masturbation crusade. On its face, Foucault's continuity claim is puzzling. The two theories have many profound differences, not least of which is that the incest theory seems to be about directed sexual interest and not about autoerotic masturbation, and Freud allows that child sexuality is natural and not inherently pathological and so offers no obvious reason for concern about masturbation.

I focused on Foucault's arguments in his 1975 lecture on the incest theory (2003) that parents' concern about child masturbation could easily and smoothly be shifted to concern about the child's incestuous sexual desire, yielding similar functional effects. Foucault provides several arguments for this claim based on how parents might react to the knowledge that their child possessed Oedipal incestuous desires. However, close analysis led me to conclude that Foucault's arguments for such ease of transition are not persuasive. Thus, some other mechanism that explained the degree of continuity in the transition had to be identified.

In Chapter 7, I undertook a textual evaluation of Foucault's claim about the Oedipal theory. I first reviewed Freud's preoccupation with theoretical issues concerning childhood masturbation in the run-up to his Oedipal theorizing. I then identified the case of Little Hans (Freud, 1909), a case cited by Foucault, as the likely source for Foucault's views of the incest theory. The Hans case was Freud's signature defense of the Oedipus complex and also offers a portrayal of the complex's effects on family life. The case in fact presents a vivid account of the intertwining of the analysis of Hans's Oedipal desires with oppressive Victorian-type attempts to control Hans's masturbation, offering a perfect illustration of Foucault's contention that the Oedipal theory extended the masturbation crusade. The question was, what is the mechanism that connects masturbation control and the Oedipal theory, given Freud's anti-crusade view that masturbation in childhood is normal? I looked for this mechanism in the theory itself and in how the theory was applied in Little Hans's family.

In the Hans case, Freud looks beyond Hans's masturbation—which he dismisses as the parents' theory of the case—to Hans's incestuous wishes as the ultimate source of his phobia. Freud did clearly reject the crusade notion that masturbation in itself was pathogenic. Despite this and other clear divergences from masturbation-crusade doctrine, many textual findings detailed in Chapter 7 resonate with or support Foucault's contention that in an important sense this is a new episode in the crusade. In particular, the concern about and relentless attempt to control Hans's masturbation without Freud's objection is strikingly apparent confirmation of Foucault's view. However, it is also mysterious given Freud's assertions in the case itself that masturbation in childhood is normal. The roots of this seeming anomaly are not immediately obvious, and I explored this question in depth as a way of evaluating Foucault's claim.

Following up clues in the Little Hans case history, I concluded that, although submerged in the Oedipal theory and subsequently obscured by the focus on incestuous desire and fear of castration, in fact the dangers of masturbation in potentially amplifying Oedipal desires to the point of triggering neurosis was theoretically central to the Oedipal theory. Underlying the theory is the assumption that childhood is healthy only when there is a balance between masturbation and Oedipal stimulation. Without the benefit of the adult's ability to engage in sexual intercourse, the only outlet for the Oedipally aroused child is masturbation, and so the successful and non-pathogenic transition through childhood depends on the proper balance between Oedipal desire and tension relief through masturbation. The Oedipal theory is inherently also a theory of childhood masturbation.

Consistent with the contemporaneous masturbation-crusade view that masturbation is distinctively pathogenic due to the intense fantasies that accompany it, the Hans case illustrates the problem that intense Oedipal fantasies can become linked to and amplified by masturbation to the point that, rather than discharging tension as masturbation theoretically should, it yields increasing and over-whelming sexual tension, threatening pathology. The postulation of incestuous sexual desire in a young child necessitated continuing concern about child masturbation as both a healthy way to reduce Oedipal tension but also a danger if it becomes associated with overly stimulating incestuous fantasies. Thus, the Oedipal theory contains central elements of the masturbation crusade's focus on the dangers of masturbation, as Foucault had suggested.

This resolves the puzzle of why Hans's masturbation is suppressed even though Freud asserts the normality of child masturbation. It also explains why Freud would hold that adult masturbation is pathogenic whereas child masturbation is not. In both cases, he is defending his sexual theory of the neuroses. In the adult case, he needs the pathogenicity of excessive masturbation to explain the actual neuroses. In the child case, he needs the normality of masturbation to explain the siphoning off of Oedipal desire that prevents universal neurosogenesis due to the buildup of tension. Yet, although masturbation is not only normal but essential in childhood, the limited gratification of masturbation and the intensity of fantasies stoked by masturbation poses a danger of psychopathology.

Foucault's continuity claim that the incest theory in some interesting sense extends the masturbation crusade's doctrines was thus vindicated. The "Gestalt" argument (described in Chapter 6) that Freud's sexual theories are obviously continuous with Victorian sexual theories was considerably strengthened by an understanding of the specific theoretical mechanisms that perpetuated an exaggerated concern about masturbation and supported tactics of surveillance and medicalization of the child's sexual life. I conclude that a careful examination of Freud's work—both his early work and his Oedipal theory—reveals a persuasive textual basis for Foucault's claims that Freud's sexual theory and its power/knowledge tactics are, in important respects, mutations but nonetheless episodes in the masturbation crusade and the deployment of sexuality. My analysis suggests that Foucault may have been a more careful reader—or intuitive extrapolator—of Freud than his lack of detailed textual discussion would suggest.

Some critics complain that when Freud gave up the seduction theory and adopted the Oedipal theory, he focused on fantasy and ignored the possibility of real sexual stimulation and sexual trauma in childhood. However, one can think of the Oedipal theory of neurosogenesis as a theory of self-induced childhood sexual stimulation in which the child's own masturbation is initially a normal response but can bring about such intense and overwhelming accompanying Oedipal sexual fantasies that the child is thereby in effect self-traumatized. This approach is Freud's ingenious response to the problem of how to save his sexual theory of the neuroses and psychoanalytic method after finding that the seduction reports he obtained from his patients were not veridical (Wakefield, 2023a).

The Oedipus complex was invented by Freud in order to evade the suggestion objection and explain how children could have traumatizing sexual experiences without any adult or other child sexually stimulating them. The focus on the dangers of masturbation in the masturbation crusade provided Freud with the basis of an answer. Masturbatory fantasy provoked by and amplifying Oedipal desire was Freud's new answer to the source of later psychopathology. Conjoined with the postulated incestuous desires, masturbation would provoke fantasies of precisely the kinds reported by Freud's early patients, and the kind that Freud found to be pathogenic, as the attempt to explain the false seduction fantasies demands. This solution expiates Freud from the suggestion accusation regarding the seduction theory and thus accomplishes what the Oedipal theory was designed to do.

Freud's preoccupation with the nature of childhood masturbation did not end when he created the Oedipal theory. Instead, the Oedipal theory fitted that preoccupation into a fuller and richer theory. The broader sensitization that Oedipal theoretic insight yields into the triadic child-parent relationship notwithstanding, the Oedipal theory of neurosogenesis was at its core a theory of traumatic masturbation, and to this extent it was a "new episode" in the masturbation crusade's and the deployment of sexuality's inflated view of the dangers of masturbation.

Foucault and the Future of Psychoanalysis

I concluded that Foucault's view of Freud's Oedipal theory is persuasive; Freud was in this respect another in a long line of theorists of the "deployment of sexuality"—the two-century phenomenon in which evidentially unsupported and spurious scientific claims about the vast pathogenic potential of sexuality were used as a rationale for intervention into family life and for intrusions of social power in reshaping the population's behavior. As I argued in *Attachment, Sexuality, Power* (Wakefield, 2023b), Freud's theory was the source of enormous iatrogenic harm as mothers were cautioned not to engage in routine attachment behaviors of cuddling or sleeping with their children. Yet, Freud was, as I have emphasized, a pivotal figure in the history of psychology for several other reasons. Thus, my conclusion does not erase Freud from the pantheon of psychological theorists. Rather, contrary to his own view and that of many of his followers, it erases the notion that the Oedipal theory is central to his contribution or even in the long term a productive and illuminating part of his work. Along with the larger spurious hypothesis that it was aimed to support—the sexual theory of the neuroses—it was a historically understandable but nonetheless disastrous misstep by a brilliant theoretician.

This book's analysis of Foucault's claims about the Oedipal theory overall supports my belief, mentioned in Chapter 1, that Foucault's "big picture" assessment of Freud has merit. Freud made major advances in several areas of psychological theory, including his postulation of unconscious mental states (Wakefield, 2018) and his rejection of the theory of constitutional degeneracy as well as his theory of psychological defense and many other contributions. However, his sexual theory of the neuroses and specifically his Oedipal theory must be seen as evidentially unsupported attempts to preserve his misconceived sexual theory of the neuroses, which was in turn an extension of the two centuries of spurious and exaggerated theories about sexual dangers to health that preceded him that had taken the form of the masturbation crusade.

My motivation in writing a trilogy on the Oedipal theory and exploring Foucault's critique of Freud goes beyond my desire to resolve questions I had long had about the status of Freud's theory. Psychoanalysis is an invaluable exploration of conscious and unconscious meaning, but its credibility has been undermined by the Victorian-anchored sexual theories that Freud defended to the end. Only by explicitly renouncing this component of the psychoanalytic tradition—not by simply shifting attention and moving on to something else, but by clearheadedly detailing and acknowledging the errors that were made and apologizing for the pseudoscientific doctrines that were perpetuated in clinical work and imposed on patients long after they should have been apparent—can psychoanalysis regain its moral and intellectual credibility.

Because the Oedipal theory took precedence in the public image of psychoanalysis and in the power/knowledge effects Freud's theorizing had on family relationships, this historic misstep by Freud extended the oppressive deployment of sexuality through a third century. The challenged condition of psychoanalysis today—just when it is desperately needed as a meaning-oriented balance to the overly biologicalist dominance in today's psychiatry—is in part due to the effects of Freud's insistence on the Oedipus complex and the sexual theory of the neuroses as the test of psychoanalytic orthodoxy, and the consequent socialization of generations of analysts to "see" sexual etiologies behind many forms of human misery. The spurious Oedipal theoretical construct got psychoanalytic concepts mostly excluded from mainstream psychiatry's diagnostic manuals, led to the use of (likely spurious) "deep" theory-generated interpretations of the unconscious when faced with the patient's lack of memory of the proffered sexual explanations, divorced psychoanalysis from mainstream psychological research, and precluded the discipline's development into a cumulative self-correcting science. Psychoanalysis has recently tried to correct this enormous distortion in its scientific development, but in leaping from one theoretical framework to another without adequate attention to developing a common under-standing of what went wrong and how to advance in a scientifically persuasive way, this effort has created theoretical fragmentation of the field into dogmatic fiefdoms that undermines scientific progress rather than provoking useful testing of ideas and evidentially supported advances.

All in all, it is arguable that Freud's devotion to the Oedipal theory was one of the great blunders in the history of medicine. It was fated to undermine not only the credibility of psychoanalysis but also the scientific reputation and legacy that Freud so avidly sought. Perhaps the trilogy of which this book is a part will help to provide a foundation for reconsidering psychoanalysis's status informed by an understanding of what has gone wrong in embracing the sexual theory, and for highlighting the many remarkable achievements that form the legitimate basis for the reputation that Freud deserves. If so, this attempt to look at the Oedipal theory through critical Foucault-tinted glasses will prove not only illuminating but useful for psycho-analysis's future.

References

Freud, S. (1909). Analysis of a phobia in a five-year-old boy. *SE* 10, 1–150.
Foucault, M. (2003). *Abnormal: Lectures at the College de France 1974–1975.* (G. Burchell, Trans.), V. Marchetti & A. Salomoni (Eds.). New York, NY: Picador.

Grace, W. (2010). *Foucault's power: A history of sexuality beyond the desires of French psychoanalysis.* Doctoral dissertation, University of Western Australia. Accessed at https://api.research-repository.uwa.edu.au/ws/portalfiles/portal/9834936/Grace_Elizabeth_Wendy_2010.pdf

Halperin, D. (1995). *Saint Foucault: Towards a gay hagiography.* New York: Oxford University Press.

Wakefield, J. C. (2018). *Freud and philosophy of mind, Volume 1: Reconstructing the argument for unconscious mental states.* New York: Palgrave Macmillan.

Wakefield, J. C. (2023a). *Freud's argument for the Oedipus complex: A philosophy of science analysis of the case of Little Hans.* New York: Routledge.

Wakefield, J. C. (2023b). *Attachment, sexuality, power: Oedipal theory as regulator of family affection in Freud's case of Little Hans.* New York: Routledge.

Wakefield, J. C. (2023c). The promise of evolutionary psychiatry. *World Psychiatry, 22*(2), 173–174.

Index

Little Hans case: attitudes towards Hans and his mother 71–72, 326; as evidence for Foucault's hypotheses 298–302; Freud's argument for the normality of child sexuality in 302–304; Hans' anxiety disorder 307–309; original Oedipal theory case 82; puzzle of Freud's explanations 311–320

MacIntyre, Alasdair 63
Macmillan, Malcolm 87–88
Madness and Civilisation 56
Makari, George 294–298
Malthusian couple 29, 244
Malthus, Thomas 125
marketing genius of Freud 80–82
Marten, John 108
Marxists on the masturbation crusade 158–164, 198–199
masturbation: in early Freudian theory 232–242; with lack of full coital satisfaction 231–232
masturbation crusade: commentary on Foucault's analysis 198–204; as concern about the education of the workforce 193–197; ease of transition to Oedipal Theory 261–268; explanations for 104–106; exported to America 114–117; extended by the Oedipal theory 2–3, 99–101, 248–251, 255–256, 325–327; Foucault's functional analysis of 157–158, 198; Foucault's lectures on 5; Foucault's question (1975) 2, 35, 157–158; late-nineteenth-century trends 148–150; Marxists on the 158–164, 198–199; medical arguments for 101–106, 133, 162; mid- to late-nineteenth-century shifts in 132–134; origins of 103, 106–113; and spermatorrhea 107, 117–125, 135, 172, 179–181,

199–200; surgical treatment 133, 186–192; Tissot's contribution 108–113
masturbatory fantasy 296–297, 320–321
Maudsley, Henry 149
"medical gaze" 16
Medical Inquiries and Observations, upon the Diseases of the Mind 114
medicalization of sexuality 33, 176–177
medical penetration of the family 274–278
medical-scientific targets 29
medical technology of control 181–186
Menand, Louis 63–64
Merleau-Ponty, Maurice 10, 15
Miller, Jacques-Alain 260–261
Mill, John Stuart 148
Milton, John 187
moral conscience development 13
motherly affection 71–72, 326, 338
myth making explanation 70–72, 89–90

nerve severing as treatment 188–189
nerve shock theory 116, 122, 128–129, 137
neurasthenia: causes of (Freud) 221, 230–232, 241; definition 210; Freud and the problem of 209–211, 242–243, 246; symptoms of 211; vs. anxiety neurosis 212–216
neurosis: actual neuroses vs. psychoneuroses 216–218; anxiety neurosis 212–216; definition 209–210; Freud's classification of causes 218–221
"nonexistence" of psychoanalysis 89–95
normalization process 156
nuclear family 163–164, 169
nymphomania 146, 147

For Product Safety Concerns and Information please contact our EU
representative GPSR@taylorandfrancis.com
Taylor & Francis Verlag GmbH, Kaufingerstraße 24, 80331 München, Germany

www.ingramcontent.com/pod-product-compliance
Lightning Source LLC
Chambersburg PA
CBHW050332270326
41926CB00016B/3414